New York (City) Bureau of city chamberlain.

NEW YORK CITY'S ADMINISTRATIVE PROGRESS 1914-1916

A SURVEY OF VARIOUS DEPARTMENTS UNDER THE JURISDICTION OF THE MAYOR

Conducted Under the Direction of

HENRY BRUÈRE
Chamberlain, City of New York

MAY, 1916

3102-16-1000

CONTENTS

CONTENTS

CONTENTS

CONTENTS

CONTENTS

CONTENTS

CONTENTS

Hon. John Purroy Mitchel,

Mayor, City of New York:

Dear Sir—This report is a statement of administrative progress made and projected in fifteen departments under the direction of the mayor during the period of your mayoralty. It is based on a survey conducted at your request under my direction as chamberlain, by examiners drawn from the board of estimate bureaus, the office of the commissioner of accounts, and the Bureau of Municipal Research. It aims to be impartial and accurate, and as complete as the time available for making it allowed.

Not all the departments under your jurisdiction were covered in the survey. No adequately equipped examiner was available at the time the survey was begun, for example, for a study of the fire department. The preoccupation of the dock commissioner in working on the New York Central, west side and other problems, made it infeasible to include the dock department. Moreover, the problems of that department were, according to plans then under consideration, to be studied by a special expert commission, whose study would presumably include the organization and effectiveness of dock and harbor facilities. The department of licenses was undergoing special investigation by the commissioner of accounts; the department of public charities was so much under discussion that it was left out of the study in order that it might be separately dealt with. I recommend, in this connection, that a special committee of three qualified persons be appointed by Your Honor to report on the work of the department of public charities during your administration, problems faced when you took office, steps taken, results accomplished, and work yet to be done thoroughly to modernize that pre-eminently important branch of government service.

This report does not deal with the work of the chamberlain's office and the special staffs under his direction, because that work had already been separately reported upon by me.

In making a survey and report there is ground always to determine and to recite the shortcomings of a department. No organization or human effort in the world can escape the criticism of falling short of complete perfection. No department under your control makes claim to perfection, or has been found perfect in administrative detail. It would be absurd at this stage of governmental development to expect any such condition. It will take many years of difficult labor and training both of administrators, civil servants and the public, before even approximate administrative perfection can be achieved. It is significant that the record shows that there has been no wanton blundering or disregard of opportunities for public service in the departments examined. On the contrary, the facts show that heads of departments have studiously and earnestly striven to do the best with their responsibilities that zeal, experience, the intrinsic difficulties of the task and the traditional methods and morale of government permitted.

A broad foundation has been laid for cumulative progress. The city has undergone an administrative reconstruction, not suddenly begun but built on the work of other administrations where that work was well done, notably during the fusion administration of 1910-1914.

New York is better governed now than in the past. Great progress has been made under your leadership. It can be better governed still, as every informed person realizes and every responsible public official would be among the first to acknowledge. Among others, the following steps are, in my judgment, essential for a progressively better government:

1 Reconstruction of the general framework of the government in order that greater emphasis may be kept on general administrative leadership and supervision. (On this point a separate report is in preparation.)
2 Special training of public employees
3 Non-partisan elections of city officials
4 Home rule powers
5 Extension of terms of leading administrative officials and wider inclusion of well-tested executives in the permanent service.

Respectfully submitted,

HENRY BRUÈRE

July 15, 1916.

INTRODUCTION

New York's present city government is the consummation of years of effort to establish a genuine non-partisan administration of the city. The existing administration was especially commissioned to fulfill the obligations of non-partisanship, to broaden the services of government and to promote the economy and efficiency of city management. It represents, in the first instance, an effort to divorce the consideration and conduct of city affairs from national politics, and to establish as permanently as possible the principle of non-partisanship (in a national party sense) in the government of the city.

For years New York has striven to this end. In this effort it has suffered the handicap of necessary reliance upon party nominations to place a city ticket before the electorate. It has had to combat the cohesive and effective machinery of the local Democratic organization which is bound together primarily by the purpose of winning and maintaining control over local affairs.

Administrative as well as political progress has been impeded in the past by these conditions. Mayors, comptrollers and members of the board of estimate and apportionment were necessarily chosen with a view to their affiliations with national parties, and often without due regard to their qualifications and purposes with respect to city affairs.

The present administration, on the contrary, is constituted, for the most part, of men who have had long experience in city government, whose views and records in this field are thoroughly understood, and who were freed from party obligations on the assumption of their duties.

This achievement of a non-partisan government has been due not only to the growth of a large independent body of voters who exercise their choice in elections irrespective of national party affiliations, but also to the increased emphasis in recent city campaigns on municipal issues. It is also attributable, in large measure, to the patriotic willingness of national party leaders of influence in New York City to subordinate political and partisan considerations to the city's welfare by lending their support to candidates pledged to good government.

The encouragement of independence and non-partisanship in municipal elections is a prime obligation of city officials. To achieve this end it is necessary to keep constantly before the public city problems and policies, and the results of effort to solve them.

The survey, of which the following is the report, was undertaken in order to place before the mayor and administrative officials a concrete summary of progress to-date in departments under the jurisdiction of the mayor. But it will also serve to acquaint the public with facts regarding the government so that it may be in a position to exercise intelligent judgment respecting city matters.

New York is one of the few progressive cities in the country whose charter does not yet make provision for non-partisan local elections. Such provision must inevitably be a part of future charter revision, as it has increasingly become a part of the recently adopted charters of other cities in America. Until such provision is made, however, reliance for independent leadership and influence in the settlement of municipal issues must be placed upon the growing number of independent voters who are determined to keep the city government out of the hands of politicians, and to prevent the confusion of local questions in the irrelevancies of national party programs.

Much of the recent administrative progress of the government of the city has been due to the continued action of independent citizens in calling public attention to the details of city affairs, and to their co-operation with public officials in rectifying archaic and ineffective administrative conditions. The Citizens' Union, the Bureau of Municipal Research, the City Club and various independent political organizations whose activities center around municipal problems, have been notable factors in advancing the cause of good government in New York City.

A militant public opinion based upon knowledge of facts and directed towards the continuance of effective government is New York's surest safeguard against the exploitation of public business for personal and political ends. In considering the present state of New York's affairs it is well to bear in mind the years of steadfast toil and self-dedication which public-spirited citizens have devoted to breaking down the dominance of political factions in city government.

The problems confronting New York City are so numerous and complicated that clear public vision regarding them is difficult to maintain. Non-partisan fusion platforms have frequently been formulated more as expressions of admirable intention than as solemn pledges for unswerving execution. In the past the high purposes of reform administrations have often been obscured by special and unforeseen difficulties arising in the course of administration.

The present administration has sought to bear in mind continuously the obligations placed upon it by the platforms under which it was elected in 1913. Many unforeseen problems have arisen, it is true, which made more difficult the carrying out of obligations then assumed. But, as this report will indicate, progress has been made along practically each of the lines of activity and betterment outlined in the fusion platform of 1913, and in many instances the results achieved must fully meet the expectations of the electorate who supported the fusion ticket.

Members of the present fusion government did not begin their work in 1914, but four years before, in 1910, when the board of estimate and apportionment was placed in the control of the first fusion officials. Much of the constructive work accomplished during the past two years is merely the consummation of the work begun at that time. From 1910 to 1914 many improvements were effected in the methods of conducting the city's business. The presidents of the boroughs of Manhattan, Brooklyn and The Bronx undertook the reorganization of their departments, prompted by the revelations of incompetence existing in them made by Mayor Mitchel as commissioner of accounts and the Bureau of Municipal Research during the years of Mayor McClellan's administration. Unnecessary positions were abolished, offices were consolidated, purchasing methods modernized, effecting large economies, improved methods of contract and public letting were installed, and better control over the maintenance of highways, sewers and public buildings was achieved. The administration of the borough of Manhattan set a high water mark for the conduct of city business and its advance was in many respects paralleled by the administration of the other boroughs.

The comptroller, who as head of the department of finance has charge of the fiscal operations of the city,—the keeping of accounts, the financing of the city and the inspection and certification of all claims,—had prior to 1914 achieved a progressive reorganization of his department. Better financial methods, the completion of accounting reorganization begun by his predecessor, more effective control of the auditing of claims, all substituted order, dispatch and information for confusion, delay and doubt regarding city business, and stimulated not only the efficiency of the central department of financial control but that of all departments of the city government.

The office of the president of the board of aldermen under the fusion administration of 1910-1913, was made an effective working instrument. For the first time in its history this office was provided with a staff of investigators whose work enabled the president to share the burden of necessary investigation and planning which devolves upon the board of estimate before it can determine broad questions of city policy. Under the leadership of its president, the board of aldermen itself began to win back public confidence in its usefulness. Measures then instituted have been continued and advanced under the present administration, until now the president of the board of aldermen is able to exercise practically co-ordinate influence with the mayor and comptroller in the work of the board of estimate.

The first fusion board of estimate and apportionment assumed, as a board, more complete responsibility for the preparation of the annual tax budget and began the work of curtailing extravagance in the authorization of corporate stock through the adoption of a budget policy with respect to public improvement authorizations.

During these years perhaps the most important problem which the board of estimate was called upon to consider was the extension of rapid transit facilities. In this time it brought to a consummation years of effort to provide proper facilities for the city. Irrespective of differences of opinion as to the merits of the detailed provisions of the rapid transit contracts, the fact remains that the administration initiated the development of transit facilities which when completed will be unparalleled in the world.

It is not necessary to review in detail the administrative progress made in the general departments of the city during the years 1910-1913. It is sufficient to emphasize again that there was unprecedented progress in placing the government on a business basis. Many things were done. Many things were necessarily, by reason of incomplete organization and the complexity and variety of the tasks to be undertaken, left undone or hardly begun. But in the fall of 1913 when the voters of the city were again confronted with the problem of determining the character of their government for the next four years, it was possible to place before them in definite and concrete form the principal issue at stake. This was, whether the city should be turned back into the hands of a government by politicians, or whether it should continue to progress along the lines laid down by the board of estimate during the preceding four years.

The fusion party (for there was in this year a complete fusion of all forces for good government) was in a better position in 1913 that ever before to impress the voters with the sincerity and single-mindedness of its program. For the first time it was able to call attention to definite constructive achievements, and to indicate specific tasks which awaited performance by the incoming administration.

The present administration was put into office principally to complete work begun and outlined by the board of estimate and apportionment in 1910-1913 inclusive. The committee of 107 citizens, on July 31, 1913, nominated a municipal ticket which was subsequently accepted in whole or in part by various anti-Tammany political organizations of the city. The candidates endorsed by this committee were as follows:

For mayor—John Purroy Mitchel
For comptroller—William A. Prendergast
For president of the board of aldermen—George McAneny
For president of the borough of Manhattan—Marcus M. Marks
For president of the borough of Brooklyn—Lewis H. Pounds
For president of the borough of The Bronx—Douglas Mathewson
For president of the borough of Queens—Leonard C. L. Smith
For president of the borough of Richmond—George Cromwell

All except the nominees for the presidency of the boroughs of Richmond and Queens were elected by overwhelming majorities.

At the same time a platform was adopted which stated that:

> "* * * municipal government should be independent of national politics and boss rule, and shall be administered impartially for the welfare of the community. This is the one fundamental issue for a fusion campaign. * * *"

Candidates for the fusion party were, in addition, pledged to specific reforms in governmental organization and administration. Foremost among these reforms was the demand for home rule.

For many years preceding, the relation between the city government and the state government had been one of hostile antagonism. The state viewed the city as the legitimate source of most of its income, and the city resented the discrimination which it felt the state exercised against it. It was determined that a vigorous attempt should be made to obtain for the city of New York home rule with regard to its purely local affairs, and that there should be established beyond the possibility of controversy or interference a definite constitutional or statutory relationship between the city and the state.

Accordingly, the fusion candidates were pledged to:

1 A consistent effort to obtain home rule for the city of New York, with especial reference to the following points:
  - a Framing and adopting its own charter
  - b Enlarging the powers of the board of estimate to make it the responsible governing body of the city
  - c Controlling the sources of city revenue including subjects and rates of taxation
  - d Determining the city's policy with respect to the control, ownership and operation of public utilities
  - e Controlling the organization of all city departments, including number, classification and salaries of city and county officials

2 Reorganization of the police department

3 Extension of the city's social service program with especial reference to:
  - a Regulation of the height, size and arrangement of new buildings in various sections of the city and the adoption of city planning on a broad scale
  - b Establishment by the city of wholesale terminal markets in each borough as a means of reducing the cost of food
  - c Inspection and supervision of foods and the continuation and extension of pure milk stations
  - d Authorization of the board of education to supply lunches at cost to school children
  - e Extension and development of trade and vocational training in the public schools, and the wider use of school property for athletic, social and recreational purposes

4 Thorough modernization of the department of public charities in the interests of economy, integrity and efficiency of administration, and for the purpose of more humanitarian treatment of the city's unfortunates

5 Development of a comprehensive, scientific system of pensions for city employees

6 Adoption of a vigorous policy for comprehensive port and waterfront development, under effective city control, with a view to the city's ultimately securing the ownership of its entire waterfront

7 Greater economy and efficiency in the city government with special reference to:

a Continuation and further development of the policies of rigid scrutiny of proposed expenditures and of drastic retrenchment

b Necessity of living within the tax income, issuing bonds only for permanent improvements and never for longer periods than the probable life of such improvements

c Establishment of a central purchasing bureau for city supplies

d Completion of the standardization of salaries of municipal employees

e Careful study of proposed public improvements in the light of relative importance rather than with regard to pressure from local or speculative interests

f Appointment and retention of city employees only upon the basis of merit and the highest obtainable standard of efficiency

g Abolition of all useless positions

These were the most important pledges.

PART I

LEGISLATIVE AND GENERAL ADMINISTRATIVE PROGRESS MADE IN FULFILLMENT OF FUSION PLATFORM PROGRAM

HOME RULE

The most important demand in the fusion platform related to obtaining home rule for the city of New York. Although a law was passed in 1913 which purported to give home rule to cities in the State of New York, its provisions are so much in dispute as to leave the situation in New York City substantially unchanged.

Attempts to Obtain Legislative Relief

The present administration has on many occasions sought relief by specific legislation from the burdens and restrictions now imposed upon it by statute. A very extensive program of legislative relief was presented to the legislature of the years 1914 and 1915, but only a small part of it was enacted into law. This year (1916), with the assistance of a legislative committee which conducted for the state an investigation of New York City's affairs, there was very much greater prospect of success in putting a more complete program on the statute books. But again attempted legislation failed.

Until the local authorities are given full control over the operation of local government they cannot be held properly responsible by the electorate for results. At the present time they are helpless in many respects. The board of estimate and apportionment, constituting the city administration, has authority over about 62% of the annual budget (exclusive of debt charges), 78% of the annual expenses from corporate stock funds, and 60% of the expenditures from special revenue bond issues. The board of education controls without restriction the expenditure of about $33,500,000* annually. There are five counties which have almost complete control over $7,100,000 of annual expense. There are other boards, commissions and commissioners who expend other moneys of the city without let or hindrance by the local authorities. In addition, salaries of municipal employees are in many instances fixed and determined by action of the state legislature, and the city of New York is therefore compelled to pay for services not what it deems to be necessary and proper, but what is decreed by legislative mandate. Steps have been taken to give the board of estimate power to abolish positions which are admitted by it to be unnecessary, but in so far as positions established by statute are concerned such efforts have been nugatory.

The whole structure of the government of the city is based upon a mass of conflicting and inconsistent provisions. Indeed, there are three kinds of

*General fund only. In 1916, the Board of Education received a special appropriation of about $5,500,000, over which it has practically complete jurisdiction.

local government: The city government, which in part has jurisdiction over the entire city; the borough government, which is a local government in respect of certain matters for each of the five boroughs; and the county government, which is a local government for each of the five counties in regard to county affairs. The first is wholly centralized; the second is partly centralized by means of the board of estimate and apportionment; the third is completely decentralized. There is no more relation between the governments of New York County and its neighbor, Kings County, than between the governments of New York County and of Niagara County, about four hundred miles away.

In the winter of 1916 the city administration, at the instance of the mayor and with an assurance of support from Senator Brown, undertook to obtain the co-operation of the state senators and assemblymen from New York City with respect to the proposals which were discussed before the Brown committee investigating the city's finances. Several meetings were held between the assemblymen and senators from New York City and the board of estimate, and substantial progress was made. As a result of these deliberations, the work of the Brown Committee, and due also to independent action of the board of estimate, more than one hundred bills were introduced into the 1916 session of the legislature favorably affecting the city's interests. A short description of the most important of those bills which are concerned with the administration of the city and county governments, follows.* Where the desired legislation was obtained this fact is indicated by the word *passed*. Measures not so marked failed of adoption.

Relative to county government:

Drafted by the commissioner of accounts, under direction of the mayor:

- Providing for the abolition of the five offices of public administrator and the transfer of their duties to the chamberlain.
- Providing for the abolition of commissioner of records, New York County, commissioner of records—surrogates' office, New York County, and commissioner of records, Kings County.
- Providing for the abolition of counsel to certain county officers, making provision instead that the law department of the city of New York shall furnish required legal assistance.
- Providing for the consolidation of the five offices of commissioner of jurors under one head to be appointed by the Appellate Division.
- Providing for the transfer of jurisdiction over civil and criminal prisoners to the department of correction.
- Providing for a constitutional amendment whereby county clerks, registers and sheriffs are no longer continued as constitutional officers, thus making possible administrative adjustments which now cannot be effected.

---

* At the request of the mayor a complete detailed report is being prepared by the law department on legislative action taken on bills presented by representatives of the city and civic organizations.

Presented by the Joint (Brown) Legislative Committee:

Placing county expenses, except salaries of judicial or elective officers, subject to referendum, under control of the city.

Turning the sheriff's fees of New York County into the city treasury, the sheriff to retain no portion of them—**Passed.**

Repealing state aid for maintaining county roads—**Passed.**

Proposing a constitutional amendment whereby county bills in the city of New York are made city bills and as such are subjected to the mayor's veto.

Vesting in the local authorities the regulation of salaries of all county officers and employees—**Passed the senate but was defeated in the assembly.**

Relative to the city government:

Presented by the Brown committee:

Changing the time of collection of taxes from May and November to January and July, so that the necessity for borrowing money on short term paper during the first months of the fiscal year may be obviated—**Passed but vetoed by Mayor.**

Enacting the "pay-as-you-go" policy into law—**Passed.**

Vesting in the local authorities the regulation of salaries of all city officers and employees. Before this bill was passed by the legislature it was amended so as to exclude the officers and employees of the board of education. When finally passed and transmitted to the mayor it afforded the city so little control over the salaries and compensation of city officers and employees beyond that which it already has that the mayor refused to accept the bill on behalf of the city.

Providing for the consolidation of functions relating to the inspection of buildings—**Passed (Lockwood-Ellenbogen bill prepared with the active assistance of Fire Commissioner Adamson).**

Prohibiting deduction from the special franchise tax of the amount of car license fees paid to the city by railroad corporations crossing the Williamsburg and Brooklyn Bridges—**Passed.**

Making more workable the present powers of the city with respect to the regulation of the areas and heights of buildings and the creation of building zones—**Passed.**

Giving to the city control over all expenditures of the board of water supply and the courthouse board.

Providing for the transfer to the state of the expense of maintaining the city's *normal* schools.

Prepared under the direction of the mayor:

Providing for the reorganization of the office of the commissioner of accounts under a single commissioner—**Passed.**

Providing for the substitution of a board of education of nine members for the present board of forty-six.

Providing for the establishment of a department of markets.

Prepared by the chamberlain:

Establishing a department of purchase, based on a previous bill prepared by the comptroller.

Providing for the creation of an enlarged department of health to take over the hospitals and institutions now under the department of public charities, Bellevue and allied hospitals and the board of inebriety, and establishing a department of public welfare—**Withdrawn by Mayor.**

Establishing a department of plant and structures to be responsible for the maintenance and up-keep of buildings and structures now maintained by various city departments, thus concentrating in one department most of the mechanical work of the city—**Passed.**

Providing for the transfer of the collection of water revenues from the department of water supply to the department of finance.

Reorganizing the teachers' retirement fund based on the studies of the mayor's commission on pensions and prepared in conformance with recommendations of the pension commission, a sub-committee of the board of education, and the pension committee of the teachers' federation. **Failed of passage by 3 votes in assembly. Passed by the senate.**

Relative to the relations of the city and state:

Presented by the Brown committee:

Charging the state with the regulative expenses of the public service commission of the first district now borne by the city, and giving the city control over expenses for construction—**Passed—to take effect July 1, 1917.**

Dividing the automobile tax now received wholly by the state with the counties, subject to the restriction that the amount so received shall be expended on roads, except that in the case of New York City the amount so received shall go into the general fund—**Passed.**

Providing that the city shall receive the stock transfer tax on transfers made in the city, and that the state shall be reimbursed for this loss of revenue by an amendment to the inheritance tax law.

Charter Revision

In addition to submitting for legislative action various bills for the purpose of improving administrative conditions, considerable attention has been given by the present administration to the problem of charter revision. On January 23rd, 1914, a committee was appointed to draft suggestions for charter revision. The services of this committee ended on January 13th, 1916, prior to the determination of any definite recommendations, though a considerable mass of material had been collected as a necessary preliminary to the actual work of charter drafting.

As a member of the committee I am preparing a report outlining in some detail a plan of reorganization for the city. The preliminary plan was submitted to the comptroller who carefully considered the principles of organization involved and approved of them.

In this plan it is proposed that the mayor as chief public representative and framer of municipal policies should be released in large part from detailed administrative responsibility, that the board of estimate should become a board of directors, and that as a corollary of these changes there should be a city manager in immediate charge of the administrative activities of the city, with the principal exception of the police department. It is suggested that certain consolidations of departments be made for the purpose of simplifying governmental procedure. The acceptance of some such plan of governmental organization as will be outlined in this report and the request for the necessary legislation to put it into force, would satisfy two of the fusion pledges: (1) obtaining power for the city to frame and adopt its own charter, and (2) the enlargement of the powers of the board of estimate so as to make it the responsible governing board of the city.

Sources of Revenue

Home rule not only means ability to organize the work of the government in accordance with the best judgment of the local authorities, but carries with it the idea that the city should have broader control over its sources of revenue as well as expenditures. The fusion platform contained the pledge that the administration would endeavor to obtain such control. On January 11, 1913, a commission on new sources of city revenue had reported, after exhaustive investigation, on the present sources of the city's revenue and had recommended new measures for adding to them. The new administration, however, felt that additional information was necessary as to the best means for developing new sources of revenue, and in February, 1914, the board of estimate and apportionment adopted a resolution in pursuance of which a committee on taxation was appointed in the following April.

This committee devoted itself to the question of the advisability of reducing in whole or in part the tax on improvements which now forms a part of the ordinary local general property tax, and to a consideration of the best available methods for increasing the income of the city. In January, 1915, it tentatively recommended an "abilities tax," composed of a habitation tax, an occupation tax and a salaries tax to be accompanied by an increment tax. In its final report made in January, 1916, substantially the same proposals were incorporated and bills embodying certain of the recommended measures were prepared and submitted to the mayor for approval.

The committee's recommendations were in summary as follows:

1 That the principle of untaxing buildings, gradually or otherwise, be not adopted.

2 That a state income tax be imposed as a partial means of securing the additional revenue required in the immediate future.

3 That if a state income tax be not feasible, an "abilities tax," composed of a habitation tax, an occupation tax and a salaries tax for the city of New York, be imposed as a partial means of securing additional revenue.

4 That the principle of a low rate tax on personal property as a means of securing additional revenue be not adopted.

5 That a tax upon the increments of land values be imposed.

Several other suggested changes and amendments of law were proposed by the committee, including the repeal of section 48 of the Tax Law, which provides for the deduction from the special franchise tax of the amount paid by the owner of the special franchise as a fee for the franchise and any sums paid which are in the nature of taxes, such as car license fees, etc.

The problem of local taxation in New York City as well as in the state has also been the subject of an investigation by a committee of the state legislature under the the chairmanship of Senator Ogden L. Mills. The legislative committee and the city's committee have been in frequent consultation and have co-operated in the interests of the city and the state.

The present board of estimate has therefore before it the report of the commission on new sources of city revenue and the exhaustive report of the committee on taxation. Sufficient material has been collected to enable the board to reach a determination as to what measures of tax relief should be advocated by the city in the near future. The expenditures of the city have increased so largely in the past few years that the burden on real estate is rapidly becoming too onerous. Unless the city, by means of administrative reorganization and readjustment, finds itself able to reduce the cost of government even more substantially than in the past two years, it will soon be necessary to seek new taxes or new sources of revenue in order to relieve real estate from a mounting tax burden.

Public Service Franchises

The administration has found itself hampered in its desire to improve present conditions with respect to franchises by the existence of many contracts between the city and private corporations which run for long terms of years. The policy heretofore adopted with respect to new franchises has, however, been continued by the present administration. A thorough investigation of each application is made with a view both to the desirability of granting the privilege requested in the interest of the public and to the fixing of terms and conditions upon which the grant shall be made if deemed desirable. An attempt is made in each case to exact proper compensation. The so-called standard form of franchise has been continued in use and has been found to be of benefit in more definitely fixing the relations of the grantee and the city. Use of this form insures equality in the treatment of applicants and avoids any possibility of partiality or favoritism.

The requirement of the charter that the full context of each franchise contract be published twice in two daily newspapers has been found to impose an unduly onerous burden upon applicants, particularly those asking for minor privileges. Accordingly, an amendment to the charter was secured in 1914, providing for the publication of a notice of the hearing upon the franchise and of a statement indicating where full copies of the contract may be obtained. This has been found to answer all reasonable requirements of publicity.

The situation with respect to the lighting companies, which has long been a matter of discussion, has become a matter of action, and the corporation counsel, under the direction of the board of estimate, is prosecuting several suits looking to a determination of the rights of the companies concerned to use the streets of the city. It is believed that the city will be successful in these cases and that as a result the companies will be required to compensate the city properly for the use of public property.

A gradual change in the city's franchise granting policy is therefore being effected so that ultimately public service corporations will make adequate return to the city for the privileges and rights which they enjoy.

Control over Public Service Corporations

The question of control over public service corporations is less easy to determine. There is no clear line of demarcation between the duties of the public service commission of the first district and the city of New York with respect to the control of public utilities. The city has, however, jurisdiction over private water companies which operate in Brooklyn and Queens, and the department of water supply has spent more than a year in making a thorough investigation of these private water companies with a view to their possible acquisition by the city. The department also may control the rates of these companies, and as an incident to the larger investigation, inquiry was made into the relative equity of charges for water supplied to private consumers and to the city for fire protection purposes. As a result of this investigation the rates were radically revised in respect of the Queens County Water Company, the city's payments for fire hydrants being increased materially and the rates charged to private consumers reduced.

The water department also has responsibility for testing the quality of gas supplied by gas companies to the city and to private consumers. The law requires that gas of certain quality be supplied, but it is defective in that it does not provide definitely for adequate penalties in case an inferior quality is furnished. The department has kept careful watch over gas supplied and has found in many cases that the candle power was deficient. It is now endeavoring to reach a satisfactory agreement in the matter with the several gas companies.

A division of complaints has been established in the law department to handle all protests and complaints against public service corporations, and to represent the city's interests in any litigation arising out of franchise grants. Citizen complainants against public service corporations may go directly to the law department and receive prompt attention.

Although the law does not specifically clothe the health commissioner with the right to control the operation of street cars or rapid transit trains, nevertheless, under broad powers conferred upon it to protect the health of the community, the health department has conducted a vigorous campaign against overcrowding in surface cars and in the subway. The railroad corporations, though at first reluctant, later co-operated to some extent, additional cars being provided on surface lines, and an agreement was reached with the Interborough Rapid Transit Company to run the same number of trains during the summer months as during the months of heaviest winter traffic.

Therefore, while the city has not as many nor as complete powers with respect to the control of public service corporations as it should have, definite and concrete steps have nevertheless been taken to improve the character of service rendered the public, and the administration is now engaged upon the problem of obtaining more effective control.

POLICE DEPARTMENT

The present administration came into office pledged to a reorganization of the police department. In 1912 the disclosures following the Rosenthal murder had sharply brought the entire police question before the public. An aldermanic committee on police investigation, generally known as the Curran Committee, was appointed soon after these disclosures and made an exhaustive study of the police department. Its final report, made to the board of aldermen in June, 1913, pointed out many defects and presented a large number of recommendations for changes in organization and methods.

The report was thoroughly considered by the present commissioner. Some of its recommendations could not be carried out without legislation; two or three were thought to be impracticable or undesirable; nearly all of the others, however, have been put into effect, either as originally presented or in a modified form.

In addition to the changes suggested by the Curran Committee, a great many other changes have been made since 1913, both in organization and methods, as a result of continuous study and experimentation by the present administration. There has, however, been no radical or spectacular reorganization. Improvement in the work of the department has come from steady, continuous effort and from careful attention to the smallest details, and is bringing concrete results.

Relation of Administrative Officials to the Uniformed Force

One of the most significant accomplishments of the present police administration is the improved relationship between the police commissioner and his staff of administrative officials, and the uniformed force. There are weekly conferences between the commissioner and the deputies and inspectors, at which departmental matters are taken up intimately and confidentially.

Commanding officers are trusted to do their work and are given to understand that they will be judged by results. All members of the force are permitted, upon application, to have an interview with the commissioner upon any subject. The position has been taken that outside influences shall not be allowed to affect the departmental conduct of business. The men are gradually beginning to understand that the only influence they can count on in their favor is their own performance of good police work, and that no man can expect to have poor police work on his part counteracted by the intercession of influential friends.

Improved Crime Conditions

Because of the inadequacy of the records prior to January, 1915, it is not possible to make complete comparisons of crime conditions now with a similar period two or three years ago. But a comparison of serious crimes reported to the detective bureau during the first three months of 1915 with the last three months of the same year shows a remarkable decrease. During the first three months, 9163 felony cases were reported and 8577 misdemeanor cases, or a total of 17,740. During the last quarter of the year, 6426 and 6009 cases, respectively, were reported, a total of 12,435, or a decrease of almost 30 per cent. The first two months of 1916 compared with the first two months of 1915 show a corresponding decrease.

For some of the most serious offenses, complete data is available for the past two or three years. This information indicates that there has been progressive improvement. For example, there were 246 murders in 1915, as compared with 257 in 1914, and 286 in 1913. In bomb cases, the record was 45 in 1915, 65 in 1914 and 151 in 1913. The reports of burglary cases at the present time are 20 per cent. less than in 1913 and 1914.

Perhaps one of the most significant evidences of improvement in the department's work is the increase in the percentage of convictions, which was 78.94 in 1915, the highest point reached in the history of the department. The record in 1914 was 74.56 per cent., in 1913, 73.67 per cent. and in 1912, 71.52 per cent.

Methods of Patrol

One of the problems taken up in the reconstruction of the department was the study of methods of patrol in use in different sections of the city and the distribution of the police force. It was found that little attempt had been made to vary the methods of patrol to suit the needs of the various sections of the city. The patrol methods originally planned for the business and more populous residential sections of the city had been extended uniformly to the suburban sections, regardless of the fact that the police problem was radically different in these sections. Practically the only exceptions to this general rule were the use of mounted patrolmen in a number of the suburban precincts and the installation of the fixed post system in Manhattan and in portions of Brooklyn and The Bronx.

Reorganization

In undertaking the reorganization of the patrol service the work was planned on two fundamental ideas. First, that the patrol service should be based upon the needs of the locality, and in determining these needs a smaller unit than the precinct should be used, *i. e.*, a patrol post or group of posts should be considered the unit, and foot, mounted, bicycle, motorcycle, or telephone booth service would be used as the conditions in different sections of the precinct demanded. Second, that there should be adequate provision for communication with the man on patrol by means of signal boxes, telephone booths, or such other means as might be devised. The importance of means of communication between the precinct station house and the men on patrol can hardly be over-estimated.

Decrease in Fixed Posts

The first step in this program was to decrease the number of fixed posts, and to transfer the men who had been covering these posts to the residential and suburban sections of the city where the service had been depleted to provide enough men for the fixed post system. The fixed post system solved one problem of patrol service. It provided a means by which a policeman could be found quickly, but this advantage was obtained at a cost of men out of proportion to its value. It required an average of 25 per cent. more men for patrol. To meet this need, approximately 1400 men had been added to the precincts in Manhattan and to the business and more populous residential sections of Brooklyn and The Bronx, with the result that the sections of the city from which the extra men had been drawn were not adequately policed. It was impracticable to operate the fixed post system as it had been planned and at the same time to give proper police service to the other sections of the city without increasing the force beyond the number which the city was able to provide.

Signal Box Service Re-established

Although a large number of the precincts of the city had been provided with signal boxes for communication between the patrolmen and the station house, the boxes had not been used while the fixed post system was in operation. The boxes which had not been used were again put in service and a plan was worked out by which the patrolman calls up from the signal box at least once every hour. A schedule is arranged for each precinct, and the patrolman is given a period of fifteen or twenty minutes in each hour during which his call must be made. This enables the desk officer to give instructions, alarms and complaints to the men on post and it assists very materially in keeping the men on patrol.

Signal Box Posts

In a number of the busiest precincts, signal box posts were established. A signal box post is limited to the territory which a patrolman can cover and still be able to hear the signal box telephone-bell. The man on the signal box post alternates with the man on the adjacent patrol post. This provides a means by which the station house can get in touch immediately with a number of men on patrol who can be dispatched more quickly to the scene of any emergency than the reserves in the station house. The man on each signal box post also covers a zone which includes many of the patrol posts. Any complaints or other matters requiring police attention within this zone are transmitted to the man on the signal box post for his attention.

Flashlights

The weakness of the signal box system is that it does not provide a means by which the officer in the station house can call the patrolman on post unless the patrolman stays close enough to the signal box to hear the telephone-bell. To solve this problem, flashlights were installed in one of the busiest precincts and tried out for several months. The plan worked so successfully that it has been extended to six precincts and is being installed in thirteen others. In addition to the precinct installations, flashlights have been placed at bridge entrances, ferries, and at other important points. The flashlight system is in reality an extension of the signal box system by the addition of a flashlight on the electric light pole above the signal box. A light can be flashed from the station house, or by pressing a button on the signal box.

Telephone Booths

A few telephone booths have been in use in the department for a number of years, but they had been located in the distinctly suburban precincts at points far removed from the station house. They had not been made an integral part of a well thought out system of police service for the suburban and residential sections. In the reorganization of patrol service for these sections, booths have been installed in twenty-seven precincts. Surrounding each booth is a patrol zone, which is patrolled by bicycle or motorcycle men. In a few cases mounted or foot men are assigned to booths and booth zones. The patrolman assigned to the booth can be reached either by telephoning to the station house or by calling the telephone number of the booth. In precincts where before the installation of the booth system it had taken from 45 minutes to an hour—and at certain times of the day even longer—to reach certain points from the station house, these points can now be reached by the men stationed in the booths within six to eight minutes.

Bicycle and Motorcycle Patrol

Bicycle and motorcycle patrol have been substituted in a great many precincts for mounted and foot patrol. Either a bicycle man or a motorcycle man can cover more territory than a mounted man. The extension of this kind of patrol has resulted in actual economies of men in a number of precincts, and has increased the efficiency of the service in other precincts which could not be patrolled properly by either mounted or foot patrolmen.

Decrease in Mounted Service

The substitution of bicycles and motorcycles for the mounted patrol has made it possible to decrease the mounted service from 506 at the beginning of 1914 to 350 in January, 1916. This has resulted in very considerable economies, since the mounted service is the most expensive branch to maintain. The annual cost of maintaining the 156 horses, by which this service has been reduced, exclusive of original purchase cost, was approximately $51,000. The cost of operation and maintenance of the equipment used in place of the horses is approximately $5,000, showing a saving of $46,000.

Reorganization of Patrol Service not Completed

During the greater part of the past two years, chief attention has been given to the reorganization of the patrol service in the suburban sections, because it was felt that the service in these sections was least efficient. In the other sections of the city, attention has been directed to the subject of communication, and improvements have been made almost solely in the extension of these facilities. For several months, however, a comprehensive study of the patrol work in the more congested sections of the city has been under way. Some changes have already been made, principally in adjusting the length of the posts to the requirements of police service on each particular post, and in eliminating the duplication of patrol service on streets which are the boundaries of adjacent precincts.

Posts in many precincts had been laid out so as to keep them as nearly an equal length as possible, without regard to the police conditions on each post. Of two posts of the same length, one might require three or four times as much police work as the other. If the busy posts are shortened and the quiet ones lengthened, more police service will be obtained without increasing the number of men. The changes already made and others which will be made as a result of the work under way, will undoubtedly result in further improvement of the patrol service.

Detective Bureau

The work of the detective bureau is good or bad according to the success of its effort along three lines:

1 Arresting and convicting persons guilty of felonies, that is to say, larcenies of amounts greater than $50, burglaries, assaults with dangerous weapons, blackmail, extortion, confidence games, etc.
2 Preventing the commission of crimes of the character above mentioned.
3 Recovering the proceeds of burglaries and larcenies and returning property to the lawful owners.

There are about 650 men in the detective bureau. These men are assigned to nine branches and certain squads which will be mentioned hereafter. There are four branches in Manhattan, one in The Bronx, two in Brooklyn, one in Queens, and one in Richmond. Each branch has a separate commander who is directly responsible for the detective work done in the territory covered by this branch, and all branch commanders are under the direct supervision of an inspector. The bureau is under the supervision of the second deputy commissioner. This system was inaugurated in August, 1914. Formerly detectives were assigned to precincts, and worked from the station houses. The responsibility for the suppression of crime and the arrest of criminals was then more or less divided between the uniformed force and the detective bureau.

In addition, one special squad devotes itself exclusively to larcenies from lofts; another squad to the rounding up of safe burglars; another looks after pickpockets; another takes care of men engaged in the manufacture of bombs and use of dynamite for criminal purposes; another squad secures evidence against " white slavers "; another looks after the so-called gunmen or gangsters; another is engaged in the suppression of the illegal sale and use of cocaine, heroin, and other habit-forming drugs; another looks after the arrest of automobile thieves and the discovery and return of stolen automobiles. The number and composition of these squads is changed from time to time according to the increase or decrease of the particular crime with which a given squad is concerned.

Selection

The best men are selected for the bureau by a careful examination of the qualifications of members of the uniformed force. No other consideration obtains or has obtained during this administration in making up the personnel of the bureau. The special knowledge of some of the more expert detectives has been made, to a certain extent, the common knowledge of the entire bureau, through a system of talks and practical demonstrations.

Promotions and Demotions

The best effort of the detective is encouraged by the fact that there are two grades of detective, the first grade, which pays $2250 a year, and the second grade, which pays $1400 a year. Promotions and demotions are regulated solely upon merit and record of performances. No political or individual considerations affect the judgment of the commissioner. Changes are made either on the basis of the commissioner's personal observation or on the recommendations of those charged with the immediate supervision of the bureau.

White Slaves

Prior to 1915 the police had not been successful in the prosecution of so-called white slave cases. In 1915, fifty-nine men were convicted under the compulsory prostitution act, and received appropriate sentences ranging in length from one to twenty years. There were more convictions in 1915 than had been previously obtained in the entire history of the city.

Automobile Thieves

Three hundred and sixty-six automobiles were reported as stolen in 1915; 298 were recovered, and others will be. Eighty-six men were convicted of grand larceny for the theft of automobiles, and it can be safely said that among these are included all of the expert automobile thieves who had baffled the police for several years, except two. Of the two, one is dead and the other is not now in the United States. This work was accomplished by a squad of six men, and resulted in the recovery of property valued at more than $300,000.

Gangmen

On the subject of the gangster and gunman no accurate statistics are available as to comparative conditions. There are still plenty of gangsters in New York, but they do not dare herd together, and for that reason are comparatively harmless.

Confidence Men

In 1915, the hotels were crowded to an unprecedented degree, and, as a result, wire-tappers and confidence men flocked to the city. Special effort on the part of the police resulted in the conviction and imprisonment of the best known of these operators. The twelve men who were sent to prison included the two best known confidence men in the United States, along with their principal confederates.

Larcenies and Burglaries

Available statistics indicate a decrease of 20 per cent. in cases of larceny and burglary reported. It is the feeling, however, of those in charge of the bureau, that much more effective work can be done than has been done, and the plan of action now followed is producing important results.

Work of Plain-clothes Men

Vice Control

There has been a marked improvement in the work of the men assigned to plain-clothes duty. These men are engaged primarily in the work of enforcing the laws relating to public morals, and particularly those with reference to prostitution and gambling. This improvement applies both to the squads under the command of inspectors, and to the special squads under the direction of the commissioner and his deputies.

During 1914 there was a very considerable increase in arrests by plain-clothes men. At the same time, a greater proportion of convictions was obtained. This increased activity resulted in bettering conditions, so that arrests were not so numerous in 1915. It may be safely said that the conditions with respect to commercialized prostitution and gambling were never better. This is indicated conclusively by official records of the department, and is borne out by investigations made by outside civic organizations.

Improvements in this branch of the service have been brought about by holding commanding officers to strict accountability for conditions in their territory, and by improvement in the administrative methods so that the work of commanding officers has been under constant supervision and review by the deputy commissioners, each of whom has jurisdiction over police conditions in one of the boroughs.

Formerly there was no system for handling complaints concerning vice conditions, and no provision for follow up on complaints or review of reports. A procedure has been established by which all of these complaints, except those handled personally by the commissioner or a deputy, are handled by the complaint clerk, who is a member of the commissioner's staff. Periodical reports covering the work of the different commands and of the individual members of the command are also required. By review of these reports and comparison of results, an effective check is maintained over the work both of the squads and of the individual members.

Drug Traffic

Until a comparatively short time ago there was little appreciation of the extent of the traffic in habit-forming drugs, and of the relation of this traffic to crime. Many of the most vicious crimes of assault, as well as a considerable portion of the crimes of theft, are the result of the use of drugs. A very large proportion of the persons arrested for the sale or use of drugs have previous criminal records. Early in the administration, one of the special squads was assigned to work almost solely upon the suppression of the drug traffic. At the time, the importance of this work was impressed upon the inspectors and other commanders of the plain-clothes squads, so that this work has constituted a considerable portion of the work performed by plain-clothes men.

The traffic has not been suppressed, but conditions have improved, and it is now very much harder to obtain drugs for illegal use than ever before. The department's work has been facilitated greatly by enactment of legislation providing for better control—the Boylan Law in the state and the federal statute known as the Harrison Law.

The following statement of arrests and convictions shows the increased activity of the department for the last three years in this class of crime:

Year	Arrests	Convictions	Discharges	Pending
1913	512	256	147	109
1914	1,950	947	612	391
1915	1,978	1,379	390	209

Mendicancy and Vagrancy

Increased attention has also been given to the suppression of mendicancy and vagrancy. A special squad has been employed on this work for the purpose of forcing the professional panhandlers and the beggars—who frequently beg not because of their need but because it presents an easy way of obtaining a living, and in many cases even more than a living—to accept employment and cease their imposition upon the public.

Traffic Service

For a number of years prior to 1914 there had been no material increase in the number of men assigned to traffic duty. On the contrary, in 1912 the force was decreased to provide additional men for the fixed post system.

Police Sergeant Talking to School Children on the Causes of Street Accidents

In 1914 legislation was secured authorizing the assignment to traffic duty of a maximum force of 1,000 instead of 550 as formerly. Since that time the force has been gradually increased until there are now 650 men assigned to this work.

The increases in force have been based upon the most thorough study of traffic conditions, supplemented by carefully collected data with respect to street accidents. Since there has been no increase in the police force during the past two years, any increase in the traffic force had to be met by a corresponding decrease in the regular patrol force, so that additions have been made only where and when traffic conditions compelled them.

In traffic work emphasis has been laid very largely upon changes which would help to reduce street accidents and make the streets safer for pedestrians. At the same time, a great deal of attention has been given to improvement in the regulation of vehicular traffic.

Street accidents have decreased in number. During the first two months of 1916 there were 1,966 vehicular accidents as compared with 2,005 accidents during January and February, 1915. This indicates that the work of the traffic force has been more efficient not only in the matter of accident prevention, but also in the regulation of traffic. The decrease is more notable if the increase in the number of vehicles on the streets is considered. The increase in motor vehicles alone, licensed in New York City between 1914 and 1915, was 18,098, or 33%.

Of the constructive work undertaken in traffic regulation, the following are worthy of special comment:

Car-Stop Safety Zones

Car-stop safety zones have been established at a large number of the principal traffic centres. These afford a space where persons may alight from a car with safety. They have been a very effective aid in the prevention of accidents. The statistics of street accidents show that in no case has a person been injured while alighting from or boarding a car at a safety zone, whereas previously there were many accidents at these places.

Play Streets

To provide places where children might play without danger from street traffic, a number of blocks in thickly populated residential sections have been set aside as play streets. On these blocks, no traffic, except on Sunday, is permitted between the hours of 3 and 6 p. m. Other streets, used largely by children, have been designated as congested streets, and the speed of traffic along these streets has been limited to not more than eight miles an hour during certain hours of the day.

Educational Talks on Street Accidents

Through co-operation with business concerns employing large numbers of chauffeurs and truck drivers, police officers thoroughly familiar with traffic regulations, causes of street accidents and means of preventing them, have been assigned to visit garages and stables and to talk with the drivers, giving them instruction in traffic regulations, and pointing out ways in which they can assist the police department in facilitating traffic and preventing accidents. Police officers have also been assigned to visit the schools to talk to school children on the dangers of playing in the street. This has been done not for the purpose of keeping the children off the streets, but rather to impress upon them the necessity of playing on streets set aside for the purpose, or on streets where traffic is light, and also to give them an idea of the most frequent causes of accidents and what they can do both to protect themselves and to assist the police in the effort to make the streets safer.

Assistance of Regular Patrol Force

Regular patrol officers have been detailed to crossings where traffic regulation is needed for a few hours a day during the rush periods, but at which the normal traffic conditions do not justify the assignment of a regular traffic officer. The precinct patrol force has also assisted in warning children and parents, and drivers of automobiles and trucks, and in other preventive work.

Changes in Traffic Regulations

Probably the most important change in traffic regulation has been the installation of the semaphore system on Fifth Avenue, between 26th and 58th streets. By this method of regulation, vehicles are permitted to move at least five blocks at a time without interruption. This innovation has very materially improved traffic conditions on the city's busiest traffic street.

Regulations for street traffic promulgated by the police commissioner were revised and distributed to all public stables, garages, and corporations or persons employing large numbers of drivers.

The number of permanent one-way traffic streets has been increased, and at times, when traffic conditions are particularly bad because of snow and ice, other streets have been temporarily reserved for one-way traffic.

Safety and rotary traffic aisles, consisting of traffic stanchions to prevent vehicles from cutting the corners, have been established in a number of places and have prevented collisions between vehicles as well as providing greater safety for pedestrians.

Need for Additional Legislation

The intensive study which has been made during the past two years of traffic conditions has pointed out the need for extension of the regulative provisions. Accordingly, a number of amendments to the ordinance have been introduced at the suggestion of the police commissioner. One of these provides for the restriction of speed of motor trucks of large capacity; others relate to restriction in the use of certain streets by commercial vehicles, hacks, etc., at certain hours, and to the use of headlights on

Police Sergeant Talking to Drivers in Garage on Dangers and Street Accidents

automobiles. Amendments to the motor vehicle law have also been proposed, providing for the licensing of all operators of motor vehicles, whether employees or owners, and for the revocation of such licenses.

Training School

The training school has been greatly improved and developed. It is now not only a school for recruits but also a school for all members of the force. Its purpose is to provide instruction and training for the new members of the force, which would qualify them to perform their police work capably and intelligently, and which at the same time would test those receiving instruction as to their qualifications to remain in police service. Other courses, for patrolmen already in the service, for those seeking promotion, for superior officers, and for those assigned to special duty, have been started in order to give men on the force opportunity for self-improvement and to increase the efficiency of the police service.

Course for Recruits

The course for recruits has been extended from six to twelve weeks, and even after leaving the school for duty in precincts the men spend one day each week at the school on review work until the end of the probationary period, *i. e.,* six months.

Promotion and Other Classes

Promotion courses for patrolmen seeking advancement to the rank of sergeant have been established, as have similar schools for sergeants who desire promotion to the rank of lieutenant. Both of these schools have been very successful, a large proportion of all men eligible for promotion having enrolled. In addition, a course for lieutenants has been provided, all lieutenants being assigned to the school for a period of two weeks in each year. Special two-week courses for men about to be promoted to higher ranks and similar special courses for men assigned to special duty have also been conducted.

Improvements in Records and Administrative Procedure

Much attention has been given to improvement of the records of the department, and to the development of a comprehensive system of reports and records. Prior to the time this work was started, the information available in the departmental records concerning crime and general police conditions throughout the city was not sufficiently complete and in most cases not accurate enough to be used by the officials of the department as a basis for administrative judgment or action.

Handling Complaints

One of the first studies had to do with the methods of handling complaints from citizens concerning crimes and conditions requiring the attention of the police. With the exception of complaints of more serious crimes, which are ordinarily handled by the detective bureau, there was no requirement that any record be made of a citizen's complaint, nor were there any rules or instructions as to the method of handling them. Complaints handled by the detective bureau were reported to headquarters and supplementary reports were forwarded, giving the disposition or action taken. Written or telephone complaints received at headquarters were forwarded to precincts and other commands for investigation and report, but equally important complaints received at precincts or other offices were not sent to headquarters. The complaints on file at headquarters were, therefore, only a portion of the total number received. An examination of the records indicated also that the procedure in handling complaints referred to the detective bureau did not show receipt of and action upon such complaints.

On January 1, 1915, a new procedure was put into effect, in accordance with which a record must be made of every complaint received at headquarters, detective bureau branches, district offices, precincts or other offices. Brief memoranda on each complaint and the action taken thereon are also sent to headquarters, where they are filed by precincts and are used in compiling statistics of conditions throughout the city as indicated by complaints from citizens.

Accident Reports

A new procedure governing street accident reports was also put into effect on January 1, 1915. Prior to this time, the patrolmen reported accidents, but the reports were not sent to headquarters, and the facts ascertained were meagre. Under the new procedure, the patrolmen are provided with special forms containing headings for the important facts about street accidents. The reports are now sent to headquarters, where they are used for the compilation of data on traffic conditions, places and causes of accidents, etc. Maps which show the places at which accidents occur are made up from the reports for the purpose of locating the danger points, so that preventive measures may be taken. Special studies are also made of locations at which accidents are most numerous, to determine the causes and factors, such as street obstructions, poor lighting, arrangement of car tracks, course of traffic, etc.

Arrest Reports

No change has been made in the procedure for reporting arrests, but the report form has been revised to provide additional information of statistical value. The method of filing has also been changed to facilitate reference to offenders against traffic regulations. All cases of traffic violations are filed in a separate file, so that the records of those who have been previous offenders may be ascertained quickly.

Statistics

The statistical work of the department has been completely reorganized by centralizing it in the bureau of statistics. Information formerly

Training for Recruits

compiled in precincts and in the detective bureau branches, and in several offices at headquarters, is now collected in this bureau. This centralization insures uniformity in method and classification, as well as accuracy and completeness. The work is being gradually extended, in response to the administrative needs of the department.

Reports for Administrative Purposes

Current reports for the police commissioner and other administrative officers are compiled in the bureau of statistics as follows: (1) Reports of crimes and offenses reported to the police, classified by the principal crime classifications, as well as by precincts and other units of command, also comparatively by periods; (2) reports of the work of the several detective branches; (3) reports of street accidents analyzed by time, causes, etc. In addition to these reports, a great many special studies are made both of crime conditions and of street accidents.

Handling Alarms

The methods of handling alarms adopted many years ago had been continued in use without revision or development to meet present day problems. As a result, the issuance of alarms and the action taken on them had become merely perfunctory. Seldom, if at all, were any results obtained. To replace this outgrown system, an improved procedure was worked out providing for central control over the issue of alarms.

All important alarms are transmitted to the men on post by means of the signal boxes and telephone booths. The patrolmen, before going on post, are required to copy in their memorandum books the alarms which have been received at the station house during the preceding twenty-four hours. They are also required to copy any alarms they may receive over the signal box or booth telephone. It was found that copying the alarm serves to impress it upon the mind of the policeman, and with the important facts of the alarm in his memorandum book, he always has an opportunity to refresh his memory. Formerly, the alarms were read to the outgoing platoon by the commanding officer or desk officer. Sometimes as many as eight or ten alarms would be read to the patrolmen, with the result that they had no definite impression of any one.

These changes have brought effective results. During the past year a number of very important arrests have been made in this way. In two cases murderers were arrested by uniformed officers. A great number of stolen automobiles have also been recovered, and in several cases, automobile thieves and persons wanted for other offenses have been detained by uniformed officers acting on information received in alarms.

Detective Bureau Records

The principal changes in the detective bureau records have been made in the criminal identification records and in the means of identifying stolen property. There has been no change in the procedure in the bureau of criminal identification, but the work has been greatly extended. During the past two years the number of finger-print records in the files has more than doubled, and including those received from other police departments, records are being added at the rate of approximately 50,000 a year. This means a very great increase in the effectiveness of the identification records as aids in the work of the detective bureau. By comparison with other cities, records are interchanged and the New York bureau is rapidly becoming a national clearing house for information concerning criminals.

There has been in use in the department for a number of years a system for the identification of certain kinds of stolen and lost property. A comprehensive plan which will multiply the effectiveness of this work has been developed. This was made possible by ordinances recently enacted providing for reports to the police department from all pawnshops and second-hand dealers of articles pledged or sold. These reports are compared with the reports of lost and stolen property, and if the description is similar, the person who reported the loss is given an opportunity to identify the property and to prove ownership, if so identified. Although these records have been in use only for a short time, they promise to be of great aid in the recovery of stolen property.

Precinct Records and Procedure:

Coincident with improvement in the records and administrative procedure at headquarters, many changes have been made in the precinct records and methods of handling reports, records and files. This work is not yet completed. A thorough survey is being made at the present time of the methods of transacting the routine work of the precincts, preparatory to the installation of a uniform procedure. No instructions have ever been prepared governing much of the work of the precinct officers. Each commanding officer has been free to develop his own system, with the result that there is no uniformity in the method and no standard in the orderliness and efficiency with which the routine work of the precincts is transacted. Of the changes already made, the following are the most important:

Revision of force and time records: Substituting separate loose-leaf forms for the former cumbersome card system, which was difficult to operate, caused duplication, and did not provide an adequate permanent record.

Revision of arrest, aided and accident records: Providing for an arrest record and a record of accident and aided cases, instead of the present combined record; also providing for the simplification of entries in the aided and accident record. This change has been worked out and will be put into effect just as soon as the new forms are ready.

Simplification of blotter entries: Instructions providing for a uniform method of making these entries have been issued. The former rules on this subject left the way open for unnecessary recording and differences in methods. Uniformity has been secured by the issuance of printed reproductions of the blotter, containing examples of the way in which entries should be made.

Crime maps and reports of precinct activity: In each precinct, maps are kept upon which are shown the exact locations where crimes have been committed. These maps, with the reports of precinct activities which are prepared weekly and monthly, enable the commanding officer to keep informed as to the conditions within his precinct and as to the particular sections where trouble is likely to occur.

Patrolmen's reporting system: Patrolmen have been required for many years to report conditions observed on their posts, such as defective highways and sidewalks, violations of corporation ordinances, street lamp outages, etc. Formerly, entries of these observations were made in their memorandum books and were copied from these books by the desk officer or clerical man in the precinct. These reports in the memorandum books were not prepared with any uniformity, and frequently did not contain all of the necessary information. Specially printed forms have now been provided. The headings on these forms show the patrolman what he should report, insure uniformity, and facilitate his work.

Merit System

The most important change affecting the precinct patrol force has been the introduction of a merit system. This system was tried out for several months in six precincts, and on March 1st of this year was extended on trial to all precincts. It is the result of study and work of over a year on the part of members of the administrative staff and a committee of inspectors. The underlying idea of the plan has been to develop a means by which the every-day work of a policeman would be made a part of his official record upon which his advancement and recognition in the service would depend. The work in the different sections of the city has been graded so that the man on a quiet post, where there is little to do, will not be handicapped in comparison with the man on a busy post, where there is more demand for police work.

Administration of Pension Fund

During the past two years, a current saving of approximately $413,000 has been effected in police pensions, in comparison with the results of the three preceding years, 1911, 1912 and 1913. During these three years the annual charge against the pension fund had been increased about $654,000, or an average of $218,000 per year. During 1914 and 1915 the average increase has been a little under $11,200, which shows a saving of $206,800 for each year.

This has been accomplished without denying to any member of the force any right to retirement to which he is entitled, and without reducing the amount which it has been customary to pay police pensioners. Nor has the service suffered because of continuing men on the force who are physically unable to perform any kind of police service. The result has been brought about through the adoption of common sense standards of physical requirements; through assignment to duty in accordance with the demands of the service, and through the preventive work of the board of surgeons.

In assignments to duty where the demands of service are not so severe, the older men who are less fit physically have been given preference. This practice has been followed without detriment to the service. These men are able to respond to an emergency and to measure up to many of the requirements of police work as satisfactorily as the younger and less experienced men. At the same time, these older men probably would not be able to stand service requiring great physical stamina and would be forced to retire if continued in such assignments. During 1915 only 55 policemen were retired for disability, as compared with 79 in 1914 and 308 in 1913.

Improvement in Department Property and Equipment

The present administration found the buildings of the department generally in very bad condition. General repair work had long been neglected, and many buildings were inadequately equipped with facilities for the comfort and health of the men, such as bathing, washing and toilet facilities.

A program was prepared which provided for: first, repairs necessary to prevent deterioration of the buildings; second, installation of shower baths and sanitary washing and toilet facilities; third, general improvements and betterments. The last plan is to be delayed, however, until the work necessary to carry out the first two items on the program has been completed.

During the past two years, in accordance with this program, provision has been made for extensive repairs in thirty buildings. It is thought that by the end of the present year practically all of the work listed under the first and second items above can be completed. If similar provision of funds is made in the budget for 1917 as for 1916, it will be possible to put the buildings of the police department in such condition by the end of this administration that the appropriations for repair work can be materially decreased for a number of years.

As a part of the program for keeping the force in better physical condition, gymnasiums have been established in over one-third of the precinct station houses. It is hoped that by the end of this year gymnasiums can be provided in practically every station house in the city.

Three additional motor patrol wagons have been added, and provision was made in the 1916 budget for complete motor installation throughout the city. Contracts for the equipment have been awarded, and within a few weeks all of the horse-drawn wagons will be replaced by motor vehicles. This change will result in a saving of approximately $30,000 a year.

EXTENSION OF THE CITY'S SOCIAL SERVICE PROGRAM

City Planning

Several specific recommendations were made in the fusion platform with respect to the assumption by the city of a broader and more farsighted social service program. Among them was the promise that city planning would be undertaken on a broad scale and that definite progress would be made in regulating the height, size and arrangement of new buildings in various sections of the city, together with a plan of districting in accordance with the character of occupancy of buildings.

In 1913 a heights of buildings commission was appointed by the board of estimate and apportionment to study the needs of the city with respect to the regulation of building heights in certain districts. On the recommendation of this commission an amendment to the charter was secured in 1914 authorizing the board of estimate and apportionment to divide the city into districts, and to regulate the height of buildings, the area of courts and open spaces, and the location of trades and industries in each district. This legislation provided, however, that before the establishment of such districts the board of estimate should appoint a commission to recommend the boundaries, and that public hearings should be held upon these recommendations.

The report of the heights of buildings commission was referred to the committee on city plan. This committee early in 1914 recommended to the board of estimate that a commission on building districts and restrictions be appointed, which should be authorized to use the staff of the committee on city plan in its work. A committee on building districts was appointed in 1914, and in March, 1916, submitted a tentative report to the board of estimate. This report, which was favorably received by the public, makes recommendations relative to the locations of trades and the heights of buildings throughout the city. Public hearings were held during March and April, 1916. If the report is accepted by the board of estimate it will be the basis for the redistricting of the city which the board is authorized to undertake by charter sections 242-a and b.*

The committee on city plan for the last two years has occupied itself mainly in co-operating with the committee on building districts and restrictions. It has not been possible, therefore, for it to furnish the board of estimate information and facts fundamental to the working out of a thorough program for rational city planning. Accordingly, the next few years must necessarily be occupied by the committee in laying the foundations for this work by the collection of essential data and statistics for a comprehensive scheme of city development. In addition, the committee will be engaged as in the past in currently investigating and reporting, in conjunction with the chief engineer of the board of estimate, on the more important proposed public improvements.

---

* Adopted April 15, 1916.

There are other problems with which the committee should deal. It should be possible to effect an increased degree of co-operation between the work of the port and terminal committee and the city plan committee, since the adoption of a broad plan for port and terminal development is an imperative need. The committee plans to make an intensive study of future rapid transit extensions in outlying boroughs, so that the needs of various sections can be met more completely and more quickly when the present transportation facilities are augmented. It is planning the location of parks and playgrounds in sections of the city which are at present incompletely developed, so that they may be as convenient of access as possible to the future population. The committee is also working for the adoption of a bill recently introduced, providing for the approval of the board of estimate and apportionment as a condition precedent to the filing of street maps laid out by real estate development companies. At the present time new tracts are opened up by real estate companies and streets are laid out with no particular regard to the general scheme of city thoroughfares. The board of estimate should have power to approve or disapprove the maps made by realty companies so that when the question of final acceptance by the city is raised the city will not have been saddled with incongruities and unnecessary expenses.

In this way the board of estimate is endeavoring to fulfill its pre-election promise to deal with the problem of city planning on an intelligent and comprehensive basis. The staff of the committee which was provided for in the 1915 budget was continued in the 1916 budget and will, for the next two years, devote itself to the questions outlined above.

Markets

Realizing that the problem of food distribution in a city the size of New York, where the private householder possesses such limited facilities for the storage of any quantity of foodstuffs, is one of the most serious economic problems confronting the community, the fusion candidates pledged themselves to undertake in a serious way an investigation of market conditions and the institution of some system whereby producer and consumer could be brought into closer relations.

The board of estimate appointed early in 1914 a committee on markets under the chairmanship of the president of the borough of Manhattan. Later in the year funds were provided for this committee so that a paid staff could be employed and detailed work commenced on the market problem.

After a study of the existing condition of markets in the city and observations as to possible market development, the committee made the following recommendations:

1 That no large sums of money be expended by the city at this time for market terminals, owing to the city's existing financial condition

Old Washington Market—Unsanitary Wooden Floor and Food Uncovered

New Washington Market—Food Sold in Public Markets Under Constant Supervision of Department of Health

2 That railroad and steamship companies be encouraged to provide adequate rail and water terminal and dock facilities at their own expense

3 That open and pushcart markets be established on available city-owned property not required for other purposes

4 That active efforts be made to induce the farmers about New York City to utilize the open markets and to increase their own production

5 That the suburban railroad companies be requested to provide adequate transportation for farmers' produce to the city

6 That a study be made of the existing markets of the city, which were established many years ago, with a view to ascertaining whether or not they serve the purposes for which they were erected and what improvements are necessary to make them more serviceable to the community

7 That private enterprise be encouraged to establish markets and also auction sales for produce, this method having already been established for the sale of poultry and citrus fruits

The chairman of the committee on markets interested himself in carrying out many of the suggestions contained in the report of his committee. He desired to make a practical demonstration of the fact that some immediate relief could be had pending the adoption of a broader plan of wholesale and retail markets, and that the immediate development of the open air market system and an improvement in the pushcart situation would be the most logical first step in the program.

Accordingly, with the co-operation of citizen committees, it was decided that temporary open markets be established at various locations throughout the city. In the fall of 1914 the board of aldermen designated permanent market sites under the Queensboro Bridge, the Harlem River Bridge, and the Manhattan Bridge. Through the efforts of the chairman of the market committee all three sites had been utilized during the summer as temporary markets. Early in 1915 the sinking fund commission assigned as sites for public markets parcels of land under the Williamsburg, the Manhattan, the Queensboro and the Third Avenue bridges. Markets are now in successful operation on each one of these sites. Stands are provided and space is definitely allotted on a rental basis to farmers who care to bring their truck and produce into the city for sale direct to consumer. Prices obtaining at the markets are materially less than prices charged at regular stores. The success of the experiment indicates that the ultimate development by the city of a comprehensive plan for public markets would result in great benefit to the public.

Another problem which has been considered by the market committee relates to the thousands of pushcart peddlers who ply their trade throughout the city, especially in the congested districts where store facilities are inadequate. Two commissions appointed by preceding mayors, and an aldermanic committee, have in recent years made investigations and submitted reports on the pushcart problem in the borough of Manhattan. No definite solution has yet been offered. The open markets, however, have attracted hundreds of pushcarts from the streets, and to some extent this has relieved the congestion, but the problem is still a serious one.

The idea of municipal markets in the city of New York is as yet in its infancy, despite the fact that for years the city has maintained Washington, West Washington, Gansevoort, Jefferson, Fulton and Wallabout markets. Fulton market, because of obsolescence, was discontinued in the spring of 1914. At the present time nine public markets (including the four opened under the bridges) are being operated by the city of New York. But, while these tend in some degree to improve the distribution of foodstuffs, their number is too small and their facilities inadequate to meet present needs.

The best method of meeting this problem is through the provision of wholesale terminal markets. This problem of terminal markets, the fundamental feature of a municipal market system, is closely connected with the problem of port and terminal development. Co-operation between the board of estimate's committees on city plan, port and terminal facilities and the committee on markets, will do much to hasten the time when the city can undertake on its own initiative, or can encourage private enterprise to undertake, the establishment of suitable and adequate facilities for the handling of foodstuffs shipped to the city.

As an incident to the outbreak of the war in 1914 there was a threatened shortage in the food supply of the city of New York. The mayor appointed a citizens' committee, under the chairmanship of Mr. George W. Perkins, to deal with the subject. The committee, among other things, conducted an educational campaign on food conservation and uses, but came to the conclusion that the conspicuous need of the city was a market department to deal consecutively and continuously with the question of food distribution for the entire city. Accordingly, the committee prepared a bill creating a market department following the lines of a similar recommendation made by a market commission appointed by Mayor Gaynor. The bill has been introduced in two legislatures, but still awaits favorable action.

Food Inspection and Pure Milk

It is scarcely necessary to call attention to the fact that the fusion platform provided for continuing and extending the vitally important work of the department of health in connection with inspection of foods and the maintenance of pure milk stations. The work of the bureau of food inspection has been extended to include inspections in hotels and restaurants, and it is hoped ultimately that physical examinations may be made of all persons employed in places where food is handled. In addition, an effective curb has been placed on the sale of fraudulent patent medicines by requiring that labels of patent medicine packages show their ingredients or that the formulae be filed with the department of health.

The bureau of child hygiene has continued to maintain infants' milk stations, and the number of such stations has been increased. In 1915 the number of infants under one year of age registered at the milk stations increased by 10,000. In Part II is given a summary of health activities in this connection and in other fields.

School Lunches

The promise of the fusion party to secure the provision of facilities by the board of education for furnishing lunches to school children at cost was redeemed in large part during 1914 and 1915. Funds were provided in the 1914 and 1915 budgets for equipping schools with the necessary utensils and fixtures for lunchroom service. When such kitchens have been equipped by the board of education, their operation is entrusted to the school lunch committee in Manhattan, which employs a staff of forty-five employees, and in Brooklyn to the Brooklyn School Lunch Association. The paid staffs are assisted in the service by pupils. In 1915, revenue bonds were issued to provide funds for altering sixty school buildings so as to make them suitable for the installation of lunch rooms. While the supplying of luncheons by the board of education is not strictly a function of the department, there are cases where exceptional conditions require such measures. The city has already gone far in its endeavor to meet the needs of this situation.

Extension of Trade and Vocational Training

In the fulfillment of the fusion promise to extend and develop trade and vocational training in public schools, the administration has taken several important steps. In May, 1914, the mayor, the president of the board of education, the chamberlain, several of the associate city superintendents and members of the board of education, went west to visit the schools in Gary, Indiana, and obtain information at first hand on the work being done by Superintendent Wirt, and to inspect the continuation schools established by Dean Schneider in Cincinnati.

As the result of this trip Superintendent Wirt of Gary, Indiana, and Dean Schneider of the Engineering School of the University of Cincinnati, were engaged to make a survey of New York City conditions with reference to the possibility of applying in its public schools many of the principles which they had successfully used in Gary and Cincinnati. After a study of the part-time problem with which New York City is constantly confronted, Mr. Wirt recommended that six schools of different types be set aside by the board of education for the demonstration of his plan. Dean Schneider recommended that the city make a practical demonstration of his plan of correlating the vocational work in high schools with the various trades and industries in the city, which gave children between fourteen and eighteen years old, who were gainfully employed, an opportunity to continue school work.

Accordingly, the board of estimate tentatively agreed to provide approximately $250,000 in the budget for 1915 for this experimental work, and the board of education assigned Associate Superintendent Ettinger as its representative to assist Mr. Wirt, and Associate Superintendent Haaren to assist Dean Schneider.

During the interval prior to Mr. Wirt's arrival, the work of fitting up the schools to meet the needs of the double session plan was entrusted to Superintendent Ettinger, who directed the expenditure of some $70,000 in equipping five model elementary schools with shops. Upon Mr. Wirt's arrival, however, it was found that the schools which had been equipped for him could better be used to demonstrate a system of pre-vocational training devised by Superintendent Ettinger, and it was then arranged that a third experiment should be carried on by the board of education under Superintendent Ettinger simultaneously with the work of Mr. Wirt and Dean Schneider. The chief feature of this third experiment was the provision for three hours a day of technical shop training for certain groups of seventh and eighth grade pupils together with three hours of related academic work. It is as yet too early to reach final judgment on the educational value of these experiments.

Because of this development of the Ettinger plan, it was necessary to make available to Mr. Wirt for his experiment other schools than those chosen by Superintendent Ettinger. In the winter of 1914-15, therefore, two schools were turned over to Mr. Wirt for his demonstration, viz.: No. 89 in Brooklyn and No. 45 in The Bronx. Both schools had been forced by reason of excessive enrollment to keep the majority of their pupils on part time. Mr. Wirt reorganized these schools and by the application of the "work-study-play" program has been able to establish a six-hour school day for all classes except those of the lowest grades in The Bronx school, where a five-hour day was substituted for the former day of three and three-quarter hours. During 1915 this work was continued and funds for the erection of additions to provide improvements such as swimming pools, gymnasiums, shops, laboratories and library rooms were provided for both schools.

In addition to the foregoing, the board of education decided to proceed with the reorganization of twelve additional schools in The Bronx. About $750,000 was made available by the board of estimate for the necessary permanent improvements in the buildings. The schools are located in a section so congested that had not some such plan been adopted it would have been necessary to construct immediately about six new buildings, at a cost of approximately $3,000,000, if all of the 12,000 pupils then receiving less than five hours instruction were to be given full time opportunities under the old plan of providing a reserved school seat for each pupil.

The services of Mr. Wirt have been continued for the year 1916 and up to the present time five of the twelve schools selected have been reorganized.

At the time of the preparation of the 1916 budget, the board of estimate, impressed by the success which had attended Mr. Wirt's initial efforts, agreed to make available about $5,000,000 during 1916 for the elimination of part-time in all schools in accordance with the " work-study-play " program.

The Gary " work-study-play " program provides opportunities for shop and laboratory work for all children above the fourth grade, eliminates part-time and increases the length of the school day to six hours, thus keeping the child under the supervision of trained teachers for a longer period each day and giving him the advantages not only of being taught definite academic and trade subjects by special teachers but also of having his recreation and play to some extent supervised and guided. It also makes possible co-operation between public libraries, recreation centers, parks, playgrounds and schools, hitherto deemed impossible of attainment.

The facilities for education and recreation which the city now offers are made available in greater measure to the people of the city by the proposed plan for the co-ordination of all welfare agencies. Moreover, these increased advantages are secured with reduced expenditures for school buildings and sites by making a more intensive and wider use of the present school plant. The reduced expenditure for sites and buildings will mean a permanent saving of interest and amortization charges. Instead of the original estimate of forty million dollars required for sites and new buildings, the board of superintendents have reported officially that twelve and a half million dollars will eliminate all part-time and also provide for some increase in register, if the " work-study-play " school program is adopted.

The practical application of the principles contained in Dean Scheider's plan was entrusted to ten regular high school teachers in ten schools, who were assigned to the work of interesting employers of labor in the utilization of high school students on a part-time arrangement under the direction of Associate Superintendent Haaren. This part-time arrangement provides for the selection of pairs of pupils who shall spend alternate weeks in school and shop and who shall follow a program of school work so formulated as to assist them in their chosen occupations. The experiment of Dean Schneider is still proceeding. Before the principles which he has established can be applied throughout the city, however, it will be necessary to impress upon the business interests the fact which has been demonstrated so far in this experiment, namely, that a successful plan of co-operation can be worked out between the high schools and employers. In order to develop further co-operation between the industrial interests and the school authorities, $15,000 has been made available for an industrial survey to be conducted by a committee of 13 to be appointed by the mayor.

The present administration has addressed itself seriously to the problem of developing trade and vocational training in the public schools. As outlined above, three definite and distinct experimental undertakings have been inaugurated—one under Associate Superintendent Ettinger, one under Dean Schneider and Associate Superintendent Haaren, and one under Mr. Wirt.

To lay the basis for a fundamentally sound plan of industrial education which shall be related to the needs of future workers, take cognizance of industrial opportunities and the requirements of employers, and which shall as well conform to proper educational standards the board of estimate recently authorized the mayor to appoint a commission to conduct an industrial educational survey of the city. This committee, under the chairmanship of Dr. C. Richards, Director of Cooper Institute, and composed of representative employers, employees and educational experts, has begun its work and before the end of the present administration should have arrived at recommendations for the permanent guidance of New York's enlarged vocation educational activities.

Unemployment

An unforeseen emergency which confronted the administration in the winter of 1914-1915 resulted from the disturbance of industrial conditions which created widespread unemployment. The distress of thousands of people furnished the opportunity for agitation and radical propaganda. Turbulency developed in the streets as an incident to the holding of public meetings at which various means for the relief of unemployed workers were urged.

By effective action on the part of the police in providing opportunity for free speech held, however, strictly within limitations imposed by law, disorder was quieted and public peace restored. It was obvious, however, that constructive measures were demanded.

As a result of a conference called at the house of Mr. Jacob H. Schiff, at which leading citizens, important employers and public officials were present, the mayor appointed a sub-committee of officials to take up questions of unemployment. This committee, consisting of the chamberlain, commissioner of public charities, commissioner of licenses and the president of the municipal civil service commission, proposed the organization of a public employment bureau to be conducted by the city government. This proposal was approved by the board of aldermen, and since May, 1914, for the first six months experimentally and subsequently under permanent organization, the city has conducted an employment bureau for the purpose of bringing about a better organization of the employment market in the city. This bureau is now rendering notable service to employers and to those who seek work.

From November, 1914, to April, 1916, over 11,000 positions have been reported as filled. The increasing value of the bureau is evidenced by the fact that in February, 1916, the bureau with its subdivisions, which are supported by voluntary organizations, found employment for 1420 persons and in March for 1926 persons, an increase of 42 per cent. A detailed statement of its work follows.

Another effort to meet the critical industrial situation was the appointment by the mayor of a committee of citizens under the chairmanship of Ex-Judge Elbert H. Gary. This committee co-operated with existing organizations for the relief of distress, and throughout the winter of 1914-1915 provided emergency relief by giving temporary work at a nominal wage to 11,073 men and women for 215,429 days. An average of 5,000 persons were employed daily. Funds used for this relief were raised by public subscription. The basis for a constructive program for the city in dealing with problems of unemployment was also laid, so that the city will not again be confronted unprepared with similar difficulties.

The results of the work of this committee have since been published in a report submitted to the mayor by the chairman and secretary of the committee.*

Following the suggestion of the committee, the mayor appointed in the winter of 1916 a small standing committee on unemployment problems representing leaders of industry, labor leaders and social workers. This committee, with funds provided entirely by private subscription, will continue to serve the people of the city in preparing against a subsequent recurrence of acute unemployment. Through conference and investigation it is developing constructive measures to eliminate conditions which promote unemployment in so-called normal times as well as in periods of distress.

Public Employment Bureau

The function of the public employment bureau is to organize in an authoritative, disinterested centre the demands made by individual employers and the unemployed workers available to meet these demands. While the service performed for the employee seeking quick and suitable connection with a livelihood is important at all times, the service to employers is especially important in periods of labor shortage. Public employment bureaus can more easily conserve the labor supply and avoid unnecessary unemployment by the fair and effective distribution of labor from places of oversupply to points of demand. Another function of such bureaus, as yet well developed only in England, is the guidance of the 50,000 boys and girls who leave school annually into constructive employment opportunities.

During the period under consideration the public employment bureau has been called upon by 11,530 employers to select and supply 17,408 employees. 51,191 men and women have registered their qualifications and desire for work. About 11,000 placements have been made. The total number is actually larger than this, because in spite of method and persistency, no report is received from a considerable number of the introductions made through the office, and credit is taken only for proved placements.

* Report of the Mayor's Committee on Unemployment, January, 1916.

The monthly average number of placements increased from **300** for the first **nine** months of 1915 to **827** for the next **three** months, and **1609** for the first **four** months of 1916. The number of placements in March (1926) was larger than the number placed in all four long-established state bureaus in Massachusetts. Two-thirds of those placed at work were men, and of these 20% were mechanics, 6% building trades help, and nearly 40% persons engaged in trade and transportation. The last group includes office help, salespeople, packers, shippers and laborers. Of the women placed, one-half were in domestic and personal service, and nearly one-half in trade and transportation.

All boroughs are served, though not evenly because of insufficient funds for branches. 97% of the calls from employers came from within the city, being distributed approximately as follows: Manhattan 80%, Brooklyn 9%, The Bronx 3%, Queens 4%, Richmond 1%. 98% of the labor supply lived in the city, and was distributed approximately 3/5 in Manhattan, 1/4 in Brooklyn, 1/10 in The Bronx, 3% in Queens.

In addition to the steadily increasing number of places obtained, and of satisfied calls for service, there is evidence of expanding good will in the fact that most of the employers' accounts received remain actively open and applications are made to the bureau for higher grades of help.

The extraordinary gain in results during the last few months is based on solid earlier preparation and cumulative relations. The ability to care for the greatly increased work has been made possible by faithfulness and energy on the part of the staff, plus new distributions and methods of work.

In March, 1915, a special branch was established in the Municipal Lodging House for the homeless unemployed. In July, a branch was opened in the East Side House for the Yorkville District, which is maintained by private organizations and persons of that neighborhood, with the exception of supplies furnished by the bureau. A local private and a temporary United States employment office are soon to be combined with this branch.

The Greenpoint office, opened in September last, is located in a Neighborhood building, but other expenses are borne by the bureau, one of whose workers is assigned to it. Though it was inactive for a few months this branch has lately proven to be a decided success in serving this industrial district.

The Chelsea branch in Hudson Guild was formerly a long established private philanthropic bureau for women day workers. It was taken over by the bureau in December, 1915. Here, too, all of the expense except supplies and one of the three workers is met by the Neighborhood Guild. Plans are under way for developing this branch so that it will meet the needs of both sexes.

The Greenwich branch, opened March, 1916, is maintained similarly to the Yorkville office by the Public Forum and Community Centres of the village. All of the branches are supervised by the bureau superintendent, and operate as parts of a growing system. The Yorkville, Chelsea and Greenwich branches are supported for the purpose of demonstrating the need of local branches.

Relations between the bureau and other departments are developing to mutual advantage. The police department assists by means of the signal system to men on beats in locating employees who have previously registered and for whom a sudden need develops. The division of repairs of the street cleaning department calls upon the bureau for extra wheelwrights, blacksmiths, and others. If satisfactory, the person is employed temporarily, and a report is made as to his ability.

The bureau co-operates with the commercial and trade extension classes for unemployed girls located in the same building and established as part of the constructive program for dealing with the unemployment situation, and the regular trade and vocational schools. It has recently arranged to give preference to persons who attend or have graduated from such classes, and does all of the placing work for one of the classes. The bureau's request that the mayor's committee on unemployment and the department of education establish similar classes for unemployed boys has been approved.

The bureau co-operates with the civil service commission by advertising its examinations, and by procuring high grade candidates. Conversely, it hopes to obtain carefully rated persons for private employment from the eligible lists. The civil service eligibility cards ought to be recognized as of primary value in obtaining employment anywhere in the occupation covered.

It is now developing a plan for the affiliation of three juvenile employment bureaus, and expects as rapidly as possible to assimilate the three score private non-commercial employment centres of New York into a single harmonious system.

The solution of the employment problem is of first rate importance to the commercial, industrial and social life of the community. Its undertaking cannot depend on political exigencies at Albany or the awakening of remote districts. The city should not wait for the general organization of its labor market until the state develops a policy and an effective organization. The bureau should be maintained under its present direction until the state has developed a satisfactory policy for dealing with the subject.

Many students of the subject believe that wherever the local problem can be affected or relieved by common action with other industrial and commercial centres, the state and federal government's part should be that of a correlating, not a local administrating, force, as in public health and education.

Opinion as to the division of this function between city, state and nation is still nebulous. For this reason the executives of the national, state and city systems of public employment bureaus have been formed into a committee to develop interrelations.

DEVELOPMENT OF A COMPREHENSIVE, SCIENTIFIC SYSTEM OF PENSIONS FOR CITY EMPLOYEES

In the summer of 1913, Mayor Gaynor appointed a commission on pensions to investigate and report on the general subject of municipal pensions. Preliminary work was begun under Mayor Kline, when a series of hearings were held relative to the city's existing funds. Intensive studies of the pension problem were not commenced, however, until the spring of 1914, when appropriations of $31,000 were made available by the board of estimate and a staff engaged for the work.

New York was the first American city to pension its employees and is the first city to undertake a scientific investigation of pension funds for the purpose of establishing them upon a sound actuarial basis. There are at present in the city of New York one general and eight departmental pension systems. Analysis of the financial condition of these funds shows that in no case had provision been made for the development of an adequate reserve to meet their liabilities. These funds are in the greatest possible confusion. They lack uniformity, soundness of financial provision and in some cases are uncertain with respect to future benefits to participants. The financial condition of some of them, particularly the police and firemen's funds are analogous to conditions that would prevail if the city issued long term bonds, falling due in varying amounts in different years, and made no sinking fund provision for them.

In order to approach the problem of reorganizing existing funds and establishing a sound general service and disability retirement system with proper information, it was necessary to make a study of the experience of the entire service of the city and to determine fundamental actuarial facts. This was a monumental task involving a census of 120,000 employees representing all persons who had been in the service of the city from January, 1907 to January, 1914. The methods employed in making this census had to be devised, for there were no suitable precedents to follow, and a vast quantity of statistical work had to be performed. In addition, an exhaustive analysis of the existing funds (actuarial computations being wholly lacking) had to be made. The difficulty of the task was increased by confusion and deficiency of records, for to this important part of its business now representing an annual outlay of $5,000,000 for 8,000 existing pensioners, the city had never before given business-like attention. This work is all completed and, in addition, a new plan for the reorganization of the teachers' retirement fund, involving 21,000 teachers has been worked out and submitted to the legislature. The plan looks to a financially sound pension plan for the teachers, making impossible the recurrence of the bankrupt condition into which the existing teachers' retirement fund had fallen. The plan devised by the pension commission follows the best precedents in the organization of European and Australian pension systems, and was agreed to by the representatives of the teachers in conference, approved by the board of education, the mayor and the comptroller, and was submitted for the action of the legislature.* It is based on the principle of equal contributions of teachers and the city to meet the cost of future pensions, but provides, as a matter of necessity, that the city shall make up the excess of accrued liabilities for existing members of the force where the excess exceeds the amount that can be met by an 8% contribution of teachers. Ultimately the cost to the city for teachers' pensions will be reduced to about 5% of the payroll for teachers, whereas the present cost to the city for the pensions of firemen and policemen already equals 14% of the respective payrolls for those forces, and is destined, unless corrective legislation is obtained greatly to exceed that proportion.

The pension commission has published two reports. One, on the teachers' retirement fund, containing a plan for its reorganization together with an estimate of prospective cost and the actuarial tables on which it is based. The second contains a descriptive analysis of the present condition of the eight other pension funds. The commission has in preparation eight reports describing the condition of the individual pension funds. A report is now in press covering the actuarial cost of all of these funds on the present plan of operation. A report is in course of preparation which will set forth proposals for the reorganization of all pension funds on a sound and lasting basis and will include those divisions of the service for which no suitable retirement provisions have been made.

This material will be the most complete municipal pension material ever brought together and will be of value not only to the City of New York but as a pension precedent for cities throughout the world. In its preparation every important municipal and state pension plan in the world has been examined.

The head of the actuarial division had the benefit of the advice and assistance of three well-known actuaries, members of the Actuarial Society of America and each employed by large insurance companies. These actuaries rendered splendid and invaluable services without cost to the city.

The present administration has gone a long way toward redeeming its pre-election promise to effect a radical reorganization of the city's pension plans, so that taxpayers of the next generation may be relieved from the tremendous burdens which would inevitably fall upon them if the liabilities of existing pension funds continued to increase, as in the past, without the accumulation of reserves to meet them. **The magnitude of this problem is shown by the fact that while the city paid but $765,472 in 1894 for pensions, in 1904 the pension charge had grown to $2,226,305 and in 1914 to $5,053,167. The continuance of past and present pension methods would mean annual cash payments of $10,000,000 in 1924, $20,000,000 in 1934, and $40,000,000 in 1944. Inasmuch as the bulk (83%) of the income of the city's pension funds is supplied by the city, such a growth in annual requirements would mean an intolerable burden**

* Passed the Senate but failed of passage in the Assembly by 3 votes.

as an annual charge. Since 1857 the city's contributions have amounted to $50,101,416. In 1914 the city contributed $4,467,610 of the total fund receipts of $5,342,507.*

ADOPTION OF A VIGOROUS POLICY OF PORT AND WATERFRONT DEVELOPMENT

The city owns 127 miles, or 22%, of its entire waterfront. This property has been acquired by state grants, by cessions from private owners, by purchase under agreement and by condemnation. Only 103 miles of the total waterfront of 577 miles, however, have been developed for commercial purposes either by the city or by private owners. Furthermore, there has never been a broad and farsighted plan to provide for a growth of terminal facilities which should keep pace with the development of the traffic and commerce of the port.

The board of estimate appointed in 1914 a committee on port and terminal facilities, and work was started through the commissioner of docks and ferries and his staff of engineers on the preparation of plans for effective port development. There is also under consideration the appointment of an advisory board of engineers to make a complete port and harbor survey in co-operation with city engineers and citizen commercial organizations.

During the past two years the department of docks and ferries has made more progress with respect to the physical upbuilding of the port than in any similar period in its history. The city has begun work, much of which is completed, providing for nearly seven miles of new wharfage space. The new piers which are being constructed furnish a deck space of approximately 45½ acres. The three most important projects which have been initiated or completed since 1914 are as follows:

1 Construction of new passenger piers at West 46th and West 44th Streets to provide three berths for the longest type of passenger steamships.

2 Construction of three new piers at 29th, 30th and 35th Streets, Brooklyn, one of which is 1,740 feet long and 175 feet wide, and so far as the records of the department show is the longest commercial pier in the world. These three piers, which provide for 9,380 feet of wharfage space and 568,500 feet of deck space, have all been rented. In addition, a very large portion of the city's adjoining upland, which has remained almost entirely unused since its acquisition in 1905, has been profitably leased.

3 Betterment of railroad terminal facilities by providing for the addition of eight new piers on the East River for the New Haven Railroad; the addition of Pier 21, E. R., for the Baltimore and Ohio Railroad; the construction of a modern pier near the foot of Catherine Slip for the Delaware, Lackawanna and Western

* The commission has recently issued a report on the operation of the nine pension funds "Report on the Pension Funds of the City of N. Y., Part I, 1916."

Railroad; the construction of a new pier at Rector Street, North River, for the Lehigh Valley Railroad and the addition of a new pier at Carlisle Street for the Central Railroad of New Jersey.

Not only have these forward steps toward the physical upbuilding of the port been taken during the past two years, but the department has also devoted much time and attention to two vitally important city problems—the New York Central Railroad Company's west side improvement and the South Brooklyn marginal railroad. A successful tentative settlement has been reached by the port and terminal committee with the New York Central Railroad with reference to the removal of the railroad tracks on 13th Avenue, generally known, because of its dangerous character, as "Death Avenue," and much of the success of the arrangement now made is due to the assistance rendered the committee, of which the dock commissioner is a member, by the engineers of the dock department. The details of the agreement entered into between the city and the New York Central Railroad are sufficiently covered in the several reports of the port and terminal committee and need not be described here.

As regards the South Brooklyn Marginal Railroad, the dock department has completed all the preliminary plans for the railroad and has placed them at the disposal of the committee of engineers appointed by the trunk line railroads which, under the proposed arrangement, would operate the system. The successful consummation of this plan is one of the most pressing needs of the city's port development. The marginal railroad would serve the ports and docks in South Brooklyn and would provide a means of necessary freight transportation now lacking. After careful consideration the board of estimate on July 2nd, 1914, set aside for this purpose the sum of $9,492,004.83 of the city's debt incurring power. It has wisely postponed, however, the commencement of actual work on this improvement until an agreement can be secured from the operating companies providing for the payment of a sufficient rental to the city to cover the cost of carrying the city's investment. Negotiations are now pending to this end.

ECONOMY AND EFFICIENCY IN CITY EXPENDITURE

In no direction has the present administration striven more earnestly to fulfill its pre-election promises than in the matter of increasing the efficiency of the city departments and at the same time making substantial reductions in the cost of administering them.

The board of estimate elected in 1913 equipped itself for the first time in the history of that important body adequately to discharge its responsibilities with respect to the fiscal concerns of the city. Two additional bureaus were established to aid the board in obtaining information on all matters upon which it was obliged to act. The bureau of standards was established to deal with all matters pertaining to the personnel of the city and to complete the work started by the salary standardization committee of the previous board of estimate and apportionment. The bureau of contract supervision was created to pass on all requests made by departments on the board of estimate and apportionment for funds for construction and repair work. In addition to establishing these two new bureaus the incoming board effected, in 1914, a reorganization of its committees for purposes of administrative convenience. The number of committees was reduced from approximately 50 major and innumerable minor committees to 16 standing committees, and definite assignments were made.

Having organized and equipped itself properly to perform its important financial duties, the board of estimate turned its attention to the problems of economy and retrenchment in expenditures. The board's functions which promised the most fruitful results from efforts toward economy were:

1 Preparation of the annual tax budget
2 Authorization of corporate stock for long-term bonds
3 Financial policy pursued with respect to financing public improvements

Annual Tax Budget

The most important single recurring task that confronts the board of estimate and apportionment is the preparation of the annual tax budget. As explained in the first part of this report the first fusion board of estimate continued and extended the work inaugurated under Comptroller Metz of improving the methods of budget preparation. The policy of segregating items of appropriation so that the board could maintain an effective control over expenditures was developed and perfected. This work resulted in great economies, for not only was it made impossible for department heads to expend funds for purposes other than those approved by the board of estimate at the time of its consideration of the budget, but the result also was that salary appropriation accruals from vacancies instead of being used indiscriminately for salary increases were automatically returned to the general fund for the reduction of taxation. A comparison of the sums thus returned to the general fund prior to 1909 under the old system and under the new system subsequent to 1909 indicates the effectiveness of this form of budget control. The following table shows the amounts of unexpended budget balances returned to the general fund for the reduction of taxation:

Year	Amount
1906	$913,852.71
1907	647,189.74
1908	940,032.43
1909	2,443,888.40
1910	5,373,108.42
1911	3,455,032.36
1912	3,417,709.69

Six months after the new administration took office it was confronted with the necessity of preparing the budget for 1915. For this work the board was well equipped, its principal members having been re-elected to office and having had several years of budget-making experience. A sub-committee was appointed by the tax budget committee of the board of estimate to review the estimates of the departments and carefully examine into their needs. In this year, however, the mayor decided to submit, for the first time, an executive budget. Formerly the estimates of department heads were submitted directly to the sub-committee. In the preparation of the 1915 budget, the mayor directed department heads to submit their estimates for his review before sending them to the sub-committee. This was done with the object of considering the budgets of the operating departments in the light of their relative needs and not as separate units of government. As a result of the mayor's visé, the estimates of departments were reduced substantially.

The results obtained from the more intensive examination of budget requests by the present administration have been most gratifying. In the two years it has held office, the total budget appropriations to the administrative group of departments* have been decreased by about $3,125,000 below the total appropriations for 1914. This decrease is all the more impressive when it is remembered that it followed a succession of annual budget increases. The following table analyzes and compares budget appropriations for 1906-1910, 1910-1914, 1915 and 1916, giving the percentage of average annual increase during this period. This table shows the facts which have been pointed out repeatedly, notably before the Brown Committee, that whereas the average annual increase in budget appropriations to this group of administrative departments in the four year period of 1906 to 1910 was 9.2% and in the four year period of 1910 to 1914 was 2.7%, the decrease in the 1915 appropriations below those for 1914 amounted to 2.1% and the further decrease in the 1916 appropriations below those for 1915 amounted to 2.2%.

It is not necessary to enter upon a detailed explanation of budget figures for 1914 to 1916. The reasons for the increase in the total budget, together with a description of the means by which such substantial economies were effected in the administrative group of departments have already been presented. Public attention has been repeatedly called to them by the mayor and the comptroller in their testimony before the Brown Committee.

Corporate Stock Allowances for Salaries and Wages

In addition to effecting reductions in the tax levy budget appropriations to the departments over which the board of estimate has control, the present administration has succeeded in reducing the budget schedules support-

* The departments under the mayor, the five borough presidents, the finance department, the staffs of the board of estimate and Bellevue and Allied Hospitals.

ing corporate stock appropriations in the 1916 budget to a sum less by about $2,000,000 than the corresponding schedules for 1914. These reductions were effected chiefly in the departments of docks and ferries, bridges, water supply, gas and electricity, and the offices of the borough presidents. For example, while the 1914 budget contained corporate stock schedules for the department of docks and ferries amounting to $1,256,064.83, the 1916 budget provides for only $102,621.95, a reduction of over $1,150,000. In the bridge department the reduction was $210,000; in the department of water supply, gas and electricity $410,000, and in the borough presidents' offices $200,000.

Although this reduction of $2,000,000 is not reflected directly by a decrease in the budget total, it is none the less of very great importance in the general economy program. One of the greatest sources of extravagance in previous years has been the more or less unrestrained authorization of corporate stock expenditures. The checking of such authorizations has, of course, been one of the contributing factors in this economy of about $2,000,000 for salaries and wages since 1914.

Corporate Stock Authorizations

Another field in which the new board of estimate could manifest its sincerity in fulfilling its pre-election pledges of economy and efficiency was with respect to the authorization of corporate stock. The city's debt had been increasing at a tremendous rate. The issue of bonds had been authorized with great liberality and in many cases for purposes which were not properly chargeable against the funded debt. During the McClellan administration (1906 to 1909 inclusive) new authorizations of corporate stock were made in the sum of $409,668,458.52, of which $206,653,694.48 was for revenue producing purposes, such as dock improvements, water supply and rapid transit. The first fusion board of estimate realized the need for curtailing to some extent the authorizations of long term bonds and succeeded in reducing the total amount authorized in the four years 1910 to 1913 inclusive, to $351,807,993.85. This reduction of nearly $60,000,000 was effected even though there was an increase of $114,000,000 in the amount authorized for rapid transit purposes.

Not even the care exercised during the preceding administration, however, was sufficient to check the rapidly mounting city debt. When the present administration took office it found itself confronted with a serious situation. Although it was powerless to reduce the amount of debt already incurred it was able to limit the incurrence of additional debt for only absolutely essential purposes. The salutary effect of its rigid economy in this respect is conclusively shown below by a comparison of the total corporate stock authorizations during its first two years of office with the average annual authorizations of the two preceding administrations:

Oversized Foldout

Administration	Average Annual Authorization
McClellan (1906-1909 incl.)	$102,417,114.63
Gaynor (1910-1913 incl.)	87,951,998.46
Mitchel (1914)	14,594,670.48
" (1915)	11,585,981.69

"Pay-as-you-go" Policy

The third great financial reform which has been brought about by this administration during its first two years is generally known as the "pay-as-you-go" policy. Those members of the first fusion board of estimate who were candidates for re-election to the board had for some time been impressed with the need for changing the city's policy with respect to long term borrowings. In the fall of 1914, the city found itself confronted with the necessity of meeting with gold $80,000,000 of foreign obligations, and applied to the prominent bankers of the city for the floating of an emergency loan to meet its indebtedness. At the conferences held between the board of estimate and the bankers for the arrangement of this loan, the bankers insisted that as a condition of its assistance the city adopt a policy of "pay-as-you-go" in the authorization of public improvements. The board of estimate saw the wisdom of this policy and adopted it by resolution on September 11, 1914.

The provisions of this plan have often been discussed and are generally familiar to the public. In substance, provision is made for the issue of 50-year corporate stock only on account of revenue-producing improvements, such as dock construction, water supply and rapid transit. All other public improvements must be financed to an increasing degree from the annual tax budget, until after 1918 the entire cost is so defrayed. This is a drastic remedy and means a considerable increase in the amount of the budget for the next ten years. After the expiration of that time, however, the city will again be on a sound footing with respect to its debt and there will be a progressive decrease in the total of the city's indebtedness.

Central Purchasing

As incidental to each of the three great financial reforms outlined above, many specific economies have been brought about.

For example, in November, 1914, a central purchase committee was appointed by the mayor to take over the purchasing work of certain departments under his control.

The committee has now taken over practically all of the contract purchasing of the departments under the mayor's control, amounting to approximately $6,000,000 annually. Through the voluntary co-operation of the departments the purchase committee is able to let consolidated contracts for supplies needed in common by several departments, with the result that more favorable terms are obtained.

The central purchase committee has made rapid progress in the development of its work, as is shown in its report to the mayor on one year's efforts.*

The full benefits of centralized purchasing cannot be realized, however, until a permanent central purchasing agency is created by statute. In the legislature of 1915 a bill was passed providing for the permanent establishment of a department of purchase which should take over, under proper legal restrictions, the purchase of fourteen millions of dollars of supplies annually for the city. This bill was vetoed by the mayor because of technical objections, and it has been necessary to continue the central purchase committee as a voluntary co-operative organization.

Another bill was introduced in the legislature of 1916, again providing for the creation of a department of purchase and the establishment of a permanent organization for handling both contract and open market order purchasing. It failed of passage. The suggested plan contemplated the appointment of a board of purchase, consisting of the mayor, the comptroller, a representative of the board of estimate, and two other members appointed by the mayor, who may or may not be city officials. This board was given power in the bill to appoint a director of purchase and a director of stores. If this bill had passed the city government could have proceeded at once with the organization of the new department, and the successful experiment in central purchasing conducted for a year and a half would have continued under much more favorable conditions.

Standardization of Salaries

Early in 1910 a committee was appointed by the board of estimate and apportionment to undertake the standardization of salaries of municipal employees. It was not until the late fall of 1912, however, that the necessary funds for this work became available. In January and February, 1913, a staff of examiners was organized to record and study salaries, grades and duties of employees in practically all city departments. This staff devoted itself to the compilation of definite facts relative to the character of employment of substantially every employee in the competitive and exempt classes. Records were prepared showing the essential facts theretofore unavailable relative to each position, and work commenced on drawing up definitions and specifications of employment.

In the early part of 1914 the work of the committee on standardization of salaries and grades was assumed by the newly created bureau of standards of the board of estimate. This bureau took over all the records and material of the standardization committee and continued the studies begun by that committee. Since 1914 the bureau has completed the preparation of tentative specifications to cover the rates of compensation paid by the city for substantially all classes of city employees except school teachers. These specifications have been printed and distributed, and as

* Report of the Central Purchase Committee.

soon as public hearings have been held upon them the board of estimate will be in a position to adopt them as a basis for determining salaries to be paid.

Prior to the formal adoption of all the specifications and rates of compensation recommended by the bureau of standards it has been possible to apply the principles of standardization quite generally throughout the city. In the preparation of the 1916 budget the recommendations of the bureau were available for use and were in many departments made the basis for personal service appropriations. This application of standard rates resulted in decreasing the compensation of 967 employees while increases were allowed to 5,517 employees.

The principle of salary standardization as applied in the 1916 budget was employed not as a measure of economy but as a measure of justice. In one department alone nearly 600 salary increases were granted in order to bring the pay of every employee up to the minimum of the grade where his work properly fell. In many cases where the arbitrary application of standard rates would have meant substantially reducing salaries, it was decided that the hardship and consequent inefficiency which would result would more than offset the financial saving to the city. In these cases either the salary remained unchanged or only a small decrease was recommended.

Ultimately when the entire city service is based on standard grades of compensation the personal service cost of government will be less than at present. During the process of adjustment, however, there will be little if any actual financial saving as a result of salary reduction. The principal savings have resulted from the abolition of positions which were no longer necessary and whose incumbents received excessive compensation.

The work in this direction which still remains to be done can be most effectively carried on if there is complete co-operation between the bureau of standards and the municipal civil service commission. It will be necessary to change completely the titles and classification of city employees now used by the municipal civil service commission, to conform to the standard titles of the bureau of standards. Civil service grades should be established so as to come within the provisions of the specifications adopted by the board of estimate and apportionment.

The basic work of standardization has now been practically completed. There remains only the necessity for the formulation and adoption by the board of estimate and apportionment of a definite plan for applying the new standards gradually in the preparation of future annual budgets. If the work which has already been started is consistently carried on during the next five or six years, city salaries will conform strictly to the value of service rendered and employees' chances of promotion within grades will be greater than ever before. The effect will be to stimulate the interest of employees already in the service and to attract to the service employees of an increasingly higher grade.

BOARD OF ALDERMEN

Stress has been laid in the foregoing account upon the election of a fusion board of estimate and the resulting good effect upon the government of the city of New York. It is true that the board of estimate is the most important governing body in the city, but the importance of the board of aldermen should not be minimized or overlooked. During the first fusion administration, 1910 to 1913, inclusive, a majority of the board of aldermen was composed of organization Democrats.

Under the leadership of the president, however, this unwieldy body became an effective instrument for supplementing the work of the board of estimate. The finance committee co-operated in the preparation of the annual tax budget, and in exercising its charter rights to reduce appropriations passed by the board of estimate, the board refrained from any drastic action without first fully informing itself of the necessity for a particular appropriation.

During the first two years of the second fusion administration, the board of aldermen contained a substantial fusion majority and was able to do splendid constructive work. The board appointed a committee to revise the building code and re-enact it as a coherent and intelligible single ordinance. This work, directed largely by Mr. Rudolph P. Miller, former superintendent of buildings in the borough of Manhattan, was prosecuted vigorously. As a result a new building code was drafted, scrutinized and adopted by the board and published in readily accessible and intelligible form. It has also laid the foundation for an annual revision of the code. In addition to revising the building code the board of aldermen for the first time in nine years codified all city ordinances, revised them and re-enacted them as a single instrument, reducing the number of sections from about 1,300 to about 980. Here again the board has made a marked contribution to the efficiency of city government.

The fusion board of aldermen also showed its sincerity in desiring to help the city administration by making no objection to the transfer of its licensing power to the central department of licenses under the mayor's control. Prior to the establishment of the central department in 1914, licensing was scattered among many city agencies. This tended to create confusion and rendered impossible the effective control of this important municipal function. Concerted opposition by the board of aldermen to centralized control of licenses would have made this improvement in organization difficult if not impossible. It is greatly to the credit of the board that it subordinated the personal prerogatives of its members to the city's welfare.

PART II

SURVEY OF ADMINISTRATIVE DEPARTMENTS

Introduction

The foregoing account shows summarily the events leading up to the fusion movement and the major accomplishments to which the two fusion administrations can point. It is desirable, however, to describe in greater detail the effect of better business methods upon departmental organization and administration. In many cases the results obtained are alike, but in order that there may be a clear understanding of what has been done by those of the mayor's departments which have been surveyed, the facts will be presented for each department separately.

First, however, it may be helpful to record the method of procedure in obtaining the present information of departmental conditions. On January 19, 1916, the mayor addressed a letter to the heads of his departments requesting them to submit to him early in February a statement reviewing the progress which had been made in working out plans for improving administrative conditions, and summarizing the work that remained to be done to carry the task forward in the next two years. On January 29th the mayor directed the chamberlain to make a general survey of the mayor's departments and to submit a report with recommendations as soon thereafter as possible. In order that the work might be facilitated, on February 15th, the mayor addressed a second letter to his department heads asking them to co-operate in making the survey. The staff necessary to make the survey was obtained by assignment of examiners from the office of the commissioner of accounts, the bureaus of standards and contract supervision, the latter obtained with the cordial approval of the comptroller, and by the co-operation of the Bureau of Municipal Research. In every case the department heads assisted greatly by giving their personal attention to the verification of facts contained in the reports on their departments and by assigning one or more members of their staffs to collate the information. The staff assigned to the chamberlain by the investigating bureaus was as follows: Bureau of standards—Messrs. Wilvonseder and Saunders; bureau of contract supervision—Messrs. Thomas Smith, Elliott, King, Reed, Murray, Rochester; Bureau of Municipal Research—Messrs. Clowes, Bassett, Parlin, Sheridan, Moses and McCombs; commissioner of accounts—Messrs. McGinley, Welton and Atlee. Mr. Paul C. Wilson, secretary to the mayor and Mr. Spencer Phenix, chief examiner, office of commissioner of accounts, assisted in the general supervision of the survey. In only one or two instances was the full time of these men available.

The purpose of the survey was to obtain a general view of the departmental conditions and a guide to administrative betterments which still remain to be undertaken. It is not desired to give the impression that the administration has a record of infallibility. Mistakes have been made but none so far as I know due to wilful negligence or intention. In every department vigorous effort has been made to render the best possible service, with what result the record best describes. The survey covered the following departments and boards:

Health
Correction
Tenement house
Water supply, gas and electricity
Parks—all boroughs
Bridges
Street cleaning
Municipal civil service commission
Law
City record
Commissioner of accounts
Board of assessors

As stated, because of the preoccupation of the commissioner of docks and ferries and his principal assistants at the time in the urgent work of settling the West Side railroad improvement problem, no survey of the dock department was attempted. Time was not available for surveying the difficult and extensive problem and activities of the police department, nor for an adequate study of the fire department. A summary of the constructive work of the police department during the present administration has been prepared with the assistance of the fifth deputy police commissioner and included in Part I.

As explained in the letter of transmittal it is recommended that the department of public charities be dealt with in a separate report.

The following pages deal with the departments included in the survey and contain not only the results of independent examination but the statements of the respective department heads as well. Because of the very close relation of the department of finance to the improved administration of the departments of the government generally, a brief reference is here made to the notable betterment of the financial and accounting administration of the city in recent years.

Relation of the Department of Finance to the Administrative Departments

In the past two years there has developed a very close administrative relationship between the department of finance and the other departments of the city government. Until 1908, when the department of finance began to install and ultimately to supervise the accounting methods of various administrative departments, the relationship between that department and the rest of the city government was largely one of antagonism. This was chiefly due to the fact that the finance department was assumed to exist principally to prevent irregularities or extravagance and misuse of funds by the spending departments.

With the development of co-operation as a result of joint effort to reorganize the city's accounts, more and more the finance department has come to be regarded as an aid to the administrative departments in the improvement of their business methods. The appointment of a staff of expert accountants to supervise the accounting reorganization brought into the finance department men who have had experience in accounting and business practices in large private undertakings. These men, in assisting departments in reorganizing their accounts have at the same time been able to assist them in improving business methods generally.

During the present administration a consistent effort has been made to render more effectual the co-operative relationship between the finance department and the operating departments. At the very outset a review was undertaken of the progress of the work of accounting reorganization and accountants from the office of the commissioners of accounts were drawn upon to supplement the staff of the finance department in conducting this work. In a number of cases improvements have been brought about through the joint effort of staffs assigned from the finance department and the individual department and brought together by the chamberlain at the mayor's request to take up specific problems. Thus, for example, there has been centralized in the department of finance all the work of payroll preparation heretofore done by special staffs in the various operating departments. Initial steps have been taken, similarly, to centralize in the department of finance all fund accounting, replacing the fund accounts now maintained by all the operating departments. Similar co-operation has been developed in reference to the preparation of the budget.

Prior to this administration the department of finance and the chamberlain's office were practically independent units of government. Beginning in January, 1914, every effort has been made to articulate the work of these two offices where they deal with common problems, and to avoid the friction and circumlocution which inevitably results from independent treatment by two officials of a task which they perform in common. Illustrations of this co-operation are afforded by the systematic advice furnished by the comptroller to the chamberlain of prospective borrowings, thus facilitating a more intelligent and judicious distribution of funds among the city depositories, and the deposit of funds by the chamberlain in banks designated by the comptroller as especially helpful in assisting the city in making loans.

The department of finance has made very great strides forward during the present administration in establishing itself as the principal office of business advice to all branches of the city government, a function which it will perform with increasing value as the government more and more approaches complete, businesslike efficiency in its operations.

DEPARTMENT OF HEALTH

Introduction

The following report on the survey of the work of the health department is in more complete form than the reports on other departments owing to the special facilities available for making this part of the study. Two representatives of the department of health, one examiner of the bureau of standards, and the health experts of the Bureau of Municipal Research jointly made the survey. All were especially well equipped for the work, and the result is a document of detailed information of constructive value.

The administrative progress of the health department has been especially notable during the past two years. Each phase of the department's extensive and varied work has been subjected to careful analysis and a program of progress and improvement formulated. Activities have been widened with a great reduction in expenditure. The salaries of more than 600 underpaid employees have been raised to standard rates prescribed by the bureau of standards. Altogether, the results obtained in the department of health indicate conspicuously the advantages which result to the community from the skilful, public-spirited and energetic administration of a public department.

It is hoped that before the conclusion of the present administration similar detailed statements may be prepared for each of the departments of the government, so that a record may be available to the public and subsequent administrative officials on which the future development of the departments may be based.

Because the report indicates the value of a close analysis it is here included in full despite the fact that its volume is very much greater than the statements on the work of the other departments. Had time and facilities permitted, the work of every department of the government would have been similarly discussed. Other department heads may find the form of the report suggestive to them for similar studies.

Scope of Survey

The survey of the department's work from January 1, 1914, to date, as presented herewith, is divided as follows:

General progress in departmental administration
Bureau of general administration
Bureau of public health education
Bureau of records
Bureau of child hygiene
Bureau of preventable diseases
Bureau of sanitary inspection
Bureau of food and drugs
Bureau of laboratories
Bureau of hospitals

General Progress in Departmental Administration

Economy in Operation

The following table shows the cost of operation of the department of health from 1913 to 1916, and a comparison between the appropriations and the expenditures for the first three years:

	1913		1914	
	Appropriation	Expenditure	Appropriation	Expenditure
Personal service	$2,434,119.50	$2,371,540.78	$2,549,455.50	$2,440,591.87
Other than personal service	932,100.00	877,134.55	975,785.00	851,006.24
Total	$3,366,219.50	$3,248,675.33	$3,525,240.50	$3,291,598.11
Unexpended balance	$117,544.17		$233,642.39	

	1915		1916
	Appropriation	Expenditure	Appropriation
Personal service	$2,572,220.50	$2,512,435.31	$2,602,393.60
Other than personal service	871,271.72	835,780.13	730,723.00
Total	$3,443,492.22	$3,348,215.44	$3,333,116.60*
Unexpended balance	$95,276.78		

* Includes $22,755 allowed to the department of public charities for the purchase of medical and surgical supplies and equipment for this department.

It should be noted that the appropriation for 1916 is only $84,441.27 more than the actual expenditures of 1913, notwithstanding the greatly increased activities of the department, and the increase in personal service cost due to added force, the changes from part-time to full time, and the increased rates of compensation.

Attention is also called to the fact that though the appropriation for 1915 was over $80,000 less than for 1914, the department was able through careful economy to save an additional $95,276.78.

Changes Effected with Regard to Personal Service

From the standpoint of general organization and departmental efficiency, one of the most important changes effected in 1914 was the requirement of full time service on the part of bureau chiefs and other important officials in the medical service receiving salaries of $3,000 or more per annum. This policy of full time service has since been extended by including almost all the higher and supervisory medical positions for which part-time service has been required heretofore. In the 1916 budget, increased compensation on this basis was granted to eleven officials.

Definite regulations fixing the time that each employee should spend on duty each day have beeen adopted and are now being rigidly enforced. Special attention has been given to the arrangement of time schedules for part-time and for other employees, whose duties require unusual or irregular service.

In cooperation with the municipal civil service commission, higher educational requirements have been adopted for medical inspectors, and the suggestion of the department of health was adopted that a year of hospital training in addition to four years of medical education be made a necessary qualification for the position of Medical Inspector.

The department has co-operated heartily with the bureau of standards to put into effect the new grades of salaries as established by that bureau. As a result, in the budget of 1916, with but few exceptions, the compensation of all the employees of the department was based in conformity with the tentative standards formulated by the bureau of standards. More than six hundred salaries have been increased to place rates of pay on the level prescribed by the standard schedules.

At the beginning of 1916, a new system of service records as proposed by the municipal civil service commission was put into effect. This will undoubtedly result in the establishment of a sound and fair basis for the rating of all employees.

The departmental board of promotions, which previously consisted of three individuals, was organized early in 1914 so as to be more representative in character by including as members the directors of the nine bureaus of the department. This type of organization has been adopted by the civil service commission as a model for all city departments.

New Pension Regulations Recommended

A committee appointed by the commissioner has made a complete study of the pension system of the department, as a result of which the following recommendations have been forwarded to the mayor's commission on pensions:

1 That the present constitution of the board of trustees of the health department pension fund and its control of the fund should be continued.

2 That the present pension law be amended, so that there should be included among its revenues, in addition to the present resources, an increase in the assessment of members from one to two per cent.; the inclusion of all moneys received from the issuance of transcripts; moneys paid for various permits issued under the authority of the Sanitary Code, and moneys obtained by reason of salary accruals.

3 That the length of service remain at twenty years. That no pension be granted unless the individual applying for it has reached the age of fifty years.

4 That to each and every individual retiring after twenty years of service an annual pension be paid during his life time of a sum not less than one-half the full salary or compensation per annum at time of retirement.

It should be known that in 1915, for the first time since the establishment of the department pension fund, the expenditures exceeded the receipts.

The pension commission does not concur in these recommendations. It calls attention to the following weaknesses in the health department pension fund and suggests more drastic measures for the reorganization of the present retirement system:

1 There is no valid reason for the separate existence of the pension fund. The employees of the department are engaged in occupations similar to those existing in other branches of the service. They should be covered, therefore, by provisions of a general system applicable to the entire municipal service. Such system, though based on the principle of equal consideration to all city employees should, however, contain variations in retirement conditions determined upon by differences in strain of work, mortality and other considerations peculiar to various occupational groups of the service.

2 The recommendation for an increase in revenue is a good suggestion with the following qualifications:

a The fund income should be actuarially determined, taking into account the present as well as future obligations of the fund. The present income is totally inadequate to guarantee the permanancy of the system.

b The city's share of the pension burden should be discharged by direct budgetary appropriations and not through the misleading method of diverting miscellaneous city revenues to the uses of the fund.

c The employees should contribute a larger proportion of the cost of their benefits. Neither the present one per cent. nor the recommended two per cent. assessments are sufficient to pay for any considerable part of the pension cost. The assessments should also vary in accordance with the number of years they are paid into the fund. The employee soon to be retired should make larger contributions than those who start paying assessments from the time of their employment. The contribution rates should also vary according to the sex and occupational group to which the contributor belongs.

d The contributions should be compulsory on each and every employee. At the present time less than one-half of the health department force contributes to the fund. Voluntary participation renders a retirement system ineffective and leaves the problem of release from service of those who did not elect to contribute unsolved. For obvious reasons this class of employee constitutes the main objective of a retirement system.

3 The suggested introduction of a minimum age limit of 50 years for retirements on demand after a service of 20 years is only a partial step in the right direction. The recommended age limit is un-

questionably too low. A much later period, at the age of about 60 or 65, would be a more logical provision, fair both to the taxpayer and the employee. The city would defeat its own interests were it to allow retirement at as early an age as 50 without satisfying itself that such retirement is warranted because of the inability of an applicant to continue in service.

4 The recommended pension scale of "not less" than one-half of the final salary is inequitable to employees of varying periods of service, as the usual interpretation of such provision results in the granting of half-pay pensions to the large majority of applicants. Those who have served and contributed for a larger number of years are unquestionably entitled to a larger pension than those who have availed themselves of an opportunity to retire promptly after complying with the minimum service requirement. The main weakness of the recommendation, however, is in the vague term of "not less" than one-half salary. The extent of favoritism by means of discretionary grants of "more" than one-half salary pensions which such vague language invites has been fully discussed in Part I of the Commission's Summary Report (pages 32 to 34).* Considerations of equity require definite provisions for grading pensions in accordance with length of service.

Deputy Commissionership Created

In April, 1914, the sanitary superintendent was designated to act as deputy commissioner of health. The departmental establishment of a deputy commissioner has greatly relieved the commissioner from various exacting obligations such as interviews, speeches and technical medical features, thus enabling the commissioner to devote his entire time to the broader and more valuable functions of public health administration and to the determination of departmental policy.

Bureau of Public Health Education Established

In May, 1914, the Bureau of Public Health Education was established in the department without additional appropriation.

Richmond Borough Office Reorganized

In the early part of 1914, a study of the work of the Richmond borough office resulted in the consolidation of activities formerly administered by several bureaus. Due to this consolidation, it was possible to transfer several employees to other branches of the department where their services could be of most value, which resulted in a saving of $4,500 in the cost of operating the Richmond office. The consequent amalgamation of the work has produced much more efficient results.

Division of Research and Efficiency

In the latter part of 1914, the division of research and efficiency, formerly limited to the bureau of child hygiene, was transferred to the

* Part I.

office of the commissioner, where its services could be utilized for the benefit of the whole department.

Under the direction of the commissioner, this division has conducted studies of the administrative methods of many of the bureaus, and in co-operation with the directors has put into effect improvements recommended.

This division organized the experimental health district, the success of which has demonstrated the value of this type of organization for public health work.

Reorganization of Laboratory Service

The bacteriological work of the department, which was under divided control prior to January 1, 1915, was consolidated on that date by the transfer of the diagnosis laboratory from the bureau of preventable diseases to the bureau of laboratories. This change has been the means of placing the diagnostic facilities under better trained supervision and provides for a more flexible laboratory organization. This change also permits more effective administration on account of the large seasonal fluctuation of the work of bacteriological diagnoses of infectious diseases.

The chemical laboratory, over 90 per cent. of whose work consists of the analysis of samples of foods and drugs collected by the bureau of food and drugs, has been transferred to this bureau from the bureau of laboratories. This change creates a more intimate relation between the laboratory and field work of food and drug control, and at the same time has placed this laboratory service under the supervision of a director specially trained in chemical laboratory work.

On January 1, 1916, the drug laboratory, a part of the hospital service, was abandoned, and the work turned over to the general drug department of the department of public charities. This change, without curtailing the work of compounding and supplying drugs for departmental use, has resulted in a saving in personal service of over $10,000. It is further expected that this centralization will result in additional economy through the purchase of drug supplies in larger quantities for delivery at a central point.

Institutional Inspectional Service Combined

The work of institutional inspection, which until January 1, 1916, was divided between the bureau of child hygiene and the bureau of preventable diseases, has been combined under the immediate supervision of one full time medical officer, who reports directly to the commissioner. This has resulted in eliminating overlapping service, which was inevitable on account of the difficulty in fixing a line of demarcation for child-caring and other institutions. Improvements have been effected already as to the control of infectious diseases, stricter enforcement of the sanitary requirements, and new regulations with respect to food supplies.

District Type of Organization Tried

Late in 1914, an experiment was started in a selected area, known as Health District No. 1, in the lower east side of Manhattan, the object of which was two-fold:

1 To test the value of local administration of the functions of the department, especially with a view to preventing over-lapping of service.
2 The development of a community spirit with respect to health matters in that district.

The functions of the department are directed locally by a health officer in charge, who has under his supervision a force adequate to perform the work in this district. Each bureau directs its service, through the district officer.

This experiment, still being continued, has proven so successful that preparations are being made to extend this type of organization to other parts of the city. It is expected to be in operation in the entire borough of Queens within the next two or three months.

Its advantages are:

1 To the inhabitants of a district the activities of the health department become concrete. The district office is recognized as a place to which they can come for guidance in public health matters.
2 The entire district staff develops an interest in and a knowledge of the general health of the community surpassing present methods by bureaus.
3 Many inter-bureau affairs can be adjusted directly at the district office without the delay involved in their reference to general headquarters.
4 Local direction by a health officer permits distribution of service according to district needs.
5 The co-operation between the medical and the nursing service is improved.
6 Nurses can satisfactorily perform an all-round health service.
7 The nursing staff is elastic, that is, it can be concentrated on infant welfare, schools, infectious diseases, or other service, as conditions or seasons of the year demand.
8 Civic organizations and public-spirited individuals are ready to aid in developing a community health program.

Departmental Co-operation Increased

During the past two years a better spirit of co-operation has been developed between the bureaus, resulting in a more effective administration of the entire department. This is evidenced by the increased assistance afforded the bureau of food and drugs and the sanitary bureau by the laboratory service; the close relations between the division of industrial hygiene in its examination of food handlers and the bureau of food and drugs; the team-work between the bureau of preventable diseases and the bureau of child hygiene in the control of infectious diseases among school children; and the aid given to the bureau of

A HEALTH CENTER

Local Direction of Local Needs—All Health Department Activities for a District of 35,000 Inhabitants Are Directed from this Office.

public health education by all the other bureaus in extending the educational features of the department.

Co-operation With Other City Departments Extended

The police department has given more extensive aid in reporting violations of the Sanitary Code and, in addition, in visiting places where violations have been reported of food, sanitation and quarantine regulations. Special efforts have been directed towards securing evidence for the conviction of unscrupulous midwives.

An interchange of information as to violations of the regulations of the health, fire, tenement house and license departments and the building bureaus has proven a source of mutual benefit.

The department has co-operated extensively in making surveys for other departments, as shown in the following brief summary:

- Department of correction—Sanitary survey of all penal institutions.
- Department of public charities—Sanitary survey of all public charitable institutions.
- Department of street cleaning—Sanitary survey of Barren Island, disposal of garbage, etc.
- Department of licenses—Examination of applicants for push cart licenses, and a survey of ventilation facilities in moving picture theatres.
- Borough presidents—Sanitary survey of comfort stations and floating baths.
- Department of parks—Survey of mosquito breeding areas in public parks, and of bathing facilities.

Advisory Council Organized

Early in 1914, an advisory council was organized, consisting of representatives of the various trades regularly coming under the supervision of the department, and persons identified in some way with public health work or with institutions and private associations whose aims are similar to those of the department of health.

The advisory council is divided into committees corresponding to the several bureaus of the department. It has rendered valuable assistance to the department in the critical study of established procedures and in the consideration of proposed new measures. One of its most important services was its assistance in revising the Sanitary Code.

Co-operation With Outside Agencies

The department has been aided very materially by the co-operation of a great number of organizations, which directly or indirectly are concerned in public health activities, such as federal, state or municipal departments, medical and charitable societies, civic clubs, newspapers and many others too numerous to mention.

The following are a few specific instances of the assistance afforded:

Bureau of Chemistry, Washington, D. C.—Receipt of advices concerning chemical analyses necessary in the control of the food supply.

Bureau of Animal Industry, Department of Agriculture, Washington, D. C.—Instruction of department food inspectors and veterinarians in better methods of inspection.

New York State Department of Health—Reports furnished of cases of contagious diseases on farms from which milk is shipped to the city.

New York State Department of Agriculture—Aid given the department in its efforts to secure pure milk for the city, through extensive tests for tuberculosis in cattle.

New York and Kings County Medical Society and Academy of Medicine—Investigation of serological laboratories of the department, for the purpose of gaining better co-operation with the medical profession.

Charity Organization Society—Survey by the Committee for the Prevention of Tuberculosis of clinics conducted by the department, with a view to securing improved service.

Association for Improving the Condition of the Poor—Investigation by the committee on school lunches to determine the need for school lunches at a nominal cost, for those children found suffering from malnutrition on examination by the department's inspector.

New York Milk Committee—Surveys made of the milk control system of the department, and aid given in devising improved records.

Welfare Activities Installed

The physical examination of department employees begun in 1914 was completed early last year, and re-examination has been started in order to measure the results of diagnosis, treatment, and preventive measures inaugurated. A sickness record is also kept which will give authoritative data on sickness in the various kinds of employment within the department. Examination and annual re-examination of all new employees is now compulsory.

A lunch room in the headquarters building was established in 1914, where the employees are furnished wholesome and well cooked food at reasonable prices. This lunch room is available also for all city employees, and is conducted without maintenance cost to the city.

Sanitary Code Rewritten

The Sanitary Code has been completely re-written, and in its new form is definitely correlated to the ordinances of the board of aldermen. Twenty or more sections were added in 1914, and further revisions made in 1915.

In the past two years all rules and regulations governing procedure within the department and requirements of the department governing outside trades or industries have been carefully revised and printed after adoption by the board.

Overcrowding of Street Cars Regulated

After a demonstration of the dangers by the bureau of laboratories of overcrowding in street cars, a limit of once and a half the seating capacity was established. The board of health has issued orders against various lines throughout the city forbidding them to exceed this limit. As a result of these orders, and an intensive campaign of education through the newspapers, a decided improvement in street car service has been accomplished.

Supervision of Private Schools in Tenements

As a result of an exhaustive study of the sanitary conditions in private schools conducted in tenements, the Sanitary Code was amended so as to require these schools to secure a permit and to be conducted in conformity with the regulations of the board of health. This amendment goes into effect on September 1, 1916.

Further Improvements Recommended

1 At present the Charter requires that representatives of the sanitary bureau, the bureau of records, and the office of the secretary of the department be maintained in each borough. In order to administer the department economically and with increasing efficiency, it is desirable that the city should be free from these mandatory specifications as to officers and salaries. It is now necessary to have five assistant sanitary superintendents, five assistant registrars and five assistant chief clerks. Only one executive officer for each borough is needed.

2 Medical examination and supervision of city employees should be provided by the establishment of a service which shall give to all city employees, particularly to the teachers in public schools, the benefit of such annual physical examination as is at present afforded in the department of health, thereby raising the standard of physical fitness of employees and giving an opportunity to determine and prevent such sickness as now results in a considerable amount of absence from work. Such a service, under the direction of the department of health, could also be used with great advantage to protect the city in its administration of proper pension funds.

3 Beginning with a consolidation of the veterinary staff of the department, now distributed between the bureau of preventable diseases and the bureau of food and drugs, it should prove practicable to combine the veterinary service of all city departments with considerable increased efficiency and economy of service.

4 The department now occupies a leased eight story building in Manhattan, originally built for loft purposes, and not well adapted to its needs. The lease expires in 1920, and steps should be taken now to provide suitable quarters for the department in a city-owned building.

5 A training school for department employees should be established which will instruct all employees in the rules, procedures and work of the department. Definite courses of instruction should be outlined, and employees detailed to the school at definite times. Upon completion of a course, examinations should be held and credit given in the efficiency ratings for satisfactory educational attainments.

BUREAU OF GENERAL ADMINISTRATION

As a result of a general reorganization of the department along functional lines under the last administration, several important activities were grouped under the supervision of the secretary of the department under the title of bureau of general administration. These activities are of a general nature and concern principally the business procedure of the department as distinguished from the medical or professional side. They include the secretarial work of the board of health, the auditing and accounting, purchase, inspection and storage of supplies, the care of buildings and grounds, supervision of construction and repairs, and other activities of lesser importance.

The segregation accomplished was far from complete, as a considerable amount of work properly belonging to a bureau of general administration was still performed by many of the other bureaus. Recognizing the value of such a bureau in the co-ordination of the business functions of the department, constant efforts have been made during the past two years to improve the procedure and segregation in order to relieve the other bureaus of activities which could be more effectively and economically administered under a central control, at the same time enabling the bureaus to devote their undivided attention to the work for which they were organized.

Conditions Corrected, Improvements Made and Activities Extended and Inaugurated

Secretarial Service

This service may be divided as follows:

1 Preparation of the board calendar
2 Recording and promulgating board orders
3 Correspondence

Improvements in the arrangement of the board calendar and in the methods of filing and indexing the minutes, whereby the work of the board has been facilitated, have been effected. Routine matters have been separated from those requiring special attention, thereby leaving the board free to give full consideration to questions of importance or policy demanding special attention.

Greater care has been exercised to secure board action, as required by the charter, in place of independent action on the part of individual officers of the department, it having been found that numerous rules and regulations governing departmental procedure were in force which had never been adopted by the board.

The former custom of officials of the department communicating directly with other branches of the municipal government has been replaced by a centralization of such correspondence in the bureau of general administration.

Law Division

As a connecting link between the health and law departments, the law division was originally established to serve as a clearing house for civil and criminal prosecutions for all violations of the health laws. The work of this division has increased during the past two years through its more extensive use as legal adviser to all branches of health service. It has afforded great assistance in framing rules and regulations supplementary to the Sanitary Code and in guiding the procedure of employees in obtaining and preparing evidence in cases for prosecution.

The noticeable increase in the number of successful prosecutions in the courts is evidence of the more careful preparation of cases:

	1913	1914	1915
Magistrates' Courts..................	7,074	7,430	8,552
Special Sessions......................	1,642	1,578	2,210
Total......................	8,716	9,008	10,762

The work of the division now includes a careful scrutiny of all proposed state legislation for the purpose of securing the necessary information to protect the interests of public health work in this city. Until 1914, this work was not systematized, and only sporadic efforts were made when matters were specially called to the attention of the department.

Purchase and Control of Supplies

More rigid scrutiny of all requisitions, exact records of stock on hand and rate of monthly consumption, together with more careful preparation and segregation of the budget, have resulted in a notable saving in supplies since 1913, notwithstanding increased activities and additional hospital accommodations.

	1913	1914	1915	1916
Appropriation................	$932,100.00	$975,785.00	$871,272.00	$730,723.00
Expenditures.................	877,134.55	851,006.24	835,780.13	....
Unexpended balance..........	$54,965.45	$124,778.76	$35,491.87	....

The expenditures have decreased every year and the appropriation for 1916 is $146,411.55 less than actually expended in 1913. It will be noted that in 1915, after the budget appropriation had been reduced under 1914 by over $100,000 the department affected a further saving of $35,491.87.

In order to show the chief of each bureau precisely where his bureau stands in the matter of supplies, and whether in a given month goods have been consumed in excess of the available appropriation for any particular purpose, a form was inaugurated for monthly distribution showing the following facts:

1 Amount of annual appropriation for supplies (each appropriation item to be separately stated)
2 Amount of monthly appropriation calculated as one-twelfth of annual appropriation
3 Amount of requisitions, item by item, during the month covered by the report
4 Amount available for the period since the beginning of the fiscal year (on a pro-rata basis)
5 Amount actually used since the beginning of the year

Definite schedules for such items as traveling expenses are arranged in advance and maximum allowances fixed.

Arrangements have been made for the transfers of overstocks, to those branches of service in need, and a system of control is being installed whereby an over-supply in any branch of the service will be detected.

Unnecessary inspections have been eliminated. For instance, in the case of drugs the laboratories report on any deviation from contract specifications, and other inspection is dispensed with.

Economy has been accomplished through the central purchasing committee, by joining with other city departments in the purchase of supplies.

To obtain uniformity and to eliminate unnecessary duplication, a committee has been appointed to pass on all new or revised forms to be printed through the board of city record. As a result a marked reduction in the number of forms and amount of printing is expected.

Audit and Accounts

The accounting work of the department until November 1, 1913, was in charge of the chief clerk, and was confused with other clerical service. On that date, a departmental auditor was appointed, and early in 1914, a separate division was established under his direct supervision. This segregation has resulted in the systematic handling of accounts and has accomplished prompter payment of bills and a closer co-operation with the department of finance.

In conjunction with the department of finance expense accounting has been developed. Salaries are now paid through the central payroll division, and semi-monthly instead of monthly.

Per capita costs for the care and treatment of patients, and the maintenance of employees are computed monthly for administrative guidance.

A complete inventory of equipment has been made, but the record of additions and deductions has not been kept up-to-date.

The accounting methods in connection with the sale of biological products were overhauled with the assistance of the commissioners of accounts. Long outstanding accounts were collected or adjusted, and a definite procedure was adopted between the revenue producing branches of the service and the division of audit and accounts.

Periodical reports and audits are being made of all receipts, including revenues from sales of laboratory products, the issuance of transcripts of records, and fees for market inspection, which apparently had little or no supervision before 1914.

Stenographic and Typewriting Service

On January 1, 1915, the stenographic and typewriting service in the headquarters of the department, until that time performed under the immediate supervision of the various bureaus, was combined in a division of stenography and typewriting, which serves the entire department in Manhattan. On December 1, 1915, the division's work was extended by the inauguration of the Brooklyn branch, and branches will be opened very shortly in the boroughs of The Bronx and Queens.

This change has resulted in a more even distribution of work, greater efficiency and economy, the necessarily increasing amount of work being taken care of by a smaller staff. In consolidation eight positions were dropped.

Furthermore, a number of clerks in the various bureaus who formerly combined typewriting with clerical service have been enabled to devote their entire attention to clerical work, thereby avoiding the necessity of providing additional force in the clerical service.

Dictating machines have been installed and are now used by about twelve of the officials, thus saving considerable time of stenographers and securing an increase in output by both the dictator and stenographer.

Mimeographic work, formerly done by the bureaus has been taken over by the division and performed by specially trained employees. The use of the multigraph has been extended so that cards and line work are handled in addition to letters and reports. An electrically-driven machine is being used which turns out from three to four times the work of the hand machines formerly used.

Form letters for routine matters have been adopted in all bureaus and specific instructions for their use promulgated, thus eliminating much unnecessary dictation and typewriting.

A complete record is kept of the cost of repairing each typewriter in order to determine the time when it will be more economical a replace a machine than to continue repairs.

Transportation

The transportation work of the department consists of passenger, ambulance and goods wagon service (delivery, dog and glanders work).

The cars and chauffeurs for the passenger service, formerly under the bureau of general administration, were, on January 1, 1916, transferred to the municipal garage.

The ambulance and goods wagon service is still directly under the supervision of the bureau of preventable diseases. In 1913 this was entirely a horse drawn service except for two ambulances and one motor truck on mosquito extermination work in Richmond, and 59 horses were kept. The service has been largely motorized since by the addition of five ambulances and six trucks, and the number of horses has been reduced to 32 and should be still further reduced to 12 when certain changes now in progress are completed.

Construction and Repairs

The work of this division consists of the inspection of building and engineering construction, enforcement of contract specifications, the writing and enforcement of specifications for repair work, and other building maintenance.

This work is performed by sanitary inspectors, and up to November, 1915, was under the supervision of the chief clerk. At that time a division of construction and repairs was organized and an assistant engineer appointed and placed in charge. Through this organization it has been possible to exercise trained supervision over the operation of the heat, light and power plants, and over other engineering activities of the department.

It is hoped that the end of the year will show a considerable saving effected in the repair work of the department through the greater care now exercised in the drawing and enforcement of specifications.

Central Filing of Correspondence and Records

Although a central filing office existed, it was found on January 1, 1914, that the facilities of this office were used only as a depository for obsolete or completed correspondence by a few branches of the service. The work has been extended to provide for current filing of all correspondence of the bureau of general administration and the bureau of records, and for the handling of correspondence and records of other bureaus that deal with general departmental and inter-bureau matters.

The method of filing and indexing has been somewhat improved by the installation of the decimal system. Many opportunities for further improvement exist.

Borough Office Supervision

An analysis of the laboring force employed in the care of buildings and grounds in Brooklyn resulted in a redistribution of the work, which made it possible to reduce the force from six to three laborers. Two of these extra employees were assigned to Queens, thereby enabling this work in Queens to be performed by departmental labor instead of by contract.

Orders for the abatement of nuisances in the different boroughs are now issued under the direction of the various assistant chief clerks instead of by the central office as formerly. This saves time and affords added convenience to the residents of outlying boroughs.

Definite time schedules for telephone operators have been adopted, rendering unnecessary the improper assignment of clerks and others to this service. Provision has been made for additional facilities outside of office hours, eliminating a frequent source of complaint from those having business with the department on Saturday afternoons and holidays.

A complete survey of all buildings of the department has been made by the fire prevention bureau of the fire department, resulting in a request for a transfer of salary and wage accruals amounting to $10,500 to provide for compliance with all fire regulations.

Further Improvements Recommended

Secretarial Service

The secretaryship of the department, now an exempt position, should be brought into the classified service, thereby guaranteeing permanent tenure of office. This position should be made second only in importance to that of the commissioner, and through its permanence and that of the sanitary superintendent, should be the means of effecting the continuity of public health service irrespective of changes in administration. As the chief officer in charge of the business administration of the department, the position should be made a co-ordinating influence among the several bureaus.

To provide for the proper performance of the secretary's duties, in case of absence or disability, the chief clerk of the department should be vested with the authority of an assistant secretary.

The present secretarial work of the board of health which is scattered among several employees under divided supervision should be consolidated into one division, under the direction of a single head reporting directly to the secretary.

Law Division

A considerable amount of clerical work is now being done in the several bureaus in connection with proposed legal prosecution, after violations of the Sanitary Code and other regulations have been established. All such clerical work should be centered in the law division as soon as the first reference is made to it.

To provide for a uniform procedure and to avoid the possibility of hasty judgment, a board of review consisting of at least three members should be established for the purpose of considering all violations of the health law before cases are taken to court. This would eliminate all poorly prepared cases, whose chances of successful prosecution are remote, and would also permit the more extensive use of authority vested in the board of health, through withholding or revoking permits. Experience has shown that the use of this authority of the board has been a more effective means of securing compliance with the health law than court prosecutions, which often result in suspended sentences or small fines.

Purchase and Control of Supplies

Anticipating legislative authorization for the city-wide purchase and storage of supplies, the department of health should immediately establish a departmental storehouse and a procedure whereby centralized control will be secured over all expenditures for other than personal service and over the proper distribution and use of all supplies, materials, equipment, etc. This should include proper control over all requisitions on the board of city record.

Audit and Accounts

All financial accounting and the control of all moneys received and disbursed by the department should be centered in the division of audit and accounts under the direct supervision of the departmental auditor.

An adequate system of cost accounting should be developed and put into effect, for administrative guidance.

Stenographic and Typewriting Service

Complete centralization of this service should be accomplished by the transfer of a few positions now remaining in several bureaus.

Central Filing of Correspondence and Records

The present central filing system should be brought up-to-date and extended to meet the filing needs for all correspondence and other records of the department. This can be accomplished by centralizing the work in the several borough offices wherever possible, and where, on account of peculiar conditions, it is necessary to maintain files in the bureaus, the same system should be used.

A definite relation should be established between the work of the central filing bureau and the work of the distribution and collection of correspondence.

To insure prompt answers to all correspondence, a definite system of follow-up should be established.

Transportation

All vehicular and stable service of the department should be placed under centralized supervision, and all horse drawn vehicles replaced by motor equipment.

A survey of the delivery service for departmental supplies and for the collection of pathological specimens from the various stations throughout the city, numbering over 400, should be made in order to establish regular and efficient service.

Construction and Repairs

A study of the numerous open market orders for general repair work should be made for the purpose of eliminating causes for unnecessary repairs and to ascertain the possible wisdom of doing this work with departmental labor.

Until this work is transferred to the newly created department of plant and structures, all repair work, exclusive of the hospitals, should be under the control of this division.

Borough Office Supervision

The care of buildings and grounds should be centered in the bureau of general administration under the charge of the assistant engineer.

The responsibility for the care of sixty milk stations, eighteen tuberculosis clinics, two day camps, the hospital admission bureau and five borough buildings, now respectively scattered among the various bureaus of the department, should be promptly combined.

BUREAU OF PUBLIC HEALTH EDUCATION

Origin

Prior to 1914 the educational publicity work of the department was not organized properly for most effective results. Material for bulletins and pamphlets was prepared by the central administrative office and by the various bureau heads, the services of workers of special talent as writers, compilers, lecturers, etc., in the bureaus being called upon as needed. Recognizing the need for a more definite organization and a broader program of publicity, the bureau of public health education was created in May, 1914. The staff was drawn from the various bureaus so that no additional expense was involved.

Cost

For purposes of comparing the cost of maintaining this bureau, the figures of 1915 and 1916 only are available, owing to the fact that prior to 1914 and during part of the same year the employees engaged in publicity work were distributed among various bureaus, and their services were therefore charged against other activities. There were no changes in staff from 1914 to 1915, nor from 1915 to 1916. The cost of the bureau for 1915 and 1916 was as follows, the figures for 1915 representing actual expenditures while those for 1916 are the budget figures for the current year:

	1915	1916
Personal service	$13,676.18	$13,430.00
Other than personal service	4,778.26	4,247.00
Total	$18,454.44	$17,677.00

Publications

1 *Weekly Bulletin*

Prior to 1914 the weekly bulletin of the department was an eight page pamphlet, and owing to its limited circulation of 2,000 copies, was not especially effective as a medium of information to physicians and the public. In 1914, the circulation of the weekly bulletin was increased from 2,000 to 12,000, and at the present time is about 15,000. The bulletin was further improved by a rearrangement of material so that six pages were given to the reading matter of the bulletin instead of the two pages formerly given—the two remaining pages containing current statistics.

The bulletins are sent regularly to every practising physician in the City of New York, to clergymen, school principals, public libraries and other institutions with which the department has official relations. This has resulted in better co-operation from physicians and others because of their better understanding of what the department is doing and why.

For the purpose of making the files of weekly bulletins available as a ready reference work, an index to the year's series of bulletins was prepared in 1914, which has increased the permanent value of the bulletins considerably. The complete index to the 1915 volume of weekly bulletins has also been published.

2 *Monthly Bulletin*

The monthly bulletin, which is a summary of the activities of the department by months and contains special articles of importance too extended for inclusion in the weekly bulletin, has the same circulation as the weekly bulletin and performs similar functions. Under the direction of the bureau of public health education, its scope has been broadened materially because of the increase of available material resulting from the scientific studies carried on in the various bureaus. A list of a few of the leading articles in the monthly bulletin during the twelve months of 1915 indicates clearly its value to physicians and public health workers:

The Social Significance of Industrial Accidents and Occupational Diseases
Syphilis as a Public Health Menace
Malaria and Mosquito Extermination

Publications Issued by the Bureau of Public Health Education

Patent Medicine Legislation of the United States and Foreign Countries
A Clinical and Sanitary Study of the Fur and Hatters-Fur Trade
The Tuberculosis Dispensary as a Center for the Education of the Patient, his family and the Community
The Barren Island Garbage and Offal Disposal Works

3 *School Health News*

In 1915 a new monthly publication was inaugurated called School Health News. This publication is an eight-page bulletin with a circulation of 22,000 copies among school teachers and others engaged in school work. It is designed to keep teachers informed of the work of the department in promoting school health and to suggest to them ways in which they may co-operate.

The department of education has at its disposal two pages of this bulletin which it may use for its announcements or instructions to teachers.

4 *Neighborhood Chronicles*

Recognizing the need for reaching social service workers throughout the city, and other organizations having a local or neighborhood field, the bureau began during the current year the issuance of neighborhood chronicles to organizations and individuals in seventeen different neighborhoods or communities. These chronicles are four-page leaflets which are designed to inform regarding health activities and needs. The seventeen neighborhood chronicles have a total circulation of 95,000 copies monthly, and there can be no doubt that the result of this wide dissemination of health information is well worth the additional expense.

5 *Staff News*

The Communicable News, a small pocket-size bulletin issued by the director of the bureau of preventable diseases to the employees of the bureau, was discontinued in 1914, and in its place was published the Staff News, which is an eight-page pamphlet with a circulation of 2,000 among the employees of the department. Its object is not only to keep all employees informed regarding the activities of the department, but also to encourage the *esprit de corps* so essential in a large organization.

6 *Otisville Ray*

To help and encourage the patients and employees at the Otisville Sanatorium for Tuberculosis, the publication of the Otisville Ray was begun in 1914. This bulletin is a monthly of four pages and has a circulation of 1,000. It is published by the patients themselves but the material is edited by the director of public health education.

7 *Reprint and Monograph Series*

The reprint and monograph series, begun several years ago, have been continued but have been published with greater frequency. The reprint series consists of special pamphlets reprinted from articles by health department employees in medical journals and other publications, while the monograph series is made up of special articles written for publication in this series by representatives of the department.

During 1914 five numbers were added to the reprint series and one monograph issued on the hygienic features of New York City. In 1915, there were added sixteen new numbers of the reprint series and three new numbers of the monograph series, while two monographs were revised to bring them up-to-date. This represents a very material and noteworthy addition to the publications of the department.

Annual Report for 1914

The preparation of the annual report of the department for 1914 was taken up by the bureau early in 1915. This report was transmitted to the mayor on January 31, 1915, and represents an attempt on the part of the department to give a readable and understandable survey of its accomplishments and program. It is a distinct improvement on previous reports. The amount of statistical matter has been reduced considerably and a beginning has been made in the use of graphs for interpreting statistics.

No report for 1915 has been published as yet. It is planned, however, to have the report for 1915, even more than that of 1914, a text book on municipal health control, and to make it more valuable than ever before as a medium of information to the average citizen.

Other Publications

In addition to the regular publications of the department, the bureau has very widely extended the special pamphlet or leaflet service. Probably no other city in the country is giving health facts and information wider publicity, and this is due to the conception of the present health administration that the public should be told. It is worth pointing out here that there has been a decided change in the attitude of the department within the period covered by the present administration as to the part which it should play in publishing the facts. Its policy has been the "public be told," and this change has resulted in the greater co-operation of the public.

Circulars and leaflets have been issued on tuberculosis, venereal diseases, infant mortality, food, flies, spitting nuisances, alcohol, and other subjects of health interest too numerous to mention. Among the most extensively distributed publications may be mentioned—

900,000 vaccination leaflets in schools, churches, department stores and factories
200,000 tuberculosis folders
250,000 miscellaneous health leaflets in co-operation with the work of Health District Number 1
A simplified health code based on the Sanitary Code of the department, in co-operation with the Metropolitan Life Insurance Company

Newspaper Publicity

The department has secured the co-operation of the newspapers in publishing news stories. Although strict censorship is maintained by the commissioner over all news stories, which are released from his office, more space in the newspapers of the city has been given health department material than ever before.

Campaign Against Intemperance

Especially noteworthy is the publicity campaign which has been waged by the department against intemperance, a large part of the work of which has been carried on by the bureau of public health education. Recognizing the fact that the intemperate use of alcohol is a serious menace to the health of the community and the source of much disease, the department has attacked the problem vigorously as one of preventable disease and not as one of morals. This is a decided departure from the older conceptions of the functions of the health department.

Lectures

As an important function of the bureau, a lecturer on part-time was employed to give lectures on health topics. The lectures are available to to private organizations, to employees of other city departments, to public school children and teachers, and to other bodies interested in health promotion. The experiment thus far has demonstrated that this is an effective means of reaching organized agencies throughout the community.

One of the most important new activities taken up by the bureau was the arrangement of courses of lectures and demonstrations to health department employees. A course of twenty lectures was given to each of the following groups of city employees in 1914; medical inspectors, lay inspectors, field nurses, hospital nurses, and clerks in the Municipal Building. Lectures were also given in 1914 at the Boys' High School, the College of the City of New York and the Labor Temple; noon day talks were given to factory employees at various factories; and a series of fifty lectures on tuberculosis was given in co-operation with the bureau of lectures of the department of education.

In 1915, without any increase of staff, the lecture service of the bureau was considerably extended. One hundred and forty lectures were arranged for and delivered under the auspices of the bureau, in addition to regular courses of lectures to social settlement nurses, police recruits, and other groups. Still further extension of the lecture work is desired by the director, particularly in the public schools. This is impossible at present, owing to the fact that only one lecturer is available for all lecture service.

Public Health Exhibits

The preparation of a permanent health exhibit in the department was begun in 1913, and completed in 1914. Further additions and extensions were made in 1915, so that there is now a very extensive and complete exhibit on all phases of the public health problem. This exhibit has been largely used for the instruction of employees and visitors from various schools and colleges in the city.

An exhibit showing the activities of the entire department was prepared for the Panama-Pacific Exposition, as a part of the general New York City exhibit, which earned a grand prize.

Eight small traveling exhibits describing the work of the department and special features, such as the patent medicine campaign, child welfare, food, dental hygiene, tuberculosis, etc., have been prepared and shown at public schools and welfare associations in neighboring cities.

In co-operation with the bureau of food and drugs, the bureau of public health education in 1915 conducted a pure food exhibit at the University Settlement, which was very well attended and received extensive press notice.

Motion Picture Activities

Free moving picture shows have been made a feature of the publicity campaign through co-operation with the film manufacturers and the proprietors of moving picture houses. This is a decided innovation in health department activity. In co-operation with the Tuberculosis Committee of the Charity Organization Society, and with the Tuberculosis Committee of the Brooklyn Bureau of Charities, thirty moving picture shows were given in 1914 and 1915 in the various parks and on recreation piers of Manhattan, The Bronx, Brooklyn and Queens.

In connection with " Clean-up Week " and " Baby Week " in 1914, the bureau prepared a large number of lantern slide announcements which were shown in moving picture theatres throughout the city.

In addition, moving picture shows have been given to the patients in hospitals, at special meetings of the public health workers, and 270 health reels were loaned in 1915 to schools, settlement houses, etc.

Library

Although an attempt has been made to conduct a departmental library, this work is as yet insufficiently organized. Many of the bureaus have private libraries of books and pamphlets suited to their varied needs. As yet no means have been provided for keeping the administrative officers in touch with the material in the library, so that the library is not fully utilized.

Miscellaneous Activities

Owing to the fact that the newly organized bureau has carried on a most extensive health publicity program, its co-operation and help has been sought by private organizations, by other city departments, and by organizations and institutions throughout the country. Co-operation was given to the mayor's food committee in 1914, in the preparation and publication of popular educational leaflets; to the Charity Organization Society and to the Association for Improving the Condition of the Poor in New York City. Health departments throughout the country have been supplied with photographic prints from department negatives and a great mass of information furnished them regarding health publicity in general.

Further Improvements Recommended

Lectures

The director of the bureau is handicapped because of the lack of sufficient lecturers to carry on a more extensive program in the public schools and among private agencies. It is recommended that the director submit an estimate of the cost of employing the private lecturers necessary for the various lecture courses desired and that this estimate be made the basis of appropriation by the city for this purpose.

In order that the purpose and program of the department may receive wider co-operation on the part of private business and industries, it is recommended that the bureau arrange for a series of conferences with the private concerns engaged in work which is under the inspection of the health department. In co-operation with the directors of the various bureaus, conferences should be arranged with the proprietors of food industries, dairymen, sanitary officers of corporations, hospital authorities, etc. A beginning has already been made in co-operation with the division of industrial hygiene.

In order that the various private organizations, such as the Housewives' League, the Woman's Municipal League, the Social Welfare Organizations, etc., may be used most effectively in health work, it is recommended that courses of lectures on municipal health service be given to these bodies. Following these lectures report forms should be given to the members of these organizations in order that they may report violations coming to their observation.

Exhibit

The health exhibit now maintained at department headquarters has not been of greatest service to the general public, owing to its location on the fifth floor of the health department building at the corner of Centre and Walker Streets. It is therefore urged that steps be taken to place this exhibit or portions of it in the various municipal buildings. The arrangement of the exhibit material upon screens placed lengthwise through the center of corridors of municipal buildings would make the exhibits available to thousands of people instead of the few who now see them at the department's headquarters.

Library

In order to make the library of general service to the department, it is recommended that all libraries and collections of books and pamphlets now in the offices of the various bureaus be transferred to the general department library and that a librarian be engaged to catalogue, index and make available for reference all such material.

Current periodicals, reports, etc., should be indexed as received and a daily summary sheet showing the character of the material received should be sent to all bureaus and department offices for reference by the officers of the department. In this way, they could be kept currently informed of such material as might be useful to them.

BUREAU OF RECORDS

Cost

While many improvements in the routine collection, tabulation and interpretation of vital statistics have been made during the period 1913-1916, there has been very little increase in the expenditures of the bureau. The following shows the increased cost during this period, the figures for 1913, 1914 and 1915 representing actual expenditures while those for 1916 are the budget figures of the current year.

	1913	1914	1915	1916
Personal service	$62,165.19	$62,510.10	$62,803.13	$65,150.00
Other than personal service	2,502.54	2,331.81	3,340.76	3,527.00
Total	$64,667.73	$64,841.91	$66,143.89	$68,677.00

The increased cost of personal service for 1916 over 1915, $2,984.81, is accounted for by the addition of five clerks and by salary increases made necessary through the adoption of the standard salary rates recommended by the bureau of standards of the board of estimate and apportionment.

Functions

The following general functions are performed by this bureau:

1 Receiving, indexing and filing certificates of births, marriages and deaths
2 Making transcripts and searches of records
3 Issuing burial permits
4 Making statistical research and preparing reports on findings

Conditions Corrected, Improvements Made and Activities Extended and Inaugurated

Receiving, Indexing and Filing Reports of Births, Marriages and Deaths

Recognizing the importance of securing as complete registration of births as possible from physicians and midwife attendants at birth, the bureau began in 1913 a definite campaign to this end. The deaths of all infants under six months were checked against the birth records to see if the infants reported as to death had been previously reported as to birth; nurses, inspectors and all field workers were required during a week's period to obtain the necessary identifying data regarding children under one week of age, and the records thus obtained in the homes inspected by them were checked against the birth records. Nurses in milk station work were required to secure identifying data regarding children brought to the milk stations in order that these records might also be checked against the birth records. As a result of this campaign and a similar one conducted in 1915, approximately 25 per cent. of all birth records were examined. From these studies it was estimated that **approximately 98 per cent. of all births** in the city of New York were being reported within the ten-day period required by law.

During the present administration a more vigorous campaign has been waged against physicians and midwives who fail to report births and prosecutions instituted against persistent violators of the law. From September 1, 1914, to March 20, 1915, 42 physicians and 12 midwives were prosecuted, convicted and fined for failure to report births as required by law.

Birth record forms were not properly filled out by physicians and midwives because of lack of clarity of the questions asked. The bureau has now revised the birth certificate so that all questions are clearly stated. The revised certificates will be shortly put into use.

In order that contact with parents might be established as soon as possible after the birth of the child, the bureau of records, in co-operation with the bureau of child hygiene, in 1915 began sending to parents a formal acknowledgment of the record of birth, this acknowledgment to be used by the child for future purposes, such as evidence of school age in applying for employment certificate, or when applying for certified copy of the original birth record. These acknowledgment letters bear a number corresponding to the original record number of the birth certificate so that searches for original records may be simplified.

Along with this letter of acknowledgment is sent a pamphlet outlining simple methods of baby care and including a directory of the infants' milk stations. The cost of this procedure is less than $1,500 a year, but it has already proved to be a most effective measure in improving registration and in establishing the contact with the mothers of the new-born which is so important in infant welfare work.

Making Transcripts and Searches of Records

With the organization of the child welfare bureau of the department of education in 1914, transcripts of the birth records of all children coming under its care were issued to that bureau by the bureau of records.

Prior to 1914, a great deal of difficulty was experienced by the bureau of records at the beginning of each school year because of the crowds of children who flocked to the department to obtain the transcripts of records necessary as evidence of age. A plan was adopted in 1914 whereby children might be admitted to school without such transcripts, the transcripts being later supplied on the application of the school principals. This very effectively did away with the disturbance of routine and inconvenience at the beginning of each school year.

It was also customary prior to 1914 for children to apply to the department of health for a new transcript of the birth certificate each time the child was transferred from one school to another. Under the present plan the transcript originally issued follows the child throughout its school career. This will eventually result in the department of education having complete birth records of all children admitted to school.

By the amendment in 1914 of Section 1241 of the Charter providing for the recording of certificates of birth of children whose birth was not recorded by the physician or midwife attendant, a large number of births not previously recorded were finally registered.

Information regarding still-births was, up to 1914, exceedingly meagre. The bureau recognizing the importance of such information, adopted in 1914 a new form of still-birth certificate which requires data regarding the occupation of the mother during pregnancy; the number of previous pregnancies; the number of previous pregnancies resulting in still-births, and the period of gestation in each case; the immediate cause of still-birth and underlying causes, such as syphilis, chronic disease of the uterus, etc. The collection of this information will permit the compilation of data upon which to base prenatal work.

Prior to 1914 all transcripts of records were made by hand or typewritten. This entailed a considerable amount of clerical and stenographic work and allowed the possibility of errors in making such transcripts. To do away with these difficulties, photographic divisions of the bureau of records were established in the Manhattan and Brooklyn offices and photographic copies of all records in these offices are now made.

An investigation of the methods of handling money received for transcripts of records, which amount to more than $30,000 annually, was made in 1915, and disclosed the fact that the transactions involved were insufficiently safeguarded. A change was effected by substituting for the three part book in use, a carbon receipt book similar to those used in the issuance of money orders by the United States postal authorities.

Issuance of Burial Permits

As a result of the discovery that the signatures of physicians on death certificates could be successfully forged, a procedure has been adopted during the current year which is designed to prevent such forgery. The physician is required to register his signature in a book and also on an index card. The signatures on the death certificates are then checked by the medical clerk against the signatures on file.

Statistical Research and Reports

In 1909 a committee of consulting statisticians was appointed by the commissioner of health for the purpose of making a survey of the statistical work done by the bureau of records upon which definite recommendations for broadening the scope of statistical work might be made. The report of this committee recommended the creation of an office of statistical research within the bureau of records, but owing to lack of appropriation this was not accomplished. In 1915, however, a division of statistical research was established within the bureau of records, and the assistant registrar of Manhattan was assigned as chief of the division. The following has been accomplished by the division since its organization:

1 An illness census was made in the experimental health district of the department for the purpose of obtaining complete and accurate data which could be made the basis of a thorough program of medical and social service. This was the first illness census ever made in New York City.

2 In order that statistical data might be more readily available for comparative purposes the city was laid out in 40 acre tracts as recommended by the United States Bureau of Census, and a beginning has already been made in the compilation of statistical data by these areas. Such compilations will be extremely valuable in presenting comparable facts as to births, marriages, deaths, including infant mortality, etc., and will be made the basis of further and more intensive statistical study and service.

3 Recognizing the fact that birth certificates which are received from maternity hospitals are liable to error, the division of statistical research undertook in 1915 a survey of maternity hospitals to ascertain the accuracy of birth reports and to secure such other information as would enable the division to redistribute these births according to the residence of parents by health areas.

4 In order that the division might be kept thoroughly informed regarding statistical work in other cities and countries, a complete file of statistical reports of such cities and countries is maintained.

5 For the purpose of showing the mortality in various occupations, the deaths of 1914 were analyzed and tabulated. This analysis affords a great deal of information of value to the department in carrying on preventive work in various industries.

6 An analysis of birth records is now being made to show the effect of age, nativity, occupation, etc., of the parents upon fecundity.

7 Prior to the annual report for 1914, practically no effort had been made to show statistical data in graphic form. In the report for 1914, a beginning was made and the work of preparing graphs for future reports is now under way.

8 A beginning has also been made in the tabulation of the illness experience of city departments and such outside organizations as employ medical examiners and desire to co-operate with the department. Because the difficulty in obtaining such data is due to the inadequacy of records kept by these departments and concerns, forms are being drafted upon which comparable data may be secured. This service will be an extremely valuable one

in indicating to the department where public health work is most needed and how it may be best accomplished.

9 Prior to the present year, the special statistical data of the various bureaus of the department had been prepared by the bureaus themselves. This reuired in each bureau the use of a number of clerks almost wholly on such statistical work, and disturbed seriously the routine procedure of the bureau. An effort is now being made by the division of statistical research to tabulate the statistical data by census areas, and considerable of the statistical work of other bureaus has been turned over to the bureau of records.

10 The Powers tabulating machine, which is the latest and most complete device for analyzing statistical matter, has been installed in the bureau of records during the past year. Its use will make possible many statistical studies whose cost would otherwise have been prohibitive.

Further Improvements Recommended

General

All routine statistical work now performed in the various bureaus, including the infant mortality statistical studies should be transferred to the bureau of records, and sufficient clerical service released from these bureaus to the bureau of records to perform the service required.

To avoid the present duplication of service, the bureau of records should be made the sole repository of marriage records. This requires an amendment to the charter.

Receiving, Indexing and Filing Reports of Births, Marriages and Deaths

In order to improve birth registration, it is recommended that, in addition to the various checks upon registration now imposed, the bureau make annually an analysis of the baptismal records of churches where such records are kept.

Further to safeguard the issuance of burial permits at the presentation of the death certificate by the undertaker, it is suggested that the bureau send to the physician certifying to the death an acknowledgment stating that the death certificate had been received and a burial permit granted. In case of fraud by forgery the physician would be apprised of the fact and would naturally make investigation.

The present register of the signatures of physicians should be thoroughly revised and brought up-to-date. In order to facilitate the work of clerks in comparing physicians' signatures on death certificates with the signatures on file, it is suggested that a visible index of the signatures of physicians reporting deaths be prepared and used.

Statistical Research and Reports

The file of statistical reports of other cities and countries maintained by the bureau of records should be turned over to the library for indexing and filing, as should also all other statistical reference works of the bureau.

In order to secure data regarding the physical health of employees in the various departments of the city government and in private corporations, it is recommended that the division of statistical research co-operate with such city departments or corporations in preparing forms for the tabulation of such data. In those city departments where no medical supervision is given employees, the data collected by the division of statistical research would be valuable in showing the need for medical service.

A beginning has already been made in the use of graphs for showing statistical data. This method should be more widely extended and applied in the annual reports of the various bureaus.

Effort has been made at various times to secure students from the colleges of the city for volunteer statistical research, but without great success. It is urged that further efforts be made to secure this service. Provided an arrangement can be made with the college authorities to allow students credit in courses for statistical work in the department, such a program could no doubt be carried out.

BUREAU OF CHILD HYGIENE

Cost

The expenditures for child hygiene work for the years 1913, 1914 and 1915, together with the appropriation granted for 1916, are presented here for comparison:

	1913	1914	1915	1916
Personal service	$594,822.66	$621,678.86	$630,152.65	$642,455.00
Other than personal service	37,795.46	37,986.30	36,846.65	21,850.00
Total	$632,618.12	$659,665.16	$666,999.30	$664,305.00

It will be noted that the expenditures for personal service have steadily increased. This is due in some measure to increases in the force, 30 nurses and 3 medical inspectors having been added in three years. The additional appropriation for the present year is due largely to increases in salary made necessary to conform to the specifications of the bureau of standards.

The 1916 personal service budget would have been much larger if the clinics for school children had been continued, as this would have required the continuance of the force necessary to maintain these clinics. By their elimination over $33,000 was saved in salaries and wages for domestics, helpers, laborers and cleaners. The expenditures for supplies continued about the same up to this year. The decrease of $2,694 in the 1916 appropriation was due to the elimination of supplies needed for the clinics for school children and to the improved system of supply control.

Functions

Up to 1913 the division of infants' milk stations and the division of clinics for school children were the only functions of the bureau administered directly from the Manhattan headquarters, the other activities of the bureau being under the direction of borough chiefs in the various boroughs. During 1913 the need for centralizing control over all the work became apparant, and in the fall of that year extending into 1914 borough supervision was replaced by the establishment of divisions administered directly from Manhattan headquarters. The bureau was then organized as follows:

Division of Midwives and Foundlings
Division of Institutions and Day Nurseries
Division of Infants' Milk Stations
Division of School Medical Inspection
Division of Employment Certificates

This centralized control permitted each function to be developed more extensively and secured more uniform results in field work. The division of school medical inspection, however, which is the largest division in the bureau, still continues the use of chiefs for directing the work in the boroughs.

At the beginning of 1916 the division chiefs and the school supervisors were placed on full time, thus allowing changes to be made which promise still further improvements in the work. The bureau is now divided into four divisions, namely:

Division of Midwives, Foundlings, Institutions and Day Nurseries: Maintains control and supervision of midwives, foundlings boarded out in private homes, and not only the child hygiene work of institutions and day nurseries, but institutional work formerly conducted under the jurisdiction of the bureau of preventable diseases.

Division of Baby Welfare: Supervises the work formerly done in the division of infants' milk stations and adds to it the physical examination of children of pre-school age. This last activity should be extended very materially in the near future and eventually may be segregated into a separate division.

Division of School Medical Inspection: Controls not only the inspection for contagious diseases and the physical examination of school children, but has direct supervision over clinical service. Nine clinics in various parts of the city have been discontinued and the work necessary for eye refractions, contagious eye diseases, and dental treatment is performed by a force which goes from school to school. A room is provided at these school centers in which is placed the appropriate equipment for this service. The treatment of nose and throat defects has been discontinued entirely and the care of these cases has been left to the various hospitals and clinics throughout the city. Changing the clinic service from a stationary to an ambulatory type has effected a saving of $40,000, by eliminating the personal service necessary to maintain clinic buildings such as domestics, helpers, cleaners, and expenses such as rent, light, coal, food supplies, clothing, bedding, and other equipment.

Division of Employment Certificates: Continues work as before.

The clerical service of the bureau was formerly distributed in the various divisions, but is now centralized under the chief clerk of the bureau.

This gives a more elastic and uniform service. Summarized weekly reports have been introduced which lessen the number of daily records sent to headquarters.

Conditions Corrected, Improvements Made, and Activities Extended and Inaugurated

Midwives

The practice of midwifery is raised to a higher level by requiring a certificate from a recognized school before a license to practice is issued. It is necessary now for the applicant to take a resident course of at least six months in a qualified school.

Stricter regulations have been adopted as to the necessary equipment of midwives and its maintenance in a clean condition. Inspections are directed especially to determine the presence of such supplies and instruments which, according to the regulations, midwives are not permitted to use.

The monthly inspections made at the homes of midwives are more thorough. The rooms are inspected as to cleanliness, records are inspected to see that they are kept in accord with requirements, and careful inquiry is made of the methods pursued by midwives in performing their work.

Effective co-operation with the police department has been instituted so that the work of unscrupulous midwives can be closely followed up. Evidence secured by the health department as to illegal practices by midwives is sent to the police department, and a special corps is detailed therefrom to try to secure evidence which will result in the arrest and conviction of these practitioners. During 1915 thirteen midwives were arrested, of which six were convicted for attempting to perform abortion.

Foundlings

Improvements have been made in the character of inspections by the nurses who visit the homes in which foundlings have been placed. The nurses not only see if the sanitary conditions of the homes are proper but are required to give detailed instructions as to the home care and general hygiene necessary to maintain and improve the physical condition of these infants.

Institutions

In 1913 the physical examination of children kept in institutions was inaugurated. In 1914 the follow-up work necessary to secure correction of defects found was begun by co-operating with the physicians on the staffs of these institutions and by arranging with hospitals and clinics for the treatment of children sent to them. These institutions in many instances were persuaded to appoint specialists on their own medical staffs to insure improved general medical attention for the inmates. This included the appointment of dentists for routine supervision of teeth of children.

The regular monthly inspection of institutions was broadened in its scope. Late in 1915, in addition to the usual inspection of sanitary conditions, special attention to personal hygiene was begun. Methods of bathing children, changes of bedding and clothing, and methods of screening the kitchen are looked into. Careful inspection of procedure in the receipt and care of food supplies and physical examination of those handling the food, to determine their freedom from communicable disease, are also made.

Heretofore it has been difficult to get these institutions to correct unsanitary conditions found on inspection. During 1915 this was improved very materially by securing the co-operation of the department of public charities which now does not admit new cases to these institutions until defective conditions are remedied. In 1915, of 1,400 items of complaint against institutions, over 60 per cent. were remedied promptly as against practically none in preceding years.

Baby Welfare

Many administrative features needed for the better control of this work were instituted during 1914 and 1915, as follows:

1 Detailed statistics of infant mortality are now made which show for each census area of the city, deaths from congenital, diarrhœa, respiratory, contagious, tuberculous, syphilitic, and miscellaneous diseases, further divided into age groups, nationalities, institutions, and private dwellings. This permits more intelligent direction of the campaign to reduce infant mortality by locating definitely the neighborhoods where deaths of a certain type are more prevalent as compared with other parts of the city or mortality of previous years.

2 In those parts of the city where poverty is prevalent much illness of infants may be prevented by securing prompt relief, and arrangements have been made with the charitable agencies by which better co-operation is obtained and help given quickly when necessary.

3 Maternity hospitals and district nursing associations are co-operating to a greater extent by reporting the names and addresses of the infants leaving their institutions. Upon receipt of this information nurses visit these homes and endeavor if possible to get these infants under milk station supervision.

4 Up to the summer of 1915 the infant mortality campaign was under dual direction, the division of infants milk stations controlling its own force, and the school nurses performing this function during the summer months under the direction of the division of school medical inspection. In 1915 the entire work was placed under the immediate supervision of the division of infants milk stations, thus securing more uniform methods in administration.

5 The bureau of records has been assisted very materially in checking birth reports by receiving from the milk stations the names and addresses of all known babies under six months of age.

The extension of baby welfare work is evidenced as follows:

1 The 55 milk stations operated at the beginning of 1914 have been increased to 59 by budgetary appropriations. Private citizens

One of the City's Fifty-nine Milk Stations

donate rent and equipment for 7 other stations during the summer, for which the bureau of child hygiene provides doctors and nurses.

2 As a rule, babies coming to the milk station are dropped from the register after an absence of three weeks. Exception is now made in cases of delicate babies suffering from malnutrition, by requiring the nurses to follow them up persistently in their homes. It is felt that by this procedure many lives may be saved.

3 "Baby Week" has been instituted and will be continued as a yearly means of stimulating community interest in the effort to save babies. This will be done by publicity methods, *e. g.*, newspapers, billboards, car advertisements, window posters, movies, baby parades, and the distribution of educational literature.

Pre-natal Work

This has become an established function of the bureau. Prospective mothers are closely supervised as to their general physical condition during this period and are given instruction as to hygiene and proper care. This promises to develop into an important factor for the reduction of infant mortality, as deaths from congenital diseases demand the greatest attention. A special corps of nurses, in addition to the regular milk station nurses, is engaged on this work. In 1914, 3,522 cases came under supervision. In 1915 the number increased to 4,338.

In 1915 educational articles were published in foreign languages in appropriate newspapers. This will develop an important method for instruction in the care of babies, as so many mothers are unable to read English.

The education of girls in Little Mothers' Leagues is made more effective by the selection for this work of those nurses who have shown special aptitude as teachers.

Children of Pre-School Age

The supervision of children between the ages of 2 and 6 has been commenced by inducing patrons of the infants' milk stations to bring their children between these ages for physical examination. While comparatively little has been accomplished in this direction its inauguration fills the last gap in the child hygiene program, which supervises the child from birth until he leaves school and applies for an employment certificate.

School Medical Inspection:

The following administrative needs have been recognized and put into operation:

1 Up to 1914 the system of records did not permit ready information for each school considered as a unit. By revision this information is now obtained and results in better co-operation with the school authorities.

2 Through the courtesy of the board of education the public school telephones are now used for transmitting official business with

this department. Reports of cases of acute contagion found in schools or on absentee visits are now telephoned immediately to the borough offices and to the inspectors.

3 Beginning 1916, 7 full-time medical supervisors have taken the place of 15 part-time officials. Borough chiefs have been discontinued and the supervision of the school work is performed by these full-time officers under the immediate direction of the division chief at Manhattan headquarters. This will give more consistent supervision at less cost than before and enable the full-time supervisors to concentrate their attention upon new developments and improvements for the service.

School medical inspection service has been extended as follows:

1 Up to 1914, children attending parochial schools had not been included in the system of school vaccination but during that year 70,000 children attending these schools in the five boroughs were vaccinated against smallpox. Parochial school children are now included in the regular vaccination program for public school children.

2 Up to 1915, all physical examinations of school children were performed by the medical inspectors of the department. In that year, arrangements were made whereby examinations by private physicians are now accepted at the time when children enter school. The records of these examinations are sent to the health department for compilation. Since September, 1914, 12,500 examinations have been made by private physicians out of a total number of 74,000 new pupils admitted to the schools. This is another step in "hitching-on" private physicians to the city's health program.

3 In 1915 high schools were included in the schedule for routine inspection and physical examination of pupils, whenever the department was requested to inaugurate this service. Thirty-three high schools now receive routine inspections, physical examination of pupils, or both.

4 Health Leagues have been inaugurated in the public schools. These are composed of the pupils, whose interest and co-operation is thus secured for personal hygiene and better conditions. Much rivalry has been developed and the pupils in these leagues have become an important factor in securing correction of physical defects and improving the general cleanliness of members.

Clinics for School Children

Up to 1914 the corrective dental work performed did not seem to have any appreciable effect considering the city as a whole, as the force of dentists was entirely inadequate to cope with the enormous amount of dental treatment necessary. The policy of the bureau was changed to one of prophylactic treatment limited to new pupils entering the schools. Children are now inspected carefully upon entering school and treatment secured. They will be reinspected at stated intervals to insure continued improvement. Cumulative results from this definite program will be much greater than the desultory efforts heretofore made.

The clinic service beginning January, 1916, is confined to eye refraction work, care of contagious eye diseases and dental work. Physicians and nurses now go from school to school. The force is no longer continued as a separate division, and is under the direction of the division of school medical inspection.

Issuance of Employment Certificates

In 1915 the records and reports in use in this division were simplified to a great degree.

The Metropolitan Life Insurance Company made a study of 10,000 physical examinations of children applying to the health department for working papers, and upon this basis have established standards of normal development of children between the ages of 14 and 16. These standards are to be used hereafter in deciding qualifications of applicants for working papers.

Better co-operation with the department of education is secured by transmitting to it daily reports of all children granted or refused certificates.

To guard against the improper use of certificates, a rule was put into effect requiring the lapse of one month before issuing a duplicate when the original is claimed to be lost.

When applicants are refused because of physical incapacity the cases are followed up very carefully by nurses to secure the correction of the defects so as to give the child a better chance to obtain a certificate upon re-application.

Up to 1915 certificates of " over age " were issued by the department of labor. During that year the work was taken over by this division.

Vaccinations

Additional vaccination centers were established without increasing the cost by including all milk stations in this classification in addition to public schools.

Further Improvements Recommended

Supervision of Midwives

Midwives and foundling keepers are to be graded into A, B and C classes, depending upon conditions found. Upon this basis a new system of inspection will be instituted which will require less field work as a whole and at the same time keep under closer observation those midwives and foundling keepers who are not up to the standard requirements. Those in Class A are to be visited every two or three months, Class B monthly, and those in Class C monthly, bi-weekly, or oftener as conditions demand.

School Medical Inspection

It is felt that medical inspectors making physical examinations of school children need training to improve the technique of their examinations. It is expected to establish courses of instruction in this work.

School teachers are to be instructed so that they may recognize symptoms of contagious diseases and signs indicating gross physical defects. With this knowledge teachers should be of valuable assistance to the medical inspectors and nurses.

It is proposed to transfer the tabulation of records and reports to the division of statistical research in the bureau of records, with the clerical force necessary to perform the work.

Most of the nurses upon entering the service have little or no conception of public health nursing. This entails a vast amount of training while they are being paid by the city. If possible, the civil service examinations for this class of service should require knowledge of public health work.

The physical examination of children of pre-school age is very important and should, if possible, be extended. Examinations at this time of life if conducted on a large scale should reduce the number of physical defects found during school life and the need for follow-up work. It is estimated that there are about 480,000 children of pre-school age. As only 1,100 examinations of this character were made during 1915 it is apparent that very little has been accomplished.

Increased activities demand more medical and nursing service in this bureau, as shown by the need for physical examinations at the pre-school age and in order to provide for the natural increase of school population. This must be met by an increased force to some degree, but to keep requests for appropriations to the lowest possible point studies should be made as to the methods employed with a view to securing greater output by the present force. For instance, in the physical examination of school children, each examination as at present made necessitates the writing of various cards and records by the medical examiner, which takes from one-third to one-half of the time required for each examination. This clerical work might be performed by clerks or by nurses at a lower cost, thus increasing the number of physical examinations made in the schools or providing service for medical examinations in other fields.

Extension of dental treatment should be secured by employing "dental hygienists"; that is, women trained to cleanse teeth and give hygienic instruction. This system has been developed in Bridgeport, Connecticut, where women are employed at a salary of $30 per month. They can do a great amount of work at a comparatively low cost.

The failure of effective co-operation between the department of education and the department of health in regard to the physical welfare and instruction of school children in hygiene and sanitation shows the need of the kind of co-operation between these two departments that exists in the school system of Gary, Indiana. In Gary, the opinion and authority of the department of health may be accepted as final in all matters concerning the health of school children, thereby abolishing the duplication of offices and duties, and the conflict of instruction to the teaching staff and children from medical representatives of the two departments.

The importance of having the children physically fit at the time they leave school to undertake their own self-support, and so instructed in matters of personal hygiene and sanitation in their homes and working places that they may avoid the diseases of advancing life, make the school the most important field for the activity of the health department. This can be accomplished without sacrificing in any way the control of fundamental problems by the department of education, simply by formal recognition of the sphere of the two departments in the lives of the children for whom they are respectively responsible.

BUREAU OF PREVENTABLE DISEASES

Cost

The following table gives the expenditures for this bureau for the years 1913, 1914, 1915 and the appropriation allowed for 1916:

	1913	1914	1915	1916
Personal service...........	$534,641.79	$522,728.20	$465,594.02	$475,700.00
Other than personal service..	86,234.37	86,133.08	59,401.98	46,560.00
Total.............	$620,876.16	$608,861.28	$524,996.00	$522,260.00

The decrease in personal service for 1915 as compared with 1914 was due to the transfer of the diagnosis laboratory from this bureau to the bureau of laboratories, and to the discontinuance of routine fumigation for infectious diseases in private homes, which reduced the force of fumigators. **The increase in personal service for 1916 was caused by salary increases made necessary to conform to the new classification of the bureau of standards.**

The decrease in the expenditures for other than personal service during 1915 was due to less use of supplies because of the transfer of the diagnosis laboratory and the discontinuance of general fumigation. The decrease for 1916 for other than personal service was made possible because of rigid analysis of the supply budget.

Decentralized Control of Infectious Diseases

Up to 1914 the care and prevention of tuberculosis was carried on by a separate division through a system of districts with branch offices throughout the city, and the control of other infectious diseases was directly supervised from the five borough offices. In 1914, these two functions were combined into a bureau of infectious diseases and the branch office system was extended to the administration of all infectious diseases. A separate force of field nurses for the care of the tubercular and another force for other infectious diseases were amalgamated, and thereafter the same nurses made visits to all kinds of cases. This resulted in a great saving of time and allowed a much extended service to be put in operation. From an administrative standpoint this system took from the division chiefs many of the routine procedures, such as keeping records and reports, and placed the responsibility for their execution in the branch offices.

In the same year the name of the typhoid division was changed to the " division of epidemiology " because of extended activities. Besides the control of typhoid fever, cerebro-spinal meningitis, poliomyelitis and malaria, this division began the study of infectious diseases as to their onset, spread, and control. The information derived from these research studies is used for guidance in the administration of the work of the entire bureau.

In November, 1915, the veterinary work up to this time performed from central headquarters was turned over to the branch offices for routine administration.

A valuable means of extending the activities of the health department is the co-operation effected with the police department whereby patrolmen are to be used as an adjunct of this department. As an experiment, in several parts of the city for the past few months patrolmen have been visiting cases where violations exist as to sanitary and food conditions, and the control of infectious diseases. The work of this division has been visiting cases of infectious diseases where violations of quarantine have occurred, and delivering cards of instruction and information for minor infectious diseases, such as whooping cough, chicken pox and mumps.

Conditions Corrected, Improvements Made, and Activities Extended and Inaugurated

Control of Tuberculosis

Territorial boundaries of tuberculosis clinics have been rearranged to conform to the new census areas. For administrative purposes this secures uniformity with other bureaus of the department and other departments of the city which are adopting these new divisions. If universally adopted for city use this system should result in more effective co-ordination of work and uniformity of records for purposes of comparison.

Up to 1916, a large proportion of the physicians in the tuberculosis clinics had been giving service voluntarily, which of course did not permit of strict control such as is possible over the paid employee. At the beginning of this year all these clinic physicians were included in the competitive class of the civil service and placed on the payroll of the department, and the better control secured should result in a much improved service.

During 1914 a special school of instruction for physicians entering the service was established, in which these medical inspectors are taught technique in physical diagnosis and methods used in branch office and clinic routine. After completing this course they are ready to give a good type of service in this particular field.

The hospital admission bureau which is under the combined direction of the department of public charities and the department of health was reorganized in 1915. The bureau of social investigations of the department of public charities, whose nurses had been making investigations of social conditions in the homes of tuberculosis patients, had overlapped the service rendered by the nurses of the health department. To prevent this duplication of work its force has been withdrawn to be used elsewhere, and this field is covered by the health nurses alone.

The institutions caring for the tubercular have been divided into two classes, (a) for patients only temporarily dependent through illness, and (b) for patients of a chronic dependent type. By this rearrangement it is possible to segregate into the hospitals of the latter class cases which are a menace to the community, and therefore require forced detention. Furthermore, in the municipal hospitals patients are admitted on positive sputum findings only, and are discharged when two sputum specimens taken a month apart are found negative and no other positive signs of activity are present. This avoids a large waiting list of applicants to these hospitals and places under care the most needy cases and those which are recognized as sources of infection.

The filing system at headquarters has been improved by establishing a file which shows the distribution of tuberculosis cases by occupation, and operating separate files for "homeless" and "not found" cases. By this system the various types of cases can be located more readily.

In 1915, the women's auxiliaries attached to the various tuberculosis clinic districts which up to that time had been working independently of one another, were organized into the Society for the Relief and Prevention of Tuberculosis, thus co-ordinating endeavors in this particular field.

In 1915, in the interest of school children provision was made for the supervision of school teachers suffering from pulmonary tuberculosis and in cases of necessity only, requiring their exclusion from school. Three new clinics have been opened as follows:

Yorkville Clinic, Borough of Manhattan, March, 1914
Parkville Clinic, Borough of Brooklyn, April, 1914
Riverside Clinic, Borough of Manhattan, May, 1915

The tuberculosis clinics in Manhattan which were formerly conducted by the New York Nose, Throat and Lung Hospital and the Good Samaritan Dispensary, respectively, were taken over by the department and installed in new quarters.

A systematic investigation by field nurses is being made of all cases discharged from the State Sanatorium at Raybrook and from the department of health sanatorium at Otisville, the object being to ascertain the final results of treatment, its social as well as its personal value.

Control of Infectious Diseases

Beginning in 1914, persons who are suffering from communicable diseases are prohibited from working in their homes upon articles intended for general consumption. This is another step in the effort to control the spread of infectious diseases.

Regulations have been made which permit the use of coffin seals in cases of death from infectious diseases. This prevents undue hardship on families who under previous rules were required to bury immediately, thus involving an additional expense if this was necessary on Sundays or holidays.

In 1914 the general practice of fumigation of private homes upon the termination of infectious diseases was discontinued in the boroughs of The Bronx and Queens and in January, 1915, was discontinued in the borough of Manhattan. The conclusions reached after six months trial of this new policy convinced the department that this procedure might well be applied to the entire city, and in July, 1915, this practice was discontinued in the five boroughs. Hereafter, as a routine procedure ambulances and library books only will be fumigated. The discontinuance of fumigation means a saving of $25,000 to the city.

The institutional care of contagious diseases has been extended to a considerable degree. Special inspections have been made of each general and special hospital, home for incurables, orphan asylums, dispensaries, and similar institutions in the city. Suitable regulations have been adopted and put into force for the care of contagious diseases in all public and semi-public institutions. Special emphasis has been laid upon the need for an isolation room in the various hospitals.

The department has discontinued the practice of transferring patients ill with contagious diseases from out-of-town institutions to the city, because it was felt that such institutions should be provided with suitable facilities for the isolation and care of contagious diseases.

Diagnosticians are required after notification to see immediately cases ill with contagious diseases which require removal to hospital. This eliminates much delay, which has been the subject of complaint. Furthermore, better co-operation of department diagnosticians with private physicians has been effected in those cases concerning which there has been some dispute as to diagnosis.

Improvements in keeping records have been inaugurated by combining the daily lists of contagious diseases formerly issued separately by boroughs. This provides the borough of Richmond with a printed list and gives to each borough a knowledge of cases in other boroughs but living very close to the borderline. Files of major and minor contagious diseases have been separated and uniform systems established in all the borough offices.

In July, 1915, the method of controlling measles was changed by eliminating some of the routine procedures in the department and permitting private physicians to exercise more control. The period of quarantine for scarlet fever cases has been reduced from 35 to 30 days. Diphtheria cases are more closely supervised by requiring two successive negative cultures to terminate cases and establishing 14 days as the definite period of quarantine.

Better information to the medical profession as to the control of contagious diseases has been given through special articles to private physicians in the Weekly Bulletins.

A section of the Sanitary Code was added prohibiting any unmuzzled dog on any public highway or in any public park or place in the city. The validity of this ordinance was sustained by the Appellate Division of the Supreme Court in a suit brought against the department of health on the validity of its dog muzzling order. Justice Collins upheld the department and his opinion was concurred in by all the justices of the court.

Epidemiology

This work, which heretofore only embraced the study of typhoid fever, has been extended to cover investigations of all other infectious diseases. The information obtained will be used for guidance to prevent the spread of these diseases. Reports from the division of statistical research in the bureau of records now include much data of great value to the studies made by this division.

The control of typhoid fever is better effected by adding:

1 A record of typhoid carriers
2 A list of domestics employed in houses where cases of typhoid are prevalent
3 A file not only of the homes of patients but of their business addresses
4 A file of all ships entering the Port which carry typhoid cases
5 Better precautions before case is terminated by requiring a negative bacterial report of the discharges in every case
6 Forcible removal of typhoid cases to the hospital if environment is unfavorable or proper care is not exercised to prevent the spread of the disease.
7 Treatment of chronic carriers by large doses of vaccine, which is being tried in the hope that control in this manner may become possible
8 Food handlers after typhoid are supervised closely to prevent its spread.

Much delay was caused by the system of sending letters when knowledge was desired from milk companies as to the milk supply of typhoid patients. Frequently days and even weeks elapsed before the information was obtained. The use of telephones for this purpose has secured prompt information, with the ability to follow up more closely any sources of infection. Delayed reports of typhoid cases by institutions and private physicians are investigated more closely and followed up carefully to learn the cause of such delay.

Veterinary Service

Better co-operation has been secured from the New York State Department of Agriculture which is permitting its force of veterinarians to aid the veterinarians of this department in making stable surveys throughout the city, for the detection and control of anthrax and glanders.

By the use of a new system of records it is possible to locate glanders cases more definitely. Vaccine treatment to control the spread of glanders was undertaken as a new feature in July, 1915. A special study of horses, their general physical condition, and the condition of their stables was undertaken in 1914.

In 1915 the division began inspections to prevent the spread of anthrax, and routine inspection of blacksmiths' shops insofar as their condition relates to the spread of infectious diseases amongst horses.

Following the outbreak of the foot and-mouth disease in the Fall of 1914 a careful inspection was made to check its spread. This inspection is now continued in order that the disease may not gain a foothold in the city.

Control of Venereal Diseases

Before 1914 physicians were required to include the full names of the patients in their reports of these diseases, whereas institutions were permitted to give either the name or initials. This has been changed so that both institutions and physicians may give either the names or initials of their patients. There is therefore less reluctance on the part of the private physician to make a report of his private cases of this character. The registration of these diseases has been very incomplete, and persistent efforts are being made to show physicians through the Weekly Bulletins that Section 88 of the Sanitary Code requires that these diseases be reported.

The Industrial Clinic reports venereal diseases of food handlers (syphilitic). These cases are then followed up by this division and satisfactory evidence is required to show that they are under medical care.

Late in 1914 the health department, in conjunction with the genito-urinary section of the Association of Out-Patient Clinics, attempted to bring up to standard requirements the conduct of all clinics of this character in the city. Persuasion only has been tried thus far, with very little success, and probably it will need some system of inspection to bring about improved conditions. At the present time those clinics which come up to the standard have cases referred to them for treatment from the advisory clinic of the department.

A systematic campaign against the advertisements of quacks has been inaugurated in an endeavor to have newspapers refuse advertisements of this nature. Furthermore, the department is making an effort to counteract the evil effects produced by quack advertisements in public toilets and lodging houses by conducting a crusade for the destruction of such signs and the substitution of a placard giving substantial advice as to the character and treatment of these diseases. A vast amount of literature has been distributed and several lectures upon the subject of venereal diseases were given by the bureau of public health education.

Division of Industrial Hygiene Exercises Supervision Over Working Conditions

The following table gives the number of cases reported to this division from 1913 to 1915:

	1913	1914	1915
Syphilis	10,623	21,155	19,449
Gonorrhoea	6,883	9,526	10,221

In 1914, an evening clinic for these diseases was opened in Manhattan and in the latter part of 1915 a day clinic was opened in the borough of The Bronx.

Industrial Hygiene

This is one of the latest extensions of the health department's activities and was begun during the present administration. During 1914 applicants for peddlers' licenses were examined, in co-operation with the bureau of licenses, for tuberculosis and other communicable diseases. In the latter part of that year this function was taken over by the health department, being conducted at the various tuberculosis clinics throughout the city. Bakers and peddlers were included in this examination. In April, 1915, the work for the five boroughs was combined into a division of industrial hygiene with an Occupational Clinic located at Lafayette Street in Manhattan.

The Occupational Clinic makes physical examinations of industrial workers in various fields. Its activities are evidenced by the following table, which shows the examinations made for 11 months beginning April 1, 1915:

Peddlers	8,028
Bakers	8,312
Food Handlers	17,943
Industrial Groups, such as painters, furriers, rug makers, etc	1,301
Total	35,584

These physical examinations, in addition to being conducted at the Occupational Clinic, are made also by private physicians throughout the city, especially of workers handling food. In the last five months of 1915, 20,000 examinations of this character were made by private practitioners. Necessarily, for public health control these examinations by private physicians must be guided by the health department, and this has been done by reviewing the records of such examinations and placing on probation or excluding from the performance of their occupation those afflicted with syphilis in an active state.

In addition to the physical examination of painters conducted at the clinic, surveys are made to determine the surroundings under which painters perform their work, with particular reference to the dangers of handling lead and wood alcohol. In these surveys are included painters employed by the various city departments, men in active labor under private concerns, and investigations of breweries so far as they refer to the painting of vats. Experiments are now being conducted to determine the possibility of using leadless paint, particularly for inside work.

Workers in the fur and felt industry come under the supervision of this division. During 1915 surveys in 113 factories of this type and over 850 physical examinations of employees were made.

In 23 of the large department stores in the city inspections were made to determine industrial hazards; as a result, procedures were modified in seven stores.

Special emphasis has been laid upon the educational features with respect to industrial hygiene. During 1915 twenty-eight lectures were given to an attendance of 11,000 people.

Citizens' complaints as to industrial conditions are investigated, and during 1915 many stores were inspected as a result of these complaints. In co-operation with the veterinary and laboratory service of the department special investigations are conducted with regard to infection by anthrax in those industries handling hides and wool.

Employers are required to use reasonably effective devices, means, and methods to prevent contraction by employees of illness or disease incident to the work or process in which they are engaged.

The co-operation of the American Museum of Safety has been secured. It provides two medical advisors, a social service nurse, and facilities for necessary relief. (These workers are stationed at the Occupational Clinic. By their aid it has been possible to follow up for correction the physical defects found in industrial workers applying for medical relief. This, in effect, inaugurates the work of adult hygiene, which aims to secure periodic examinations of adults with the necessary follow-up to secure correction of defects. In a complete program this should include a re-examination at specified intervals.

Further Improvements Recommended

Tuberculosis

A more uniform service in the throat and nose division of the tuberculosis clinics should be established. It is proposed therefore to appoint a supervising laryngologist and through him to see that methods adopted are uniformly administered in all department clinics. Studies are to be made to secure possible improvements in existing routine methods and procedures as conducted for exclusion from school and forcible removal from homes of individuals affected with tuberculosis.

New standards of diagnosis of pulmonary tuberculosis in children have been proposed by the Association of Tuberculosis Clinics of this city. The National Association for Tuberculosis is expected to adopt these standards, and it is planned to accept them as a basis in the operation of clinics.

In order to develop advanced methods for controlling and supervising cases of tuberculosis, it is planned to require all clinics to submit to headquarters regular reports giving facts as to the onset and spread of the disease, housing problems, and other data of a similar nature. This information will be collated and will serve as a basis for better administration.

The division of tuberculosis expects to take up shortly the problem of tuberculosis in lodging houses and Mills' hotels. Already systematic examinations are being made by physicians of the department of public charities of inmates of the Municipal Lodging House, and the department is preparing to make prompt examinations and reports on sputum specimens with the intention of removing those inmates found to have positive sputum.

Many of the nurses at present employed in the tuberculosis clinics perform routine clerical work which could be done by second grade clerks, allowing the nurses to be utilized for regular nursing service.

Janitorial service should be provided when feasible for the tuberculosis clinics in order to insure proper care of city property and to avoid the performance of this work by nurses attached to these clinics.

Infectious Diseases

It is proposed to extend the co-operation between the health department and private practitioners, to the end that they may formally assume, under the supervision of the department, many functions with respect to the control of preventable diseases now held strictly in the hands of the department. At the present time this is being tried out experimentally in the borough of Queens, where private physicians known to the department as members of the medical profession who have heretofore co-operated, are given the name of " Associate in Public Health," and assume public health control of their infectious disease cases under the guidance of the department. If the experiment in this borough is successful it is expected to extend its application to other parts of the city. This illustrates the possibilities of " hitching-on " the medical profession to the public health program. Thus a vast extension of service is secured without added expense to the city or increase of departmental force.

It has been suggested that a method for controlling whooping cough now being tried out in other cities be used in New York, that is, the use of a red ribbon or band around the arm of the infected individual, as a warning to other children as to the presence of the disease. The difficulty of keeping the whooping cough cases indoors during the period of infection is well known.

Typhoid Fever

Better co-operation should be secured from the state department of health to obtain the examination of the water supply of villages in which are located creameries which pasteurize milk for New York City consumption, in order to prevent the possible spread of typhoid fever through infected water.

Typhoid immunization should be inaugurated as a routine procedure in all institutions governed by the city.

Means should be devised to give to the division of epidemiology data from the branch offices for epidemiological studies. If possible this data should be submitted in form for tabulating by machines.

Venereal Diseases

To secure uniformity of methods pursued at the various genito-urinary clinics in the city, it is suggested that a license to conduct such clinics be required.

Industrial Hygiene

Follow-up incidental to the physical examination of industrial workers and other groups of adults might be extended considerably without additional cost by detailing this service to the branch offices, and having the nurses under their jurisdiction visit these cases.

1 Considerable extension of the adult hygiene program might be effected by giving to applicants at the tuberculosis clinics a complete examination. In addition to the present heart, lung, nose and throat examination, the examination of urine and the blood pressure test should be used. This could be secured by a comparatively small addition to the present examining force.

2 The examination of adults could be extended by requiring physicians employed in other city departments to make this type of examination for employees under their care. For the purpose of harmony and uniform methods the work performed by them should be under the general guidance of the department of health.

3 In order that the department may be what it is capable of being—the medical adviser to the entire administration, and the administrator of medical services for the benefit of all city employees—it is considered essential that it should maintain supervision on behalf of the city of all work done by or for the city which involves industrial hazards, whether these occur in the great construction works of subways or water supply, or in the activities of the painters, repairers and cleaners of city property. Well-recognized preventable disabilities, resulting from neglect of precautions by the large contractors who carry out great undertakings for the city could be avoided if expert medical opinion were availed of in the preparation of contracts involving the expenditure of city money.

Co-operation with the State Department of Labor should be more effective; or better still, there should be an amendment to the State Law which will provide that the supervision of factories, etc., at the present time under the supervision of the State Industrial Commission, be placed under the health department of this city. Much of the work of the State Industrial Commission, as performed in New York City, duplicates work which the health department has authority to conduct.

At present no effort is directed toward the supervision of the health of individuals at the adolescent age. It might be possible by co-operation between the division of employment certificates and the division of industrial hygiene to follow up more consistently those children who have been physically examined and have received employment certificates. The suggestion is made that this be done by requiring the employer to secure a permit for every individual employee, in addition, or in place of the present procedure, which gives to the applicant an employment certificate with no further control over the character of work in which these growing youths are employed.

BUREAU OF SANITARY INSPECTION

Prior to 1914 the work of the sanitary bureau was largely confined to the investigation of citizens' complaints and the supervision of places and premises under sanitary regulation by the department. In the attempt to reorganize this bureau and to direct its work along the most productive lines, it was clear that a great deal of effort was being wasted in this kind of sporadic inspection. In 1914, therefore, a number of limited surveys were undertaken to determine the extent and location of conditions and occupations which were detrimental to public health. A general survey of the entire city was determined upon as a result of the limited surveys mentioned, and this survey by house and block is still in progress.

Cost

The following figures show the cost of this bureau in the period 1913-1916, the figures for 1913, 1914 and 1915 representing actual expenditures, those for 1916 being the budget figures for the current year:

	1913	1914	1915	1916
Personal service...........	$273,311.65	$231,597.63	$232,003.58	$241,310.00
Other than personal service..	19,279.55	17,674.07	9,266.35	9,925.00
Total.............	$292,591.20	$249,271.70	$241,269.93	$251,235.00

The very considerable decrease in personal service in 1914 under 1913, is accounted for by the transfer of eighteen sanitary inspectors from the sanitary bureau to the bureau of food and drugs; by the reduction in salary of the sanitary superintendent from $7,000 to $5,000; by the reduction of the number of medical inspectors attached to this bureau from nine to six, and by extensive reduction and transfer of the clerical force made possible through better organization.

The reduction of cost in 1915 under 1914 in other than personal service was due partly to the transfer of the cost of the automobile passenger service to the bureau of general administration and partly to general economies in the purchase of supplies and equipment.

Functions

The functions of the bureau may be described in general as follows:

1 Investigating all citizens' complaints regarding nuisances
2 Inspecting certain premises operating under permits from the department of health, except those which are inspected and supervised by other bureaus of the department more directly concerned
3 Conducting surveys of various localities, occupations and businesses requiring supervision by the health department.

Conditions Corrected, Improvements Made and Activities Extended and Inaugurated

Citizens' Complaints

In the performance of the functions indicated above, perhaps the most important change in procedure made during the present administration was the substitution of a systematic house and block survey for the former sporadic method of inspection upon citizens' complaints. This survey was begun in 1914 and is still in progress. As a result, the number of complaints filed by citizens has been decreasing steadily. Nuisances which were formerly left uncorrected until complained of by citizens are now found and corrected by the inspectors themselves.

Inspections of Premises

Following the policy of making surveys of various localities, occupations and businesses which may be a source of nuisance, or of conditions which may become detrimental to the public health, the following special surveys have been made:

1 A survey of 132 city lodging houses, resulting in the improvement of equipment, lighting, ventilation, plumbing, toilet facilities, etc.
2 A survey of 5,000 barber shops in Greater New York and the enforcement of existing regulations.
3 A survey of comfort stations maintained in public buildings and places by city departments and those maintained by the transit companies, resulting in the temporary improvement of these places, and the co-operation of city officials and private agencies has been enlisted in efforts to keep them so.
4 A survey of 4,000 roof tanks disclosed that departmental regulations relative to their construction, covering and cleansing were being ignored. As a result, 3,000 notices were issued requiring compliance with departmental regulations.
5 Realizing that improperly kept stables were the chief source of fly breeding in the city, a general survey of over 10,000 stables of the city was made. Conditions warranting action were found in more than 4,500 cases and these conditions were corrected. New regulations regarding such places were adopted.
6 To prevent further the fly nuisance, a survey was made of all inland dumping grounds and orders issued to the owners of the premises regarding the use of disinfectants, covering of garbage, etc.

Draining Large Areas of Swamp Land to Prevent Mosquito Breeding

7 Recognizing the fact that office workers are frequently subjected to conditions injurious to health, the sanitary bureau has undertaken a survey of office buildings upon which will be based recommendations for the correction of improper conditions.

8 A survey of commercial laundries in order to determine whether or not the methods of cleansing articles were sufficient to destroy all pathogenic organisms, has resulted in the passage of new regulations by the department.

9 A sanitary survey of homes for the aged was made for the purpose of stimulating the interest of their managers in sanitation.

10 A sanitary survey of private schools was conducted which disclosed many unsanitary conditions. The co-operation of the private school authorities was secured for the correction of such conditions.

11 A survey was made of all river baths and as a result many of them were ordered discontinued as unsanitary. Following a study made of the mikveh baths by the representatives of the department of health, definite regulations for such establishments were made and agreed upon by the department of health and the board of rabbis of the Mikveh Owners' Association.

12 At the request of the commissioner of correction, a sanitary survey was made of the penal institutions on Blackwell's Island with a view to the correction of defects in the physical plant and in the methods of preventing the spread of disease.

13 A study was made of the horse troughs of the city for the purpose of regulating them to prevent the transmission of glanders through their common use. As a result of the study an order was issued for the abolition of common horse troughs and the substitution of drinking fountains requiring the use of individual pails.

14 By a survey of theatres, department stores, public institutions and other places, a more general compliance with the law relative to common drinking cups and common towels was secured.

Mosquito Extermination

The work of eliminating the mosquito nuisance has been done under the supervision of the sanitary bureau. A great deal of progress has been made during the present administration, and the success thus far attained indicates that the mosquito may be practically eliminated in Greater New York if the present work is continued. Plans have been drawn of areas yet to be drained, and the areas deriving benefits from such drainage are to be assessed for its cost. The following is an estimate of the area still to be drained and the cost:

Acreage undrained—	
Salt marsh	9,000 acres
Inland swamps	1,000 acres
Cost per acre—	
Salt marsh	$15.00
Inland swamp	100.00
Total estimated cost	$250,000

Disposal of Garbage and Offal

A thorough study has been made during the past two years of the garbage and offal disposal works on Barren Island. Court proceedings were begun in 1914 against certain corporations operating on Barren Island, but were temporarily discontinued at the request of the president of the board of aldermen pending an investigation by an engineer of the board of estimate and apportionment. The report of the engineer showed the existence of nuisances such as to constitute cause for action by the health department. The department then again brought action and this action, after many delays, is now pending. Conditions, however, have materially improved on Barren Island due to the action of the department.

Smoke Nuisances

During 1914 an active campaign was waged to eliminate the smoke nuisance. Several railroads and other corporations were prosecuted and fined for violation of the sanitary regulations, with the result that a very considerable improvement has resulted throughout the city.

Regulation of Chicken Yards

In the ten months prior to November 1, 1914, over 4,000 complaints were received in the sanitary bureau from citizens who were annoyed by the sound, smell and other nuisances arising from chickens. New regulations controlling the maintenance of chicken yards were drawn and put into force, resulting in a very considerable reduction of the number of complaints.

Co-operation With Other City Departments

The co-operation of the police department has been secured in requiring all policemen on their beats to observe and report violations of sanitary regulations. Each patrolman has, therefore, been made an auxiliary health officer.

The co-operation of inspectors and field workers with the department of street cleaning in preventing the throwing of ashes, garbage and other refuse into the streets has resulted in making more effective the work of both sanitary inspectors and the street cleaning department.

The co-operation of the tenement house department has also been secured to enforce the law relative to the standards of ventilation in tenement houses.

Sewage in Queens

Due to the activity of the sanitary bureau in 1914 a long standing nuisance at Maspeth, L. I., was in a large measure abated. Formerly sewage direct from privies, sinks, wash tubs and cesspools was permitted to flow into the street gutters and thence into Newtown Creek. Pending the construction of permanent sewers, the co-operation of the residents of this section was secured and temporary drains and sewers installed by them at their own expense.

Quarantine Against Bubonic Plague

The sanitary bureau has during the past year assisted in preventing the introduction of the bubonic plague into this country by enforcing the regulations of quarantine relative to the use of rat guards on the hawsers of ships docking at the port. Many night inspections have been made by the policemen of the health squad to see that ships comply with the regulations regarding the raising of gang planks after dark.

Manure Nuisances

Nuisances in connection with the transportation of manure to places in the various boroughs have been eliminated through inspection and by the requirement of cement roadbeds where cars are loaded so that they may be readily cleaned and fly breeding prevented.

Sanitary Instruction to Janitors

In June, 1915, the first of a series of conferences with janitors was held at the department of health for the purpose of instructing them in health department regulations and to secure their co-operation in improving the sanitary conditions of premises.

Ventilation of Street Cars

A series of studies has been made by experts of the sanitary bureau for the purpose of determining all available facts regarding the ventilation of street cars. As a result of these studies recommendations for improving ventilation will be made to the transit companies concerned and definite regulations established.

Further Improvements Recommended

1 Analysis of the duties of the members of the police force—a lieutenant, two sergeants, and fifty patrolmen—detailed to the sanitary bureau of the health department leads to the belief that patrolmen at $1,400 are now employed on work which could as well be performed by sanitary inspectors at $1,140 to $1,320. It is, therefore, recommended that more thorough study be given to this matter with a view to reducing to a minimum the number of policemen actually necessary. By more thorough co-operation with the police department, the regular patrolmen could be used in many cases. Additional sanitary inspectors should be given the department of health, the number to be determined after careful investigation.

2 Section 1299 of the charter should be amended so as to permit the department to order the vacation of premises where nuisances exist which are or are likely to become detrimental to the health of occupants of *neighboring premises* as well as the occupants of premises in which the nuisance exists.

3 Section 1172 of the charter should be amended so as to permit the department to exercise jurisdiction over the storage of fertilizers and manure upon unimproved property used for farming purposes in the city of New York, in order that a broader program for the elimination of the fly nuisance may be carried out.

4 The charter should be amended as approved by the board of estimate and apportionment, which will give the department authority to drain marsh land for the purpose of mosquito elimination and the abatement of other nuisances, without the use of the present cumbersome and expensive method of acquiring easements after condemnation.

5 An amendment to section 383 of the charter is recommended, which will transfer the sanitary control of public comfort stations, public baths and public urinals from the borough presidents to the department of health.

6 The present practice in investigating complaints is to require an inspector to visit and interview each complainant personally. While this may be necessary in certain instances in which the nature and circumstances of the complaint is not clearly stated, it is a waste of time and money in many other instances, as the inspector is unable to get any more information than is contained in the original complaint. It is recommended, therefore, that this practice be discontinued as a routine procedure—the determination of whether or not a personal interview with the complainant is desirable being left to the director of the sanitary bureau.

BUREAU OF FOOD AND DRUGS

Reorganization

Prior to January 1, 1914, this bureau was called the bureau of food inspection. Throughout 1913 it was the target of a great deal of criticism. Charges of incompetency and graft came from many sources and the records of the department and methods of supervision of inspectors in the field were so inadequate that it was felt by the then commissioner that reorganization of this bureau should be pushed forward as rapidly as possible. Accordingly, a general survey of the bureau was made by its director with the co-operation of other interested agencies, certain definite and serious defects were discovered, and a beginning made to correct them.

Early in 1914, however, no great progress had been made in the reorganization of the bureau. Owing to the irregularity and incompetency of much of the clerical service and the large amount of purely routine work made necessary by the complicated and inadequate recording methods in use, the latter part of 1913 and the early part of 1914 were spent largely in perfecting these methods. The daily reports of inspectors were in such form as to make impossible the exercise of proper supervision of their activities. There was obvious need of the adoption of a scoring system for food industries under inspection, so that they could be properly classified. Records of the arrest and conviction of offenders were incomplete. The filing system in use was not properly adapted to the use of clerks so that time was wasted, and the frequent changes in the personnel of the clerical staff made efficiency well nigh impossible.

It was also evident that great duplication and overlapping of inspectional service existed. Owing to the division of the bureau according to the character of inspections there were three distinct groups of inspectors, viz., food inspectors, sanitary inspectors assigned to the bureau of food inspection, and milk inspectors covering in large measure the same fields.

The reorganization under way in 1913 and 1914 was finally completed early in 1915. The title of bureau of food inspection was changed to bureau of food and drugs, and a director selected on the basis of an open competitive examination was placed in charge on June 23d, 1915. The office of assistant director was created, and the former chief of the division of milk inspection was appointed. Four main divisons of work were defined as follows:

1 Division of Food and Drugs
2 Division of Milk Inspection
3 Division of Meat Inspection
4 Division of Laboratory

Functions

These divisions indicate in a general way the functions of the bureau which are:

1 Inspection of production, distribution, storage and sale of food products, except milk and meat.
2 Registration and supervision of the sale of drugs and pharmaceutical preparations, including all so-called "patent" medicines.
3 Supervision of entire milk supply, including the inspection of dairies, shipping stations, pasteurizing plants, transportation facilities, local sale or distribution.
4 Supervision of all places where meat is handled, stored or sold, including both abattoirs and markets.
5 Analysis of all specimens of food and drugs taken by inspectors, for the purpose of obtaining evidence of contamination, adulteration or unwholesomeness.

Cost

The following table gives the expenditures for the years 1913, 1914, 1915 and the appropriation allowed for 1916:

	1913	1914	1915	1916
Personal service...........	$145,481.53	$167,564.54	$186,560.10	$229,190.00
Other than personal service..	33,550.13	30,931.91	38,553.46	35,919.00
Total.............	$179,031.66	$198,496.45	$225,113.56	$265,109.00

The increase in personal service of 1914 over 1913 is accounted for chiefly by the transfer of 18 sanitary inspectors, formerly attached to the sanitary bureau, to the bureau of food and drugs. The increase of 1915 over 1914 is accounted for chiefly by the addition of 16 food inspectors, while in 1916 the still further increase is due to the transfer of the chemical laboratory, representing a cost for personal service of $21,000, from the bureau of food inspection, and, in addition, to the modification of salary range made necessary by the adoption of the standards of salaries and grades by the bureau of standards of the board of estimate and apportionment.

It should be noted that, although the service of this bureau has been greatly extended by virtue of added functions since 1913, the increase of the budget figures of 1916 over the actual expenditures for other than personal service for 1913 is only $2,369.87. The great part of the cost for other than personal service is for the transportation of inspectors, particularly inspectors on country milk inspection, approximately $30,000 annually being spent for this item alone.

Conditions Corrected, Improvements Made and Activities Extended and Inaugurated

Administration

It was apparent at the very outset of the reorganization of the bureau that administrative control of the inspection service was very defective in that the reports of inspectors and the methods of record-keeping did not furnish the administrative head with an adequate basis for judgment. In order to correct these defects, the following improvements were made:

1 To prevent duplication of inspection and to make possible a comparison of all district activities, the bureau districted the city in forty-acre tracts, and placed a field supervisor in charge in each district. All work of inspection, whether food, sanitary, or milk inspection, is under the immediate supervision of these field supervisors. All records are now tabulated by districts, and by comparison of districts the director of the bureau is able to keep himself informed as to the comparative efficiency of his force and the conditions in the districts.

2 In view of the many new activities of the bureau, and in order to ensure uniformity of action by the various supervisors and inspectors, bi-weekly conferences of employees were inaugurated, at which the rules and regulations of the department were discussed and the supervisors and inspectors given instructions as to their interpretation and application.

3 Field supervision of inspectors has been greatly improved by placing a supervising inspector in charge of each district. At the close of the day's work, all inspectors are required to meet the supervisor at an appointed place, usually the health department clinic, where the day's work of each inspector is reviewed by his supervisor.

4 A complete new uniform card system of inspectors' reports has been adopted. This report card is so framed as to make note of every violation of the sanitary code or departmental regulation. This record furnishes an absolute and accurate index on the

condition of places inspected, and furnishes the director with information upon which places may be graded.

5 Prior to 1914 all records of the bureau were kept in open files which were freely accessible to any of the employees. In order that these very important records might be properly safeguarded, a steel cage was erected and a clerk placed in charge of this cage, so that no record may be removed except by proper authority and after notation has been made of the fact.

6 In order to facilitate the filing of reports as soon as possible after their submission and to prevent errors in filing, all reports of inspectors are first assorted in a cabinet in which the pigeon-holes are arranged alphabetically and by districts. This greatly facilitates the use of these reports before they finally reach the permanent files.

7 In order to facilitate procedure in sending out communications to inspectors and supervisors in the field and to save postage, all communications to inspectors and supervisors are assorted and pigeon-holed in a cabinet according to districts. Instead of mailing these communications out as soon as they are prepared, two mails a day instead of five or six as previously are sent out. This has meant considerable saving in postage.

8 Considerable difficulty was formerly met with in checking the reports of inspectors to see that reinspections were properly made as required. In order to keep a check upon these reinspections, a tickler file is now maintained stating the inspector's name and the date on which reinspection is to be made. If the inspector makes reinspections and reports, upon the same date, the card in the tickler file is removed and destroyed—but if he does not make the reinspection, a memorandum is sent to the chief of the division responsible, stating that proper reinspection has not been made. This has produced very definite results in enforcing reinspections at the proper time and in correcting improper conditions.

9 It was discovered in the investigation during 1913 that persistent offenders against food regulations were being brought to court as first offenders, because no adequate records of previous convictions were available in the bureau. The inspectors could not properly present such cases to the courts and were obliged to trust to their memories as to previous conviction. A very complete record of previous prosecutions is now maintained so that now the court has all the evidence available regarding the career of the offender.

10 Considerable difficulty was formerly experienced in keeping track of records of complaints and prosecutions that were in transit from one official to another, and the progress of such records. A method has been devised and is in operation by which a card record is maintained of the progress of all such records through official channels. When the original record reaches the permanent file, this card furnishes a brief history of each case. These cards are filed according to districts and are an index to conditions within the various districts.

11 A new method has been devised for the tabulation of statistical data regarding the work of inspectors. One tabulating sheet is designed for each district, the total being brought down to the

bottom of the sheet. At the end of the week these sheets are put together in order according to the number of districts. Each successive sheet is a trifle longer than the preceding one, so that when all sheets are placed together, the totals for each sheet fall under one another. The combined total is thus very quickly ascertained and the summary shows the amount of work being done in each district. It is estimated that this procedure will cut down the time of tabulation approximately forty per cent.

12 Other minor improvements in the methods of controlling the clerical force and in making information available to the public have been adopted, such as:

a Definite assignments of duty to the clerical staff, one copy of such assignment being given to the clerk and one signed by the clerk being retained by the chief clerk.

b Instruction of clerks in their duties and deportment and in proper methods of dealing with officials, citizens and others with whom they come in contact.

c Better facilities for attending to the wants of the public by the establishment of an information desk, which may be used by applicants for permits, etc.

d Posting signs indicating the location of the various officials and employees with whom citizens may wish consultation.

e A record of all telephone calls and requests so, that in the absence of the person called, all information will be available to him on his return.

f Erecting a railing which prevents visitors from invading the space occupied by employees.

Inspection of Food and Drugs

Due to the improved methods of supervision indicated, a general improvement of routine inspectional service has resulted. The division of food and drug inspection has in addition taken on many new activities of primary importance.

Proceeding on the proved theory that reform in food handling comes rather from education of food handlers than from prosecution, the director of the bureau has inaugurated the policy, except in very flagrant cases and where ill-intent was obvious, of holding hearings in his own office and instructing and advising offenders, instead of bringing immediate prosecution. This has resulted in better co-operation of food handlers with the department.

An active campaign has been inaugurated for the prevention of disease through the handling of food by persons afflicted with communicable disease. A particular effort was made to exercise supervision over the handling of foods in hotels and restaurants. As a result more than 13,000 persons have been notified that they must procure health certificates and more than 7,000 have been examined by the division of industrial hygiene.

Taking the position that cases of preventable diseases are more difficult to cure when the patient uses harmful patent medicines, the department has rigidly regulated the patent medicine business. An amendment to the Sanitary Code requires the naming of ingredients of patent medicines on the labels of the packages, or in lieu thereof the registration of the ingredients with the department. The registration of patent medicines has necessitated greatly increased work on the part of the bureau of food and drugs. Special men have been assigned to the collection of samples and at the present time an efficient control of the patent medicine business is maintained.

Regulations have been enforced prohibiting the distribution of free samples of proprietary medicines, the sale of bichloride of mercury except upon a physician's prescription, and the use of wood alcohol in preparations intended for human use.

In order further to safeguard the public from contaminated foodstuffs, physicians and hospital authorities are required to report to the department suspected cases of food poisoning. Careful investigation is made of all such cases by the bureau.

In view of the fact that complaints of fraudulent practice on the part of manufacturers, importers and dealers in bottled waters have been frequent, the department requires that such persons file with the bureau of food and drugs a statement as to the character and composition of the water.

A new procedure has been instituted for the disposition of spoiled canned goods, large quantities of which are condemned annually by the department's inspectors. Formerly, these goods were sent to the offal dock and disposed of at the expense of the city. At present all canned goods are condemned only in the hands of the retailers and emptied on the spot, the empty cans being returned to the jobber or manufacturer. The city is thus relieved of the cost of taking care of these goods which is an item of considerable expense in the course of a year.

Among other minor but important new regulations adopted by the department and enforced by the bureau of food and drugs are the following:

1 Definite regulations governing the handling, storage and sale of food in stores, factories, hotels, restaurants, etc.
2 Regulations prohibiting the use of common eating utensils on free lunch counters.
3 Regulations governing the cold storage of foods.
4 Regulations governing the conduct of poultry slaughter houses so as to prevent nuisances and to ensure fair competition among dealers.

Milk Inspection

In order to co-ordinate the activities of all inspectors having to do with the milk supply of the city, the former divisions of city milk inspection, country milk inspection and pasteurizing plants were consolidated in 1915, and a definite program established for safeguarding the supply from production to consumption. Among the most important of the new procedures adopted were the following:

1 Realizing the necessity of more adequately protecting the public from the dangers of contaminated milk, and recognizing the inability of the department to furnish sufficient inspection of milk at its source throughout this state and neighboring states, the department requires that all milk intended for human consumption except that which is produced under ideal conditions, amounting to about one per cent. of the entire milk supply, shall be pasteurized.

2 Prior to 1914, the department omitted the inspection of dairies producing certified milk which were conducted under the auspices and approval of the county medical societies. However, after careful consideration, it was decided that all such dairies should be inspected by the milk inspectors of the department. This has been done and the maintenance of adequate standards is assured.

3 More stringent tuberculin tests of cows producing Grade A milk have been established, experience having shown that the former procedure was not sufficient to make certain the exclusion of tuberculous cows from herds producing Grade A milk.

Meat Inspection

At present only half a dozen slaughter-houses in Brooklyn remain under the supervision of the department. In addition, however, a large quantity of country-killed meat comes into the city which must be regularly inspected. For the slaughter-house inspection and the inspection of large markets, a special division of meat inspection has been organized under the direction of a trained veterinarian. The following new procedures and extensions of service have been adopted:

1 Prior to 1914 the inspection of slaughter-houses of the city which were under the jurisdiction of the department was performed in part by lay inspectors. In order to improve the service, it was found necessary to employ only trained veterinarians. Nine veterinarians are now employed instead of three veterinarians assisted by lay food inspectors. Further necessary improvement in the strict enforcement of regulations is expected.

2 The inspection of country-killed meat which has required a considerable expenditure of time and money by the bureau of food inspection was made self-supporting early in 1915. The merchants of the West Washington and other city markets are now assessed fees based on the number of carcasses inspected by the bureau of food inspection. This method of meeting the cost of inspection of meat has been adopted with success in other cities.

Laboratory Service

In 1913 the food and drug laboratory of the department was under the direction of the bureau of laboratories. Although this laboratory did work

A Difficult Task—Maintaining Sanitary Conditions in Small Slaughter Houses

almost solely for the bureau of food and drugs, it was impossible, owing to the division of authority, to secure the most effective results. In the general organization and improvement of the service of the bureau, however, the following changes have been made:

1 The chemical laboratory was detached from the bureau of laboratories in 1915, and made a division of the bureau of drugs, thereby fixing responsibility for its procedure and control upon the director of that bureau.

2 Formerly the chemist of the laboratory examined food samples only for substances or ingredients designated by the chief food inspector. As a result the chemist was allowed no leeway in making his examinations, and the entire purpose of the examination was often nullified. By departmental ruling, this procedure was changed in 1915, and the chemist now has authority to exercise his own judgment in making analyses.

3 Prior to 1914, a great deal of chemists' time was spent in making analyses of samples of drugs submitted by the police department. With the increase of food supervisory functions, it was impossible for the laboratory to do justice to this phase of the work. In order to relieve the food and drug laboratory of this extra burden, this work was transferred to the standard testing laboratory to which chemists were assigned by the board of estimate and apportionment.

4 The routine examination of the city's water supply by the food and drug laboratory was discontinued as a result of a careful study of the city's needs in this regard. These examinations were also being performed by the department of water supply, gas and electricity, and the examinations by the laboratory of the health department were therefore a duplication.

Further Improvements Recommended

General

In order to put the inspection service of the bureau of food and drugs upon a self-supporting basis as far as possible, it is recommended that a change in the charter be made which will permit the requirement of fees for permits issued by the bureau for the conduct of all food and drug industries. The success of the bureau in applying this principle under a local ordinance to the inspection of country-killed meat offers a precedent for the practice recommended.

Ice cream manufacturers should be required to obtain permits which should be granted only after thorough inspection and approval by the department.

All statistical work of the bureau should be transferred to the division of statistical research and reports of the bureau of records, and an arrangement made for the transfer of such clerical force as may be proper from the bureau of food and drugs to the bureau of records.

Inspection of Food and Drugs

The grading of all premises now under inspection by the bureau of food and drugs should be begun as soon as possible. Certificates of merit based on the grading of such premises should be issued as a means of educating the dealers and the public to an appreciation of the necessity for improved control. The director of the bureau is now formulating a plan to carry into effect this suggestion.

In order that the inspection force may be used most effectively, it is urged that the bureau further concentrate its efforts upon the inspection of food products at the source, in the factory and at points of arrival into the city, so as to eliminate as far as possible, the inspection of such articles after they are scattered over the entire city.

In order to raise the standard of inspectional service, it is recommended that the department adopt as soon as practicable the plan proposed by the director of the bureau of food and drugs of placing all newly appointed inspectors under a definite system of instruction for a period of not less than sixty days before sending them out independently into the field.

In co-operation with the bureau of public health education further efforts should be made to hold conferences with groups of manufacturers, producers and handlers of various food and drug products in order that they may be informed fully of the purpose of the department and their co-operation enlisted.

Efforts should be made to secure the same kind of co-operation from the police as has been secured in the experimental health district in the enforcement of regulations throughout the entire city regarding the sale of foods which are unprotected from street dust and dirt on sidewalk stands and push-carts. At present the department's regulations regarding this matter are difficult of enforcement owing to the impossibility of providing sufficient inspectors. The policemen could, however, very effectively prevent violations of this kind.

Milk Inspection

In order that skimmed milk, which is a valuable cheap food, may be made available to the people of the city, it is urged that efforts be made, as recommended by the director of the bureau of food and drugs, to repeal existing legislation prohibiting its use in Kings and New York counties, when it has been produced in said counties or in other counties of the state. Protection against fraud in its sale could be provided by the department by the enforcement of proper standards and regulations as to labeling.

Although the department has established definite bacteriological standards for the various grades of milk, the change of inspection methods necessary to secure control through the enforcement of these standards has not been made. During the coming year more emphasis should be laid upon the enforcement of proper conditions of production and handling of milk through the taking of milk samples along the entire line from producer to consumer. This will require the discontinuance of much of the routine dairy inspection now practiced and the dependence by the department upon the analysis of milk samples for its judgment as to conditions in dairies. A dairy that is producing clean milk as demonstrated by bacteriological tests does not need inspection. The efforts of the department should be concentrated on those dairies which are shown to need correction by the bacterial counts of their product.

In view of the fact that the above recommendation advocates the discontinuance of reliance upon routine dairy and creamery inspection for control of the milk supply, it is believed that the routine bacteria count of milk should be transferred from the control of the bureau of laboratories to the bureau of food and drugs. The entire program of control of the milk supply, the efficiency of inspection, the direction of the inspection force, the enforcement of milk standards, etc., should be dependent upon the bacteria count, and it is obviously in the interest of economy and efficiency that the instrument of control should be in the hands of the officer who must exercise control.

Meat Inspection

Veterinarians in slaughter-house inspection are required to perform very arduous duties for long hours and at low salaries. These veterinarian inspectors are considered as giving part-time service "averaging not less than eighteen hours a week" and are paid at part-time rates. It is believed that greater efficiency would be secured if veterinarians were paid for full-time service according to the rates established by the bureau of standards of the board of estimate and apportionment.* On days when no slaughtering is done these veterinarians could be used in the inspection of meat throughout the city.

Chemical Laboratory

Provision should be made for the transfer of the chemical or food and drug laboratory to a location more convenient for inspectors of the food and drug bureau, and in order that the director of the bureau may exercise more direct supervision over laboratory work. Although now a division of the food and drug bureau, the laboratory is located at 16th Street and East River, about a mile and a half from the headquarters of the food and drug bureau. Inspectors taking samples to the laboratory must spend considerable working time on the road between their field territory and the laboratory, since all samples must be delivered in person by the inspector to the chemist.

*The recent exposures relative to the alleged bribery of health department veterinarians by the proprietors of slaughter-houses under inspection, emphasizes the necessity of placing health department veterinarians on a full-time basis at adequate salaries and under more rigid supervision.

BUREAU OF LABORATORIES

Cost

Expenditures for laboratory service for the years 1913, 1914 and 1915 are herewith presented, together with the appropriation granted for 1916:

	1913	1914	1915	1916
Personal service...........	$117,429.00	$120,366.96	$163,246.73	$164,220.00
Other than personal service..	35,900.14	34,609.74	52,353.83	44,478.00
Total............	$153,329.14	$154,976.70	$215,600.56	$208,698.00

The increase which is shown for personal service in 1915 as compared with 1914 was due to the transfer of the diagnosis laboratory, which up to that time had been under the direction of the bureau of preventable diseases. The figures for the latter bureau show a decreased expenditure for this same period. In 1916, there was a considerable increase in salaries in order to conform to the specifications of the bureau of standards, but this was offset in great measure by dropping five bacteriologists from the service who were doing special investigative work. The increase for other than personal service in 1915 was due also to the added function of bacteriological diagnosis, but this amount was reduced for the year 1916 by $7,500 as a result of careful scrutiny of the supply request for the present year.

Reorganization Effected

Up to 1915, the laboratory work of the department was under divided control. At this time the diagnostic laboratory was taken from the bureau of infectious diseases and placed under the immediate supervision of the director of the bureau of laboratories. This brings the entire bacteriological laboratory service under one head and has resulted in better supervision of the work, more uniform methods and a considerable extension of the service.

A further change was effected in the latter part of 1915 by taking the chemical laboratory of this bureau and placing it under the direction of the bureau of food and drugs. This was done because the entire work of the chemical laboratory consists of examinations of food, which is very closely connected with the routine administration of the food bureau. This permits better administration and gives a more elastic service.

By the two changes just mentioned, the bureau of laboratories now does the entire bacteriological work of the department, and takes over the supervision of the chemical analyses.

In the spring of 1915 the division of research and efficiency began a careful analytical study of the policies and especially the business methods of the bureau of laboratories. Among other things attention was given to the business aspects of the preparation, sale and distribution of the biological products of the laboratory; general accounting methods; time given to laboratory duties by all classes of employees; cost of research work and its practical application to the administrative policies of the department; limitations of civil service requirements on the scientific efficiency of the laboratory staff; and cost value and legal basis for the employment of voluntary research workers. This analysis resulted in recommendations to the commissioner which are still under consideration and which, if put into operation, it is thought should result in a more effective administration of the bureau.

Conditions Corrected, Improvements Made and Activities Extended and Inaugurated

Bacteriological Diagnosis

A special fund in the Bureau of Social Research of the Rockefeller Foundation, which had heretofore been used to support the diagnostic laboratory work in venereal diseases, was exhausted at the end of 1914. Provision was made in the 1915 and 1916 budgets to carry on this work as a municipal function.

The diagnosis of bacteriological specimens has been increasing year by year. The following table shows extension of service.

	1913	1914	1915
Typhoid	9,064	11,716	22,164
Tuberculosis	41,644	49,761	61,080
Diphtheria	80,150	154,169	151,151
Syphilis	18,750	29,891	49,212
Gonorrhoea	3,526	9,441	10,640

The department is being called upon to enlarge its service in this field constantly. It may be mentioned that the increase in the number of typhoid examinations made for 1915, as compared with the previous year, was due in large measure to the routine examination of discharges from food handlers and from inmates of institutions where this disease is endemic.

In the examination of water, milk and other food products, revision of the methods employed resulted in an increased output from 20% to 40%. The following table shows the increased number of examinations:

	1913	1914	1915
Milk	54,379	76,014	106,023
Water	1,103	1,113	1,331

At the beginning of 1916, examinations were begun of well and spring water sold in bottles in this city.

A service inaugurated within the past two years is the bacteriological examination of oysters, in recognition of their possibility as a factor in the spread of typhoid fever. During 1914, 620 examinations of this nature were made and in 1915, 1,270 examinations.

For several years part of the bacteriological work of the New York County Milk Commission was carried on in the laboratories of this department. Following an opinion by the corporation counsel that the provisions of the law did not warrant the use by the Milk Commission of employees, supplies and apparatus of the department of health, an arrangement was made whereby the Milk Commission withdrew its work from these laboratories.

Preparation, Sale and Distribution of Biological Products

During 1914, at the request of the commissioner of health, a study of accounting methods and care of valuable stock, etc., at the branch laboratory at Otisville was made by the office of the commissioner of accounts. Based upon this investigation, various recommendations made regarding accounting methods were adopted.

The preparation, sale and distribution of biological products are made from the research laboratory in this city and also at a branch located on the grounds of the Otisville Sanatorium. In general, the crude products are prepared at Otisville and the refining and bottling conducted at the New York City laboratory. In September, 1914, the Otisville service was placed under the supervision of an assistant director with marked improvement in the character of the service. A new barn to be used in connection with the antitoxin production was completed and an equipment installed which allowed a much increased output of these products. It is possible now to do more of the refining at Otisville than heretofore. Studies are being made at the present time by the assistant director to standardize tuberculin, which, if successful, will make the use of this vaccine more certain.

Studies have been made to determine the efficacy of a vaccine for the treatment of whooping cough. These experiments were conducted at a special whooping cough clinic established at the corner of Avenue C and East 16th Street, borough of Manhattan. The results have been of such a positive character that it has been decided to use this vaccine for the treatment of this disease in the future.

The war in Europe placed an additional demand upon our laboratory facilities for tetanus antitoxin and anti-meningitis serum. Receipts for the sale of surplus products amounted to over $100,000 during the past two years, and represents sufficient antitoxin to immunize at least 500,000 wounded men. The money received for the sale of this product was turned over to the city sinking fund.

Bacteriological Research

Studies have been conducted during the past two years with a view to securing better methods of bacteriological service. One of the most important results of these studies is an improved and rapid method of examining discharges for the detection of typhoid bacilli. This has made possible, as a general procedure in the department, the examination of the discharges of every typhoid convalescent and typhoid carrier, and the results of these examinations must be negative before the case is discharged from observation. This gives an effective control similar to that exercised over diphtheria.

Another experiment of practical importance was made to determine whether a single dose or repeated doses of diphtheria antitoxin should be given for treatment, the size of the dose and the method of administering. It was found that one dose is fully sufficient, provided it is given in a comparatively large quantity; also that the intra-spinal method for acute cases reduces the mortality to 50%. Limiting the injection to a single dose has resulted in a saving in the amount of antitoxin used.

Another valuable feature which has been developed is a new test for diphtheria known as the Schick test. By its use it is possible to separate the immune individuals, so as to avoid unnecessary antitoxin injection. This method saves a large quantity of antitoxin, which otherwise would have been used for immunization of all exposed individuals and is the first experiment in America to estimate the value of the procedure and put it into effect.

Extensive examinations of the mouths of school children were made and material obtained for laboratory analysis. From these studies a new procedure in mouth hygiene may be established for practical application in the schools.

Investigation with respect to some of the procedures connected with routine bacterial analysis of milk conducted in 1914, resulted in new methods such as simplifying the testing of serums and the use of more suitable bags for inspectors for carrying samples of milk for bacterial analysis.

Further Improvements Recommended

It is proposed to establish in the culture stations in the city an all-night service which will permit physicians to leave diphtheria culture tubes up to a much later period in the day than is now possible. As an experiment, in a few of these stations some incubators are to be installed in which these culture tubes will be placed by private physicians and kept at a proper temperature until collected by the department. If this proves successful and practical, it will be extended to other parts of the city, and this phase of the diagnostic service should be improved materially thereby.

The system of preparation, distribution and collection of diagnostic and therapeutical outfits for culture stations is not satisfactory, and steps are now under way for a rearrangement of the present methods. It is expected that this will result in a much improved system of preparing these outfits, and by a reorganization of the entire culture station service many superfluous stations will be eliminated and a more economic and effective administration of this function secured.

An analysis of the entire bureau made during 1915 shows the need for its reorganization for better administration. The bureau should be divided into well-defined divisions, with executive officers at the head of each division and responsibilities clearly outlined. All the bacteriologists doing special research work should be placed in the division of special investigations so that accurate records of time taken for this work will be possible.

The accounting system should be revised and methods developed which will show more clearly the various steps in the production of laboratory products, stock on hand, and stock distributed. A better system of records should be installed to show all the transactions in the sale of laboratory products. The entire stock and shipping service needs to be segregated under one control. At present it is performed under the jurisdiction of several executive officers and, therefore, is not uniform in character. The increased demands upon the diagnosis laboratory undoubtedly will require an additional force to keep up with the work. Before doing this, however, intensive studies should be made of the present distribution of the force, to determine whether the maximum output is being secured at the present time.

The field of scientific research is such a vast one that it is difficult to determine what special studies should be undertaken with the limited force available. It is suggested that at the beginning of each year a program be arranged which will show as clearly as is possible for this peculiar type of work those studies which it is planned to take up for the coming year. From this list those studies should be selected which promise results, and which will improve administrative procedures when applied practically. This program for research work is in effect at the present time in the Bureau of Chemistry of the Department of Agriculture at Washington, D. C., under the direction of Dr. Carl Alsberg.

The further development of facilities and the improvements made at Otisville should make possible not only the production of a larger amount of crude products, but also an extension of the refining processes. In this way the expense of production could be much reduced, because the necessary buildings and equipment could be maintained at a much lower cost in Otisville than in New York City.

At the present time the therapeutic application of serums and vaccines for meningitis and sepsis is under the direction of this bureau because of the technical procedures necessary. When these procedures have been better effected, their direction should be placed under the bureau of preventable diseases.

BUREAU OF HOSPITALS

The department of health operates four hospitals and a tuberculosis sanatorium for the care and treatment of preventable disease patients, viz.: Willard Parker in Manhattan, Kingston Avenue in Brooklyn, Riverside on North Brother's Island, Queensboro in Queens (to be opened May, 1916), and the Sanatorium at Otisville, New York.

Cost of Operation

Personal Service	Expenditures		Appropriation	
	1913	1914	1915	1916
Willard Parker	$80,674.62	$132,914.07	$139,150.59	$133,471.60
Kingston Avenue	70,047.95	100,553.84	103,247.21	116,655.00
Riverside	93,414.43	104,545.44	108,166.80	116,557.00
All Hospitals	126,821.83	75,587.68	85,570.78	101,382.00
Tuberculosis Sanatorium	91,146.73	92,037.40	94,532.11	91,908.00
Total	$462,105.56	$505,638.43	$530,667.49	$559,973.60

The increase in the cost for personal service is due to:

1 Added bed capacity of 660 beds as follows:

Willard Parker	320	Kingston Avenue	100
Riverside	160	Tuberculosis Sanatorium	80

2 Increase in number of nurses, in order to provide an adequate staff for the care of contagious disease patients, approaching more closely the number of patients per nurse which conforms with the recommendations of the Medical Board and the nursing methods of other hospitals. It is now on the basis of one to ten patients, during the day, and one to fifteen at night. Formerly the number of patients to a nurse was double this number.

3 Increase in pay of nurses and doctors in accordance with the recommendations of the Hospital Inquiry Committee and prevailing rates of pay, and in the case of the resident physicians as a recompense for their increased executive responsibilities. Nurses now receive on entrance into the service, $50 a month instead of $40 as formerly, and the compensation of resident physicians has been increased from $1,800 to $2,400.

4 The increase of 1916 over 1915 is principally due to the wage and salary increases to conform with the recommendations of the bureau of standards.

Other Than Personal Service	Expenditures		Appropriation	
	1913	1914	1915	1916
Willard Parker	$98,070.06	$98,073.15	$105,823.40	$95,413.00
Kingston Avenue	89,203.59	75,846.50	75,555.58	69,165.00
Riverside	147,950.90	143,358.35	141,335.86	118,137.00
Queensboro	....	....	....	12,830.00
Sanatorium	163,718.16	143,971.37	139,207.35	118,365.00
Fixed Charges	2,671.00	7,682.54	6,095.00	6,850.00
Total	$501,613.71	$468,931.91	$468,017.19	$420,760.00

The reduction in the cost of supplies has been due to improved methods of control of distribution and care of supplies, the establishment of standard dietaries, and because in 1916, on account of former methods of basing contracts on actual consumption, ignoring stock on hand, a sufficient stock, exclusive of perishable foodstuffs, remained over from 1915 to last the first quarter of 1916.

The total appropriation for the bureau for 1916 is only $17,014.33 more than the expenditures in 1913, though the bed capacity, through additional buildings, has been increased from 2,332 to 3,072, or almost a third more.

Conditions Corrected, Improvements Made and Activities Extended or Inaugurated

The work of the bureau of hospitals is divided under two distinct functions, administrative and medical, and for the consideration of the work, the bureau is separated into two units, the city hospitals and the tuberculosis sanatorium at Otisville, New York.

General Administration—City Hospitals

On January 1, 1914, experimental administrative conferences of the executive officers of the institutions, held with the director, were established on a permanent weekly basis, and have resulted in a closer control and knowledge of institutional matters by the director, in building up a spirit of hearty co-operation among the officers, and in increased efficiency and reduction in cost of operation.

Early in 1914, the administrative office of the bureau was organized and located at Willard Parker, thus centralizing the control of all administrative features and establishing a much closer supervision.

An efficiency committee was formed, consisting of the director, executive clerk and three resident physicians, to pass on the tentative ratings of all employees for the use of the board of promotions. Reports were also required from the executive heads on the work of all employees in the labor and domestic classes.

On January 1, 1916, the resident physicians were placed in full charge of each hospital, thereby relieving the director of routine details of administration.

In 1915, with the co-operation of the central payroll bureau, the payment of all employees by check instead of by cash was instituted.

On account of the nature of the service and the inaccessibility of the hospitals, an effort has been made to provide more attractive social relations among the nurses, which is necessary in order to maintain a standard of service which will compare with other institutions more favorably located. Beginning in October, 1914, lectures have been given every two weeks at each of the hospitals throughout the winter months.

On January 1, 1915, dispensaries were established in the hospitals for the treatment of all minor injuries and ailments of the employees. These are attended for two hours a day by members of the resident staff.

A dietitian was appointed in 1915 and placed in full charge of the kitchen and dining room service of all the hospitals. A menu committee was appointed composed of the dietitian and the executive officials, and the greater part of the saving of $12,218.65 effected in foodstuffs in 1915 is directly traceable to their work in the re-arrangement of menus and proper apportioning of foods.

In October, 1915, a training school for dietitians was started. Two graduates from dietetic courses in schools are serving as pupil dietitians at Willard Parker, and it is expected to secure graduates next June to serve at Kingston Avenue and at Riverside. The hospitals secure the services of theoretically trained dietitians at the nominal cost of twenty dollars a month and practical schooling is given the pupils.

In July, 1915, the practice of sending nurses with the ambulance surgeons in responding to calls was instituted. This has resulted in:

1 Instituting in the minds of the parents confidence in the hospital before the children leave home.
2 Insuring proper care of the child in transit.
3 Relieving the hospital of the responsibility of the care of the child's personal clothing, as the child is dressed in hospital clothing and wrapped in warm blankets before being removed.

The work formerly performed by the fire drill expert of the department has been carried on by the formation of a committee on fires and fire prevention.

The State Charities Aid Association accepted an invitation to make periodic inspections of the hospitals. This work has been done by members of the Association's New York City Visiting Committee.

A saw mill purchased for the Otisville Sanatorium was utilized first at Willard Parker to saw 941 cut off piles remaining from the dock work construction of the sea wall at foot of East 16th St. The motor used was an antiquated one obtained from the board of education. 54,200 feet of rough lumber and 29 cords of fire wood were cut and stored at a cost of $794.70 for departmental labor and $250 for materials, a total of $1044.70. The lumber was used for the construction of fences and walks, for the sewage disposal work at Queensboro, and general work around the hospitals.

In 1914, a squad for repairs and replacements was established, consisting of laborers skilled in painting, carpentry and masonry, which is sent from hospital to hospital, as necessity arises. By utilizing the laborers in large numbers it is possible to complete a big job in a short time, as for instance, painting twelve pavilions at Riverside in twelve days. The size of this squad depends entirely upon the activities in the hospital wards. When the census is low it is possible to assign the laborers doing orderly and porter work to this repair squad. The only repairs requiring outside labor with special experience are those which have to do with roofs, cornices, expert machine work and painting which require hanging scaffolding.

Since 1914 the following changes for improved service have been made:

1 At the Reception Hospital, Willard Parker, large glass windows were built in the partitions of the rooms and a porch constructed around the west wing, 170 feet by 4, at a cost of $465.70; labor being $291.29, materials $174.41. By contract, the cost would have been at least double this amount.

2 A fire caused by the incinerating chimney at the disinfecting plant at Willard Parker made it necessary to transfer the incinerator to another part of the grounds and to rebuild it. In doing this, the hospital utilized the smokestack of an abandoned furnace of the Consolidated Gas Company on the river front between 15th and 16th Streets and built a new incinerator at a cost of about $300 equal to the former one, which cost by contract in 1890 about $2,000.

3 An old coal-hoisting engine-house at Willard Parker has been reconstructed by departmental labor at a cost of $501.95 and turned into a morgue and mortuary chapel. Hearses and undertakers' wagons, which formerly gathered in the heart of the hospital grounds and under the windows of the wards, are now sent to East 15th Street, where they are not seen by patients or visitors as formerly, thus avoiding the depressing effect such scenes invariably produced.

4 Sputum at Riverside was formerly collected in individual receptacles in each ward and incinerated with the garbage, and was under no scientific control. An incinerator building for sputum has been erected, which also serves for storing sterile sputum cups and gauze handkerchiefs. This is really the administrative point of control of infectious sputum from tubercular patients. Twice a day patients have to visit this building, leaving their used sputum cups and receiving fresh ones. The building, which is 9½ feet long by 5 feet 9 inches wide and 8 feet high, was erected by departmental labor at a cost of $363.26.

5 On account of repeated violations placed on the various buildings in Willard Parker because of insufficient tank capacity, a three-inch water line has been laid through the pipe tunnel, so that the standpipes of every building can be connected up with the large fire pumps provided in all the new buildings. This means that every building in the plant has a sure and ample supply of water under all conditions.

6 With the construction and occupation of four new cement buildings on the newly filled-in land at Riverside (street refuse and ashes), it became necessary to construct a hard bottom road to transport patients and supplies to the building. A road 1,000 feet long was constructed with a Telford base and gravel surface (by department labor at a cost of $1,000), using rock from excavations of the pipe tunnel.

7 Up to 1914, all the sewage of Kingston avenue was received in an open settling tank, located where the new kitchen building was erected. With the addition of new buildings, it was necessary to build a new system to provide adequately for the care of the sewage. A disposal tank has been built for the reception of the hospital sewage, which is then pumped to the nearest sewer.

8 Extensive improvements in the appearance of the grounds both at Riverside and at Kingston avenue have been made through the construction of lawns, flower beds, walks and roads.

Additional Buildings Completed or in Course of Construction—City Hospitals

WILLARD PARKER

Measles pavilion—capacity 320 beds
Female help dormitory and staff house will be ready for occupancy this year.
Sea wall from 15th to 17th Streets nearly completed.

KINGSTON AVENUE

Isolation Pavilion—capacity of 100 beds.

This pavilion replaced four portable beds and relieved the heavy strain on five others. The patients are in far better sanitary surroundings and the employees are no longer exposed to the dangers of contracting colds and other affections, due to exposure to elements, which was formerly the case on account of their having to pass to and from the various buildings.

A new kitchen building, which also includes the pantries and dining rooms for all non-professional help, and dormitories for forty maids, has been completed except for the equipment. The equipment includes a bakery, which will be able to supply the breadstuffs for all the hospitals of the department in the city, and effect a saving.

A diphtheria pavilion has been started and will be ready for use in 1917.

RIVERSIDE

Two cement pavilions—capacity of 80 beds each
Addition to Nurses' Home
Pavilion for venereal diseases—capacity of 80; two cement pavilions, 80 beds each, and a maids' dormitory, are in course of construction

QUEENSBORO

There was considerable opposition to the building of a contagious disease hospital in the borough of Queens, on the site known as the Haacke Farm, between Jamaica and Flushing. In 1914, at the final public hearing held by the board of estimate and apportionment, the commissioner of health was able to convince the board of the necessity for such a hospital in that borough, and that its presence would not be deleterious either to the property or health interests of the community.

In 1915 a hospital was completed on this site, which is a distinct acquisition to the architectural quality of the buildings in the vicinity and represents every modern convenience for the proper treatment of contagious diseases. It will be open for the reception of patients by May 1st, 1916. In order that the opening might not be delayed on account of lack of sewer facilities, a cesspool for temporary relief, 16 feet wide, 35 feet long and 11 feet deep, has been constructed by departmental labor at a cost of $528.14. An appropriation has been made for the construction of a sewer to connect with the existing sewer system.

Medical Administration—City Hospitals

On January 1st, 1914, the medical direction of Kingston Avenue Hospital was turned over to a medical board consisting of twenty-two members. Under its direction are fifteen assistant attendant physicians and surgeons.

The Willard Parker Hospital Board has been enlarged from twenty-seven to thirty-two members by the addition of two attending physicians, one neurologist, one pathologist, and one special anaesthetist. A roentgenologist will be added this year. The assistant attending physicians and surgeons now number twenty-eight.

In 1914, a definite and uniform organization of the visiting medical service in all the hospitals of the department was accomplished. Schedules providing for definite service by all visiting physicians were promulgated and methods adopted replacing uncertain and irregular medical attendance in the hospitals by the visiting staff.

A more careful selection is made in filling vacancies on the visiting staff, resulting in a higher calibre of service. Two or more candidates are now insisted on before any appointment is made.

In order to acquaint the private physician with the progress in hospital care and application of new methods of diagnosis and treatment of contagious diseases in the hospitals, clinics for private physicians were inaugurated at Willard Parker in 1915, under the direction of members of the medical board.

In addition to the clinics that are held by four universities at Willard Parker and at Riverside, this privilege was extended to the New York Medical College for Women.

As a result of the activities of the medical board at Riverside, thirty chronic cases simulating tuberculosis were discovered and transferred to other institutions, thereby upholding the policy of the department to avoid the treatment of chronic disease and to eliminate surgical cases for which facilities are not available.

In July, 1915, twenty-three cases of chronic laryngeal stenosis (tube cases) were transferred from Willard Parker to a farm house on the grounds of the Otisville Sanatorium, for a stay of three months, with a view to improving their general condition. As a result all showed great improvement and six are apparently cured who have been in the hospital from two to six years. The cures among these patients have hitherto been very infrequent, and their care, on account of the necessity of constant medical and nursing attendance, has been very costly.

The treatment of septic cases of scarlet fever by the transfusion of blood from donors convalescing from that disease, was inaugurated in 1914 with a considerable degree of success. Several septic cases in which the prognosis appeared to be wholly unfavorable recovered after this treatment.

The detail of special nurses to patients who are very ill from measles is believed to have played an important part in lowering the death rates in the hospitals.

Quarantine periods for contagious disease cases throughout the city have been changed, the most marked change being in the case of scarlet fever, a reduction from forty-two to thirty days, provided discharges from nose and ears have ceased. This will result in an economic gain through the much earlier release of patients to the resumption of useful activities, as well as the corresponding reduction in time and effort in caring for and supervising the care of the patients.

Since any history of contagious disease is incomplete that does not show the sequela, and as these sequela frequently develop after patients have been discharged from the hospital, a follow-up system has been inaugurated whereby nurses or physicians visit the houses of discharged patients and secure the necessary information to complete the histories. The statistics gathered in this important work will be most valuable as to the actual cure of cases of contagious disease and the economic loss in persons permanently disabled by complications subsequent to the primary disease. This follow-up system also determines the number of return cases and shows the necessity of sufficiently long and effective isolation.

Studies of the Schick test (the reaction shown in the skins of individuals who have no anti-toxin in their blood, after the injection of a minute amount of toxin) made in the department's research laboratory, proved its absolute value in locating susceptibles to diphtheria amongst the employees and patients in the hospitals. Its protective and economic value in permitting the authorities to separate all persons susceptible to diphtheria from contact with that class of patients being recognized, an order was issued in 1914 to test all new admissions and new employees before being detailed to the wards.

Revised rules for medical treatment of patients have been adopted which have resulted in a notable reduction in the number of cases of mixed and secondary infections. In the case of scarlet fever, as the secondary infection, the number was reduced from 14 in 1914 to 8 in 1915. A checking system on all employees who have been in contact with cases in the hospitals, developing cross infection, has been inaugurated in an attempt to fix definite responsibility.

In 1914, routine Widal tests for typhoid were ordered on all employees handling food, and cooks had also to undergo the Wassermann test. A closer supervision of typhoid carriers is being enforced and the state board of health is co-operating in the treatment of those now in the hospitals.

In order to extend the knowledge of the hospital physicians in the branches of medicine collateral to the specialized care of contagious diseases, an order was issued in 1914 directing the hospital physicians to attach themselves to clinics and regularly to attend them.

The resident staff of each hospital was organized in 1914 as a medical society with a constitution and by-laws. Monthly meetings are held dealing with character of diseases received in the department's hospitals.

In order to extend facilities for the study of contagious disease nursing, the department of health offered a post graduate course of instruction in this subject to be given in its hospitals. This was brought about by the statements of the heads of large training schools that such opportunities were necessary for the proper training of nurses who contemplated the care of contagious disease cases.

The privilege of sending pupil nurses to the department's hospitals for instruction was extended to the Presbyterian Hospital of Newark, N. J., and, so far, two have taken advantage of it.

The medical service at Riverside was extended in 1914 by furnishing dental attention to the patients.

Wassermann and complement fixation tests for the presence of venereal diseases in tubercular patients admitted to Riverside or the Otisville Sanatorium, were made a routine feature on June 1st, 1914.

Through an arrangement made with the department of public charities in 1914, whereby the department of health furnishes the materials, Riverside Hospital patients can be sent to the Metropolitan Hospital for X-Ray photography. Funds have been provided in the 1916 budget for the purchase of an X-ray outfit.

To carry out the policy of the department forcibly to remove and detain at Riverside all cases of tuberculosis that are menaces to public health, it became necessary in 1915 to provide a detention ward. In October, 1915, an order was issued requiring all tuberculosis cases to remain for a period of at least four days, in order that home conditions could be investigated.

Tuberculosis Sanatorium—Otisville

On January 1, 1914, the sanatorium, hitherto administered independently, was incorporated into the bureau of hospitals. The administration of the sanatorium has been reorganized into three divisions: Hospital, under the physician in charge of the medical administration; general administration and farm industries, immediately under the director; and construction and repairs, under the assistant director.

Conditions have been corrected, improvements made and activities extended and inaugurated as follows:

Medical

A comparative study in diets has been made where milk has been substituted for eggs as the principal proteid food at breakfast. The study has

Otisville Sanatorium—A View of Some of the Buildings

proven that this ration is equal in food value to the former one, and considerably less expensive.

A study of the effects of human blood in the treatment of tuberculosis by transfusion from healthy donors to patient recipients was carried on for a period of over nine months, and the results, while showing no ill effects on the patients, were not of sufficient value to warrant the adoption of this practice.

Coincident with the order that the length of stay of patients would be determined by positive sputum, all sputa is examined, after treatment with hypochlorides (Formin method) and centrifugalization. It was found that the number of positive cases was materially increased.

An X-ray apparatus was purchased in 1914 and a laboratory established for the study of tuberculosis. The results up to date have been of material assistance in the diagnosis and location of tubercular lesions.

Coincident with the formation of the medical societies in the contagious disease hospitals in the city, a series of weekly lectures to the medical staff of the sanatorium and medical practitioners in the surrounding towns was established. The lectures are given by prominent members of the medical profession on subjects collateral to the care and treatment of tuberculosis.

Administrative

The administrative offices have been transferred from the residence of the assistant director to the storehouse, thereby centralizing all of the administrative activities and clerical force at one point.

A committee was appointed in 1914 to prepare a general plan for the lay-out of the sanatorium, showing the grouping of future buildings, service, roads, paths and other approaches, disposition of lawns, terraces and the general location of plantations. The plan which has been adopted is sufficiently flexible to permit of minor changes from time to time as new conditions arise, but is definite enough to serve as a practical guide in the location of future buildings and the development of roads, drives and walks.

In 1914, the State Conservation Commission, on request, sent a forester to survey and make recommendations relative to the conservation of the present wood lands and to future plantings. It is proposed to follow these recommendations systematically. Ten thousand red pine and Norway spruce saplings have been planted.

Arrangements were perfected in 1914 with the lecture bureau of the board of education to extend its services to the sanatorium, and bi-weekly lectures are given of the same character as those in the public schools of the city.

Permission was granted the patients to publish a monthly paper for the purpose of promulgating a spirit of good-fellowship and courage among themselves. On July 1, 1914, the first number of the Otisville Ray appeared, and it has been published monthly since, with the co-operation of the bureau of public health education.

A time limit of nine months has been established for the treatment of patients at the sanatorium, with the understanding, however, that an extension of time may be allowed by the commissioner in cases specially recommended by the attending physician for further treatment. The adoption of this time limit followed an investigation which disclosed the fact that a number of patients were retained at Otisville for extremely long periods, to the disadvantage of applicants awaiting admission.

An investigation is now made to determine the financial ability of all prospective patients for the sanatorium to pay for treatment. Where possible, patients are required to pay for treatment at a figure within their means and not to exceed the cost to the city. This was started in April, 1915.

Prior to 1914 the maintenance allowed employees was determined in each individual case and great discrepancies resulted. After a careful study, in which the bureau of standards assisted, the maintenance of all the employees has been standardized.

Through an agreement between the commissioners of health and of correction, and by formal action of the sinking fund commission a transfer was made from the sanatorium to the New Hampton Farms of the necessary horses, cows and agricultural implements to start work there, thus enabling them to plant their 1914 spring crops.

When prisoners arrived at the farms they were without proper medical supervision, and upon request of the commissioner of correction, the physician in charge at the sanatorium was instructed to furnish such medical assistance as might from time to time be required. A close supervision was exercised by the sanatorium physicians over the care of the health of these prisoners. A number of cases of epidemic diarrhœal disease were removed from contact with other inmates and an incipient epidemic through the institution was thus prevented. Every inmate was immunized against typhoid. The lack of sewers and proper sanitary control at the start of this institution would have made the inmates particularly susceptible to typhoid, if a carrier should have been among those sent to the farm.

The board of inebriety in 1914 requested the commissioner of health to allow the assistant director at the sanatorium to draw the plans and specifications for a dormitory at their farm at Warwick, which is near Otisville. The request was acceded to, and the construction was also supervised.

In November, 1915, a new boiler plant was erected at Randall's Island, and the department of health received permission to dismantle the old plant. This was done by departmental labor, and two boilers totalling 275 horse power were sent to Otisville. These will be installed, when funds are available, replacing the present small and inadequate ones. The purchase of new boilers has thus been avoided and a considerable saving effected.

In 1914 a contract was made for the purchase of light and power. The plant at the sanatorium was entirely inadequate for the needs of the institution. All machinery had to be hand operated, thus increasing the cost of construction and repair work and lessening the output.

Farm Industries

On January 1, 1914, fifteen tubercular cows in a segregated herd, were held according to the Bang method. After a survey of the dairy condition, it was considered unwise to carry on this work any further, and they were slaughtered in accordance with the laws relative thereto. All the other cattle were tuberculin tested and six, giving a suspicious reaction, were slaughtered, so that the herd as now constituted is absolutely free from tuberculosis.

The herd has been increased by the production of 22 heifers in 1914 and 21 in 1915, and now consists of 55 milch cows, 24 two-year-olds, 23 three months to one year, 1 one month old, and 1 bull two years old, 1 ten months and 3 bull calves. Seventeen calves have been sent in the two years to the laboratory for the production of vaccine. There were 178,387 quarts of milk produced in 1915, or about half the consumption, at a cost of .0545 per quart delivered at points of use.

A piggery was established in April, 1914, consisting of two sows and a borrowed boar. It now numbers one hundred and thirty. Sixteen pigs were butchered in 1915, yielding 3,000 pounds. The pigs are cared for and butchered by patient employees. The only feed outside of garbage that is used is corn produced on the grounds that is fed to them about a month before butchering in order to harden them.

The increasing need of the piggery for room was supplied by utilizing the old hen houses, and an addition of six lean-tos.

The hennery, when originally started, was supposed to be conducted by the patients and hen houses were erected near the male unit. This kind of administration proved a failure, and the hennery was removed to a point where the houses could have adequate constant supervision. A hen house, accommodating about 1,000 hens, and twelve colony houses for young chicks were built. In 1915, 2,770 dozen eggs and 2,386 pounds of poultry were produced, and in addition 5,000 eggs for incubation.

In order to help clean the pastures and meadows, as well as to aid in their fertilization, five sheep and a ram have been purchased as a nucleus of a small flock to be kept for these purposes. It is expected that there will also be some financial return from the sale of the wool.

About 3,000 tons of ice are harvested annually. By the installation of a modern ice conveyor and elevator, operated by power, the cost has been reduced from 33 1/3 cents a ton in 1914 to 20 cents in 1915.

In 1915 the cultivated area for farm and garden products was increased by the addition of about ten acres in corn and five acres in various garden vegetables. The production of corn will be increased by adding about ten acres from meadows that at present do not yield a sufficient amount of hay to warrant cutting. The two silos were filled with ensilage for the first time in 1915, and a large amount of corn fodder was stacked.

The general plan that is to be followed on the rest of the land available for agricultural purposes is to place it under actual cultivation for one year, followed by rye and seeding to timothy, so that in the third year there will be a well set crop for hay. In this way it is hoped eventually to reclaim the meadows which up to this time have been allowed practically to run out.

The overflowing of Bear Creek has been prevented and a considerable area of black dirt land has thus become available for reclamation. About seven acres were developed in 1915, and it is planned to reclaim the rest at a rate of about five acres a year for the next five years. It costs about thirty dollars an acre for drainage and clearance of trees and undergrowth. It is expected that this area will produce sufficient onions and potatoes to supply the sanatorium, and also enough carrots for all the experimental animals at the Research Laboratory at Otisville.

In 1915 a cannery was started and produced 1,165 cans of No. 10 and 300 of No. 3 tomatoes, equivalent to 1,232 gallons. The cost per gallon was .177 as against the contract price of .2027.

Construction and Repairs

Practically all work of this class is done by departmental labor, including improvement of the grounds.

The following buildings have been completed since January 1, 1914:

Two pavilions at the women's unit—capacity of 40 each.
Antitoxin stable, 3 story, 32′ x 162′ 6″
Ice house—3 units
Greenhouse 18′ by 36′, except heating and electric service.
Laundry, except equipment.

The recreation building and another pavilion will be finished about July of this year.

Bath and toilets were put in the children's shack at the female unit, thus obviating the necessity of having them travel to other shacks.

A telephone switchboard with one hundred extensions has been installed, taking the place of the former one-wire system with twenty-seven code calls.

The Evans cow barn was repaired and the lower story rebuilt, making it a sanitary cow stable with thirty-two stalls.

A striking advance has been made in the improvement of the grounds, the work being performed partly by departmental labor and partly by volunteer patients.

At the women's unit several old stone walls have been removed, unsightly and dangerous wooden steps and walks have been replaced by concrete with iron railings, the ragged and rough, rugged hillside has been replaced by smooth grass plots, and thousands of evergreen trees have been planted in the larger spaces. The grounds at both units have been cleared of stones and weeds and graded and sodded. In order to prevent further surface erosion by heavy rainfalls, drains have been placed caring for several acres of grounds.

The Bear Swamp Reservoir has been dredged and cleared of dead trees and stumps by contract, and has been in use since November, 1915. It now has a capacity of 40,000,000 gallons.

An Imhoff tank system has been constructed, thus insuring proper disposal of sewage. This will be ready for use early this year.

Further Improvements to be Secured or Desirable

The present responsibility for hospital care of the city poor, divided as it is among three departments, allows of waste of administrative forces and extravagance in operation. In the interests of public health, and to further the legitimate activities of the department of health, a single city department should have entire charge of all hospital and dispensary services operated by the city. The many advantages of such an administrative centralization for hospitals and dispensaries are not simply in the saving of personnel, plant and equipment, but in the opportunity to use these great instruments of public welfare as part of the city's machinery for the prevention and correction of disease.

At those periods of the year when the census of the hospitals is very low, the hospital activities should be extended so as to care for contagious diseases other than those at present treated, such as chicken pox, whooping cough, erysipelas and cerebro-spinal meningitis. The overhead expense of the hospitals cannot be materially lessened during these low periods, hence fuller advantage should be taken of the hospital facilities for the care and treatment of contagious diseases.

Sufficient additional funds should be granted so that a contagious disease hospital of three units could be constructed on the site at Seton Falls Park, borough of The Bronx, thus enabling the department to transfer all its contagious disease work from Riverside Hospital on North Brother Island. With the construction of this hospital, the number of cases treated could be vastly increased, and there would undoubtedly result a considerable reduction in the prevalence of common contagious diseases in The Bronx due to the curtailment of the spread of a disease if the patient were promptly removed in all instances where there was the slightest doubt that he would not be properly isolated. Many cases are not ordered removed to Riverside Hospital, because of danger from exposure during the long ambulance ride and trip on the boat.

The heating plant of the King's County and of the Kingston Avenue hospitals are to be consolidated, centralizing the boiler plant at the former, which will furnish heat, light and power for both institutions.

By joint inter-departmental action it should be possible to consolidate the steamboat services of the departments of health, correction and public charities, thereby effecting considerable economy.

The Kingston Avenue Hospital grounds and the premises immediately adjoining them are about ten feet below the sewer level of the nearest sewers. These grounds represent the lowest point to which surface water converges after a rain pour in a district approximating three-fourths of a square mile. The volume of water to be disposed of is far greater than the capacity of the three departmental pumps and one owned by the department of water supply, gas and electricity which are supposed to pump the excess water into the Clarkson street sewer. On August 4, 1915, a disastrous flood occurred due to this surface water which flooded the diphtheria wards, the cellars, engine rooms and pipe galleries, causing damage of about $10,000. This flood completely put out of commission the pumping plant, flooding the motors and switchboard, and made it necessary to call in the fire department to pump out the sewage of the institution.

A repetition of this flood is always imminent. In order to protect the property a dike has been built about three feet higher than the level of the surrounding streets, but it proved inadequate on February 24, 1916, when the water rose so rapidly that it was flowing over the top of the dike within four hours after the rainfall commenced, and the hospital again had to call on the fire department for aid.

Steps should be immediately taken to relieve the hospital of this deplorable condition by the co-operation of the city departments having jurisdiction in removing the legal technicalities which now prevent the bureaus of sewers from building a sewer which would care for all this excess water, and for which all preliminary surveys have been made. An example of the legal technicalities referred to is the present inability to secure an easement on Remsen Avenue.

Winthrop Street from Albany Avenue to Kingston Avenue and Kingston Avenue from Winthrop to Rutland Road should be paved. At present patients are conveyed over 1,400 feet of these roads which, when frozen, are distinctly dangerous to the patients' welfare and on which springs of ambulances and other vehicles are often broken. Immediately after a thaw the mud is hub deep and the roads are well nigh impassable for motor vehicles. In summer they are a constant source

of dense clouds of dust that float into the hospital wards and are decidedly detrimental to the health of the patients.

Additional Buildings or Improvements Needed

Willard Parker

A new power plant is an imperative necessity, as the present one cannot supply sufficient heat for the hospital plant, and it will be impossible to care for the two additional buildings that will have to be heated this coming winter.

A new kitchen building is needed, including dining quarters for the help. The present kitchen is overtaxed and the dining quarters are located in the research laboratory, an unsuitable place and where they are a source of constant inconvenience to the laboratory.

The enclosed glass and iron fire-escapes on the scarlet fever hospital are unsafe and should be rebuilt.

Pavilion number one, six stories high, built in 1883, is a non-fireproof building and lacks present-day hospital facilities. It should be razed and replaced.

Kingston Avenue

Administration, nurses' and staff home: The present quarters for nurses and doctors are inadequate and greatly overcrowded. When the new building is erected, the present administration building will be reconstructed into a dormitory for the help.

A new storehouse is necessary to replace the present non-fireproof building, which is so small that stores have to be kept in cellars and other improper depositories.

A new pavilion with a capacity of one hundred is needed and the present wooden buildings which are not properly constructed for the care of the cases housed should be razed.

Roads and walks should be constructed on the hospital grounds, in order to make the various buildings easier of access.

Riverside

A new kitchen building is needed. The present kitchen building is poorly constructed and inadequate to take care of the present needs of the hospital. The kitchen facilities must be increased to meet the augmented census requirements when the three new ward buildings now under construction are completed.

The fire-escape at the south end of Pavilion No. 1 should be rebuilt in accordance with the recommendations of the fire department.

New electric installations should be made in order to comply with the regulations of the department of water supply, gas and electricity. The present installations were originally made twenty-five years ago and repairs and reconstructions have been made from time to time by departmental labor.

An addition on the north end of the nurses' home should be constructed, thus completing this building and providing sufficient accommodations for the nurses necessary to the proper administration of the hospital.

A new dock to replace the present old and worn-out one should be built one hundred feet north and extended to the pier line, thus providing a decent landing place and permitting the docking of large boats at both sides and end of the dock.

Five cement pavilions, of a capacity of eighty each, should be constructed for the care of tuberculosis patients. The present wooden buildings should be removed. This is in direct line with the proposed development of Riverside as a hospital for tuberculosis and venereal diseases and the removal of all contagious cases to The Bronx.

Roadways and walks should be completed in conformance with the plan laid out and approved by the municipal art commission.

Tuberculosis Sanatorium, Otisville

Infirmary and Reception Units: This building, if constructed, will probably save the lives of a number of patients, who in the early stage of acute tuberculosis are now transferred from the sanatorium to the city, but whose condition might remain stationary, if they were permitted to stay in the altitude of the sanatorium in an infirmary properly equipped for their care, until they have passed the acute stage and returned to a normal temperature. The lowering of their resistance, due to the transfer to the city and the depressing effect of the knowledge that they are supposed to be too sick to stay at the sanatorium, has probably resulted in rapid advance and final death of cases that might have been saved, had there been proper infirmary facilities at the sanatorium.

Five pavilions should be constructed, of eighty beds each, bringing the capacity up to one thousand.

Additions to the cow barn to house the steadily increasing herd should be constructed. It is planned eventually to supply practically all the milk for the sanatorium.

The fire and sewer systems should be extended, roadways constructed and grounds further improved.

The land available for agriculture should be developed to its utmost, with a view to furnishing all the farm products necessary for the care of the sanatorium patients.

DEPARTMENT OF CORRECTION

Modern Penological Methods Lacking in 1914

For a number of years prior to this administration, no department of the city government was as neglected as the department of correction. It was principally a department of jails. The buildings were of antiquated construction, and the department was administered with scarcely any regard for modern penological requirements and methods. One or two unsuccessful efforts were made by former commissioners to infuse a new spirit and modern ideas into correctional work but these efforts, except in the establishment of the reformatory, failed.

Even as early as 1895, it was recognized that Blackwell's Island was an unsuitable place for the proper development of the institutions of this department. The legislature of that year enacted a law which prohibited further construction for the department of correction on Blackwell's Island. In 1905, a law was passed requiring the commissioner of correction to classify all criminals and misdemeanants under his charge, so that youthful and less hardened offenders should not be rendered more depraved by association with older and more hardened offenders, and designated the institution established at that time for youthful offenders on Hart's Island as the New York City Reformatory for Misdemeanants. This law also provided that, after January 1, 1905, any male person between the ages of 16 and 30, upon first conviction of any offense other than a felony, might be sentenced to the reformatory in the discretion of the magistrate or the court for an indefinite period not exceeding three years, the term of such imprisonment being determined by the board of parole. The establishment of the board of parole of the New York City Reformatory was authorized by the same act. Very little was done, however, to develop this as a reformatory until two new buildings, one for a shop and one for an office and dormitory, were completed in 1909.

The board of estimate from 1910 to 1913, began in earnest the task of improving the conditions and conception of the needs of this department by approving the substitution of modern outside cell construction for the old interior cell block, supplemented wherever possible by the cottage plan in conjunction with industrial and agricultural work. The board in 1910 rescinded an authorization of $2,250,000 of corporate stock, approved by the preceding administration, for a huge penitentiary of obsolete design upon Riker's Island, estimated to cost $4,000,000, and changed the old prison plan for the new reformatory institution on Hart's Island to a combined custodial and cottage type of institution to be erected upon a large farm tract in the country.

While the board of estimate was considering plans for the new reformatory in 1911, the New York Prison Association submitted to certain members of the board a general scheme for the re-organization and relocation of the institutions of the department, providing ultimately for the removal of the reformatory on Hart's Island to a farm, the removal of the women's workhouse from Blackwell's to Hart's Island temporarily, and ultimately to a farm, the removal of the men's workhouse from Blackwell's Island to Riker's Island, and the removal of the penitentiary from Blackwell's to Hart's Island.

Although this project was not formally approved by the board of estimate, it became substantially effective through the fact that funds authorized subsequently for permanent improvements and new construction were predicated upon it. The plan was based upon the theory that in providing additional funds for this department, the city's first duty was to improve conditions for those persons convicted and serving sentences before providing funds for the improvement of conditions for those held for trial, and in the case of those convicted that its first duty was to facilitate the work of reformation and rehabilitation.

Pursuant to this general scheme, late in 1913 the city acquired a large farm at New Hampton, Orange County, New York, for the reformatory, and additional facilities have been provided at the branch workhouses on Riker's and Hart's Islands where better conditions prevail than on Blackwell's Island. This plan has only been departed from, since 1911, in two instances which give precedence to improvements in the condition of those held for trial rather than of those already convicted. The preceding administration authorized funds for the construction of a new 3d district prison and court, commonly known as the Essex Market Court, and a central court and detention home for women, both in Manhattan.

The plans of both of these institutions have been completed and have been approved by the bureaus supervising construction plans. Sufficient funds, however, are not available to cover the estimated cost of either institution, and until additional funds are granted these plans must be held in abeyance.

On January 1, 1914, Dr. Katharine B. Davis, formerly superintendent of Bedford Reformatory, was appointed commissioner. After studying the general project discussed above, the commissioner approved it substantially, worked out the details for the changes proposed, and added thereto a plan for the removal of the women's workhouse and the women's penitentiary to a farm colony, because investigation has demonstrated that there is no necessity for separate institutions for women committed to the workhouse and to the penitentiary.

Since January, 1914, undivided effort has been given to repairing the city's neglect of its great penological problem. On account of this accumulated neglect, as well as because of the limited time for the preparation of this report, less emphasis has been placed upon a critical analysis of work yet to be done than on the work accomplished to date. At present the administration is more interested in what may be done to forward a general program for the whole department than in developing a new theory of management in a single institution. This report makes clear the fact that the department is fully alive to the still uncorrected short-comings in its equipment and methods.

The mid-term record of the present administration of the department shows not only substantial gains, but contains the assurance of specific betterments begun and of further progress under way for the remaining period of the administration. Better than that, the character of improvements made and the program initiated will make a return to the backward methods of the past difficult as well as undesirable. The city is definitely launched upon its new program of correction, sane, conservative, but firmly grounded.

Perhaps the most significant forward step of the past two years is the establishment of the new indeterminate sentence and parole law by the legislature in 1915. The parole commission appointed pursuant to this law will determine the period of commitment or the period of parole for all persons committed for indeterminate sentences, and will exercise supervision over all persons paroled by the commission. This means that the majority of the inmate population of the department of correction will come within the jurisdiction of this new parole commission. The old board of parole had jurisdiction only over the inmates of the New York City Reformatory. The parole commission has jurisdiction over the three classes of inmates committed to the department of correction, those in the New York City Reformatory, the workhouse, and the penitentiary. In a host of ways the power of this new commission may be utilized as a constructive agency for the prevention of crime and for the reduction in the number of repeated offenders who are both costly and disheartening in any community. So important are the possibilities of this new work, that the mayor felt it wise to place at its head the commissioner of correction, who had prepared the way for its effective operation. Mr. Burdette G. Lewis, who served four years as a member of the sub-committee on the city budget and two years as deputy commissioner of correction, was fully prepared to assume the duties of commissioner when appointed in December, 1915.

The task which the commissioner assumed in January, 1914, was enormous, involving a complete break with old methods and a thoroughgoing reorganization of the department's methods and rehabilitation of its plant. In view of the many improvements which have already been achieved, still more rapid progress may be expected during the remainder of this administration.

This report is divided into three subdivisions, as follows:

1 Conditions prevailing January 1, 1914.
2 Accomplishments and work initiated during 1914 and 1915.
3 Program of work for the years 1916 and 1917.

Conditions Prevailing January 1, 1914

Scope of Activity

Some conception of the magnitude of the problem involved in reorganization may be gathered from the following facts. The department has jurisdiction over 120 buildings, most of which are of antiquated construction and wholly unsuitable for their purposes. The average annual inmate census has grown from 3872 in 1910 to 6410 in 1915, an increase of 65.5%. The number of employees has grown from 576 in 1910 to 706 in 1915, an increase of 22.5%. The annual budget for operation and maintenance has grown from $1,271,351.00 in 1910 to $1,312,220.51 in 1915, an increase of only 3.2%, and the amount of the budget, plus special revenue bonds authorized, has grown from $1,275,251.68 in 1910 to $1,492,555.51 in 1915, an increase of 17%.

The following tables show departmental statistics for the period of 1910 to 1915, inclusive, with respect to the average annual census of inmates, the number of departmental employees, the annual budget, the amount of the budget plus special revenue bonds authorized for the years 1910 to 1915, and the per capita cost per annum:

AVERAGE ANNUAL CENSUS—INMATES

Year	Men	Women	Total	Increase Over Preceding Year	
				Number	Per Cent.
1910	3,132	740	3,872	....	....
1911	3,464	701	4,165	293	7.5
1912	3,675	734	4,409	244	5.8
1913	3,955	776	4,731	322	7.3
1914	4,530	808	5,338	607	12.8
1915	5,456	954	6,410	1,072	20.0

DEPARTMENTAL EMPLOYEES

Year	Number	Increase Over Preceding Year	
		Number	Per Cent.
1910	576	...	....
1911	575*	...	....
1912	591	16	2.7
1913	618	27	4.5
1914	628	10	1.6
1915	758	130	20.7

*Decrease 1.

Annual Tax Budget

Year	Amount	Comparison With Preceding Year			
		Increase		Decrease	
		Amount	Per Cent.	Amount	Per Cent.
1910..........	$1,271,351.00	....	....	....	...
1911..........	1,266,714.50	....	....	$4,636.50	.3
1912..........	1,299,437.00	$32,722.50	2.5	....	
1913..........	1,269,246.87	....	...	30,190.13	2.3
1914..........	1,270,456.07	1,209.20	.1	....	...
1915..........	1,312,220.51	41,764.44	3.2	....	...
1916..........	1,466,209.08	153,988.57	11.7	....	...

Budget Plus Special Revenue Bonds Authorized

Year	Amount	Comparison With Preceding Year			
		Increase		Decrease	
		Amount	Per Cent.	Amount	Per Cent.
1910..........	$1,275,251.68	....	....	....	...
1911..........	1,268,963.20	....	....	$6,288.48	.49
1912..........	1,343,041.16	$74,077.96	5.8	....	...
1913..........	1,339,053.27	....	....	3,987.89	.29
1914..........	1,315,280.10	....	....	23,773.17	1.7
1915..........	1,492,555.51	177,275.41	13.4	....	...

Maintenance Cost Per Capita Per Annum

Year	Budget Plus S. R. Bonds	Average Annual Census	**Per Capita Per Annum**	Decrease Over Preceding Year	
				Amount	Per Cent.
1910......	$1,275,251.68	3,872	**$329.35**	.....	.....
1911......	1,268,963.20	4,165	**304.67**	24.68	7.49
1912......	1,343,041.16	4,409	**304.61**	.06	.019
1913......	1,339,053.27	4,731	**283.04**	21.57	7.08
1914......	1,315,280.10	5,338	**246.40**	36.64	12.94
1915......	1,492,555.51	6,410	**232.85**	13.55	5.49

The census shows a normal increase practically constant from 1910 to 1913 inclusive. During 1914 and 1915 there was an abnormal increase in the census. From an average of 4,853 in January, 1914, the census increased to 6,259 in December, 1914. The average census in 1915 was 6,410, or an increase of 36% above that for 1913. During the month of February, 1915, the census reached its highest point, 7,280. The regular capacity for the institutions of the department under normal conditions on December 31, 1913, was 5,300. The budgets for 1914 and 1915 were based upon an estimated census of 4,600 and 5,000, respectively, whereas, the average census for these years was 5,338 and 6,410, respectively. Additional funds were provided by authorizations of special revenue bonds to care for this large unexpected increase in the census. Substantially the same general statement could be made with respect to the number of departmental employees throughout this period; but it is noteworthy that while the census in 1915 was 65½% greater than in 1910, the number of employees increased only 22½%.

Throughout this period, there were authorized $344,718.97 special revenue bonds, for deficiencies due to increased census and other causes, to supplement the original budget appropriation; so that the increase of 3.2% in the 1915 budget above that for 1910 is much less than the increase, 17%, in the total funds available, exclusive of corporate stock for new construction.

The fact that the per capita cost per annum has decreased each year from 1910 through 1915, whereas the service has been improved and extended, is evidence of what can be accomplished by improvements in organization and more careful administration. The annual per capita cost decreased from $329.35 in 1910 to $232.85 in 1915—96.50 or 29.3%, and from $283.04 in 1913 to $246.40 in 1914—$36.64 or 12.9%, in spite of the fact that for the last two years of this period there has been a marked increase in prices.

The 1916 budget represents the largest increase for any year since 1910, so that the budget funds for 1916 may be sufficient for all purposes, without supplemental authorizations of special revenue bonds. The census during 1916 already shows a considerable decrease compared with 1915. For the first quarter of 1915, the average census was 7,137, an increase of 2,170, or 43% above the first quarter of 1914, whereas, the census for the first quarter of 1916 was 5,455, a decrease of 1,682, or 23% below the first quarter of 1915.

In detail the main defects of the department on January 1, 1914, were as follows:

1 The system of sentencing inmates to the workhouse and penitentiary for definite and usually short terms seriously prevented the department from fulfilling its proper functions of correction and reformation. Measures for physical, moral and economic rehabilitation were seriously handicapped because arbitrarily limited to stated and usually short periods.

2 The labor of the inmates was not properly organized nor utilized, nor was it suited to the best interests of the individual and the city. Women inmates especially, to a large degree, were entirely idle.

3 The department's equipment for extension of the industrial, agricultural and educational training of inmates was entirely inadequate.

4 Departmental buildings, almost without exception, were of antiquated construction, faulty in design and unsanitary.
5 The buildings, almost without exception, were congested and overcrowded due to increased census above capacity.
6 The number of keepers and other departmental employees was entirely inadequate.
7 The "prison stripe" clothes used for men and women inmates of the workhouse and penitentiary were unnecessarily conspicuous and degrading, and other articles of clothing were unnecessarily uncomfortable.
8 Many of the disciplinary rules and practices were unnecessarily harsh and needlessly petty and oppressive in character.
9 The food served inmates and employees was of poor quality, monotonous, and did not constitute a properly balanced diet. Such conditions mean extravagance and waste.
10 The hospital, medical and surgical facilities of the department were totally inadequate.
11 The drug traffic throughout the institutions was uncontrolled. It was estimated that between 15 and 40% of the inmates were drug users.
12 The inmates who were drug addicts or suffering from contagious diseases did not receive proper medical care and treatment.
13 The duties of the administrative personnel were not properly distributed, and the administrative procedure did not produce the best results.
14 The accounting and recording systems were wholly inadequate and in many respects were erroneous and misleading.
15 The prisoners committed to the various institutions were not properly classified and segregated.
16 The work of the department was not organized to produce economy of operation together with improvements in service.

Accomplishments and Work Initiated During 1914 and 1915

It was not possible to introduce modern reformatory and correctional methods in all of the institutions of the department at the beginning of this administration for the following reasons: (1) Faulty design and inadequacy of structures and plants; (2) congestion due to the extraordinary increase in census during 1914 and 1915; (3) marked inadequacy of industrial shops and equipment for carrying on constructive training; (4) lack of medical supervision and facilities; (5) inadequate appropriations for new buildings; (6) construction of new buildings with funds granted soon after the administration took office could not be completed until practically the end of the administration.

In view of the magnitude of the problem involving, as it does, 18 institutions and a daily census of from 5300 to 6400, as compared with Sing Sing, for example, a single institution having an average of from 1200 to 1500 inmates, it was necessary to adopt a general working plan which would provide for the fullest utilization of existing plant after the necessary improvements had been made, for the gradual introduction of modern reformatory and correctional methods, and for progressive modification of laws affecting the department. In the reformatory, the discipline was changed from the old prison type to the modern reformatory type. The penitentiary and workhouse government and discipline were gradually modified along similar lines. It was obviously impossible, however, to eradicate in a brief space of time the generally prevailing laxity of discipline and administration, although the improvement of these conditions was an imperative prerequisite to any intelligent and proper reorganization of the department.

Therefore, though improvements have necessarily been slow, the work of the first two years has amounted to a veritable revolution in the laws and conditions under which this department was formerly operated and administered, and has laid a firm foundation for the larger changes which must be built upon it.

Changes in Laws Affecting the Work of the Department

The body of laws governing this department was chiefly responsible for its continuance as a department of jails instead of a department of correction. While the department is an integral part of the state's judicial and administrative system, the laws in force in January, 1914, did not sufficiently correlate its work with that of the courts, the offices of the district attorney, and the police department, so that it could function to the best advantage of the community and the individual delinquent.

Judges were required to impose definite sentences upon persons committed to all institutions of the department, save the New York City Reformatory. The sentences, usually for short periods, prevented to a large extent the reformative work of the department. The institutions of the department were constantly congested with prisoners who were continually being received and discharged at short intervals. The number of repeaters received at the workhouse in 1914 was approximately 40% of the total, 21,396; in 1915, it was approximately 48% of the total, 20,116. The number of repeaters received at the penitentiary in 1914 and 1915 was about one-third of the total, 3,974 for 1914, and 4,393 for 1915.

Some of these unfortunates were received at the workhouse under sentence twenty different times during each of these years. The unnecessary duplication of work performed by the courts, the offices of the district attorney, the police department, and the department of correction, involved an excessive and unjustifiable expenditure on the part of the city, and seriously interfered with correctional work. The department was required to discharge persons from time to time who were clearly in need of further moral, physical or industrial training. The succeeding arrests, trials and convictions of these repeaters clogged the calendars of the courts and prevented these departments from giving a greater amount of attention to more important work. The definite sentence law seriously hampered the study of the causes of delinquency and of the measures necessary to prevent and check crime.

With practically no exception, six months was the maximum sentence which could be imposed upon any person committed to the workhouse. Except in the cases of four specified felonies and for certain offenses committed by youthful offenders, the maximum sentence which could be imposed upon any person committed to the penitentiary was one year and $500 fine. The fine imposed worked inequitably, because those who had funds, or friends able to raise funds, were able to make payment and escape imprisonment, whereas, the very poor, and those without friends, were frequently required to serve their full term of imprisonment plus one day for each dollar of fine imposed.

Indeterminate Sentence and Parole Law

While it was recognized early in 1914 that the definite sentence was the most serious defect in the law governing the department, it was not deemed wise to submit an amendment to the legislature during the first two or three months of this administration.

The department's experience during 1914 with the definite sentence law was utilized in formulating the indeterminate sentence and parole law, which was passed by the legislature in 1915, amended by Chapter 287 of the Laws of 1916, to abolish the imposition of fines as alternatives to sentences upon penitentiary inmates. Under this law, all persons committed to the penitentiary must be sentenced, without a fine, for an indeterminate period which shall not exceed three years. All frequent offenders committed to the workhouse for six specified offenses must be sentenced, without a fine, for an indeterminate period which shall not exceed two years. The parole commission, established by this law, is authorized to make all necessary rules governing the parole of all persons committed to the reformatory, workhouse and penitentiary, under an indeterminate sentence. No person, however, may be released from the penitentiary short of the maximum period without the approval of the committing judge or court.

The correlation of the courts, the police department and the department of correction is further secured by a provision authorizing the magistrates making commitments to the reformatory and to the workhouse, to sit as members of the parole commission with power to vote on the eligibility for parole of persons committed to either of these institutions. The commissioners of police and of correction are ex-officio members of the parole commission and are required to sit at all meetings of the commission.

The new parole law authorizes the adoption of methods and practices for institutions of this department which have been applied with so much success in the New York City Reformatory, in the New York State reformatories for many years, in all state prisons of Indiana during the past nineteen years, at "Cherry Hill" Penitentiary, Philadelphia, since 1909, in the Ontario Province Prison at Guelph, Canada, and to first offenders committed to New York State prisons for several years. It has made necessary the transformation of the workhouse and penitentiary from the prison into the reformatory type of institution. Under this law, a prisoner must show by his work, by his conduct, and by his physical and mental condition that he is fit to be discharged on parole before he can be released. The law puts a premium upon self-control, self-improvement and self-development. It authorizes rational treatment which may act as a positive deterrent to delinquent tendencies, and facilitates the inmate's re-instatement as a member of the community.

Other Legislative Changes Affecting the Department

Institutions of the department of correction are not equipped to provide proper treatment for the aged and infirm dependent persons who were formerly committed to its custody on the charge of vagrancy. Accordingly, early in 1914, the legislature passed an amendment to Section 88 of the Inferior Criminal Courts Act authorizing magistrates in their discretion to commit to the department of public charities aged and infirm persons convicted of public intoxication or vagrancy.

In order to carry on the physical rehabilitation of departmental buildings, it was necessary to secure from the 1914 legislature an amendment to the law empowering the board of estimate to authorize the commissioner of correction to erect minor extensions to existing buildings on Blackwell's Island.

In order to facilitate the administration of the department, the 1914 legislature amended the law giving the commissioner of correction power to transfer the warden and the superintendent of industries from the penitentiary to the other institutions of the department. This has allowed the department as a whole when necessity arises to secure the services of these two officers.

The Inferior Criminal Courts Act and the county law were amended in 1914, designating the Queens County Jail as a city prison, and authorizing the magistrates to commit thereto for certain minor offenses.

The indeterminate sentence and parole law of 1915 empowers the custodial officers and employees of the department of correction to act as peace officers. This has greatly improved the administrative work of the department as it raises the official status of these officers. The same law directs the parole commission to facilitate the establishment of a central bureau of identification. This is a broad grant of power to the local authorities and provides the basis for fundamental changes and correlations which should be worked out in the future through the co-operation of the courts, the offices of the district attorney, the police department and the department of correction.

The work of these departments has been made more difficult in recent years by the great increase in the number of persons arrested who use habit-forming drugs. Frequently, persons held for burglaries, assault and other serious offenses, are found to be drug addicts. Therefore, a law was enacted by the legislature of 1915 authorizing the courts to stay proceedings at any point, and to commit the drug addict to a hospital or other institution for medical treatment until such time as the medical officer of such institution certifies to the court that the addict has ceased to crave drugs.

Under a previous amendment of the Inferior Criminal Courts Act, a person committed to the penitentiary as a vagrant might be released upon the recommendation of the warden of the penitentiary with the approval of the commissioner of correction and the committing magistrate. As a result, the department of correction and the magistrates were constantly importuned by the friends of such persons. A law was enacted by the legislature in 1915, which made it impossible for persons to be released who had been committed to the penitentiary on charges of vagrancy; so that, as the law now stands, releases may be secured only from the institutions of the department of public charities, the state reformatories, and the private and semi-private institutions to which the courts may commit.

Labor of Inmates

Idleness has been the chief defect in the care and treatment of inmates. This was due, first, to the inability of the institutions to find sufficient work to be done; second, to the shortcomings of the law; and, third, to the somewhat improper administration of the commutation law permitting time off for good behavior. An abnormal increase in inmate population, coupled with the failure of the city to provide means whereby the great majority of inmates might be employed, was perhaps chiefly responsible for this idleness, but when men received definite sentences in court which could not be changed by their conduct in the institution, it was quite impossible to offer sufficient incentive to work.

In the case of the penitentiary, however, the officials of that institution failed to take proper advantage of the commutation law, which authorized the warden to recommend that the state superintendent of prisons make certain reductions in time for good behavior during imprisonment. If the warden had more frequently made his recommendation with reference to the amount of work done or the willingness of the prisoners to perform service, the inmates would have had a stronger incentive to work.

Some improvement has already been made, but much remains to be done. Suitable and hard work for the able-bodied, under wholesome conditions, with proper opportunity for training and improvement, is essential for modern correctional and reformative institutions. Care should be exercised that the work done and the services performed interfere as little as possible with free labor outside. But we may as well recognize that little interference is possible in the city institutions, because of the short sentences and woeful inefficiency of inmates due to their lack of stamina and training.

The shops at the New York City Reformatory were insufficiently and improperly equipped. The industrial machinery installed in the penitentiary industrial building was primitive. The workhouse on Blackwell's Island had a number of so-called shops, but the equipment was of such primitive character that little real shop work was possible.

The Penitentiary—Men

The foreman of industries at the penitentiary was responsible for developing the work in all shops at that institution. The keepers were broken in by the shop foremen to act as foremen of individual shops. The shoe shop was the only one in which there was a trade instructor. There were two school teachers at the penitentiary, but their work was not properly developed. There were few books and no serious attempt was made to use modern methods in teaching English to foreigners and elementary subjects to other inmates.

The chief reason why more extensive improvement in shop work has not taken place is that the ultimate plan calls for the removal of the penitentiary to Hart's Island. It was not deemed wise to request large sums for an old plant which would soon be abandoned or transferred to the new site. However, funds were provided in the 1915 budget for an instructor for the bed shop; minor improvements in equipment and processes were made—for example, the installation of three new machines for the shoe shop and new equipment for making underwear and stockings. Arrangements have recently been made at the penitentiary for the development of school work at night. The first assignments to classes total 200 inmates. English to foreigners, simple civics and other elementary subjects will be taught. It is possible to undertake this work at this time because the Yale Club has offered to provide the service, and 25 Yale graduates have begun work.

The Workhouse—Men

The attempt to introduce shops at the workhouse had failed largely because short-term prisoners committed had never received industrial training, except in rare cases, and were not sentenced for sufficient terms to show definite improvement. A great deal of industrial work was performed, of a kind that did not develop ability, and no educational work was undertaken.

The men were assigned to the various so-called shops, to the greenhouses, the cleaning and maintenance work of the institution, the charities department bakery, the department stables on Blackwell's Island, the transportation and storage of materials and supplies for the whole department, the unloading of coal for the departments of charities and correction, and the care of grounds and buildings generally.

The department expects to abandon the workhouse on Blackwell's Island at an early date. It has not been thought wise, therefore, to provide for extensive improvements on the present site. Changes have been limited for the most part to improving the quality and increasing the quantity of work. New sewing machines and cutting tables have been installed in the work rooms. Some shop equipment transferred from other departments has been provided. The men have had the advantage of some training afforded by building bath-houses, sidewalks and walls.

Inasmuch as the workhouse population is almost wholly unskilled, provision has been made for the transfer of the men inmates of the workhouse to Riker's Island, where they have been employed building new quarters and developing the filled-in land for agricultural purposes. The plan of the department provides for the cultivation of about 300 acres of Riker's Island as a municipal farm, so that the unskilled inmates serving short terms may be given an opportunity to do simple work in the open air under such circumstances that the ever-shifting population of the workhouse may be regularly and usefully employed.

Women Inmates

To a great extent, women in the penitentiary and workhouse were unoccupied. Those at the penitentiary were occupied exclusively with the ordinary housekeeping duties of their section. Those at the workhouse did some sewing, but, for the most part, were occupied with the housekeeping duties, while a special squad of women helped clean some of the buildings of the department of public charities. The clothing of the women inmates of the penitentiary, to a large extent, was made by the men. The women in the penitentiary now make all their own clothes, and are occupied in other productive needle and dressmaking work. The women in the workhouse are allowed to do some needlework in their cells since there is not sufficient accommodation in the workrooms.

New York City Reformatory

At the New York City Reformatory four trade school instructors were employed to teach the young inmates various trades. The instruction given was very poor and inadequate due to lack of machinery, equipment and materials; and because there was no co-ordination between the shop-work and the school-work. Excellence in shop and school work did not earn merit marks toward parole of the inmates, although the rules of the old board of parole required that such reward should be made. The regular maintenance and repair work of the institution was not fully utilized for purposes of trade training. Whenever the boys did work, it was as assistants on a repair job, with little or no reference to its educational value. The book school work was as inefficient as the trade school work. It was improperly planned and the school was almost without equipment.

The problem at the reformatory has been solved by transferring the inmates to the new farm at New Hampton, where both agricultural and industrial work has been provided. Evening class room instruction in elementary subjects has been commenced at the farm, and will be extended gradually as funds and conditions warrant. On March 18, 1914, the first

New Hampton Farms: Inmate Working with Sulky Plow

New Hampton Farms: Excavating Foundation for Main Building

inmates were transferred from Hart's Island to the new farm home of the reformatory, when twelve boys took up their residence there. This number was gradually increased to fifty.

During the year 1915, the average census at the farm was about 100. At present, practically all the inmates have been transferred to the farm. The census in April, 1916, was 278. The value of the first year's work was about $15,000; the cost of operation about $8,000. During 1915 the excessive rains interfered with tomato and potato crops.

On April 1, 1916, the reformatory was moved from Hart's Island to New Hampton. The inmates care for about 500 chickens, 20 horses and 10 cows, and have assisted in the reconstruction of barns and houses, and in the construction of temporary quarters for a larger number of inmates.

The department's program has been most fully realized in the case of this institution. It is planned that the inmates shall do all the rough construction work such as the permanent reservoir and water plant, the sewage disposal plant, all excavations and foundations for buildings, and the bulk of construction work for the permanent buildings. Competent instructors of the various trades have charge of the different squads of inmates who are engaged upon this work.

The removal of the reformatory to New Hampton Farms leaves the old reformatory buildings on Hart's Island free for use as a part of the penitentiary. The penitentiary shoe shop and bed shop are now being moved to that island and others will follow gradually. A thoroughly modern, up-to-date, shoe manufacturing plant is being installed in one of the buildings. Improved equipment for the bed shop and power-driven machinery for the manufacture of clothing are being installed. Upon the completion of these shops, a large number of penitentiary inmates will be transferred to Hart's Island where they will have opportunity to work under greatly improved conditions.

A radical change has, however, been effected in the utilization of inmate labor on the construction and repair work of the department. Skilled artisans, employed by the department, are now engaged upon the work for which they were employed. Squads of inmates have been organized to work under their direction. Only a few of the inmates have had any training, and it has been necessary to train them to do this work. Wherever possible inmates serving longer terms are assigned to this type of work.

Equipment for Industrial, Agricultural and Educational Work

Plans for the ultimate development of the agricultural, industrial, and educational training for the men and women coming under the care of the department have been discussed above. Most of the women have had very little training. More than 80% of them are below a normal mental standard and are also suffering from serious blood diseases. Emphasis must, therefore, be placed upon simple work, with proper medical care and treatment.

A farm colony situated several miles from the city affords the best opportunity for a modern institution of this type.

Since practically all of the male inmates of the institutions of the department come from the city, and upon discharge must return to urban conditions, the department must furnish industrial training and education which will make possible effective rehabilitation. Investigation, however, has demonstrated that about one-third of the total average male population might, with profit to themselves and the community, be given special industrial training to enable them to secure employment at rates above those paid to day laborers. Accordingly, the plans for the new penitentiary contemplate the erection of an industrial workshop type of institution on Hart's Island. Under the power vested in the commissioner, it is possible to transfer to this institution those prisoners who are best fitted for industrial training in contrast to those who must be transferred to work at the farm colony. It is planned to lay equal emphasis upon education and work in connection with the industrial shops to be built on Hart's Island. On account of the magnitude of the problem and the lack of funds for new construction, progress along these lines has been slow. The installation of new shoe and bed shop machinery at Hart's Island is a step in this direction.

An industrial penitentiary cannot be developed, however, without the hearty co-operation of the different city departments which are called upon to purchase its products. In the first place, the departments must surrender their prejudices against goods manufactured in correctional institutions, and in the second place, they must co-operate with this department in improving the product. Most of the criticism of prison-made goods could be eliminated if the purchasing agents of the various departments co-operate with the superintendent of industries of the department of correction. This has been demonstrated conclusively during the last two years by co-operation with the state prison department, and during the last year with this department.

Improvements and Changes in Buildings and Plant

In January, 1914, the buildings and physical equipment of none of the institutions met even the minimum of modern penalogical requirements. By more economical administration of the funds appropriated by the board of estimate for the up-keep of these departmental buildings and plant, the changes and betterments listed in detail below were made with very slight increase in appropriation above that provided for the years preceding 1914.

During 1914 and 1915, the chief defects in plant and buildings, due to neglect of from one to ten years' standing, have been corrected. It was possible to secure a greater amount of betterment and improvement at smaller expenditure because, instead of having the bulk of this work done by private contractors, it has been performed to a large extent by the inmates under the supervision of departmental employees. In addition to the economy involved, it has substituted useful labor for idleness and monotony

New Hampton Farms: Interior Temporary Hospital—Inmate Playing Santa Claus on Christmas Day

for both inmates and employees, and improved the conditions under which they live. It has also given opportunity to the employees of the department to demonstrate their fitness to assume greater responsibility and to receive increased compensation.

The character and date of construction, wherever possible, and the physical condition on January 1, 1914, of the several buildings and the improvements made since then are summarized:

City Prisons

Manhattan—101 *Centre St.—The Tombs*

Reconstructed in 1902; obsolete masonry construction; small dark inside steel cells, originally intended for one prisoner each, with additional upper cot in each cell in order to provide sufficient accommodation. No facilities were available for hospital treatment or exercise.

Unhygienic bed hangers were replaced by an improved type of hangers. A ventilating plant which cost $100,000 originally, not operated for the previous five years, was placed in operation. Antiquated electric lighting fixtures were removed and a new modern system installed at a cost of $700 instead of $5,000, as previously planned. Fire alarm apparatus was installed. The warden's house was reconstructed as a visitors' building to eliminate visiting on tiers and in corridors of the main prison, thus making it unnecessary to search prisoners for drugs, knives, pistols, and other contraband, since the visitor now does not come in personal contact with the inmate.

Brooklyn—149 *Raymond St.—Raymond St. Jail*

Constructed in 1909; masonry construction with the usual small dark interior steel cells. The addition for women prisoners, constructed in 1910, provided facilities for bathing, and open air ventilation. No facilities were available for hospital treatment or exercise. An expensive isolated electric plant was left idle.

The unsanitary inside drainage was changed to a modern outside drainage system thus preventing dampness throughout the prison. A special section of the prison was fitted up for visiting, for the same reasons and with the same results as in the case of the Tombs. A fire alarm signal system was installed. The electric lighting plant, installed some years ago but never operated, was placed in operation.

Queens—Court Square, Long Island City—Queens Co. Jail

Constructed in 1898; outside walls of brick; dark interior iron cells.

Unsanitary cot hangers were replaced by hangers of hygienic construction. Four additional shower baths were installed. Defective plumbing and bathing facilities were put in first class condition. A visitors' building was erected in the yard for the same reasons and with the same results as in the case of the city prisons, Manhattan and Brooklyn. Individual electric lights were installed in all cells so that inmates may read at night. Inmate labor was utilized in adding six feet to the wall surrounding the yard and in laying down cement walks, thus affording better facilities for open air exercise. Structural alterations on the third floor provided room for a new chapel. The old interior store-room was torn out and replaced by a small outside building erected in the yard.

District Prisons

Manhattan—Jefferson Market Prison—2nd District Prison, 10*th St. and Sixth Ave.*

Constructed in 1875; small inside cells of heavy obsolete masonry construction; insufficient accommodation; two sections, one for men, one for women.

Since January 1, 1914, the leaky roof was replaced by a new slate roof. The defective main chimney was torn down and rebuilt. A new ice-box, steel-jacketed steam cooking kettle, coffee, tea and hot water urns, and hood for the range were installed, thus affording necessary facilities for preparing good, wholesome food, and preventing disagreeable odors from spreading throughout the building. New bath tubs and washing trays were installed with hot and cold water connections in place of the old, dirty sinks, which formerly were the only bathing and washing facilities. New flooring was provided in many sections to replace the old, dilapidated floors. The iron grills of the office were re-located to provide more space for the receiving room and office.

Essex Market Prison—3rd District Prison, 1*st St. and Second Ave.*

Detention cell only; insufficient space, with consequent congestion.

The detention pen was considerably enlarged. Two additional windows and a ventilating fan were installed. The walls were strengthened by the erection of a steel lining. These changes considerably improved the old temporary detention pen.

Yorkville Prison—4th District Prison, 57*th St. and Lexington Ave.*

Reconstructed in 1863; small institution; with heavy masonry cells of obsolete construction.

A new water-line service and new lavatories were installed, eliminating the low pressure which formerly restricted washing and bathing facilities to the first floor. The plumbing throughout the institution was placed in first class condition.

Harlem Prison—5th District Prison, 121*st St. and Sylvan Pl.*

Constructed in 1885; obsolete heavy masonry construction, small interior cells.

New and additional steam heating pipes were installed throughout the institution. Formerly, inmates and employees complained continually of the cold and being kept awake at night by the pounding in the old radiators. A new distribution of space was made in the office and receiving room to eliminate the close contact of inmates with employees.

West Side Prison—7th District Prison, 53*rd St. and* 8*th Ave.*

Constructed in 1896; obsolete design, with the usual small, dark, heavy, inside steel cells.

New window sashes were installed to secure better ventilation and afford opportunity to clean windows. Large openings were made in outer walls and iron grills installed, to secure light and better ventilation, thus eliminating the darkness and gloom which formerly pervaded the institution. The use of gas was discontinued and electricity installed with light for each cell. An electric pump and a hot water tank were installed for reserve and emergency purposes, thus eliminating break in water supply due to occasional shutting down of the courthouse plant.

Bronx—6th District Prison, 162nd St. and Brook Ave.

Detention cell only, sufficient for its purpose.

No change was made except necessary application of paint.

Other Institutions

Blackwell's Island

The Workhouse

Constructed by inmates of the penitentiary and almshouse in 1850; heavy masonry cells of different sizes, at variance with all modern ideas of prison construction; no toilet facilities; cell buckets necessary; no provision for outdoor recreation or exercise; practically no provision for regular industrial employment. The small shops operated are inadequately equipped.

A new bath house was constructed with 36 individual showers, affording adequate facilities so that each inmate can take a daily bath if he desires. These facilities replaced 12 shower baths, which were inadequate to meet the needs of 900 to 1,400 inmates. A small building was constructed at the end of the new bath house so that the clothes of inmates deposited upon admittance can be sterilized and stored for safe-keeping. The interior of the woman's section was changed. New operating devices were installed, making it possible to open the windows and to secure plenty of fresh air. The visitors' sections were partitioned off for the same reasons and with the same results as in the city prisons. Wooden partitions and interior walls were replaced throughout by modern fireproof interior construction. A yard, enclosed by a wooden fence, was provided at the north end of the women's prison, affording opportunities for outdoor exercise and recreation in the open air. The women's sewing room was enlarged by the relocation of a supporting wall.

The Penitentiary

The old section was constructed in 1832 and the second section completed in 1909; small dark cells of heavy masonry, 4 2/3 x 7 x 8 feet high.

Inmates were "doubled up" in these small cells which were constructed for one person only. No toilet facilities available; unsanitary and disagreeable cell buckets necessary; single electric light in each cell; isolated electric plant in operation; no steam or mechanical laundry facilities; two extractors installed in 1910 were never operated; no provision for roasting meat; steam and odors from kitchen permeated the mess hall which afforded insufficient accommodation for the inmates.

A light brick kitchen with an adjoining store and refrigerating building has been constructed. The old mess hall has been enlarged, by utilizing the space formerly occupied by the kitchen and by an addition at one side for segregating boys committed to this institution. The old punishment cells were removed, and the south end of the south prison was bricked up, providing 24 well lighted cells for disciplinary purposes. Twenty-four new cells were erected at the north end of the south prison. A new boat-house and coal-dock have been constructed. A second-hand steam laundry equipment, released by the department of public charities, has been installed in the laundry building, and a sterilizer, seldom used at the Jefferson Market Prison was set up at the penitentiary. These additions to the equipment provide facilities for washing and sterilizing all the clothing and blankets.

The industrial building afforded insufficient space for the penitentiary shops. The equipment was obsolete and inadequate. Without materially impeding the work of the shops, the old wooden floor beams were replaced by iron supporting beams. A modern shoe manufacturing plant is being installed in one of the old dormitory buildings on Hart's Island. When this is completed, the manufacture of shoes on Blackwell's Island will be discontinued. The bed shop will likewise be moved to Hart's Island. Modern equipment is also being installed at Hart's Island for the manufacture of socks, underwear and clothing. When this is installed, the clothing industry will be discontinued on Blackwell's Island.

Only the most necessary structural improvements have been undertaken at the workhouse and penitentiary because these old, obsolete structures should be abandoned as soon as adequate facilities are provided elsewhere in accordance with the general plan of the department.

Riker's Island—Branch Workhouse for Men

This institution consisted of four large frame dormitory buildings, the warden's house, a store-house, a kitchen and mess hall, and a chapel. These buildings were constructed in 1900 by a contractor at a cost of about $5,000 each with a capacity of 100, or $50 per capita. They were in a wretched state of disrepair. The bathing, cooking and lighting facilities were primitive in character and entirely inadequate. The steam heating plant produced practically no heat. There was only one kerosene lamp for each dormitory.

Early in January, 1914, it was necessary, in order to secure heat, to buy scorcher stoves and install them in each of the dormitories, because the frozen ground made it impossible to excavate in order to correct the defects in the heating plant. The defects were corrected later. Additional kerosene lamps were provided immediately, and an electric lighting system has been installed. Three new dormitories have been constructed by the inmates, working under the supervision of departmental employees. Each of the new dormitories has a well cemented basement which can be utilized later as shops when new quarters have been erected on Riker's Island for all workhouse men. Each of these buildings cost about $3,000 with a capacity of 150, or $20 per capita, that is, an increased capacity of 50 and a reduction of $2,000 in cost compared with those built under contract. The old buildings had poor basements, whereas the foundations of the new buildings are strong enough to carry any permanent structures which may be placed on them. In these new buildings, 40 shower baths and toilet facilities have been installed. A new sewer line is being constructed and a modern building for disciplinary purposes with a capacity of 80 is about half completed.

Hart's Island

Branch Penitentiary

The old buildings of this institution were formerly used by the Manhattan State Hospital for the insane, and were transferred to the department of correction when that institution was moved to Ward's Island. The buildings are of the old dormitory type, fairly serviceable, but dilapidated, and with practically no provision or equipment for industrial work. The new heating plant completed in 1909 is inefficient on account of defective steam lines which poured steam into the ground at numerous points. There was a separate sewer line for each building, all terminating on the beach above high-water mark.

New grates were installed in the boilers, and the steam lines were reconstructed by departmental labor at a cost of $9,000 instead of at an estimated cost of $25,000, by contract. The floors of the dormitory buildings were repaired; the interiors painted; a new cement floor placed in the building used as a mess hall; facilities for roasting meat installed; a new refrigerator constructed; the artificial ice plant put in first class condition; and a store room was constructed for food supplies, made possible by tearing out several brick walls in a space formerly not used. Some half dozen temporary wooden structures were rebuilt, and a new kitchen was added to provide facilities for the segregation of all women committed to the institutions of the department suffering from tuberculosis. The board of health orders were complied with in reconstructing the interior of the stable which was completed in 1909. Each of the old sewer lines was extended to a point below the low-water mark.

New York City Reformatory for Misdemeanants

A new administration building and dormitory, and new industrial buildings were completed in 1909. The administration building of the old insane asylum had been transformed into a combination kitchen and mess hall, hospital, and school building for the reformatory. The contractor had plastered directly on the brick walls without any lathing or furring. About a third of this plaster had fallen off, and the interior of the buildings was unsightly because the walls were damp. The plumbing was in bad condition and the kitchen facilities were totally inadequate.

These buildings were made as habitable as possible, pending the transfer of the inmates to the new farm colony at New Hampton, and will be entirely overhauled before they are used for the branch penitentiary.

Generally, a systematic effort has been made to keep all departmental buildings fresh and bright by the use of light colored paint, and to keep them free from the usual institution odor by the frequent use of disinfectants and cleansers.

Inadequate Number of Employees

Early in January, 1914, it became evident that the department was seriously handicapped on account of the abnormal increase in the census and the insufficient number of keepers and other employees. Accordingly, 10 additional employees were secured in 1914, and funds for 130 were provided in the budget and by revenue bond authorizations for 1915. In addition to the regular custodial staff the following employees were secured in order to improve the correctional and reformative work of the department:

1 Woman superintendent for women at the workhouse
1 Woman physician at the workhouse
1 Woman trained nurse at the workhouse
2 Men trained nurses giving full time at the workhouse.

6 Practical nurses
1 Resident physician on full time at the reformatory
1 Additional resident physician at the penitentiary
1 Assistant engineer in charge of maintenance
1 Painter for maintenance work
1 Plumber
1 Mechanical engineer and electrical engineer for maintenance and construction work
1 Inspector of foods and kitchens
1 Fuel and mechanical engineer

The budget for 1916 made financial provision for a new superintendent of industries, who has already made many improvements. The medical work of the department is not properly developed. The services of a capable medical superintendent on full time should be procured at once.

It is believed that in order to produce the best results throughout the department it is necessary to establish an 8-hour day for custodial employees, with certain requirements for reserve duty. The present 10 and 12 hour day with requirements for reserve duty cuts down the number of hours during which inmates can be kept at work. The inmates are idle in the morning and evening while the employees are eating breakfast and dinner, and when the shift is changed. They are thus kept idle for about two hours daily when their labor should be utilized. The change to the 8-hour day would undoubtedly produce real economy, and would improve the tone and discipline of the various institutions. An appropriation of $57,000 for fifty additional custodial employees would make it possible to introduce the 8-hour day throughout the department. The greater part of this amount would be saved by decreasing the expenditure for food now supplied the employees, who receive three meals per day. The employees state that they would prefer the 8-hour day to the one or two additional meals at the city's expense.

It must be clearly emphasized and understood that inmates of correctional institutions are in need of supervision and friendly counsel. An increase of capable employees means a reduction in the number of inmates assigned to each employee, and consequently an increase in the possibility that each employee will give more careful attention to each inmate. The number of inmates assigned to each employee throughout the department to-day is too large. The better reformatories of the country usually have one paid employee for every five inmates, while in the department of correction there is one paid employee for every nine inmates, including administrative and office employees.

Improvement in Clothing for Inmates

It is necessary to clothe prisoners in a distinctive uniform, but it is not desirable that the uniform be grotesquely conspicuous. The "prison stripe" uniform found in use for both penitentiary and workhouse men was unnecessarily conspicuous and degrading, and since it effected no useful or beneficial purpose, it was immediately decided to discontinue its use. A considerable amount of preliminary study was required, however, before the change could be accomplished, since a uniform had to be secured which, in color and cut, could not be confused with other uniforms, but would be sufficiently conspicuous for its purpose.

Specifications were finally determined upon, and a plain cadet gray cloth was prescribed for penitentiary men inmates and a grayish blue for workhouse men. It was impossible, due to the European war, to secure as good a quality of cloth as the old "prison stripe" cloth. On account of the supply of striped uniforms on hand at the time, neither was it possible to make the change at once, but during the year 1915 most of the men serving sentences in the institutions have been provided with these new uniforms.

In addition to these changes, plain khaki, properly marked to facilitate identification, is to be used by men working under conditions which easily soil their clothing.

The departmental rules now require that all men shall upon admission be clothed in the new plain uniform, but, in the event of misconduct, the plain uniform is to be taken away and the "prison stripe" uniform substituted.

The uniform provided for the workhouse and penitentiary women inmates was made from a wide stripe bed ticking, such as is used for mattresses, and was unsightly. A small-striped pattern seersucker has been substituted, which is not too conspicuous in pattern, and is certainly more appropriate and comfortable for dresses than mattress ticking. The uniform for matrons and women orderlies was changed in 1914 from a blue check seersucker to plain white chambray. This change was made to secure greater distinction between the dresses of the inmates and those of the matrons and orderlies.

Shoes and clothing for men and women inmates are made at the penitentiary shops. Funds were provided in the 1916 budget for the first time for the manufacture, by the women at the workhouse, of light underwear for women and some of the light underwear for men. The winter underwear is warm, thick and durable, but improvements are contemplated which will make it more comfortable. During 1914 and 1915 the specifications of shoes for both men and women were revised and materially improved, so that the shoes turned out in the latter part of the year were decidedly superior to the former product. Each woman inmate is now provided with a right and a left shoe, whereas, formerly, the shoes were identical in shape for both feet.

The 1916 budget provides sufficient funds so that each inmate may be supplied with two pairs of uniform trousers, a coat and a vest; and, in addition thereto, for those inmates whose work requires it, two pairs of khaki trousers and a khaki shirt. Provision for the first time was made in the 1916 budget for sheets and nightgowns for all inmates, which are now being made, principally by the women inmates of the various institutions. Formerly blankets were used in place of sheets. This change should work a substantial economy, since the frequent washing of blankets destroys them within a short period. Prior to 1914, there was no standard uniform for the custodial officers of the department. The rules of the department now require the wardens, superintendents, keepers and all other custodial employees to wear the prescribed uniform of the department.

Disciplinary Rules and Practices

When this administration took office, the discipline at the several institutions was woefully lax. The authority of wardens and keepers had been undermined to such an extent that certain inmates knew they need not obey orders issued by the warden and other officers. Penalties for infractions of the rules were not sufficiently varied. Too frequently blows or confinement in isolated cells were ordered. General laxity was condoned until serious trouble arose. As a natural consequence, severe disciplinary measures had to be taken occasionally and the inmates were often punished severely and excessively.

The authority of wardens and keepers was undermined by the frequent assignment of inmates to easy work, and by the transfer of inmates from one institution to another upon orders from the central office. These assignments and transfers, too frequently, were not for purposes of classification; and, in fact, were often clear violations of section 698 of the Charter, as amended, which requires the commissioner of correction

> "to cause all criminals and misdemeanants under his charge to be classified, as far as possible, so that youthful and less hardened offenders shall not be rendered more depraved by association with and evil example of older and more hardened offenders."

The central office repeatedly conducted inquiries as to alleged brutalities. The inquiries themselves were proper enough, but the method of carrying them out was often quite improper, as the keeper was frequently reprimanded in the presence of the complaining inmate. The difficulties of disciplinary problems were increased because favors were granted to prisoners by a few dishonest or weak employees, who did not scruple to violate the law and the rules of the department by bringing in contraband articles, including habit-forming drugs and whiskey. An investigation of conditions at the workhouse showed that money or influence could secure from the resident physician a bed in the hospital for healthy prostitutes to the exclusion of women who were actually sick and in need of hospital treatment.

While many of the former disciplinary rules, such as limitation on the amount of reading and writing, may not seem important, nevertheless excessive and unnecessary irritation was caused because the inmates felt that they were deprived of minor privileges without adequate reason. For instance, there were general rules governing large groups of men and women in the penitentiary that not more than two letters could be written per month, and that a daily newspaper could not be read or in the possession of an inmate. These rules were rigidly enforced and irritated those who did not abuse the privilege in any way, and who, whenever they requested that an exception be made in their cases, felt they were entitled to consideration.

Prior to 1914, inmates of the penitentiary were confined or locked up for excessive periods at the end of the week and during holidays.

The public at large must share with the politician and the departmental officers responsibility for many special favors requested and granted to inmates both for and without the payment of money. It is generally a relative or friend of the prisoner who asks that an exception be made in his favor, whereas, theoretically, the public always demands equality of treatment.

The central office interfered, as outlined above, in the details of administration, but it failed to lay down general policies for the management of the institutions and for the benefit and guidance of the local administrator. Indeed, it was quite impossible for a central office, which constantly directed the wardens to make exceptions to general rules, to devise and formulate any general policy.

The failure of the central office to formulate general policies allowed serious conditions to develop at the reformatory, which finally made it necessary for this administration to remove the overseer of that institution. It was found that the overseer violated the prison law and the charter by personally inflicting blows and by allowing others to inflict blows upon inmates, and that he had, without authority, inflicted the kind of unusual punishment known as a "stand-up" or a "starve-out." This punishment required an inmate to stand from 8 p. m. to 11 p. m., in the same place in the hall, with his arms folded; then he was allowed to retire until 2 a. m., whereupon he was required to leave his bed and stand in the same place in the hall from 2 a. m. until 3.30 a. m.; he was then permitted to retire until 5.30 a. m., at which time he was required to dress himself and fall in line with the other inmates. This form of punishment, with attendant loss of sleep, would be continued for periods of five to ten and even twenty nights. If the inmate became sick or collapsed, he might be taken to the hospital. In some cases, boys were put in the isolation cells for several days following this stand-up punishment. Sometimes the punishment was accompanied with orders that the inmate be deprived of his regular rations—the boys called this a "starve-out." This type of punishment was forbidden by the rules of the department.

Many changes have been made in discipline, at the reformatory and at other institutions since the removal of the overseer. Conditions at the reformatory were easily remedied by the appointment of a competent new superintendent, who has been able by modern methods to maintain good order and discipline, and at the same time to improve the reformative work of the institution.

The use of isolation cells has been greatly curtailed throughout the department. Plenty of water and one good meal a day is allowed all inmates in such cells, which was not the case under the preceding administration. In the penitentiary and at Hart's Island, inmates are allowed the use of beds in the isolation cells, which are kept in sanitary condition.

In the penitentiary, inmates are allowed recreation periods during certain hours each day, whereas formerly recreation was not permitted. Women committed to the workhouse who, previous to January 1, 1914, were allowed no exercise or recreation privileges, have been provided with an open-air recreation ground.

Self-government or co-operative government of inmates has been introduced in a modified form at the New York City Reformatory and at the penitentiary. The inmates are not allowed, however, to exercise authority over other inmates without supervision by officers. At the farm branch of the reformatory, a group of fifty boys were placed under the supervision of four farm instructors who lived under the same conditions as the inmates. These inmates were allowed practically unrestricted liberty in their work about the farm until their number increased to three hundred.

A league of inmates at the penitentiary has been established which is empowered to make recommendations and suggestions to the warden for the betterment of the institution on any matter that affects the welfare of the inmates.

As in other matters, progress has been achieved in this respect through gradual and constant change. The purpose of the administration in this phase of its work, as in all others, has been to transform the discipline and government of the institutions from the old prison type to the modern reformatory type, recognizing the fact that reformation of inmates depends upon enlisting their co-operation in the government and work of the institution. Improvement in discipline which amounts almost to a revolution has resulted from these changes.

Under the rules and regulations of the department promulgated as a part of the policy of the present administration, no employee may ill-treat, abuse, or assault an inmate or another employee without inviting and subjecting himself to vigorous discipline, nor is any inmate allowed to assault or intimidate any other inmate without serious consequences to himself. Several inmates have been prosecuted and convicted in the courts for such assaults. Brutality is not permitted. Employees have been made to understand that they will be judged in efficiency ratings and for promotion by their humane and intelligent treatment of inmates. Since the new parole law went into effect, inmates have been made to understand that their chances for parole and subsequent rehabilitation may be greatly improved by good conduct and fair dealing. Under this administration small privileges for the inmates have been increased and extended, which gives them greater opportunity for reading, writing, visiting with their friends and mingling with their fellows.

Improvements in Food

The food served both prisoners and employees has been very considerably improved. Economy has been effected in the preparation of food, and serious waste has been eliminated. The amount of meat was slightly reduced so that more vegetables, cereals, jellies and dried fruits could be served. The daily per capita cost for food had been about 18 cents up to the beginning of the present adminstration. The department was allowed 16 cents in the 1914 and 1915 budgets, a reduction of 2 cents per capita. About 35 cents per day was allowed previously for each employee; this has been reduced to 31 cents. All improvements have thus been carried out despite the reduction in the daily allowances for inmates and employees, and despite the increase in the price of food.

Formerly, sufficient care was not given to the preparation of food, so that considerable waste resulted. Much bread was wasted because slices were cut too thick. Investigation showed that one-third of the bread supplied at the penitentiary and about one-fifth of that supplied the workhouse was wasted. This condition was remedied by slicing the bread in pieces of uniform thickness.

Full information as to these changes and improvements may be found in the annual report to the mayor for the year 1914.

Hospital and Medical Facilities

When constructed none of the institutions of the department were provided with real hospitals. At that time the departments of public charities and correction were one department known as the department of charities and correction. What is now the City Hospital is a development of an institution which was originally called the Penitentiary Hospital. Before the workhouse was built, its population was housed for the most part in the almshouse. The old almshouse had its own hospital. The workhouse was built as a place for the detention of the able-bodied members of the almshouse; consequently, no provision was made in the workhouse for hospitals. The City and District Prisons in Manhattan and The Bronx were dependent upon Bellevue Hospital, while the City Prison in Brooklyn, was dependent upon Kings County Hospital for medical service.

No hospital wards had been provided in any of the City or District Prisons up to the time this administration took office. Application has been made for funds to transform the dormitory section of City Prison, Manhattan, into hospital wards, but funds have not yet been provided by the city. The serious cases are transferred to the regular hospitals. This practice should be discontinued as soon as possible. It is wasteful in time and in service because a guard must usually be sent for day and night service.

On the other hand, sections of the penitentiary and of the workhouse on Blackwell's Island, of the reformatory and branch workhouse on Hart's Island, and of the branch workhouse on Riker's Island had been utilized for hospital wards. The hospital equipment in these various institutions, when this administration took office, was pitiably inadequate. Early in 1914, additional wards were provided at the workhouse for the segregation of men and women drug patients, for women afflicted with blood diseases and for surgical cases. At the Hart's Island branch workhouse, provision was made for the transfer of men and women inmates seriously afflicted with tuberculosis from all the other institutions of the department, and opportunity afforded for moderate exercise out of doors and for necessary segregation.

The dark room used as a hospital at the reformatory was abandoned and a section of the industrial building set apart for that purpose.

Medical service furnished in the department was also inadequate. A board of visiting physicians supervised the medical service at the workhouse. This board was created many years before the department of correction was separated from the old department of charities and correction. An interne staff carried on the routine medical work of the institution under the supervision of the visiting staff. The visiting staff performed all operations and gave attention to the more serious cases. There was a resident physician at the penitentiary to care for the 1600 inmates of that institution; one resident physician at City Prison, Manhattan, to care for the 800 inmates of that institution, while a visiting physician gave some medical attention at the City Prison, Manhattan, and at the Jefferson Market Prison. One visiting physician was assigned to the remaining 10 District Prisons in Manhattan and The Bronx. One visiting physician was provided for City Prison, Brooklyn, and another for City Prison, Queens. One physician was provided for the 500 inmates of the reformatory and the 600 inmates of the branch workhouse on Hart's Island, and one for the Riker's Island branch workhouse. The workhouse had one trained male nurse, and one trained woman nurse; no other institution had a trained nurse. Orderlies, hospital helpers, or so-called practical nurses, were employed in the hospital wards of the other institutions.

Illicit Drug Traffic Reduced

The drug traffic throughout the institutions was uncontrolled. It was estimated that between 15% and 40% of the inmates were drug users when this administration took office. A study made by the department in 1914 showed that some 1344 men and 226 women were committed to the penitentiary, workhouse or reformatory for various infractions of those sections of the Penal Law which are concerned with the illegal use or possession of drugs. This number, while large, by no means indicates the total number of habitual users of drugs who are confined in the institutions of the department. The percentage of such users among misdemeanants and felons is very large. Immediate attention, therefore, was required, in order to prevent this disease from destroying all effective correctional and reformative work.

Under most favorable circumstances, the limitation and eradication of the drug evil is a most difficult and delicate problem. Under the conditions prevailing in the department at the beginning of this administration, and even at present, it is extremely hard to deal with its effectively. The congestion in the institutions puts obstacles in the way of ascertaining who are drug users and who are not. The short sentences interrupt and seriously interfere with the regular medical treatment provided in the various institutions. The visitors to the hospitals of the department of public charities greatly increase the difficulties of preventing the smuggling of drugs into the two correctional institutions on Blackwell's Island which are located very near these hospitals. The practice of permitting friends and relatives to bring food to inmates opened an avenue for illicit traffic in drugs and required correction. In order to secure proper control the manager of a restaurant established several years ago in City Prison, Manhattan, was given the exclusive privilege of furnishing food to prisoners awaiting trial. A caterer was installed at Jefferson Market Prison and at City Prison, Brooklyn, and given the same exclusive privilege. A commissary has been established in the penitentiary on Blackwell's Island, where inmates may purchase, at low prices, a few articles which their friends were formerly allowed to bring to them.

The old warden's house at City Prison, Manhattan, was transformed into a visitors' building, so that it is no longer necessary for the 250 daily visitors to enter the prison and to have access to the various cell block tiers where the prisoners are confined. The presence of these visitors within the prison opened a channel of communication which served as a means of smuggling in drugs, knives and other contraband articles. Before the visitors' building was ready for use it became necessary to search all visitors. This was disagreeable both to the visitors and the employees.

Screens have been put up in the visitors' rooms at City Prison, Brooklyn; City Prison, Queens, and at the workhouse, Blackwell's Island. This has helped to prevent smuggling of drugs and contraband articles by visitors.

The department assisted in drafting bills dealing with drug traffic and drug treatment, which were enacted into law. These have been discussed at the beginning of this report.

Treatment of Contagious and Drug Addiction Diseases

Especial consideration has been given to the treatment of persons suffering from drug addiction and to persons afflicted with venereal diseases. A study made in 1914 of 489 consecutive admissions of women to the workhouse showed by blood tests that 388, or 80%, suffered from blood and local contagious diseases. Inmates are received first in the detention prisons. In these institutions the most careful medical inspection and treatment is necessary in order to prevent the spread of diseases and the continuance of the use of drugs. Throughout the department a practice was instituted early in this administration of making a medical examination of each inmate admitted, so that the affected inmate could be immediately segregated and properly treated.

Under the former practice, drug addicts and inmates suffering from contagious diseases were frequently distributed indiscriminately throughout the institutions. The congestion in all institutions, the unsanitary and unhygienic plumbing, and the lack of facilities for proper ventilation accentuated the dangers of contagion and contamination. In each institution, certain portions are now reserved for those inmates who will most probably affect other inmates because of their personal habits or physical condition. Medical treatment is given in all cases where needed. This branch of the service is not as efficient as it could be, however, if more physicians and nurses were provided.

Inmates held on detention only, who could not be sent to an institutional hospital for treatment, are treated by the visiting or resident physician as ambulatory cases according to their needs. Very serious cases are, of course, transferred to the hospitals of other departments.

A member of the visiting medical board has exercised general supervision over the treatment of those suffering from drug addiction disease at the workhouse. The results obtained there have received the most favorable commendation. Persons suffering from such disease, who are responsible in every other respect, have appeared before committing magistrates and have requested that they be committed to the workhouse for treatment. The resident physician of City Prison, Manhattan, has successfully treated many persons so afflicted. The results of treatment in the other institutions have been good.

The workhouse hospital has been made the central administrative hospital for cases requiring operation. Inmates of other institutions are transferred to it for this purpose.

A woman physician at the workhouse now examines all women prisoners upon admission, so that those suffering from blood and local diseases can be immediately segregated for proper medical treatment. In co-operation with the department of health blood tests are taken of all women inmates.

A light, roomy, temporary hospital has been erected at the New Hampton Farms Reformatory, where the less serious cases can be treated. Physicians from Otisville Sanatorium have visited the farm from time to time to give the resident physician the benefit of their advice and help in the treatment of cases.

In order to safeguard the health of inmates, a general rule has been promulgated and strictly enforced, that no inmate shall be assigned to kitchen and dining room work unless previously examined by the department physician and a blood test taken for the detection of communicable or infectious diseases. The Widal test is given to these inmates before assignment to ascertain whether or not they are suffering from typhoid. In this also the co-operation of the department of health is necessary. This department has co-operated continuously with the department of correction since the administration took office.

Improvement of Central Office Supervision

The duties of the administrative personnel at the beginning of this administration were not properly distributed.

The supervision exercised by the central office was inadequate because the personnel was not organized with respect to the functions each division of the service performed. Some of the purchasing procedure was carried forward by the departmental storekeeper, some by the purchasing agent, and some by the chief auditor and bookkeeper. To remedy this situation a division of purchase and supplies was established. A complete double entry stores account system (devised by the department of finance during the last administration), was installed early in 1914, and is now operating satisfactorily.

A new per capita standard has been devised to control food distribution and consumption and to improve the menus of all institutions. The organization of the new bureau of registration and passes has enabled the division of purchase and supplies to receive a statement daily showing the current census of each institution so that all supplies may be distributed upon a proper basis.

Stores ledgers, simple in form and necessitating little clerical work for their up-keep, have been installed at all of the institutions.

The central bureau of audit receives monthly duplicate sheets of these stores ledgers advising it of the distribution of supplies in all the institutions after they have been received.

Standard requisitions have also been prescribed for use by heads of institutions and bureaus so that all supplies are used only after requisitions therefor have been approved.

The repair, construction and engineering work of the department was not properly co-ordinated. The department had no general engineer. The warden of each institution undertook construction and repair work without regard to the financial provision for the department as a whole and without regard to the importance and necessity of the work required at any other institution.

Since a lump sum appropriation for repairs and construction was made for the department as a whole, each institution took " pot luck." This meant that some wardens, more fortunate or more energetic than others, undertook construction work of minor importance while other work of more urgent necessity elsewhere was curtailed or deferred.

Little, if any, attention was given to the scientific planning and execution of repair and construction work. The warden of each institution was his own construction engineer. In order to remedy this defect in organization, a central bureau of construction, repairs and engineering was organized early in 1914. An engineer has been placed in charge of this bureau, who is responsible for and exercises supervision over the entire construction, repair and engineering work of the department. Central records have been installed in this bureau for all construction and repair work. A mechanical and fuel expert was also secured who made a study of the heating and power plants. As a result of this expert's work an annual saving of approximately $40,000 in fuel cost has been effected.

The auditing division of the department was not properly organized, and consequently it failed to produce satisfactory results for administrative purposes and for the use of the board of estimate in formulating the annual budgetary appropriations for the department. The departmental secretary undertook the reorganization of this division early in 1914. Mechanical tabulating devices were installed so that expenditures now are properly coded and classified. The annual report for 1914 presents for the first time the segregation of actual expenditures by functions and by institutions. The disbursement statements required by the comptroller are now furnished regularly. During the year 1916, the auditing division's methods of handling vouchers has been changed, so that it is now possible to pass vouchers promptly.

Improvements in Accounting and Statistical Methods

At the beginning of this administration it was not possible to ascertain exactly how many persons were held in custody at any particular time. The actual inmate census of an institution, that is, the number of persons supposed to be physically in the custody or upon the premises of an institution, was in many cases different from that shown by the institution's official records. Each institution maintains its own register.

The Charter fixes upon the commissioner of correction responsibility for the proper registration of prisoners and for their discharge upon the exact legal termination of a sentence. Section 709 of the Charter provides that each correctional institution must maintain an accurate and current register of all inmates received and discharged. These registers are of the utmost importance since they constitute the official record which shows whether a sentence imposed by the court has been legally and properly enforced and whether prisoners are properly discharged. At the beginning of this administration, it was not possible for the central office to exercise this supervision because it did not possess the machinery whereby it could supervise and check up the registers of each institution. Investigation showed that as a result of this lack of supervision the records were erroneous and unreliable. Errors in recording names of prisoners, and other discrepancies of a grave nature, considering the official character of the prison records, were also found. The commissioner found it impossible to ascertain the whereabouts of an inmate committed to the department except by individual inquiry at each of the several institutions. The situation demanded a central bureau of information where the commissioner, the public, the courts, and the police might inquire concerning inmates, and secure such other information as might be required.

A study of this part of the department's work had been undertaken by the commissioner of accounts during the latter part of 1913, and upon his recommendation, early in 1914, the new bureau of registration and passes was established, the executive head of which is the prison registrar. A uniform system of official registers and of registration cards was installed throughout the department for each institution. An official procedure was established, and the wardens were made directly responsible for its proper maintenance.

This procedure provides that the bureau of registration and passes shall maintain a daily check upon the admission and discharge of inmates to and from all the institutions, and shall audit the discharge or transfer of each inmate, to determine whether all discharges and transfers are proper and in accordance with legal requirements. A duplicate copy of the official registration and census record of each institution is forwarded daily before midnight to the central bureau. This serves as a basis for compiling registration cards for every inmate which constitute a permanent current index of inmates.

Under the new system full information concerning the incoming inmate is on file in the central bureau by the morning of the day after he is received into custody. The department can now furnish immediately information in regard to any individual who is, or has been in its custody. The loss, escape, irregular discharge of an inmate, or mistake in the census of any institution, can be immediately discovered in the bureau by means of check reporting which is a special part of the system.

The activities of the bureau have made possible vast improvements in the compilation of statistics concerning the inmates. When this administration took office, the statistics relating to inmates were practically worthless because of the many inaccuracies which had crept into the records. Each institution followed its own method of compiling inmates' vital statistics and presented different kinds of information without regard to the form or character of the information presented by the other institutions. With the exception of certain statistical information required by the State Prison Commission, there was no uniformity of presentation. Even the statistics compiled for the Prison Commission were in many respects incorrect. These errors were due in part to the transfer of inmates. Thus an inmate committed for six months, who in the course of his sentence was confined in one district prison, one city prison, the penitentiary and the workhouse, would be recorded statistically as four prisoners, each serving a sentence of six months. Four crimes, instead of one, were statistically entered under the particular religious faith of the individual concerned.

It is essential that reliable statistics concerning inmates be compiled; the number cared for, the average daily, monthly and yearly census, are facts required in order to reach an intelligent judgment concerning the cost and effectiveness of administration. If the city is attempting to prevent crime, it must understand conditions and the results of particular conditions. Consequently, statistics concerning the life of the inmate are of great importance from a penological point of view.

The function of keeping and compiling statistics is now lodged in the central bureau of registration and passes, where use is made of the latest scientific, electrical and mechanical sorting and tabulating machines. The State Prison commissioner was conferred with and the form of statistics required by that commission was subsequently changed. A comparison of the inmate statistics presented in annual reports of the department previous to the year 1914, with those presented in the report of that year, illustrates the value of the new method.

The granting of passes was also centralized in this bureau, so that all inmates should receive similar and fair treatment. The number of visits from the public to this bureau has been curtailed by issuing passes for a period of three months to persons designated by the inmate.

In January, 1914, cash fines and bails were received at each institution and turned over to the chamberlain and other authorities without any check upon these receipts by the commissioner. The cash fines and bails received annually by the department approximate $500,000. The receipts for 1915 amounted to $535,370.50. To correct this defect, a triplicate receipt form was devised and every person who paid a fine or bail is required, under the new system, to accept the original of this official receipt. The duplicate, under the controlling procedure promulgated, must be forwarded to the bureau of registration and passes so that it may be compared with the terms of fine or bail as shown by the Court's commitment. The prison registrar assembles these duplicate receipts monthly and makes a statement therefrom for the purpose of comparing the cash fine and bail returns with the actual monthly returns which are made directly by the wardens to the chamberlain. Under this procedure the possibility of irregularity in the handling of cash has been reduced to a minimum.

At the beginning of this administration, fingerprint records were taken of some classes of offenders committed to the workhouse, and concluding records were taken at the penitentiary. In felony cases, the police were permitted to take the fingerprint impressions, if they so desired. This method of identification has been extended to all classes of offenders committed to the workhouse, the penitentiary and the reformatory, and the work has been centralized in a single bureau. In order to prevent the substitution of persons undergoing sentence and to check the accuracy of the records of discharge, the fingerprint records taken in the Magistrates' Courts are compared with the fingerprint records of the inmate when received, and with those of the inmate when discharged. This method of checking has put an end to the substitution of inmates.

Another defect in the central supervision of the department was due to the fact that the commissioner found it impossible or difficult to exercise adequate control over the manufacturing industries. The New York County Grand Jury, early in 1914, severely criticised the conditions existing at the penitentiary, because no accounts of any value or reliability were maintained and because there was no proper supervision over the operations of the manufacturing industries. The secretary of the department made an investigation and installed a new accounting system for the prison industries. A summary of this work can be found in the 1914 report of the department to the mayor.

Late in December, 1915, the commissioner promulgated a body of rules and procedure for governing the business of the department as a whole, which makes it possible for him to direct the work of the department properly and to hold each employee responsible for work assigned to him and for results secured. The procedure outlined insures the discontinuance of those conditions which permitted the various institutions to operate independently of each other and without proper regard to the work of the department as a whole. The department is no longer a federation of more or less independent institutions.

Classification of Inmates

District and City Prisons

Some attention had been given to the classification and segregation of inmates in City and District Prisons during the year 1913, but the possibilities of such work had not by any means been exhausted. Under the policy established by this administration the inmates held under detention at City and District Prisons are classified primarily to segregate those afflicted with the drug addiction disease. It has not been possible to give inmates even of this class complete hospital treatment. Separate parts of the institution have, however, been assigned for the colonization of drug addicts, and each inmate has been given relief and treatment. Inmates have also been segregated for special observation of their mental condition. First and youthful offenders suffering from blood and local contagious diseases have been segregated, so that they may receive local treatment and to prevent the spread of their disease. In these prisons during 1913 improvements have been made in the prevailing bases of classification, which has been continued with further modifications.

Penitentiary, Workhouse and Reformatory

It has been somewhat difficult to classify and segregate the inmates committed to the different institutions. In the first place the order of the court committing an inmate to a definite institution must be complied with as soon as possible, and in the second place the department has not adequate facilities for making the preliminary examinations.

The old workhouse and penitentiary are on Blackwell's Island, the new branch workhouse is on Riker's Island, a branch of the penitentiary is on

Hart's Island, and the reformatory is at New Hampton, 55 miles from New York. During 1914 and 1915 it was necessary to deliver the inmates to one of these institutions as soon as possible because the law did not permit sending them to a classification and observation station where each case could be studied before final commitment. This procedure has heretofore made it impossible to centralize medical and examination work, and has interfered seriously with carrying out Section 698 of the Charter, previously referred to.

An intelligent and proper classification cannot be carried out by dividing inmates into two groups—those who are less than 21 and those who are more than 21 years of age. Under modern conditions many inmates with long institutional and criminal records are under 21 years of age. The mandate of the Charter can be carried out only after careful investigation and examination has been made. Pursuant to the provisions of a bill which recently became a law, the commissioner may transfer inmates to central clearing houses, where they may remain for study and observation not more than 30 days. At these central stations it will be possible to secure the services of qualified specialists as consultants in addition to the regular staff to determine upon a proper classification as required by the charter.

In the same way the industrial training of the inmates can be ascertained at the central clearing houses, and the inmate can be transferred to do that type of work for which he is best fitted, or where he can secure the kind of training he most needs. Under the existing plan those who are physically unfitted for work are segregated as much as possible. For example, the tubercular men and women are transferred to Hart's Island, whereas the workhouse and penitentiary women afflicted with blood diseases are all segregated on Blackwell's Island, and the penitentiary and workhouse inmates afflicted with the same diseases are for the most part segregated on Hart's Island.

Greater Economy in Operation and Improvements in Service

Earlier in the report attention was called to betterment in the service which has been secured through improvement in the personnel. It is proper to point out here, however, that the absurd organization which placed the male deputy warden in charge of 500 women regularly confined to the workhouse has been changed by securing a woman superintendent. Under this new method the treatment of women inmates has naturally improved. Each woman receives individual study and attention, so that she can be placed in the proper section of the institution or given the proper kind of work. The services of a woman superintendent and a woman physician have made it possible to transform the woman's section of the workhouse.

In order to develop the construction and repair work of the department as fast as possible, and at the same time train the inmates, a new title "Instructor of Industry" was created with the approval and co-operation of the municipal civil service commission. Men secured for these positions are artisans who are also able to take direct charge and custody of inmates. Squads of inmates assigned to construction and repair work are placed under the charge of these instructors, who, together with the custodial employees transferred from the board of water supply police, have enabled the department to utilize more fully the services of inmates. It has been difficult to secure artisans who have a proper appreciation of the disciplinary requirements in a correctional institution. The custodial force of this department has a keener appreciation of the need for discipline than the instructors of industry. It is hoped that the experience of these two forces working together will develop in the instructors sufficient appreciation of the disciplinary requirements, and in the keepers sufficient appreciation of the industrial requirements of institutional and reformatory work.

At the New Hampton Reformatory special attention will be given to agricultural work, and farm instructors have been secured to aid in raising the standard of farm work. The superintendent of food supplies and the paid cooks have enabled the department to administer the new dietaries much more effectively than would otherwise have been possible.

Physical Plant

A request for corporate stock was formulated and submitted to the board of estimate on January 1, 1915. This estimate embraces a definite construction program for the years 1915 to 1919, inclusive. The period beyond the term of this administration was included so that the program as outlined could be viewed in its entirety. The keynote of the projected plan provides for farm and industrial colonies for the reformatory and workhouse men and the workhouse women, and for an industrial institution on Hart's Island to replace the present penitentiary on Blackwell's Island.

The corporate stock request amounted to $1,898,284, of which it was contemplated that all but $355,000 would be expended within the period of the present administration. In 1914 the board of estimate approved plans for the erection of the new Detention Home for Women, for which the previous administration had authorized $450,000 corporate stock. It was contemplated that the inmate capacity of the enlarged and improved institutions would be as follows: New Hampton Farms 747, Farm Colony for workhouse and penitentiary women 800, Detention Home for Women 298, Farm Colony for men on Riker's Island 1,200, Industrial Penitentiary on Hart's Island 1,600.

The abandonment of the large and expensive institution on Blackwell's Island would enable the department to develop an institution of improved and less expensive character where there would be adequate opportunities for work and industrial training. The two large institutions on Blackwell's Island could be transferred to the department of public charities to be utilized as hospitals. Blackwell's Island is better suited for hospital than for correctional institutions. For hospital use its nearness to the city is essential, whereas inmates of correctional institutions other than hospital cases should be removed as far as possible from their old environment while they are undergoing imprisonment.

A beginning has been made to put into effect the building program outlined in this corporate stock estimate. Three large dormitories, each with an inmate capacity of 70 have been erected on Riker's Island. A new addition for a modern kitchen has also been erected, and an addition has been made to the boiler plant. A shop for the manufacture of cement blocks and bricks was erected and equipped in 1915. Frame buildings have been erected at New Hampton which accommodate 260 inmates. In addition to erecting these buildings a large amount of excavation and foundation work for permanent buildings has been completed. Wells, drains and an emergency system of water supply have been installed. Additional land adjoining the original farm was acquired and a railroad spur constructed which connects with the main tracks of the Erie Railroad.

Economies in Operation

Economies in operation have been achieved as shown by the reduction in the per capita costs. In 1913 the per capita expenditure per annum was $283.04, in 1914 it was $246.40, and in 1915, $232.85. This economy has been brought about through steady and persistent effort and at the same time the several departmental services have been improved. Food supplies have already been discussed. The operation of the heating and power plants has been modernized and brought up to a high state of efficiency.

A thorough technical study of all the heat and power plants was undertaken in 1914 by a fuel efficiency expert. As a result of this comprehensive study plans for structural changes and repairs considered necessary for the efficient operation of the plants were outlined and carried out. The capital outlay was less than $25,000, and as a result an annual saving of approximately $40,000 was effected in the use of fuel.

Under this reorganization the same maximum plant capacity was obtained with a reduced operating cost, which was made possible by the introduction of mixed fuel, by improved methods of stoking, and by discontinuing wasteful use of steam. The operating engineers and firemen were given specific technical instructions by the fuel expert. Operating records were installed and a reporting system adopted which gives the central office control over the operation of each plant.

To transport inmates, employees and supplies to the institutions situated on Blackwell's, Riker's and Hart's Islands, two boats were in operation up to May 1, 1914, in addition to other boats operated as passenger ferries.

As a result of a study of the operation of these boats it was found possible to discontinue the services of the steamboat " Massassoit," affecting a saving thereby of over $40,000 per annum.

Other economies in operation are departmental generation of electric power in substitution for outside service; the utilization of old dismantled and discarded equipment obtained from other city departments through the co-operation of the sinking fund commission; the application of modern administrative and supervisory methods over the purchase, consumption and distribution of supplies, materials and equipment; the utilization of inmate labor wherever possible, etc., already discussed in various sections of this report.

Utilization of Inmate Labor

The dormitories which were erected on Riker's Island by the inmates only cost $20.00 for each inmate accommodated. Other dormitories previously erected on the same plan under contract cost $50 per capita. On these same comparative figures a saving of $6,300 is shown, in spite of higher prices for materials prevailing in 1914 and 1915. Additions to the boiler plant on Riker's Island and kitchen, storeroom, boat house and coal shed at the penitentiary buildings were erected. The new bath house at the workhouse on Blackwell's Island, and a new storage building, were built by inmate labor at a considerable saving under contract prices.

The departmental ice plant at the branch workhouse on Hart's Island was overhauled and repaired by inmates. All the buildings at the New Hampton Farms branch of the New York City Reformatory were erected by inmates.

Additions to the City Prison, Queens, and City Prison, Brooklyn, were also undertaken by inmates. A large scale for the weighing of coal was installed by inmate labor at the City Prison, Brooklyn. The visitors' building at the City Prison, Queens, was built completely by inmate labor. The surrounding or guard wall of the City Prison, Queens, was raised six feet in height for a distance of nearly 800 feet, by inmate labor at a cost of $1,500, whereas the estimates and allowances for this work to be done by contract amounted to $8,000.

The work on the power plants was carried out by inmates under the direction of departmental plant engineers at an estimated saving of $10,000.

Practically all the electrical, plumbing, masonry, carpentry, roofing, locksmithing and iron work of the department, except where it was of a peculiar or technical nature, was undertaken and completed by inmates.

In every instance a distinct saving resulted to the city. But the financial saving is no more important than the educational and reformative value of this work to the inmates, a result itself justifying the adoption of this new policy.

PROGRAM FOR 1916 AND 1917

1 The development of a definite and scientific system of releasing or paroling prisoners under proper supervision. Such a system must be developed as rapidly as possible in order to secure the best results from the

Parole and Indeterminate Sentence Law and from the various amendments to the Public Health Act which were passed by the Legislature of 1915. It will also be necessary to reorganize the various institutions of the department as reformatories rather than prisons, to establish clearing houses, centrally located, where most careful medical examinations may be made immediately after commitment, to reclassify the inmates and to transfer them to those institutions best adapted to the particular cases.

2 The further development in all departmental institutions of educational, industrial and agricultural training and medical treatment for inmates, requiring of them in return useful labor for the department or the community. All such training and treatment will be planned to encourage the inmates to become self-supporting members of the community upon their release.

3 Every effort will be made during the next two years to secure the following improvements:

(*a*) Completion of the new reformatory for boys and men at New Hampton, New York;

(*b*) Development of a farm on Riker's Island for the employment and training of workhouse men;

(*c*) Acquisition and development, outside the city, of a farm-colony and reformatory for women inmates of the penitentiary and workhouse;

(*d*) Development of an industrial penitentiary for men on Hart's Island;

(*e*) Removal of inmates from the penitentiary and workhouse on Blackwell's Island as rapidly as facilities are provided elsewhere, utilizing old buildings as clearing and classification stations until they are finally surrendered to the department of public charities.

4 The buildings of the department will be kept up to the improved standard established during this administration.

5 Correctional methods will be modernized and administrative improvements extended as rapidly as funds and conditions warrant. Special attention will be given to the development of definite administrative standards. Clothing and food will be further improved and standardized. Approved methods of treating different classes of offenders will be developed and adopted as fast as possible.

6 The organization and procedure of the department will be continued along business lines.

7 A training school will be developed for departmental employees. Men will be given credit for actual service performed. The 12-hour day for employees will be shortened as necessary funds are provided. Salary increases will be recommended for those employees who show the greatest improvement in character of services performed.

TENEMENT HOUSE DEPARTMENT

The tenement house department was established on January 1, 1902, as a result of the report of the New York tenement house commission of 1900, for the purpose of maintaining the tenements* of the city in a safe and sanitary condition, and of supervising the erection of tenements built thereafter. It placed the improvement of housing conditions under a single authority, a responsibility that previously had been scattered among the departments of health, fire, buildings and police.

The new department was charged with the maintenance of all existing tenements in a safe and sanitary condition, with the supervision of alterations of old law tenements (those erected prior to April 10, 1901) to comply with the requirements of the law as then enacted, and with the supervision of the erection of new tenements. The first two problems were the most difficult, as conditions in the poorer class of tenements were extremely bad. Not until 1909 did the department succeed in obtaining sufficient inspectors to find out what structural alterations needed to be made, and even when that information had been obtained, it was difficult to compel owners to spend on alterations the amounts necessary to bring the old law tenements up to the requirements of the new law.

Improvements Under New Law

The administration of the tenement house law has resulted in improved housing conditions, not only because of the direct requirements of the law as to both new and old houses but indirectly, because of the competition of the new law houses with the old. Among the improvements effected on the old law houses because of direct legislation are the following:

1 Practical elimination of dark rooms (258,573 windows provided or enlarged from January 1, 1902, to January 1, 1916)
2 Elimination of school sinks
3 Improvements in fire-escapes and methods of fire egress
4 Concreting cellars, making them damp proof
5 Improvement in interior lighting from improved skylights
6 Control of overcrowding
7 Control of basement occupancy
8 Fireproofing
9 Tenements kept clean
10 Tenements kept in repair
11 Vagrancy lessened

---

* Sec. 2, Par. 1. A "tenement house" is any house or building, or portion thereof, which is either rented, leased, let or hired out, to be occupied, or is occupied, in whole or in part, as the home or residence of three families or more living independently of each other, and doing their cooking upon the premises, and includes apartment houses, flat houses and all other houses so occupied.

Par. 11. * * * Wherever the words "is occupied" are used such words shall be construed as if followed by the words "or is intended, arranged or designed to be occupied."

In addition, improvements not required by law have voluntarily been made by owners in order to put their houses into competition with new law houses.

Housing conditions are also constantly improving because the proportion of new law houses is increasing not only by building but also by the demolition or conversion into non-tenements of old law houses. On the first of January, 1916, out of a total of 103,883 tenement houses in New York City, 77,960 were old law tenements and 25,992 new law tenements. These contained 600,372 old law apartments and 356,244 new law apartments. These new law apartments were practically all built since the first of January, 1903 (only 562 houses were constructed in 1902).

Handling of Violations and Complaints

On January 1, 1914, there were 20,340 structural violations on old law tenements still pending; during 1914 and 1915 there were 1,708 additional violations filed, making a total of 22,048. During 1914 and 1915, however, 10,141 of these violations were dismissed so that on the first of January, 1916, there were only 11,907 structural violations still pending. In other words, during the two years under consideration, this type of violation was practically cut in half.

Similarly, on January 1, 1914, there were 22,330 rooms and 5,778 halls not legally lighted and ventilated. By the first of January, 1915, these figures had been reduced to 10,456 rooms and 4,679 halls. By December 31, 1915, however, an even greater reduction had been effected, as there were pending only 3,812 cases of illegally lighted rooms, a reduction of 83 per cent. of the total number on January 1, 1914. The reduction in the number of public halls not legally lighted and ventilated amounted to about 600 during 1915, a reduction of 29 per cent. since January 1, 1914. As regards the 4,087 hall cases still pending in January, 1916, however, it should be borne in mind that the conditions are not sufficiently bad to warrant legal action by the department for the removal of these violations. The department has learned that it is useless to take a case to court unless dangerous conditions exist, or the violations are serious and of long standing.

One of the important duties of the department is the investigation of complaints from citizens and from other departments. The following table gives briefly the conditions regarding these complaints:

Large light colored surfaces show yards and courts of New Law tenements; note block ventilation afforded by yards running through from street to street. Compare with the old style shafts indicated in the foreground.

Complaints Received	1914	1915
Signed	16,244	11,548
Anonymous	23,618	21,241
From other departments	.....	7,783
Total	39,862	40,572*
Action Taken		
Violations issued—Old building	13,100	11,298
New building	1	1
Alterations	156	178
Prostitution	460	332
Previously acted on	3,750	2,814
Cause removed	8,359	10,602
Referred to other departments	2,164	2,617
No basis	7,104	7,218
No action necessary	4,359	5,309
Total acted on	39,453	40,369*

*The discrepancy between the number received and the number acted on each year, represents the complaints received too late to be acted on before the first of the next year.

This table shows that the total number of complaints for 1915 is about 700 greater than for 1914. In 1914, 13,717 or 34-4/10 per cent. necessitated the issuance of orders, and in 1915, 11,809 or 29-3/10 per cent. In 1914 almost 10 per cent. and in 1915 almost 7 per cent. of the complaints were duplications in that they covered conditions that had already been reported to the department. In both years, approximately 7,000 complaints were found to have no justification in fact, and on 4,300 complaints in 1914 and 5,300 complaints in 1915 it was unnecessary for the department to take any action. On 8,300 in 1914 and 10,600 in 1915, the cause of the complaint was removed without the issue of any violation orders. In 1914, 2,100, and in 1915, 2,600, were matters over which this department has no jurisdiction. These complaints were, therefore, referred to the departments interested. A detailed table giving the nature of the complaints received follows:

Nature of Complaint	1914	1915
Chimney defective or obstructed	751	1,033
Lack of cleanliness	15,961	19,959
Dampness	648	662
Drainage imperfect	2,440	2,529
Danger from fire	5,411	6,325
Garbage and ashes	727	606
Light inadequate	2,394	2,728
Plumbing defective	3,850	4,838
Repairs to building	5,074	5,723
Unlawful use	3,553	3,776
Ventilation	377	257
Water-closets	6,320	5,666
Water supply	4,223	3,132
Miscellaneous	3,983	5,255
Total	55,712	62,489

The work accomplished by the tenement house department can be estimated in two ways:

1 Nature of orders issued
2 Actual work accomplished in removing violations of the law.

The following tables give the nature of the orders:

Nature of Orders Pending	1913 Dec. 31	1914 Dec. 31	1915 Dec. 31
Paving and grading	6,132	4,564	6,406
Lighting and ventilation, rooms	3,360	1,779	803
Lighting and ventilation, halls (day)	2,851	1,185	921
Lighting of halls (night)	471	1,033	5,748
Other lighting and ventilation	830	579	413
Repairs	27,060	19,726	34,140
Unlawful use of premises	2,669	1,588	1,169
Protection from fire	**35,038**	**23,553**	**17,535**
Drainage	2,588	2,254	2,791
Toilet accommodations	12,572	10,778	13,016
Sinks	2,051	1,775	1,927
Plumbing fixtures	8,320	8,266	10,699
Plumbing pipes	4,205	4,312	5,636
Leaders and gutters	2,596	2,165	2,599
Water supply	2,520	1,855	1,769
Cleaning	23,167	16,538	21,605
Shafts and courts	708	480	369
Alterations	7,508	7,892	9,587
Prostitution	217	610	773
Other orders	1,230	857	3,873
Total	146,093	111,789	141,779

The most significant item in this table shows that the pending violations under the heading "Protection from Fire" have been decreased almost 50 per cent. in the past two years.

The next table shows the items filed for the two years under consideration.

Nature of Orders Filed	1914	1915	Total
Lighting and ventilation, rooms	570	241	811
Lighting and ventilation, halls (day)	539	555	1,094
Lighting of halls (night)	5,111	7,981	13,092
Other lighting and ventilation	426	196	622
Paving and grading	3,278	7,621	10,899
Repairs	30,599	53,760	84,359
Unlawful use of premises	966	588	1,554
Protection from fire	35,279	18,685	53,964
Drainage	2,204	3,303	5,507
Toilet accommodations	22,030	25,081	47,111
Sinks	2,331	2,768	5,099
Plumbing fixtures	15,210	18,408	33,618
Plumbing pipes	8,008	9,857	17,865
Leaders and gutters	6,992	5,537	12,529
Water supply	4,434	5,391	9,825
Cleaning	23,007	35,249	58,256
Shafts and courts	357	246	603
Alterations	8,217	9,539	17,756
Prostitution	434	309	743
Other orders	1,817	6,056	7,873
Total	171,809	211,371	383,180

This table represents the violations of the tenement house law reported by the inspectors of the department. During 1915 almost 40,000 more violations of the law were reported than in 1914. An increased number were reported under practically every heading with the exception of "Protection from Fire," which was reduced to about half of 1914.

It will be noticed that more than half of the increase for the previous year is found under the heading "Repairs." It will also be noticed that almost a third of the increase is in the item "Cleaning." These two together, therefore, account for five-sixths of the increase. This seems to indicate that the department has reached a stage where the inspectors have sufficient time to watch carefully for even the minor violations of the law which in former years they may have been compelled to overlook in order not to slight more important violations.

In considering this table, however, it should be remembered that the work of the tenement house department is to administer the law, and that the inspectors are working under instructions to report all violations they find every time they visit any tenement house. The figures, therefore, can be taken to indicate the relative prevalence of the different conditions indicated.

The following table shows the items dismissed or cancelled for the two years under consideration:

Nature of Orders Dismissed or Cancelled	1914	1915	Total
Lighting and ventilation, rooms	2,151	1,217	3,368
Lighting and ventilation, halls (day)	2,205	819	3,024
Lighting of halls (night)	4,549	3,266	7,815
Other lighting and ventilation	677	362	1,039
Paving and grading	4,846	5,779	10,625
Repairs	37,933	39,346	77,279
Unlawful use of premises	2,047	1,007	3,054
Protection from fire	46,764	24,703	71,467
Drainage	2,538	2,766	5,304
Toilet accommodations	23,824	22,843	46,667
Sinks	2,607	2,616	5,223
Plumbing fixtures	15,264	15,975	31,239
Plumbing pipes	7,901	8,533	16,434
Leaders and gutters	7,423	5,103	12,526
Water supply	5,099	5,477	10,576
Cleaning	29,636	30,182	59,818
Shafts and courts	585	357	942
Alterations	7,833	7,844	15,677
Prostitution	41	146	187
Other orders	2,190	3,040	5,230
Total	206,113	181,381	387,494

In considering this table it must be remembered that an item can be dismissed only by compliance or cancelled only when in the judgment of the officers of the department it is too trivial to be considered a violation of the law.

For the two years, the total items cancelled or dismissed exceeded by about 4,000 the total number of items filed, so that it is evident that the department is making a gradual gain in forcing compliance with its orders, although in 1915 orders filed exceeded by 30,000 the orders dismissed.

The three preceding tables have all considered only the number of orders issued. In many instances, however, one order covers the same condition in different locations in the same tenement house. The following table is therefore submitted giving not only the actual number of violations of the law removed, but also a more detailed subdivision of the nature of the violations than the previous tables. It represents the actual work accomplished in removing violations of the law.

Work Accomplished	1914	1915
Accumulation of filth removed	12,837	15,935
Ashes and garbage, receptacles provided for	1,053	1,555
Ceilings repaired or replastered	9,097	15,896
Ceilings cleaned and whitewashed	18,584	30,123
Cesspools cleaned	22	67
Chimneys cleaned, repaired or provided	1,769	2,846
Drains cleaned, repaired or provided	2,029	4,773
Disinfections made	124	209
Fire-escapes painted, repaired or provided:		
Painted	24,339	16,758
Repaired	85,027	42,936
Provided	8,394	7,085
Fireproofing	1,932	1,801
Floors cleaned or repaired	15,478	18,998
Janitor provided	20	8
Hall lighting provided	15,664	10,640
Leaders and gutters cleaned or repaired	6,110	7,302
Oilcloth and carpets cleaned or removed	19,277	15,554
Plumbing fixtures repaired or provided	15,581	20,271
Plumbing pipes cleaned, repaired or provided	19,760	30,841
Paving and grading	3,559	8,466
Privies cleaned or removed	70	216
Roofs cleaned or repaired	5,927	7,255
Rooms, interior—windows enlarged or provided	13,787	9,948
Shafts and courts—walls whitewashed or rubbish removed	10,744	13,766
School sinks removed	29	46
Unlawful use of premises ended	3,164	3,720
Wall paper removed	4,901	5,754
Walls cleaned and whitewashed	22,221	35,010
Walls repaired or replastered	3,940	8,243
Water-closets cleaned, repaired or provided	73,217	75,826
Water supply—appliances repaired or provided	2,671	4,557
Woodwork cleaned	3,587	6,560
Cleaning, miscellaneous	73	96
Repairs, miscellaneous	22,047	28,832
Total	427,034	451,893

In this table also the most noteworthy item concerns fire prevention. In 1914, fire-escapes represented almost 25% of the work accomplished; in 1915, fire-escapes represented about 14% of the work accomplished; and for the two years, they represented 21% of the total work accomplished. Here, as in the previous tables, the 1915 figures show a marked reduction below 1914.

It is, however, obvious that the work of the department is by no means

Modern Fire Escape with Easily Lowered Sliding Drop Ladder

"Old Law" Fire Escape: Dangerous and Inadequate

accomplished. The housing conditions of the city demand constant supervision. As old structural conditions are improved more and more attention must be given to conditions of occupancy that militate against the health and safety of the city's vast tenement population.

Internal Reorganization

Early in the present administration it was felt that with the completion of the major part of the tenement house department's preliminary work it would be possible to perfect a reorganization which would simplify the work of the department and result in substantial administrative economies while increasing its effectiveness in supervising housing conditions. Accordingly, in the spring of 1914, the chamberlain, with the concurrence of the commissioner, detailed a special examiner to the department for the purpose of making an independent study of its needs.

The investigation made by this examiner was directed first toward a study of the office problem, because it seemed that there would be a greater field for helpful results in this direction than elsewhere, inasmuch as the force of clerks, stenographers and typewriters outnumbered the inspectional force by about two to one. The stenographic division of the Manhattan office was the first division of the department chosen for reorganization, but a hasty survey of the whole department was made shortly thereafter in connection with the preparation of the 1915 budget. At that time it was estimated that on the basis of the results which it was demonstrated could be obtained by reorganizing the stenographic division, the annual cost of the department could be reduced at least $95,000 without in any way decreasing the effectiveness of its work. As the time available for this investigation was limited, it was not deemed wise to cut the budget appropriation more than $54,000 under the 1914 condition. This saving, however, was considered sufficient justification for the continuance of the studies, and the examiner who had been assigned to this work was in the first part of the next year made secretary to the department at the request of the commissioner, so that he might continue his work with the advantage of having official connection with the department.

The value of the effort to establish better administrative methods was clearly demonstrated by the fact that the 1916 budget carried an appropriation for the department less by $107,283.78 than the 1914 budget. This was a decrease of 14%. During the same period the number of employees was reduced from 702 to 588, a decrease of 114 or 16% of the 1914 total. This reduction in the number of employees and expense was accomplished without loss in either the quantity or quality of the work performed by the department. It was brought about by no sacrifice of efficiency. The savings have been due to the substitution of new for antiquated equipment, the consolidation of positions due to reorganization, the dropping of superfluous employees and the institution of a new method of controlling inspectional work.

Results Accomplished

In brief, the work of promoting administrative efficiency has been conducted along the following lines:

1 *Equipment:*

One of the most serious defects in the department in 1914 was its exceedingly poor equipment. Chairs were rickety, desks were out of repair and the files, especially those used for the so-called "pending violations," were entirely unsuitable and were in addition so heavy and ponderous to handle that they were actually dangerous to the clerks employed upon them. For these reasons one of the first steps taken was the planning of modern metal equipment to take the place of the heavy wooden files.

The 1915 budget contained provision for the purchase of new metal files for two of the three offices involved. Their introduction resulted in a great improvement in appearance, and so facilitated the handling of work that it was found possible to reduce by one-third the number of clerks working thereon. In the 1916 budget the third office was supplied with metal files, so that at the present time the entire equipment for the "pending violations" files is of the most modern type. There are still, however, divisions of the department where old and dilapidated wooden files are used. In order that the expense in any one year may not be too great, it has been decided to spread the cost of substituting new equipment over a series of years. It will be necessary soon, however, to provide in the Manhattan office clothes lockers, chairs, desks, files for the bureau of records, shelves for "dismissed violation" cases, files for the re-inspection division, files for the legal division and additional typewriting desks for the stenographic division.

2 *Stenographic Division:*

The stenographic and typewriting work of the tenement house department forms one of the largest parts of its activities. At the time of the first survey in 1914 the conditions which obtained in the office greatly militated against efficiency. This was due not to lack of appreciation on the part of the commissioner and his subordinates of the handicaps under which they labored but rather to the fact that the board of estimate had neglected to provide sufficient funds for the necessary equipment. At the time of the first survey in 1914 practically all the typewriters were of the old blind model. Many of them in fact had been in use from seven to ten years. The second and more detailed study made in the summer of 1914 showed that the time wasted in the use of this machine by lifting the carriage to compare the work done with the copy from which it was made, was equivalent to the time of six operators, or more than 5% of the entire force.

In the 1915 budget a start was made to replace these machines with modern typewriters, and in the 1916 budget an appropriation was secured sufficient to equip practically the whole division with modern machines. There are only a few operators in the Manhattan office and a few in The Bronx who are still using the old type machines, and it is planned to ask for an appropriation in the 1917 budget sufficient to meet their needs.

The average daily outgo of letters from the tenement house

department is about 1,150. Prior to the study made in 1914 these letters were sent out in ordinary envelopes. It was then suggested that the use of window envelopes would obviate the need of rewriting names and addresses, thus saving a substantial amount of the time of stenographers and typewriters. This recommendation was put into effect early in 1915, as soon as the stock of old stationery had been used up. The change effected a saving of the time of six operators.

In the Manhattan stenographic office the operators occupied a large room crowded with all kinds of dilapidated desks and chairs. The equipment was all old and entirely unsuited to the requirements of the office. Accordingly, provision was made in the 1916 budget for the purchase of enough modern typewriting chairs to furnish one for each operator, and for half the necessary number of small typewriting desks so designed as to occupy the minimum of space and yet afford the maximum of convenience. These substitutions have improved the appearance of the room materially and have increased its available floor space substantially.

3 *Duplicating Letters*

Under former conditions much of the time of the stenographic division was occupied in copying orders sent by the department to owners, directing them to make certain changes and alterations in their property so as to conform with the law. For each one of the 400 or more orders which are sent out the department has a standard form. These forms were printed in a pamphlet and a copy placed in the hands of each stenographer. In writing out the orders the stenographer used to consult her book and copy the exact wording therein, filling in only the necessary word or words to make the order meet the conditions of the inspector's report. As it was necessary to make five copies of every such document the amount of time taken in arranging cards, letters and carbon paper in the proper manner was considerable.

The new secretary of the department therefore suggested that this method be changed on the longer letters and that a duplicating machine be used instead. Each one of the orders used by the department was printed in hecktograph ink, typewriter type, on gummed paper. On letters containing several orders these printed forms are picked out, pasted on sheets of paper, and the necessary words, together with the names and addresses filled in on the typewriter. This dummy letter is put in the duplicating machine, and from the impression left on the gelatine surface as many copies are taken as needed. The same machine is used in preparing letters or other papers of which more copies are needed than can readily be made by the use of carbon paper. The new method has worked even better than was expected and is now being extended to cover the letters furnished owners and title insurance companies to show the violations existing in any tenement house. During 1915 more than 17,500 of such letters were issued.

The net result of the changes outlined above in new typewriting machines, the use of window envelopes and the use of the duplicating machine has been that the total number of typewriting operators in the department has dropped from 120 in 1914 to 96 in 1916, a reduction of 20%.

4 *Organization changes*

Early in 1915 the files containing records of pending violations were removed from the custody of the bureau of records and placed in the executive division under the superintendent. This was done to make these files more available to the superintendent, who uses them most frequently.

At the same time the chief clerk's office was consolidated with the secretary's office. As a result two of the three stenographers were released to the stenographic division and the work formerly done by one $1,200, two $480 and one $300 clerks, was turned over to two clerks, one at $480 and the other at $300, so that there was a saving in this one division of $3,480 out of a total of $12,360.

In 1914 the legal work of the department was handled in three separate divisions. In 1915 these three were combined under the supervision of one clerk and resulting economy in operation was obtained. At the same time the police officers detailed to the department, and who were formerly attached to the vacation division, were put under the jurisdiction of the old building bureau, because they did practically the work of inspectors although used only in cases where the powers of a police officer are necessary.

A further saving of $3,000 was effected by dropping the position of registrar of records from the 1916 budget. The responsibility of this position had become too slight to warrant the retention of so high-priced an executive and his duties were therefore transferred to the acting chief clerk.

Other reorganizations and consolidations have been effected in the Brooklyn office, and a saving has been made in the number of stenographers, inspectors and clerks required to maintain that division. The Bronx office is so small, being less than 10% of the department, that there has not been much room for consolidation. Some economies, however, have been brought about by combining the inspectional forces of the old and new building bureaus and by dropping the position of chief inspector of the old building bureau.

5 *Changes in the duties of inspectors*

Next to the reorganization of the stenographic division, one of the most important problems to be considered was that presented by the field work of the department's inspectors. For years the practice had been for each inspector to come to the office every morning at nine, get his papers in shape, and make up a route slip covering his proposed day's work. When these duties were performed he would leave the office for his district, seldom reaching it before ten. It was also the practice for the inspectors of a given squad to meet their supervisor at some pre-arranged rendezvous in the afternoon. This meant that the inspectors were compelled to leave their districts anywhere from fifteen minutes to three-quarters of an hour before the hour at which they were due at the meeting point, and as a result more time was lost from actual field inspections, the average time for inspections being not more than four and one-half hours per day.

In the fall of 1915, however, after many conferences and discussions, a change of practice was inaugurated. The inspectors now report direct to the supervisors in the field on three mornings a week and come to the office on the other three mornings. Furthermore, the afternoon rendezvous has been discontinued on three days a week. The time thus saved results in an increase of about one-sixth of the actual available inspection hours of the field force. It is possible that further changes may be effected which will increase still more the time for field work. At present the inspectors cease work at four o'clock and go home and write up their reports. If some practicable method can be devised for simplifying and decreasing the amount of clerical work required from inspectors, they can be kept in the field later.

At the same time that these administrative changes have been brought about and these economies effected, the department has done more intensive work in many directions, because the completion of certain of its duties has made it possible to devote a larger measure of attention to such specific items as the reduction of the number of dark or illegally lighted rooms, the occupancy of basements without a permit, the encumbrance of fire escapes, the provision of workable fire-escape drop ladders, the installation of self-closing doors on dumb-waiters, and the provision of additional lighting fixtures in inadequately lighted hallways. The department has also considered itself especially charged with the duty of fire prevention and the prevention of loss of life in tenement houses.

The records of the department show that the total inspections for 1914 were 25% greater than in 1913. In nine months of 1915 the total number was about equal to the entire year of 1913. The fact that the figures for nine months only are used is due to the census work conducted by the department for three months in 1915 by its assignment twice, during that year, of the greater part of its inspectors to assist the United States government in a census of unemployment.

Not only has the inspectional work of the department been more effectively conducted, but a comparison of the number of items filed and dismissed in the department during 1913, 1914 and 1915, as shown in the following table, is evidence that the department's work has in no degree suffered from the economies and consolidations brought about by the co-operation of the commissioner in the survey and study which was inaugurated in 1914.

	Filed	Dismissed	Total Items Handled
1913	175,226	190,817	366,043
1914	171,809	206,113	377,922
1915	211,371	181,381	392,752
Total	558,406	578,311	1,136,717

In this table the heading "Filed" shows the number of specific violations of the law reported by the inspectors and the heading "Dismissed" shows the number of items on which the owners have complied with the law by doing the work ordered by the department. The items "pending" at the beginning of each year are not given in the above table, as they do not affect the volume of items handled during the year. It is evident, however, that the greater part of the items "dismissed" in each year are items which were "pending" the first of the year, not the items "filed" that year.

In each year since 1913, there has been a considerable increase in the "Total Items Handled," as shown by the above table, almost 12,000 (about 3%) in 1914; about 15,000 (about 4%) in 1915; and 26,700 (about 7%) more in 1915 than in 1913, and this increase has been accomplished in spite of a reduction of thirty-one inspectors in 1914 and 1915.

This table also shows that in 1915 the number of items "filed" increased 20% over 1913. Moreover, the table shows that for the three years, 19,905 more items were "dismissed" than were "filed." There were 146,093 items "pending" January 1st, 1914. The number has been reduced to 141,779 items "pending" January 1st, 1916; or a 3% reduction in two years.

Reorganization Still to be Effected

The most obvious and apparent opportunities for economy and reorganization of the tenement house department have been seized. Several things, however, remain yet to be done. **The most necessary perhaps is the arrangement of the inspectors' work, so that they will be relieved more completely from clerical duties and be freed for the more important task of field inspections.**

BOARD OF ASSESSORS

The work of the board of assesors consists chiefly in levying assessments to defray the cost of original local improvements, such as the grading, curbing and laying of sidewalks, paving streets and constructing sewers. Also where the grade of a street is changed, resulting in damage to property, the awards for this damage are determined by the board and included in the cost of the improvement. The following table shows the extent of the board's work during the past three years:

Year	Apportioned and Advertised	Confirmed
1913	$6,174,244.97	$6,408,105.86
1914	9,855,332.74	9,030,822.31
1915	7,672,640.68	7,318,294.08

In view of these large sums which the board levies against the property owners of the city, it is of extreme importance to the public that the work of the board of assessors be conducted in as orderly and expeditious a manner as possible. When the present administration took office in January, 1914, there were many defects in the methods of administering the work of the board. Chief among them were the following:

1 The notice given to property owners in respect of proposed assessments and of the filing of claims for damages on account of change of grade was inadequate, both as regards contents and time allowed.

2 Substantial delay occurred in the confirmation of assessments (a) due to delay in the offices of the borough presidents in preparing assessment lists and maps; (b) due to the joint exercise of jurisdiction by the street opening bureau of the law department and the board of assessors in the matter of making awards in cases of change of grade incident to street opening and widening proceedings.

3 Because of division of responsibility, it frequently happened that an owner of property, who received an award from the bureau of street openings for intended regulation of the street many years before the physical change was effected, sold the property to an innocent purchaser who, when the physical change of grade was effected, suffered the loss by damage without recourse because the previous owner had already received an award.

4 A substantial injustice to property owners resulted from the board's inability to make awards under section 951 of the charter for damages to unimproved property due to abnormal and unusual changes of grade. Under the old practice it was necessary that special statutes be enacted in specific instances to remedy such injustices.

5 Considerable confusion arose from the apportionment of assessments by the collector of assessments after confirmation. This apportionment often resulted in inequities.

If all of the assessments levied for improvements in the City of New York were levied by the board of assessors there would be no occasion for the appointment of a commissioner of assessment, so-called, in a street opening proceeding, nor would there be any occasion under the law for the assessments (which is an exercise of the power of taxation) to be passed on by the courts. The board of revision of assessments would be a better check on inequitable assessments, by reason of their special knowledge and experience in assessment matters, than any court, and much time would be saved to property owners and to the law department if all these assessment matters were handled by the board of assessors.

The equitable apportionment of assessments for benefit cannot be done except after a careful consideration of all that the property has paid and will pay, and it is practically an appraisal of the value of the property before and after the improvement. Experience is necessary in order to secure proper results, and there is no arbitrary rule which can be framed to meet these situations. In practice, assessments for street openings are levied in such a way as to be a *direct contradiction* of the values before and after as fixed by the department of taxes and assessments.

There is a deep-seated resentment on the part of property-owners, which is recognized by everybody who has knowledge of these matters as being well founded, against the present method of acquiring title to streets and defraying the expense. The matter of assessment is nominally passed upon by the board of estimate and apportionment. The assessment areas are, however, actually fixed in the office of the chief engineer of the board of estimate. As the officials in the chief engineer's office do not attend the hearings at which the objections are developed, nor obtain the arguments made at these hearings, they are not in a position to understand the effect of a series of assessments on a property owner. It is only natural that great injustices are frequent, and when the hearings upon objections develop that a change in the assessment area is desirable, another public hearing must be had before the board of estimate, with advertised notices, causing delay.

The expense of levying assessments in the bureau of street openings is much more than that in the board of assessors, although assessments for sewer construction are very much more complicated.

With the improved method of determining the damage in street opening proceedings by the courts, it would seem logical to have all assessments determined by the board of assessors.

Substantial deficiencies in the collection of assessments, with consequent loss to the city, result because the board of assessors does not report in *advance* of the authorization of the improvement on the ability of the property to sustain the expense. As a matter of practice, the board of assessors urges that it would be a decided advantage if the procedure for local improvements were changed so that upon the receipt of a petition for a certain improvement, accompanied by an engineer's estimate of the probable cost, the board were required to fix a tentative assessment on the various parcels deemed benefited. If, in its judgment, there were any question as to the enhancement of value, the tentative assessment might be submitted to the department of taxes and assessments, so that that department could also pass upon the question as to whether the improvement would enhance values by at *least* the *amount* of the tentative *assessment.* It seems illogical and sometimes entirely unfair for a property owner, after he has been compelled to pay a heavy assessment for an alleged improvement, to find that the department of taxes and assessments *reduces* his valuation.

Permission was obtained from the board of estimate and apportionment to notify property owners by mail of pending assessments. The cost of this notification is included in the cost of the work and assessed against the benefited property. It has been found that this method is much more convenient for property owners, inasmuch as the old practice of merely inserting advertisements in the corporation newspapers and the City Record was not a successful means of reaching every owner involved.

The city loses each year large sums in paying for building damages under Section 980 of the Charter, and under Section 947, which limits assessments to fifty per cent. of the fair value. The city is all the loser by reason of placing large assessment liens for which there are no purchasers, and above all because of the fact that in some cases tax values are lessened after large assessments are made against the property.

In 1915 the board succeeded in obtaining an amendment to the charter which removed from the street opening bureau its jurisdiction over the making of awards for intended street regulating, and gave exclusive jurisdiction to the board of assessors over awards for change incident to opening and widening proceedings. In this way the possibility, above mentioned, of making two awards for one change of grade (usually resulting in a loss to the latest owner) was obviated and responsibility centralized.

A bill was prepared by the board of assessors empowering the board in making street grading assessments to make awards for damage to unimproved property, in the event that the board of estimate and apportionment shall certify that the street grade is abnormal and due to unusual conditions. The law will relieve the injustice which has hitherto resulted to owners of property adversely affected by these unusual street grades.

The time required for determining damage claims and confirming assessments has been reduced by advertisement on receipt of maps in advance of the certification of the assessment certificate, by the prompt transmission by the collector of assessments and arrears of confirmed assessments for apportionment by the board of assessors, and by the preparation of assessment lists in the office of the board of assessors without the aid of maps.

The methods of recording computations have been improved, so that inequities have been obviated when the same property is assessed several times for the same general improvement, as in the case of sewer assessments.

The board has since 1914 initiated legislation giving the board of revision of assessments final appellate jurisdiction in respect of awards made by the board of assessors, thus removing one more link in the legal chain between improvement and final collection of assessments by the city; and legislation containing time limitations with respect to the filing of claims for damages, thus preventing intentional delay and a liability for interest on awards obtained on such delayed claims.

Many changes in procedure have resulted in adding to the work of the board. In spite of this fact, however, the administrative cost of the office has been consistently decreased since 1914. The budget appropriation in 1914 was $42,088.50, for 1915 it was $40,429.50, while for 1916 it is but $34,639.50. In the latter budget a saving of $5,000 per annum was effected without in any way impairing the efficiency of the department by eliminating the office of secretary of the board and assigning its duties to a member of the board without adding to his compensation.

A fact as significant as the reduction in cost is the reduction in the time elapsing between the receipt from the comptroller of the assessment list with interest certificate and the date of confirmation. In 1913 the interval averaged 92 days; in 1915 the average length of time was reduced to 62 days. As the city can under the law collect from property owners interest for only sixty days of the interval between the transmittal of assessment lists and the confirmation by the board of assessors, this reduction of thirty days in the average length of time between these two operations has resulted in a large saving to the city, as there is now practically no time during which the assessments do not carry interest.

Several steps remain to be taken, however, before the work of levying assessments for local improvements can be considered to have reached the highest possible level of efficiency. The board of assessors is alive to the situation and recommends that the following steps be taken as soon as possible:

1 That the entire preparation of assessment lists and maps be placed under the control of the board so as to avoid delay and reduce the expense of the present system.
2 That there be complete co-ordination between the authorities undertaking local improvements and the board with respect particularly to the preparation by the board of a report on probable deficiencies, prior to the authorization of an improvement instead of after the authorization, as at present.
3 That the force of computers in the bureau of street openings be transferred to the board, and that all street opening assessments be computed in this board so that the clerks doing this work may be centralized and may perform their duties more economically and with less delay.
4 That the cost of administering the board be included in the cost of assessing local improvements and apportioned fairly with the cost of the improvement, instead of remaining a charge in the annual budget.

5 That some means be found to determine in advance the proportion of the city's payroll which can be included in the cost of improvements financed through the street improvement fund. At the present time there is a wide disparity in payroll cost between the several boroughs, as is shown by the following table. This cost ranges from 6% in Brooklyn in 1914 to 31.9 in Richmond for 1915. The overhead and engineering cost of local improvements should bear a reasonably definite relation to the total cost of the improvement. Such wide disparities are startling. In the borough of Manhattan, for example, the payroll cost for street improvements in 1914 was 10.6% of the total, while in 1915 it jumped to 17.1%, although more than half as much work again was done in 1915.

AMOUNTS ADVANCED FROM THE STREET IMPROVEMENT FUND

For Assessment Work, 1910–1915 Inclusive, All Boroughs

Years	Contracts	Payrolls	Miscellaneous	Totals	Percentage of Payroll of Contract Cost
Manhattan					
1910	$341,092.82	$21,727.00	$7,179.77	$369,999.59	.0637
1911	344,330.18	26,449.48	9,427.52	380,207.18	.0768
1912	363,708.74	27,207.13	9,761.98	400,677.85	.0748
1913	325,885.24	24,679.78	14,786.11	365,351.13	.0757
1914	187,472.33	20,026.17	1,783.13	209,281.63	.1068
1915	299,957.26	51,492.95	9,991.56	361,441.77	.17167
The Bronx					
1910	1,802,942.12	198,728.17	1,706.45	2,003,376.74	.110224
1911	1,931,764.24	180,138.34	5,443.51	2,117,346.09	.09324
1912	1,742,937.20	193,014.43	5,971.95	1,941,923.58	.1108
1913	2,474,082.41	206,450.69	160.52	2,680,693.62	.0835
1914	1,944,658.75	200,850.92	1,301.44	2,146,811.11	.10328
1915	1,325,117.96	135,600.81	649.33	1,461,368.10	.10233
Brooklyn					
1910	1,586,788.32	139,171.15	8,384.01	1,734,343.48	.0877
1911	2,636,508.28	181,545.34	10,813.05	2,828,866.67	.06886
1912	2,572,264.39	189,511.94	44,722.07	2,806,498.40	.07368
1913	3,525,283.44	212,555.63	9,793.89	3,747,632.96	.06029
1914	3,454,873.43	207,917.77	6,024.91	3,668,816.11	.06018
1915	2,036,066.43	173,742.51	7,156.85	2,216,965.79	.08533
Queens					
1910	435,398.18	50,545.41	1,352.80	487,296.39	.11609
1911	1,058,169.72	67,433.69	3,918.31	1,129,521.72	.06372.
1912	1,766,117.32	99,795.83	10,769.17	1,876,682.32	.0565
1913	2,163,125.03	158,656.16	15,575.45	2,337,356.64	.07334
1914	1,574,997.69	190,569.34	9,707,79	1,775,274.82	.1210
1915	1,177,578.39	170,658.40	3,191.93	1,351,428.72	.14492
Richmond					
1910	524,307.17	57,520.89	448.72	582,271.78	.1097
1911	311,670.16	48,902.21	1,547.62	362,119.99	.1569
1912	287,789.68	37,414.64	4,045.85	329,250.17	.1300
1913	223,828.68	27,734.15	243.49	251,806.32	.1239
1914	35,194.47	3,900.37	227.06	39,321.90	.1108
1915	42,229.22	13,481.54	40.00	55,750.76	.319

6 That the "pay-as-you-go policy" be applied to local improvements, so that owners in neighborhoods desiring local improvements may be afforded an opportunity to pay their assessments, or a substantial proportion, in advance. This would eliminate the accelerated projects of real estate developers, who auction property to innocent purchasers before assessment for the improvement is confirmed. Title companies do not report pending assessments and the victims of this sharp practice often claim that the government is in collusion with the real estate dealer. The requirement of a deposit in advance is also a test of the good faith of the property owner and of his ability to pay for the improvements.

The board urges that attention be directed at once to the remedy of these conditions and that the board of estimate devise some plan whereby the matter of local improvements may be handled in a more systematic way. Legislation must be obtained to remove many restrictions and disabilities under which the board of assessors now labors.

COMMISSIONER OF ACCOUNTS

Prior to 1914 the office of the commissioners of accounts was utilized by the mayor chiefly for the purpose of making investigations of illegal practices. Little effort was directed towards utilizing this force of expert examiners and accountants in a constructive program for the betterment of administrative procedure.

In January, 1914, the chamberlain made an examination of the organization of the office and submitted a report* to the mayor in which he suggested that the commissioners of accounts' office be availed of to a greater extent for affording administrative assistance to the mayor, and that in place of two commissioners there should be a single commissioner and two deputies.

A bill embodying these recommendations was defeated in the legislature in 1914 and 1915, but was finally adopted by the 1916 legislature in modified form. A single commissioner and two deputies were created, but the powers of the office were not increased, nor was the name changed to the Division of Administration as originally proposed.

During the first five months of 1914 the office was practically assigned to the chamberlain to assist him in his studies for the administrative reorganization of the city government, and since then the commissioner of accounts' office has constituted practically a division of administration, assisting the mayor and the chamberlain in carrying out a constructive program for the betterment of administrative procedure.

Thus in 1914 and 1915 it completed a survey of the entire city and county government, comprising 145 boards, commissions, departments and offices. The survey was entirely uncritical, the purpose being to develop the facts as to the functions of each governmental unit, its organization and duties, and the numbers, salaries and activities of officers and employees. The Bureau of Municipal Research loaned men to assist in this work which in its final form was submitted to the Constitutional Convention. This survey has served as the basis for later critical studies.

In 1915 the office accurately determined for the first time in dollars and cents the effect of mandatory legislation upon the budget of the city. The many miscellaneous statutes affecting appropriations were assembled so that the makers of the 1916 budget could for the first time hew appropriations to the exact line of mandatory requirements. The mandatory legislation study, together with similar studies as to mandatory expenditures from special revenue bonds and corporate stock, and as to miscellaneous revenues diverted from the general fund by mandatory legislation, proved extremely valuable to the Legislative Committee of which Senator Brown was the chairman in its investigation of the city's finances and led to the introduction of legislation to give the city a greater measure of control over its budget.

---

*A Division of Administration

In the summer of 1915, in co-operation with the chamberlain, the office undertook a critical study of county government within the City of New York and recommended the consolidation of county offices and the merger of certain of them with offices of the city government. These recommendations if adopted would have effected an aggregate economy of over $2,000,000 a year. Sixteen bills to effect this result were drafted by the office and introduced in the legislature. The bill precluding the sheriff from participation in the fees of his office, which will turn over to the city approximately $50,000 annually, was enacted to take effect on the 1st of January, 1918.

Many other studies have been undertaken resulting in suggestions for reorganization and reduction in expense. A list of some of the economies which have been suggested during the past year follows:

Janitorial service, Bushwick High School	$7,616 00
Sheriff, New York County: Fees (approximately per annum)	50,000 00
Bonding City and County Employees (approximately per annum)	10,000 00
Coroners (approximately per annum)	50,000 00
Magistrates' Courts: Deficit recovered	147 00
County Government (approximately per annum)	2,000,000 00
Board of Elections: Annual salaries	10,000 00
City Printing: Bellevue reports	1,872 60
Department of Public Charities: Plant, equipment and stores service	18,000 00
Department of Docks and Ferries: Adjustment of salaries	9,460 00
Board of Education: Janitorial service	62,000 00
Board of Education: Repairs to buildings	905,204 21
Libraries: Repairs	13,499 00
Department of Public Charities: Check payment system	3,794 41
County detectives: Kings County	8,000 00
Department of Public Charities: Additional allowances requested	42,673 38
Department of Public Charities: Bureau of Social Investigations	19,100 00
Motor Vehicle Service: Central garage	76,000 00
Total	$3,287,366 60

Although emphasis has been given to administrative studies and to the use of the staff for constructive effort, the investigative work has not declined. Most productive among the investigations of illegal practices was the examination of the accounts and methods of the coroners' office, which resulted in the abolition of the coroners' system by a law which takes effect on January 1, 1918.

The investigation of the board of building examiners helped to prove the necessity for vetoing the Lockwood-Ellenbogen bill of 1915, which proposed increasing the power of this board without reorganizing it, and resulted at the recent session in a revision of the bill in this respect, so that, as finally enacted, the board is made appointive by and responsible to public authority.

An investigation of the "marriage bureaus" in Manhattan and Brooklyn disclosed an intolerable condition, which resulted in legislation in 1916 prohibiting aldermen from officiating at marriage ceremonies, and conferring this power upon the city clerk.

A thorough investigation of the methods of the board of elections disclosed many unsatisfactory conditions, resulting in the introduction of legislation providing for the examination by the municipal civil service commission of candidates for appointment as local election officers and for other beneficial changes.

The office has protected the rights and interests of the public by the investigation of complaints. During 1915, 75 complaints of citizens, city employees or civic associations as to municipal conditions or against public servants were investigated and 15 inquiries made relative to alleged irregularities or abuses, financial or administrative.

Continuously throughout the past two years, the commissioner of accounts, in addition to carrying on his own work, has supplied several members of his staff to assist in constructive work under the direction of the chamberlain and to investigate and report on current administrative matters referred to the chamberlain by the mayor. He has also assisted the various heads of departments in their work of reorganization. Especially noteworthy assistance has been rendered to the commission on pensions in its investigation of the city's pension funds, and to the temporary central purchase committee organized to purchase supplies on contract for all departments under the jurisdiction of the mayor. The commissioner of accounts has co-operated in the preparation of the annual budget by detailing examiners to analyze departmental requests prior to their approval by the mayor for submission to the board of estimate and apportionment. The volume of constructive work done by the office is greater than that done at any previous period and indicates the necessity for continuing as a branch of the executive force an administrative staff to deal with general questions of a constructive nature.

BOARD OF CITY RECORD

The board of city record publishes the city's official daily "The City Record" and contracts for substantially all of the printing and stationery used by the departments and offices of the city and county governments.

In general, two factors contribute to make real economy in the administration of the work of the board of city record difficult of attainment. The first is the fact that the law stipulates much of the material which is printed in the City Record. If the board had discretion as to what to include and what to exclude from the publication, a considerable reduction in volume and cost would be possible without detriment to the public interest. The second, lies in the division of responsibility between the board as a purchasing agent and the several departments as consumers of the supplies which the board provides. In this latter respect, particularly, the division of responsibility has made it easy for extravagance to creep in. Excessive amounts of printing and stationery have always been requested by the departments because, inasmuch as they have no interest in making their expenditures for these items meet a specific appropriation, they do not always consider as carefully as they should the relative need for the supplies requisitioned.

As a result of this lack of co-operation and as a result of the inadequate supervision which was exercised by the board of city record prior to 1910, the annual budget appropriations to the board had increased from about $796,000 in 1906 to $1,540,000 in 1909, an increase of nearly 100%. The total appropriation in 1909 (including special revenue bonds) was $1,902,692.12. The special revenue bonds were issued to cover "arrearages."

When Mayor Gaynor took office in 1910 he realized that a very great degree of economy could be effected in this branch of the city's service. Accordingly, a man of practical printing knowledge and wide business experience was selected to serve as supervisor. The result obtained by the substitution of modern business methods for the former loose administration of the department was most gratifying. The annual budget appropriations were decreased in spite of rapidly growing needs, until in 1913 the appropriation was but $1,070,000, a reduction of $470,000 below the 1909 budget appropriations, and $832,000 below the total 1909 appropriations. No special revenue bond authorizations were requested or granted in 1913.

Administrative Defects Found

The present mayor continued the work started in 1910 and retained the supervisor in his position of responsibility, for there was still much to be done in further enlisting the co-operation of the departments, in standardizing the quality of printing, and in removing the legal handicaps to the most economical administration of the board's work. Chief among the defects which existed in 1914 and which the present administration desired to remedy were the following:

1 The provisions of law requiring the publication by both the board of city record and the board of elections of the annual registration lists.

2 The provisions of law requiring the publication, twice a year, of the civil list supplement containing the names, addresses and compensation of all city employees.

3 The printing of the budget in seven, eight, or nine issues of the City Record and in the pamphlet minutes of the board of estimate and apportionment and the board of aldermen.

4 The publication of the minutes of the board of estimate and apportionment, the board of aldermen, the sinking fund commission and the municipal civil service commission in unnecessary detail.

5 The printing, in extended detail, of the commissioner of accounts' quarterly examination of the chamberlain's office.

6 The excessive length of the quarterly reports made by some departments and by law published in the City Record.

7 The lack of uniformity and the resulting needless duplication of printing in the advertisements of bids submitted by departments for insertion in the City Record.

8 The printing of departmental budget estimates in full as supplements of the City Record.

9 The excessive quantities of printing and stationery requested by departments and the use of engraved stationery and expensive paper for general routine correspondence.

10 The lack of central control over supplies requisitioned by municipal courts.

11 The needless drain on the City Record's printing appropriation caused by the free distribution to the public of such publications as the building code.

12 The printing in book form for individual departments of extensive annual reports not required by law.

13 The use by departments of an excessive number of copies of the City Record.

14 The direct purchase by some departments of office supplies in small quantities at prices ranging from 25 to 300 per cent. higher than City Record prices.

15 Frequent requests from departments for rush work.

16 The frequency with which substantial changes in copy are made after the matter had been set up in type, with the resulting expense for authors' corrections.

17 The need for centralization of the city's advertising and the immediate repeal of that section of the charter requiring the annual payment of $20,000 to each of five Brooklyn newspapers for "advertising."

Progress Made in Remedying Defects

Immediate steps were taken by the present administration to remedy such defects as those above enumerated and to bring about increased economy in the administrative work of the board of city record. A brief summary of these steps follows:

1 A bill was prepared by the supervisor and introduced in the legislature of 1915 providing for the repeal of the statutory provision requiring the printing of a list of registered voters in the City Record. This bill was not, however, passed, so the annual waste of some $13,000 continues. The same bill was presented again this year in the hope that it might pass.

2 A bill, suggested by the board of city record, was introduced in the legislature in 1915 providing for the printing of the civil list in April of each year instead of in January and July, as now required by law. If the civil list were printed in April to cover a period of twelve months from April 1st to March 31st, it would not only include the names of all officials elected to office January 1st and their appointees, but also all changes in positions and salaries provided for in the budget to be effective as of January 1st, as well as all changes made in February in the salaries of the teaching staff of the board of education. The civil list would thus be made an accurate source of current information and would not be as now out of date before published. This bill was referred to the committee on affairs of cities but was never reported out. A similar bill was introduced this year.

3 After numerous requests the city clerk's office finally, in 1914, agreed to substitute for the budget on three occasions where it had formerly been printed in full a reference to the date when it was previously printed in the City Record. In 1915 this practice was continued in every case when the budget came up before the board of aldermen, a reference being made to the date of the City Record in which the budget had originally been printed as part of the minutes of the board of estimate and apportionment. As a result the budget was printed but twice in 1915, the minimum number of times required by law, once as passed by the board of estimate and apportionment, and the second time as finally approved by the mayor, comptroller and city clerk.

4 It had formerly been the practice to print the budget estimates of the various departments in full as supplements to the City Record. This entailed a very considerable expense and served a questionably useful purpose. A material reduction has been effected in the cost of printing by substituting foot notes for columns used only occasionally to convey information.

The supervisor now recommends that only a summary of the departmental estimates be printed in the City Record and the matter is being studied by the commissioner of accounts. So many changes are made in the departmental estimates between the time of original and final submission to the board of estimate for action that there is little value in the printed copy based on the original estimate. Furthermore, it has often happened that the printed estimates were not available for distribution until after the adoption of the budget by the board of estimate. The publication of an abstract would serve substantially every purpose now served by the printing of the full estimates and would save tremendously in the cost of printing the City Record.

5 The office of the city record several times called the attention of the mayor to the manner in which the minutes of the board of estimate were prepared for publication in the City Record, and suggested that an intelligent condensation be made in the same

manner in which the calendar of the board of estimate is now prepared. The committee on organization of the board directed the secretary and the supervisor to co-operate and report to that committee, but no satisfactory agreement could be reached although some minor improvements resulted, such as the substitution of summaries for full reports, communications, etc. There is still room for at least a fifty per cent. reduction in the volume of these minutes and the commissioner of accounts has recently been requested to make a further investigation. This work is now being prosecuted.

6 The former practice of printing the quarterly reports of the commissioner of accounts in full was called to the attention of the present commissioner. It was agreed that the details of these reports had no public value. Accordingly, a summary form was adopted which clearly presents the important facts, and which takes but two pages of the City Record instead of the sixty pages covered by the detailed report.

7 The charter gives the mayor the right to prescribe the form in which the quarterly reports of the various departments are to be submitted to him. The supervisor of the City Record therefore suggested that the mayor delegate some one authority to go over these reports and, with the co-operation of the departments, condense the material presented so as to eliminate repetitions and useless information. This has been done and a saving of more than fifty per cent. in volume has been effected.

8 A standard form of advertisement for publication in the City Record of contracts to be let by city departments was prepared by the supervisor and submitted in 1913 to the corporation counsel for approval. Its adoption would mean a saving of about $4,000 a year. The matter has again been taken up with the mayor, and it is hoped that a speedy determination may be made.

9 In the matter of obtaining the co-operation of the various city and county departments for effecting economies in the quantity and quality of supplies requisitioned by them, the present administration has been particularly successful. The number of costly binders furnished has been reduced materially by persuading the departments to transfer the contents of such binders to serviceable but much cheaper loose sheet holders for filing purposes, so that the binders may be kept in continual use instead of being placed in storerooms containing dead material. Furthermore, the board of city record adopted a resolution in 1914 providing that printed letter heads and envelopes be furnished the various departments for general use, and that engraved stationery be furnished only to the heads of the principal departments for their personal official use. The saving thus effected approximated $18,000.

10 The question of central control over supplies requisitioned by the municipal courts has been taken up with the chief clerk and the justices of the municipal courts, who agreed that such centralization would be advisable and economical. It was found, however, that there was no clerical staff available for the work and the matter was therefore temporarily dropped. In the preparation of the 1917 budget some provision should be made for a change in the present practice.

11 No action has yet been taken on the suggestion made by the supervisor that a charge be made to the public for such books as the building code. This would be a very desirable step because it would limit the issue to persons really interested. Under existing conditions repeated editions of the building code of several thousand each have been printed at the request of the five superintendents of buildings, so that they might distribute them free to all applicants.

12 The question of substituting for individual annual reports now printed for all departments a consolidated report or Year Book, forming a single reference book of real value, has not yet been settled. The mayor has detailed a representative from the office of the commissioner of accounts to go over the material submitted by the departments for printing in their annual reports and a considerable reduction in volume has been made through the co-operation of this representative with the department heads. There is still, however, an opportunity for real economy if the administration determines that the number and size of annual reports should be reduced. Even under the present arrangement a great amount of extraneous material creeps in. In a recent report, for example, pages were devoted to listing the deaths among zoo animals by months.

13 As a result of the suggestion of the supervisor, the mayor's office sent out letters asking departments to revise downward their requests for copies of the City Record. In this way the daily edition was substantially reduced and an annual saving of $1350 in printing and $1250 in binding was effected.

14 The co-operation of the finance department has been enlisted in reducing the amount of stationery and office supplies purchased by departments from their own appropriations at prices greatly in excess of those which the City Record could obtain. The auditing division now questions any bill for such supplies and exerts its authority to prevent such purchases.

15 To reduce the number of rush requisitions sent in by departments the office of the City Record has devised a stock form for the guidance of stores and supply clerks. This form if kept up daily automatically draws attention to material which is running low and which should be replenished, and also acts as an accurate control over consumption. Some departments have installed this system with the result that their rush requisitions have been greatly decreased in number. Its general adoption would bring about even greater economy.

16 One of the most difficult sources of waste to control is the tendency of department heads to insist upon changes in printers' proof. The city's printing bill could be reduced very greatly if all copy were submitted to the City Record in final form. As this is a matter, however, over which the supervisor has no jurisdiction or authority, it is possible only to make the general suggestion.

17 The supervisor of the City Record recommended in 1914 that an amendment to the charter be prepared providing that all advertising for any of the city departments paid for by the City of New York or any of its counties be placed under the direction of the board of city record, so that a uniform method for handling advertising would be provided. At the present time adver-

tising is paid for from several budget appropriations and there is no central control. An attempt was also made to obtain the repeal of that charter section requiring the payment of $20,000 a year to each of five Brooklyn newspapers, but the requested legislation was not even reported by a committee.

In addition to taking these steps toward the elimination of those defects which were known to exist when the present administration took office, several other reforms have been inaugurated by the board of city record resulting in further economies.

For example, a new arrangement of the facts presented in the civil list was devised and a saving of over $4,000 was made in the cost of printing the 1915 civil lists as compared with 1914. Similar economies effected in printing departmental budget estimates reduced the number of pages occupied by them from 1250 in 1913 to 950 in 1914 and to 704 in 1915.

In addition, a saving was made by changing the style of printing of the lists of assessed valuations in 1914 and a further saving will be made in printing the 1916 lists by using six-point instead of eight-point type and by arranging the matter in narrower measure. It is also possible, by arranging with the printer to keep a large part of each of the law department's quarterly reports standing in type, to make the necessary alterations in the type rather than to reset the whole material. This resulted in a saving of $1,300 in printing the last two 1915 reports as compared with the previous year.

At the same time that these economies have been effected in the city's printing and stationery bills, the City Record has been required by the growth of the city's activities to furnish printing and stationery supplies to an increased number of departments. Since January, 1914, the service of the board of city record has extended to twenty-eight departments, bureaus, boards, etc., not theretofore provided with printing, stationery and blank book supplies. The most important of these are the board of estimate's committees, the department of licenses, the bureau of public health education and the offices of the newly formed Bronx County.

Next Steps Necessary

As has been stated above, the cost of the city's printing and stationery can be still further reduced if the following steps were taken:

1 Condensing and revising all reports issued by the departments and their publication preferably in one volume. The supervision over such publications by a trained writer possessing a technical knowledge of printing would result in very great economies.

2 Centralizing the city's advertising.

3 **Repealing the law requiring the city to advertise in the five corporation newspapers of Brooklyn at an annual expense of $100,000. The City Record is the official organ for advertising in all the other boroughs and there is no reason why it should not serve the same purpose in Brooklyn.**

3 Standardizing the forms of advertisements used by the various departments for contract work.

4 Standardizing letterheads and envelopes, with respect to size, quality and style, for all branches of the city government.

5 Legislation providing for:

  a Printing the civil list in April instead of in January and July.

  b Repealing the law requiring the City Record to print the list of registered voters.

  c Amending section 1544 of the charter so as to exempt the quarterly report of the commissioner of accounts of the receipts and disbursements of the chamberlain from the provision requiring all quarterly reports to be printed in the City Record.

6 Printing an abstract of the proceedings of the board of estimate instead of the full minutes.

7 Printing summaries of departmental budget estimates instead of the details in full.

8 Printing an abstract of the minutes of the commissioners of the sinking fund instead of full detail.

9 Printing an abstract of the minutes of the board of aldermen instead of full detail.

10 Eliminating from the City Record the approved papers of the board of aldermen now printed therein.

11 Centralizing the requisitioning and the delivery and distribution of supplies furnished to the municipal courts.

12 Imposing a small fee for copies of certain reports and pamphlets issued by the city.

13 Adoption by all departments of a stationery supply control form.

MUNICIPAL CIVIL SERVICE COMMISSION

Conditions Requiring Correction, January 1, 1914

1 Necessity of making a change in the positions of secretary and assistant secretary of the commission.

2 Existence of an independent and uncontrolled labor bureau in the Criminal Courts Building, administering all steps from application to certification for positions in the labor class.

3 Absence of proper business procedure and methods in the progress of examinations from application to certification; the need of a new procedure, new forms, new equipment, new filing methods and labor saving office devices in all bureaus of the commission.

4 Necessity for more effective planning, organization and direction of the examining division.

5 Inadequacy of the force of examiners; lack of proper organization and control of the examining division and of examination work; lack of contact of examiners with work in departments; absence of proper examining standards; lack of proper material with which to work.

6 Need of new types of examination for high grade positions and of recognized experts to conduct them; need for the development of oral examinations and extension of practical examinations; need for the revision of the system of promotion examinations so as to provide wider opportunities and more adequate tests.

7 Need of a proper system of advertising examinations and of publicity methods.

8 Lack of an accurate and standard classification of all positions supported by definitions of duties; qualifications and salary limits to be used in holding examinations for entrance and promotion, in checking the performance of duties under proper titles, etc.

9 Lack of proper co-operation between the physical examiners and the examining division; lack of proper physical standards for all positions; lack of proper materials, procedure and methods in the conduct of physical examinations.

10 Lack of an adequate permanent force of investigators in the investigation bureau.

11 Lack of a proper system of service records with adequate supporting materials.

12 Lack of proper comparative statistics and a well-presented statistical report.

13 Necessity of a central payroll system and of improvements in the checking of payrolls.

14 Lack of a proper system of identification of candidates for positions in the labor class.

Steps Taken to Correct These Conditions Between January 1, 1914, and May 1, 1916

1 The secretary of the commission was dropped and the secretary of the Civil Service Reform Association was appointed in his place. The salary of the assistant secretary was reduced from $4,000 to $2,400.

2 The labor bureau was abolished as a separate bureau and its functions were distributed among the various existing bureaus in the commission, i. e., the receipt of applications to the application bureau, physical examinations to the physical examination bureau, etc. The labor files were consolidated with the files of the commission and the office in the Criminal Courts Building given up. By the reorganization of the labor bureau three unnecessary positions were abolished. The administration of the rules governing the labor class was centralized in the Municipal Building and closer supervision of this work was made possible. As an incidental effect, the removal of the labor bureau from the Criminal Courts Building cleansed the atmosphere. In the past, district leaders were accustomed to frequent this bureau, and their presence gave rise to suspicion. Now these leaders make their labor requests under the same conditions as any other citizen.

3 With the assistance of the Bureau of Municipal Research a study was made of all forms in use in the commission, of the proper procedure in transacting its business, and of the equipment and filing methods needed to place the commission on a modern business basis. As a result of this study, new standard forms were introduced, modern business machinery was purchased, the procedure of all units was clearly definitized, the amount of material to be filed was limited, and a report was made to the board of estimate and apportionment on shelving and filing equipment and furniture, which led to the appropriation of over $10,000 to provide for these needs. The new equipment is now being installed.

4 The commission is completing the reorganization of the examination division. Through the death of the chief examiner a vacancy exists, and a promotion examination will be held to fill it. As soon as this competition is decided a proper organization of the examination division will be built up under the new chief examiner.

5 Improvements in the examining division and in examination work:

a Expert examiners: The commission has secured the co-operation of experts of high standing to conduct examinations for high grade positions, such as $5,000 positions of directors of the bureaus of the health department. It has been aided considerably by men and women at the head of their professions in giving these examinations, among whom are the following:

Henry R. Seager, Professor of Economics, Columbia University
Dr. J. A. Miller, Member of Public Health, Hospital and Budget Committee, Academy of Medicine
Cyrus C. Miller, Chairman, Committee on Markets
Professor Samuel McCune Lindsay, Columbia University
Dr. J. H. Huddleston, Academy of Medicine
Lee F. Hamner, Director, Division of Recreation, Russell Sage Foundation
Edmond F. Butler, former tenement house commissioner
Lillian D. Wald, Henry Street Settlement
Dr. William J. Schieffelin, Citizens' Union
Homer Folks, State Charities Aid Association
Dr. George M. Price, Board of Sanitary Control

b When the commission came into office there were nine regular examiners. It has gradually improved the division and augmented the force by the appointment of eight examiners on full time, among them two who specialize in engineering work, one specialist on accounting and business methods, and other men of broad education and experience. The personnel and *esprit de corps* of this division is better than at any time in the history of the commission.

c Work records and control: The organization of the examination division has been improved through the installation and current upkeep of progress charts and through greater efforts to anticipate examinations. Examiners are given field assignments which bring them into contact with the actual work of departments. The experience requirements have been raised, examination papers have been made more difficult and the standard of rating has also been raised.

d Library: A library has been established and special attention is being given to the building up of files containing the records of previous examinations, materials on the methods and standards of other commissions, departmental reports and essential reference books.

6 The use of practical examinations has been extended and oral examinations have been more frequently used than before in the case of executive positions or of positions in which personality is an important factor. Definite regulations governing oral examinatons have been adopted.

7 There has been great improvement in the recruiting of properly qualified applicants. For this purpose an advertising expert was engaged to improve the advertising methods and to place them upon a proper business basis, in order that the particular class of persons best qualified to fill the positions might be attracted by advertising through the proper channels. The results of this new publicity were immediately apparent. Not only was this important and neglected phase of the commission's work placed upon a sound basis but a saving of over $10,000 was effected in expenditures for this purpose. The commission has established a carefully prepared mailing list of educational, social, professional, civic and other institutions to which advertisements are constantly sent. News and editorial publicity is also stimulated in connection with positions of importance in the city service.

8 The commission held a number of conferences with representatives of the bureau of standards and the Bureau of Municipal Research for the purpose of agreeing to and adopting the substance of the salary and grade specifications drawn up by the bureau of standards. Modifications were made according to the needs and requirements of civil service rules and practice. The commission is now preparing a detailed plan for the complete revision of the rules and classification and the adjustment of titles of employees, in order that there may be no delay in putting standardization into practical effect on or before January 1, 1917. Presumably, in the near future, the work of keeping up-to-date the standard specifications, excepting the parts governing rates of compensation, will be turned over to the commission.

9 With the assistance of the Bureau of Municipal Research the commission made a complete study of the work of the physical examination division, the result of which was that physical standards were set up and published governing all positions in the competitive and labor classes. The examining physicians are now able to use physical standards definitely approved by the commission and adapted to the physical requirements of the position, and candidates know just what physical examination they must undergo to qualify. A definite procedure was established with improved materials, forms, etc., for the proper examination of candidates.

10 The number of permanent investigators was increased from five to

thirteen, and clerical assistance provided for investigation work. The chief investigator has put this unit on a satisfactory working basis.

11 In July, 1914, the commission established a board of review, consisting of the president of the commission, the examiner in charge of service records, and a representative of the department in question. This board reviews the ratings of employees, and acts, at times, as a court of appeals whenever an employee feels that an injustice has been done him. In connection with the fundamental revision of the entire service record system, the commission, with the assistance of the Bureau of Municipal Research, made a comprehensive study of service and efficiency records, and a new system was agreed upon, including a program for supporting records. It is planned to use this system in connection with salary increases, lay-offs and reinstatements as well as with promotions. The new system is installed in a number of departments and will be put into effect generally after the experimental period. A new bureau of service records has been established with a former examiner of the department of finance in charge, two permanent assistants, and the part-time assistance of regular examiners in the examining division. A plan has been prepared whereby examiners will be assigned to keep in touch regularly with certain departments, to attend all meetings of promotion boards, and thus become thoroughly acquainted with the work and personnel of the departments. The commission will thus be effectively represented by specialized examiners who are in constant touch with the departments. The same examiners will cover the same departments as far as practicable for purposes of promotion and other examinations. In the new service record bureau a complete set of cards will be maintained giving the duties of all employees, prepared alphabetically by the bureau of standards and which will be kept up-to-date currently to serve as a basis to check the performance of duties under proper titles.

12 Statistics are being prepared currently which can be summarized in the annual report, and which will be of great use to this and other commissions in preparing and defending a budget for general administrative and comparative purposes.

13 In connection with the development of the central payroll system, the payroll bureau of the commission was moved to the offices of the central payroll division in the department of finance, its methods of checking payrolls revised, new forms prepared, and complete co-operation established with the central payroll division.

14 In order to establish beyond doubt the identity of candidates in physical examinations for positions in the labor class with the persons actually accepting appointment, a plan was introduced whereby finger prints are taken at the physical examination and filed for comparison with finger prints taken in departments at the time of appointment.

Extension of Activities and Further Plans for Progress

Executive Direction of the Commission

It would be desirable to consider carefully, with a view to getting the necessary legislation, the possibility of reducing the executive officers of the commission to three, one of whom should act as secretary and be a permanent employee in the competitive class, the other two commissioners having overlapping terms of four years each.

The present division of administrative work among the three commissioners seems to be sound, one commissioner supervising the examining divisions and examination work, another supervising all administrative and business machinery, the clerical forces, the budget, personnel, all expenditures for salaries, equipment, supplies and repairs, and the installation and supervision of the new service record system; the third commissioner acting as the committee on appeals, transfers, reinstatements, changes of title and the like. The commissioner last mentioned should also take up the supervision of secretarial work if the secretaryship and one of the commissionerships are combined.

In the interest of efficient civil service in municipal government there is need in some cases for revising the civil service law and rules to keep pace with improvements and higher standards in administrative departments. Something more is required in the civil service at the present time than solely to protect public employment from politics. Members of the commission should have more detailed knowledge of problems of administrative or departmental machinery and of the plans of department heads. Considering that the commission, at the beginning of the present administration, was face to face with the more urgent and fundamental problems discussed in the preceding pages, a great deal has been done toward meeting the needs of departments. With the additions made to the examining force, the improvements in procedure, business methods, forms and equipment within the commission, the organization of the new service record division, and with the closer co-operation of the commission with representatives of the board of estimate and apportionment, it will be able to consider the administrative problems of city departments more effectively in the future.

Centralization of Clerical Units

The following scheme for reorganizing the clerical units of the commission involves many practical difficulties if all the readjustments indicated are to be made at once. Most of these difficulties, however, are due to the fact that particular individuals will be affected, either by elimination of positions or by a reduction of authority, which would necessitate reappraisal by the bureau of standards, and that the physical arrangements regarding rooms and floor space do not lend themselves easily to rearrangements. The plan is therefore proposed as an ideal scheme, taking no account of individuals and assuming that the head of the consolidated clerical division will be properly equipped to maintain close supervision and to perform all the functions required of a chief clerk, and also that the physical difficulties can be coped with. The plan will probably have to be modified in detail to fit conditions as they exist at present in the commission.

Essential Features of Proposed Plan

The proposal contemplates grouping the units at present known as the office of the chief clerk, the mailing and filing room, the certification bureau and the application bureau in a single large office. The essential features of the plan are as follows:

1 A chief clerk will have immediate supervision over all the employees of the clerical division and will be responsible for all the work of this division. The five groups of functions noted in "2" do not require five separate offices, each under a highly paid head, provided close supervision is maintained by the person in charge of the whole division.

2 The functions of the clerical division will be divided into five groups:
 a Receipt and handling of applications
 b Making certifications and recording appointments
 c Handling incoming and outgoing mail, including notices to candidates; filing correspondence and keeping up rosters and various other card indexes
 d Audit, accounts, purchases and stores
 e Central stenographic

3 The work of the application bureau will be so greatly diminished by the consolidation of the roster work that it could hardly be called a distinct bureau. The employees who devote the greater part of their time to receipting, checking and recording applications ought to work merely as a functional group under the chief clerk.

4 The work of the certification bureau, which is hardly sufficient for a separate office, should be co-ordinated, as planned, with the other clerical work of the commission, a separate functional group of employees being assigned specifically to these duties.

5 The work of keeping up the rosters and of handling incoming and outgoing correspondence, at present carried on in the office of the chief clerk, the mailing and filing room, the application bureau and the certification bureau, would be consolidated under the immediate supervision of the chief clerk.

6 The work of purchasing and handling supplies would be consolidated with the accounting work of the chief clerk. At present, purchasing is distributed between the mailing and filing room and the chief clerk's office and stores are handled by the person in charge of the mailing and filing room. It seems logical to gather all these various functions into a single group. They should properly be under the immediate supervision of the chief clerk.

7 A central stenographic bureau would be organized in charge of a head stenographer responsible to the chief clerk. The physical layout of the building does not permit locating this bureau near the proposed clerical office. Even if this were possible, a more central location is desirable. It is not thought that any laxness in supervision will result, provided the head stenographer is held strictly responsible for the work of the bureau. There would be twelve stenographers and typists in this bureau.

8 The offices noted, with the exception of the stenographic division, would be located in the rooms now occupied by the application, investigation and service record bureaus. It may be impracticable to place this group of offices in a single room. In that case, glass partitions should be used.

Savings in Expenditure

The present force is composed of the following employees:

1 Chief clerk	$3,000 00
2 Clerks at $2,100	4,200 00
1 Clerk	1,650 00
1 Clerk	1,500 00
1 Clerk	1,350 00
2 Clerks at $1,200	2,400 00
1 Clerk	1,050 00
2 Clerks at $1,020	2,040 00
3 Clerks at $750	2,250 00
3 Clerks at $540	1,620 00
1 Clerk	480 00
2 Clerks at $360	720 00
3 Clerks at $300	900 00
1 Stenographer	1,800 00
3 Stenographers at $1,500	4,500 00
1 Stenographer	1,320 00
3 Stenographers at $1,200	3,600 00
1 Stenographer	960 00
2 Stenographers at $900	1,800 00
3 Stenographers at $780	2,340 00
1 Stenographer	720 00
1 Stenotypist	840 00
1 Dictaphone Copyist	600 00
Total	$41,640 00

The proper distribution of force can be determined only after careful investigation of all the operations to be performed and the volume of work to be done in connection with each. It will doubtless be found possible to simplify many operations, to dispense with certain files and to make other changes in methods and procedure which could not be made under the present organization and location of the clerical units.

A preliminary study of the problem indicates that the work can be done with a force consisting of:

	Minimum	Maximum
1 Senior clerk	$1,980	$2,580
3 Clerks	3,960	5,400
4 Assistant clerks	3,360	4,800
8 Junior clerks	4,720	5,760
3 Office boys	900	1,440
1 Senior stenographer	1,320	1,800
1 Senior stenographer	1,320	1,680
4 Stenographers	3,840	4,800
4 Junior stenographers	2,880	3,600
2 Typists	1,680	2,040
2 Junior typists	1,200	1,560
Total	$27,160	$35,460

The minimum payroll on this basis would be $27,160, the maximum $35,460. It is probable that the actual payroll under normal conditions would be about $30,000, indicating a saving of about $12,000.

Immediate Steps to be Taken

It is, of course, realized that this plan, while it is entirely logical and would probably be adopted by a private corporation under the same need for economy as the city, would work injustice to a number of individual employees if put into immediate effect. It is therefore recommended that the commission adopt such a scheme as an ideal toward which to work, and that **the following definite steps be taken at once:**

1 Relocate the clerical units as recommended.
2 Give the chief clerk immediate supervision over the work of the consolidated clerical units and hold him entirely responsible.
3 Redistribute the functions of the individual employees, as outlined without, however, making any changes in the present force.
4 Establish a central stenographic bureau, using twelve of the present scattered force of stenographers and typists.
5 Utilize every opportunity to reduce the present force to the limits set in the proposed plan, and make this plan the basis for acting on every vacancy, request for increase, etc.
6 Notify employees of the proposed plan in order that they may make such arrangements for continuance or transfer as may seem to them desirable in view of the conditions and opportunities in the commission.

Extension of Control Over Non-Competitive Appointments

There are a large number of non-competitive positions, especially position as helpers, artisans, etc., in institutions. The commission exercises a nominal control over these assignments, although it is endeavoring to increase that control through amendments to the rules and the adoption of new forms. Lack of an adequate force to supervise these examinations has prevented the commission from fully carrying out these plans. It would be desirable to establish in the commission a central agency for registration of applications for non-competitive positions somewhat similar to the registration of applicants for positions in the labor class. If such a plan can be worked out, the commission should open a roster of applicants for non-competitive positions and certify names from this roster to heads of departments. This certification would have to be informal, and heads of departments would have to be allowed some discretion in selecting applicants certified or other applicants because of the frequency of changes in non-competitive positions in institutions and the difficulty of selecting and controlling this class of employee. The resources of the Municipal Employment Bureau and other employment bureaus should be utilized in building up such a non-competitive roster.

Charging Fees for Examinations

It has been suggested that all candidates for original appointment should pay a fee ranging from 25c. for positions paying $900 per annum to $2.00 for positions paying over $3,000 per annum. We are not, however, prepared to recommend this innovation. At all events it would require very careful consideration.

Proper Quarters for Examinations

Special efforts should be made to put into effect the plan, which has long been under consideration, of holding the larger examinations in an armory instead of paying rent for private premises. The principal obstacle is that of storage or transportation of desks and chairs. If there is no space available for storage in an armory it might be possible to rent space in the immediate neighborhood. Perhaps a co-operative arrangement may be made with other examining bodies such as the State Board of Regents and department of education for the use of chairs and tables.

Standardization and the New Classification

There are a number of problems connected with the program of standardization of titles, grades and salaries which will shortly devolve upon the civil service commission, and which the commission must be prepared to take up if the program is to be realized:

Problem of Amending and Interpreting Rules to Allow the Greatest Flexibility in Making Adjustments of Present Personnel to Proper Organization of Departments

The proper method of reducing the number of city employees and the cost of personal service is by abolishing unnecessary positions as they become vacant, by filling vacancies by transfer of employees from positions which are unnecessary, by consolidating the duties of positions as vacancies occur, and by other internal adjustments. The municipal civil service commission should be prepared to co-operate in every way with the agencies which are attempting to reduce the number of employees and the size of the budget, and at the same time to protect present employees by giving them an opportunity to earn the salaries which they are receiving. Sometimes it is a tendency of civil service commissions to take a narrow view of their function in this respect, and to limit this function merely to the protection of all employees in their present duties. Such a view generally serves to justify the criticism that civil service is a stumbling-block in the way of proper administration.

Problem of Maintaining Standard Titles

An amendment to sections 56 and 226 of the Charter was prepared making the municipal civil service commission the official agency in creating and certifying to the accuracy of all titles.* Thus the budget as submitted to the board of aldermen by the board of estimate would contain only standard, appropriate titles. Similarly, all titles in modification of the budget would be approved by the municipal civil service commission. Only standard titles would be used in all official publications and transactions. If the proposed amendment to the charter is not effected, provision for similar action by the commission could be made temporarily by a resolution of the board of estimate and apportionment.

By taking an official part in the preparation of the budget, the commission will obtain an entirely new and very desirable point of view on the organization of departments and on the necessity for economy. It is suggested that the following simple rulings should govern the creation of new titles:

1 The generic standard titles, such as clerk or assistant clerk, engineer or assistant engineer, physician or assistant physician, should be used wherever possible.

2 Specialized titles should be created only when it is impossible to place proposed duties of specific positions under the standard generic title. In many cases, it is possible to fill specialized positions by transfer under a general title where it would not be advisable to fill these positions from an open competitive list under the same general title. For example, many specialized engineering positions can be filled by the transfer of an employee performing similar duties under the title of "junior engineer" where it would not be advisable to fill the position by the appointment of the first man on an open competitive list for "junior engineer."

3 Specialized titles should be created as far as possible by adding a descriptive word or words, in brackets, after the standard generic title. For example, if a specialized position requiring the services of an assistant engineer conversant with fire telegraph installations is to be created, the title should be "Assistant Engineer (Fire Telegraph)" and *not* "Fire Telegraph Expert or Fire Telegraph Engineer."

4 All long or vague titles should be avoided. No titles preceded by the word "expert" should be used. Titles should not be created which refer to a specific department, bureau or other existing organization unit. If the department chooses to give an employee a special office title, this is no concern of the civil service commission provided the standard title is followed in communications to the commission, on payrolls, in the budget, etc.

The question of checking the performance of work inappropriate to title is discussed under the new bureau of personnel. The same records which are used in the departments and in the bureau of standards or budget bureau to maintain a current control of the work performed by each employee in the unit to which he is assigned should be maintained in the commission.

*This amendment, although approved by the mayor, was not submitted to the legislature because of the pressure of other bills. Pending its submission next year, a resolution should be submitted to the board of estimate and apportionment committing the board to the fixation of titles by the civil service commission.

Problem of Keeping Specifications Up-to-date

This function is more properly that of the civil service commission than of the bureau of standards, which will probably develop into a budget bureau to prepare, criticise and report on the budget, to control current modifications of the budget, to report on requests for corporate stock and revenue bonds, especially those relating to personal service, and to make studies of the present and proper organization of departments.

The standard specifications should be republished every year. This will be a comparatively simple thing if one person, preferably the secretary of the commission, is charged with the duty of keeping the specifications up-to-date by making all entries currently on the blank pages provided for each grade. Examiners in the civil service commission should be encouraged to report to the secretary currently all criticisms and suggestions regarding the specifications. The secretary should also hold conferences on the specifications several times a year, particularly before the publication of the revised edition of the specifications, with the examiners of the bureau of standards and with representatives of departments.

Problem of Maintaining Proper Standards in Examinations in Order to Recruit the Best Available Material for Positions Filled by Original Appointment or Promotion

This subject is discussed under the examining division.

Establishment and Maintenance of a Proper System of Service Records

The success of the system of advancement within grades recommended in the standard specifications depends largely on proper service records. This subject is discussed under the bureau of service records.

New Bureau of Service Records

The new bureau of personnel or service records has before it three tasks:

First, the extension of the new service record system to all departments of the city: This involves not only the preparation of final records in all departments, according to the new regulations, but also the adaptation and development of supporting records and the preparation of directions to govern rating officers in each department. It is not necessary or desirable to establish supporting records which will determine beyond question the value of an employee's work to two or three decimals. It is necessary to establish very clearly the relation between proper administrative records of work performed and time served, etc., and the final ratings fixed three times a year. A tentative plan has been prepared providing for the assignment of examiners in each of the specialized divisions to the various departments for which they are responsible, for the purpose of keeping in touch with the personnel of these departments, attending all meetings of the personnel board and sub-committees, and making recommendations to the commission on the acceptance of final ratings. This plan should be improved and extended as opportunities present themselves.

A much more careful supervision than now exists should be exercised over the records of the uniformed forces. The new records now being developed in the police department experimentally should be adopted by the civil service commission if they prove successful.

Service records should also be extended to the skilled positions in the labor class, and a simple semi-annual report should be required in the case of other employees in the labor class. Similarly, the record system should gradually be extended to the non-competitive class so that an employee's service record may be available for purposes of advancement within grade even where there is no promotion.

Second, the use of the service record system in making advancement within grade: The commission should urge the use of service records to determine increases in salary. It should co-operate with the budget-making agencies in bringing this about. The following are the most important considerations in determining upon a proper plan of salary increases for employees:

1 The city's ability to pay, that is, the plan must be actuarially sound.
2 It must encourage economy by department heads.
3 It must attract, retain, encourage and stimulate employees and reward merit.
4 It must be as definite as possible so as to give present and prospective employees a clear idea of opportunities for advancement.
5 It must be based on periodic service records reviewed by the departmental personnel board and by the commission.
6 It must not involve mandatory increases, but bring about a standard rating which should be higher in each successive grade.

Such a plan is being developed by the bureau of standards. It will involve competition among employees for higher ratings, and will immediately stimulate an interest in service records which has not existed hitherto. When all increases in salaries depend upon service ratings, employees can be depended upon to make every effort to get fair and higher ratings, and administrative officers can ultimately be depended upon to give much closer thought to their function as rating officers than they now give. When they are told that only the five highest out of a group of ten employees can receive an increase and that the determination of relative standing is made in the service records, the rating officers will recognize that they have a judicial responsibility which cannot be avoided.

Third, the establishment of a file of duties performed by all employees which will serve as a basis for a check on the performance of duties appropriate to titles: This involves a duplication of the system of records to be maintained in each department and in the bureau of standards. Duplicates of all duties cards in the bureau of standards have been prepared for the civil service commission. Methods must be adopted to keep these cards up-to-date. The only possible method of doing this is to have a chart of existing organization and duties kept up-to-date in each department for administrative purposes, to have a personnel clerk appointed to keep the system up-to-date, and to notify the bureau of standards and civil service commission of all transfers and changes in duties of employees.

The plan now being worked out in the health department by the bureau of standards and the Bureau of Municipal Reesarch, which involves the use of the index visible system should, if successful, be extended to all departments. It will not be desirable to use the visible index system in the civil service commission. The same information can, however, be recorded on cards and filed vertically.

The examiners in each specialized division should be expected to be in close touch with the personnel in the departments to which they are assigned, to check up periodically the duties performed by each employee, and to report to the commission all complaints. Up to the present time the commission has had no specifications to guide it in determining the duties appropriate to each position, and has made investigations only upon complaint of disgruntled employees or through some other chance advice or information. In future, the specifications with such additions or notes as may be made should determine the duties of each position, and the file of duties of employees should serve as a current check upon the performance of duties appropriate to titles.

Publications

The following material should be gathered together and published:

1 A complete, revised edition of the rules and regulations incorporating the new standard classification and new rules governing promotion, transfer, etc. The revised edition should be a simplification of the present rules and regulations and should restate clearly such passages as are now ambiguous or hazy. A number of new rules and regulations should also be added, governing oral examinations and other improvements in examination work.

2 The minutes of meetings are now being indexed currently. Simple rules should be drawn up stating the more important principles governing the action of the commission in enforcing the rules and regulations, with illustrations of these principles.

3 Complete the manual which was begun by the commission in cooperation with the Bureau of Municipal Research, for the use of department heads, employees and other civil service commissions throughout the country, covering the purposes, organizations, powers and duties of the commission (including a simple and non-technical summary of the law and rules), examination procedure in the commission, opportunities in the service, plans for examinations for the coming year, a skeleton of the standard specifications, regulations governing service records and fixing standards, and an alphabetical list of positions, etc.

Trial Board

Following the recommendation of the commission to the mayor, a trial board should be established with power to try all important disciplinary cases, to fix demerits and fines, and to dismiss employees from the service. This is a logical explanation of the quasi-judicial functions of the commission. It is closely related to the whole question of the supervision of service records. It provides an administrative tribunal in distinctly administrative cases. In order to establish such a trial board it will be necessary to enact legislation adding to and changing the Civil Service Law, and it will also be necessary to add new rules for the local commission.

Examining Division

Organization

There is vital need for a head of the examining division with proper executive and planning ability. Another essential quality in a chief examiner is an open and progressive mind. A chief examiner should constantly try to apply practical business methods in examination work, and take the broadest view of the possibilities of oral and practical examinations, of engaging experts for examinations, of non-assembled examinations, etc. There is not merely the need of keeping the complex examining machinery running smoothly, but of developing new ideas so that civil service methods may keep up with modern business procedure. Under present political conditions it is impossible to do without civil service examinations. They protect administrators from political pressure, protect employees from favoritism, and serve to apply a single standard in all departments. But the necessity of over-emphasis on these purely negative features of civil service control is steadily decreasing, and the time has come to conduct civil service examinations on broader principles, more nearly like those which are applied by successful corporations in recruiting and advancing their employees.

Under present conditions there is need of one assistant chief examiner to assign and control examiners, and one to plan in advance the dates, clerical details and progress of examinations. Within the next two years there will probably be need of another assistant chief examiner to take charge of all engineering and related examinations. This position should preferably be filled by promotion from the present engineering examiners.

The examining division has been divided into four specialized units and one non-specialized unit as follows:

Division of Engineering, including work in the following departments:

Borough presidents
Bridges
Docks
Water supply, gas & electricity

Bureaus of the chief engineer, contract supervision, franchise, under board of estimate, the armory board, the park department and the department of street cleaning, also including all practical labor examinations.

Accounting and Administration, including work in the following departments:

Finance
City chamberlain
Commissioner of accounts
City record
All board of estimate reporting agencies excepting those mentioned above
Board of aldermen
City clerk
Taxes and assessments
Education
College of the City of New York
Mayoralty

Health and Welfare, including work in the following departments:

Health
Public charities
Bellevue and allied hospitals
Board of inebriety
Tenement house
Weights and measures
Licenses

Protection and Law, including work in the following departments:

Police
Fire
Correction
Law
Courts

Non-Specialized Division, to include all other examiners than those mentioned above who can be assigned at the discretion of the chief examiner.

At the present time examiners have been assigned on equal terms and are responsible directly to the chief and assistant chief examiners. It would be desirable shortly to assign an examiner to be the head of each division and to make all future appointments to the division on the basis of the needs of each unit and the special training or experience required. Promotions from Grade 1 to Grade 2 of the Civil Service Examiner Group should be made, so far as possible, on the basis of special knowledge of the work of a certain unit. The physical re-arrangement of the examining division providing for separate small rooms for examiners in the same group would be a great improvement over the present conditions.

It may be desirable at some future time to divide the work on a slightly different basis and to add more divisions. Examiners in each division should be held responsible for keeping in touch with the current work of departments or groups of employees assigned to them, should represent the civil service commission in all service record conferences affecting these departments or groups, should be prepared to report on all work performed inappropriate to titles, and should be ready to perform all work on original or promotional examinations covering their field which may be assigned. They should also enter on the blank pages in the standard specifications all criticisms or suggestions for the improvement of these specifications. This quasi-functional arrangement of the examining division should, of course, be flexible. That is, the chief examiner should at all times be able to make such assignments as pressure of work may require even though they involve transferring examiners in one division to work temporarily in another division. For example, it may be necessary to use a large part of the whole examining force on a police promotion examination. Examiners should not be encouraged to think that they can work only in the specialized fields assigned to them.

Expert advisers should ultimately be appointed by the commission under the provisions of Rule XII—6 in each of the fields covered by the permanent divisions. This would be a desirable extension of the present feature of appointing experts for a particular examination. For the time being it will be desirable to appoint an adviser to the divisions of health and welfare, and engineering. These advisers should be persons conversant with city work and of recognized standing in their professions. For example, it might be possible to obtain the services of a former health commissioner as adviser on medical and institutional positions, or of the head of the Board of Fire Underwriters as adviser on promotional examinations in the fire department.

Planning of Work and Control of Its Progress

The examining work for each year should be planned in advance as far as possible. Facts regarding unanticipated examinations, unexpected delays and other variable quantities present some difficulties which are not, however, insuperable. It seems a comparatively simple matter to anticipate the great majority of examinations, both original and promotional, and to fix certain dates for them. A program should be made of the regularly recurring open and promotional examinations. The proper life of the eligibility of each list should be fixed. It will then be known beyond a doubt when a list will come to an end. It may happen that some lists will be exhausted before they expire, but this occurs rarely in the larger examinations, and experience will indicate how often it is likely to occur in the smaller examinations.

The program of examinations should be prepared with due regard to the organization of the specialized divisions of the commission, to the number of examiners, the season of the year, the peculiar needs of the department, etc.

The plan of examinations should be shown on a chart maintained by the chief and assistant chief examiners, using the visible index or a similar system, which will provide for quick readjustments in dates, examinations and names of examiners. At the same time the control charts should be revised so that there will be one record for all open examinations and one for all promotional examinations, the whole history of the progress of an examination appearing on one page, which can readily be referred to during the examination and filed when the examination is completed.

Technique of Examining

Methods of advertising examinations should be still further studied and effort made to reach the most desirable candidates. This should be done at a minimum cost through the development of mailing lists, the use of bulletin boards, etc.

Although great progress has been made in raising qualifications, the commission should increasingly demand still higher qualifications. In order to allow flexibility to the commission, the qualifications in the standard specifications have been left very general. It therefore has an opportunity to create the highest standards which should ultimately be incorporated in the specifications. In as many examinations as possible there should be eliminating papers on which 70, 75 or even 80% should be required.

In rating experience for higher positions, no attempt should be made to maintain secrecy as to the names of candidates. In these cases the investigation of the accuracy of statements by candidates should be made not by the bureau of investigation but by the examiners who rate the experience papers. The examiners should satisfy themselves by whatever inquiries and communications are necessary not only of the accuracy of the statements but of the exact value of the kind of experience set forth, as indicated by the investigation.

Practical examinations should be extended to almost all positions in the labor class where skill is required, and also to a number of positions in the competitive class, such as "multigraph operator." The present methods of conducting practical examinations are very good. They merely need extension and development.

Oral examinations should be extended and employed wherever personality or administrative ability are important factors. The plan recently adopted by the commission which provides for definite factors for each type of position, numerical values for the various standard ratings which may be given to these factors, and rating sheets on which definite impressions of the oral examiners are recorded, should prove useful in establishing confidence in the minds of candidates and in guarding against unconscious favoritism on the part of examiners.

The use of non-assembled examinations should be extended. These examinations, especially in the form of theses, should be extended to promotion examinations for the higher positions in the service, such as positions of senior assistant engineer, senior physician, senior municipal examiner, chief social investigator.

The present system of promotion examinations is in need of revision. Except the promotion examinations in the uniformed forces, it is the least successful part of the examination work. At the present time the smallest administrative divisions constitute separate promotional units. Specialized duties papers governing the work of these divisions have been prepared for rating at short notice by examiners who have not been in a position to do justice to employees. The new organization of the examining division and the specialization of examiners should stimulate the planning of a new promotional system. As far as possible, promotion examinations, especially for the lower clerical grades, should be department-wide. In some cases several small departments should be combined for purposes of promotion, but this would require an amendment of section 16 of the Civil Service Law. For example, there should not be separate promotional lists for 2nd or 3rd Grade Clerks in the various small divisions in the civil service commission.

The more the promotional field of employees is extended the greater are the opportunities held out to them and the better able is the civil service commission to hold adequate and fair examinations. Naturally, in many cases the work of a department or bureau is highly specialized and promotion must be limited strictly to these departments or bureaus, but in so far as possible employees under the same title and in the same grade should all compete on equal terms for positions in the next higher grade in the same department or in a group of related departments.

There is an additional reason for widening the promotional opportunities, namely, that it is very likely that there will be a change in the form of the budget which will enable heads of departments to assign employees to any bureau within the department. This is not only a sound and economical arrangement as regards the assignment of employees according to current emergencies, but also provides a basis for teaching employees, especially in the lower grades, all phases of the work of a department and keeps them out of a rut.

Increasing Opportunities in Public Service

Pensions

No scheme of salary and grade standardization or of improvement in administration and personnel can be successful without a proper general pension system for the whole city. Such a general plan is being developed by the commission on pensions. The civil service commission should be in constant touch with the pension commission in the development of the new plan.

Practical Educational Courses for Present and Prospective Employees

The co-operative courses now being given by the College of the City of New York and the New York University should be only the beginning of a general system of public instruction for entrance into, and for advancement and promotion in public service. It is obvious that the city with its educational facilities and its highly paid administrative officers in all fields should be able to devise a system of public instruction for employees which will supplant the various private civil service schools, which are conducted on a purely commercial basis by instructors whose sole purpose is to cram candidates for an examination. The question of training for public service and the relation of original examinations to the work of high schools and college has been discussed in a pamphlet published by the College of the City of New York and in various reports of Professor Beard of Columbia University and of the Bureau of Municipal Research. Stripped of exaggerated ideas regarding the attractiveness of public service to persons of superior training and intelligence but without practical experience, the plan for a closer relation of education, particularly higher public education, to civil service has great possibilities. There are many positions in the service where a sound education, energy and honesty are the primary requisites and where such practical knowledge as is required of the job can be taught in training schools during a probationary period. For example, a City College graduate who has taken several courses in chemistry and public health work would with a little training make a far better food or sanitary inspector than the average man of forty who has had unsuccessful experience in a slaughter-house or candy factory. The director of the bureau of foods in the health department is attempting to develop a school for recruit inspectors in which practical instruction during the probationary period will be given. The civil service commission is assisting him by holding a proper examination under the new title of "health inspector." It is true that the field of advancement and promotion for inspectors is limited, but the initial salary offered and the possibilities of advancement in the first few years are superior to what the average graduate without a professional education finds in other fields.

Educational courses for employees in the service who seek to fit themselves for advancement or promotion should be studied in connection with the new classification and the new lines of advancement. The sub-professional service presents a particularly fine field for educational courses leading to promotion to the professional service. The civil service commissioners have already taken a leading part in the development of these educational courses, and the chief and assistant chief examiners should be encouraged to assist in this work.

Organization of Employees for Representative and Social Purposes

The Conference of Employees, consisting of representatives from the rank and file in each department, for the purpose of providing the proper form of machinery for discussion of administrative problems, and a recognized channel of communication between the employees and the executives, should be strengthened through the judicious co-operation of administrative officials. This general organization and the local departmental organizations should be encouraged to develop athletic and social clubs and be given all possible facilities for these purposes. The Women's Lunch Room in the Municipal Building should be run on a co-operative basis. All these efforts will tend to extend a civic spirit among the employees and promote the wide assumption by subordinates of responsibility for the efficient conduct of city business.

LAW DEPARTMENT

When the present administration took office in January, 1914, it found several serious defects in the organization of the law department. The most important of these are listed below:

Administrative Defects Existing

1 There was an excessive number of separate offices and divisions which had grown up in the department and which were scattered throughout the city in separate buildings. The main office of the department was located in the Hall of Records, Manhattan, the Brooklyn office in the Brooklyn Borough Hall, the bureau of penalties at 119 Nassau Street, the personal tax bureau at 280 Broadway, the tenement house branch at 44 E. 23rd Street, the division for board of water supply matters at 66 Broadway, the Manhattan office of the street opening bureau at 90 West Broadway, the Brooklyn branch of that bureau at 166 Montague Street, Brooklyn, and the Queens branch of that bureau in the Municipal Building, Long Island City. To a large degree these offices were formerly conducted without close central supervision.

2 The work performed in the bureau of penalties and the tenement house branch office was so similar in character that it was unnecessary to maintain the two separate organizations to handle this class of litigation. It had for years, however, been the custom to maintain these two separate organizations.

3 No audit had ever been made of the accounts of the bureau for the collection of arrears of personal taxes, so that the exact amount of such arrears and the amount of uncollectible taxes had never been determined.

4 There was no central, up-to-date index of the actions and proceedings pending in the department including the litigation of its several bureaus.

5 Collections of money were made by thirty or forty persons in different bureaus and offices of the department and there was no adequate centralized control over such receipts.

6 Each bureau of the department had a separate telephone switchboard and operator.

7 There was no reliable work record of stenographers, typewriters, process servers and other persons whose work was capable of exact measurement. Similarly, the daily record sheets of the assistants and other persons in the legal force were kept in a manner which made them of little value as records.

8 There was no functional cost accounting system in the department nor any statistical records from which the cost of each particular function or sub-function of the office work could be speedily and accurately determined.

9 The work of the Brooklyn and Queens branches of the bureau of street openings could have been performed without inconvenience to the public by the Manhattan office of the Bureau, and such consolidation would have increased the effectiveness of the bureau's work.

Correction of Administrative Defects

One of the first duties of the corporation counsel, therefore, was the correction of such conditions as militated against the efficient and economical administration of the department.

The completion of the new Municipal Building and the removal of the central office to that building made certain improvements in organization and arrangement easy of attainment. The scattering of offices all over the city had been due largely to the fact that the city had no central headquarters for its departments. In September, 1914, the main office, the personal tax bureau, the tenement house branch office, the bureau of penalties, the division for board of water supply matters, and the Manhattan office of the street opening bureau were removed to the Municipal Building. This made possible for the first time the effective control of the department by the corporation counsel, and so centralized the stenographic and clerical forces of these various offices and bureaus as to bring about a greatly increased degree of administrative efficiency.

At the time of the preparation of the 1916 budget, it was determined that a consolidation of the bureau of penalties with the tenement house branch office could be effected, and that a material saving would result. Accordingly, provision was made in the budget for such consolidation, positions were dropped, and early in 1916 the actual combination took place, saving annually over $17,000 in salaries alone.

During 1914 and the early part of 1915 a complete audit was made of the personal tax cases transmitted to the law department by the receiver of taxes since consolidation, January 1, 1898, and statements were drawn up as of December 31, 1914, and December 31, 1915, showing the exact condition of all personal tax litigation. For the first time there was thus made available an official and accurate account of the city's outstanding personal taxes.

Another change put into operation by the present administration was the centralization of collections. Two clerks were designated as cashier and assistant cashier, respectively, and a new system of accounting was devised with the assistance of the auditor of receipts, department of finance. All moneys are now collected and accounted for by the cashier instead of being collected as in the past by any one of thirty or forty persons and accounted for very loosely.

The housing of the greater part of the department in the Municipal Building made possible the substitution of one central telephone switchboard for the former separate boards of the several bureaus. This was done early in 1915.

Work record systems were devised and installed and the daily records of the legal staff were improved so that the corporation counsel now has for his information and for the records of his office a sufficient and detailed account of the activities of each one of his subordinates.

A complete detailed functional cost accounting system was installed on

January 1, 1915, which gives the exact cost, by bureaus and divisions, of each function or sub-function of the office work and in connection therewith statistics showing the actual work results. As a result of this system, it will be possible by a comparison of cost and work results to show whether there is an increase or decrease in the cost of any particular class of work.

The result of these changes in the law department is reflected in part in the annual budget appropriations and expenditures therefrom as shown below:

Year	Net Appropriation	Actual Disbursements
1914	$880,303.52	$838,095.77
1915	851,370.00	818,786.69
1916	831,085.00	....

A further saving not shown by the above figures has been made in the bureau of street openings, the expenses of which are paid from the street and park opening fund; the greater part of such expense is repaid to the city in assessments upon the property benefited. The annual payroll of the bureau of street openings for 1913, 1914 and 1915 was $176,120. This has been reduced for 1916 to $141,820, an annual saving of $34,300. The actual expense of maintaining the department for 1916 will therefore be from $65,000 to $75,000 less than for 1913. Including economies in water supply condemnation proceedings, the department is being conducted at a net annual saving of over $100,000. These savings have been effected in spite of the fact that there had been a substantial increase in the amount of work handled by the department.

During the past two years there has been much closer co-operation between the law department and other city departments and boards. The gathering of so many important departments in the Municipal Building has made this possible, and it has been the policy of the administration to encourage such co-operation in every practicable way. Whereas formerly it was the custom of departments to ask for written opinions on all matters where advice was needed, officials often now find it more convenient and helpful to visit the offices of the law department in person and obtain directly the needed legal assistance. As a result there are held every day many important conferences of this sort. The legal business of the city is now co-ordinated and the law department endeavors to co-operate with every department in the most friendly and helpful way.

A conspicuous example of increased activity and efficiency resulting from this co-operation is found in the litigation brought under the fire prevention law. The number of prosecutions since January, 1914, has practically doubled. Proceedings are now brought on behalf of the fire department to vacate buildings recognized as fire traps and guilty persons are proceeded against criminally as well as civilly.

Total number of fire department civil complaints acted upon during the years 1912 and 1913	1,100
Total number of fire department civil complaints acted upon during the years 1914 and 1915	1,954
Furthermore, during the year 1915 the fines imposed in fire department criminal cases aggregated the sum of	$19,313 00

New Work Undertaken

The department has assumed many new activities. In co-operation with the health department it has actively enforced the laws relative to impure and improperly labeled drugs and medicines; rewritten the Sanitary Code; obtained a large number of convictions against individuals and corporations for selling and offering for sale food unfit for human consumption; and has aided in preventing to a large extent the over-crowding of surface, elevated and subway cars.

Number of cases prosecuted in the Court of Special Sessions during the years 1912 and 1913	2,997
Number of cases prosecuted in the Court of Special Sessions during the years 1914 and 1915	4,545
Fines imposed in health department criminal cases in the years 1912 and 1913 aggregated the sum of	$61,270.00
Fines imposed in health department criminal cases in the years 1914 and 1915 aggregated the sum of	$67,088.00

Closer co-operation with the Court of Domestic Relations has resulted in more thorough prosecution in abandonment and bastardy cases and in bringing more actions to compel the support of poor relatives. In 1915 more abandonment proceedings were prosecuted than in any previous year, the number of such cases determined in the Court of Domestic Relations being 7,146, as compared with the greatest number of such cases theretofore prosecuted (5,591 in 1912).

The procedure with respect to the foreclosure of tax liens has been improved. At the various tax sales held since the amendment of the charter in 1908 the city itself has become the purchaser and now holds several hundred of such liens. The mode of enforcing a tax lien is by an action to foreclose. Before such action can be instituted an examination of the title of the premises affected must be made to ascertain all persons claiming any interest therein, as necessary parties defendant in the action. Frequently the examination reveals a defective title. For the average case a title examiner requires about one month to make the necessary search. The work has therefore proceeded slowly.

As a result of a careful investigation it was found that the large title insurance companies in the city, because of their extensive plants, could do the work cheaper than the city. An agreement has been made with these companies to make the necessary searches at a fixed price, and the work will now be brought up-to-date and action commenced to foreclose all liens where the amount of taxes is large enough to justify the cost of foreclosure.

For a number of years the collection of arrears of personal taxes had been treated in a most lenient fashion. No actions have been commenced against foreign corporations or non-residents since 1907, for the reason that no way had been discovered to collect judgments when entered. The bureau for the collection of arrears of personal taxes has been reorganized and actions have been begun to collect, by means of examinations in supplementary proceedings, the arrears of personal taxes on non-residents and foreign corporations upon capital invested within the state and upon personal property located within the state. The city's contention that defendants in these proceedings may be examined in supplementary proceedings has been sustained by the Supreme Court, at special term, and if the decisions of the Supreme Court is sustained in the Appellate Courts, it will be possible for the department to collect each year a very large sum of money,—possibly as much as a million dollars.

There has also been a change of policy in relation to applications to vacate judgments entered by default in personal tax cases. Such applications are now vigorously opposed. All persons applying for reductions or cancellations of claims for personal taxes are subjected to a very careful examination, under oath, and every effort is made to sustain the assessment. The policy of the department will be to occasion as little trouble and inconvenience as possible to those who have been erroneously taxed, but none-the-less to insist upon the payment of the tax in every case where the person or corporation has been properly assessed.

In 1914 a policy was inaugurated in the department of active participation in franchise and public utility matters in which taxpayers, householders and the general public have a special interest. The franchise division has investigated complaints of excessive charges by the electric light, gas and telephone companies, and improper service on some of the street railways, and has appeared before the public service commission, not merely on behalf of the city (as a user of these public utilities), but also to safeguard the interests of the inhabitants of the city and, as their representative, to take the action which has hitherto been taken by private individuals. A representative of the franchise division is now appearing before the public service commission for the second district, in opposition to the New York Central's proposed increase in passenger fares, and before the public service commission for the first district, to safeguard the interests of the city and of the public in the investigation now being conducted to determine and fix a standard method of gas testing.

Further Steps to Increase Efficiency of Service

Although substantial progress has been made toward the centralization and simplification of the work of the law department, there are several steps yet to be taken before the department can be placed upon a really businesslike basis. It will be necessary to work these problems out in detail and no hasty action should be taken. A considerable saving in salaries, rents and miscellaneous expenses could be brought about by closing the branch offices of the bureau of street openings in Brooklyn and Queens and handling all of this work through the central office. This would result in better co-operation in the bureau and would greatly enhance its efficiency.

The commissioner of accounts has reported in detail on the question of special counsel to county officers. If the board of estimate is given complete control over county appropriations, the abolition of special counsel can easily be brought about, otherwise an amendment of the charter will in many instances be necessary. The law department is sufficiently equipped with legal assistants to take over the added work of advising county officers on legal questions without increasing its staff.

A very important administrative change which should be instituted immediately relates to the civil service classification of persons appointed with the title of "assistant corporation counsel." It is strongly urged that the civil service classification in relation to positions in the legal service be revised. There are now seventy-five assistants in the "exempt class" in the department, the title "assistant" being applied to all positions carrying salaries of $3,000 or over. It is suggested that the title of "assistant corporation counsel" be used only for positions carrying salaries of $5,000 and upwards. This would reduce the number of assistant corporation counsel from seventy-five to thirty. The legal service valued below $5,000 per annum should be divided between the exempt and competitive class, paralleling each other with respect to compensation. In the exempt class there should be a title of "deputy law assistant," carrying salaries of from $2,250 to but not including $5,000. The corresponding title for the competitive class should be as at present "deputy assistant," with the same range of salary. There should be a title of "junior law assistant" for positions in the exempt class of the legal service with salaries ranging from $900 up to but not including $2,250 annually, and a corresponding title in the competitive class as at present of "junior assistant" with similar salary limitations.

The main reason urged for this change is the fact that the minimum salary for positions in the exempt class—$3,000—is too high and the maximum salary allowed for positions in the competitive class—$2,850—is too low. One advantage of the proposed change would be that it would not be necessary for the corporation counsel to pay to a person entering the service in the exempt class the sum of $3,000, but persons so appointed might be started at salaries as low as $900 annually. A further advantage would be that persons entering the competitive service would not be limited, as at present, to $2,850 per annum but their salaries might be increased up to but not including $5,000 without loss of civil service status due to a transfer from the competitive to the exempt class.

The final result would be that the number of exempt positions required for the law department would soon be reduced considerably below seventy-five, probably to not more than from forty to fifty, and possibly much less than that. There would be a saving to the city from the fact that persons in the legal service receiving salaries of from $2,250 to $4,500 would be willing to accept less in the competitive than in the exempt class and appointments could be made to the exempt class at salaries of considerably less than $3,000.

If exempt positions at low rates of pay are provided and if the salaries of competitive positions are increased to $4,500 it will be possible for the law department to attract to it young lawyers who are seeking experience in legal work but who have not taken the civil service examinations in the past for the reason that the choicest positions in the department are exempt and are not likely to be open to them. A system should be provided which would permit persons entering through competitive examination to be promoted to salaries of $4,500 in the department if they prove their worth, and there are equally good reasons why persons who enter as exempt appointees should begin with low salaries. The satisfactory solution of this problem is most important.

DEPARTMENT OF WATER SUPPLY, GAS AND ELECTRICITY

Functions

The department of water supply, gas and electricity has control over and is responsible for the:

1 Sources of supply of all water furnished to the city, including the care of numerous reservoirs
2 Quality of the water
3 Distribution of an adequate supply of water to about five million people, both for domestic purposes and for fire protection.
4 High pressure fire service
5 Collection of water revenue (amounting to about $13,000,000 per annum)
6 Inspection of water meters and their installation in places where water is furnished for business consumption
7 Regulation of the rates charged by private water companies, and the supervision of quality and sufficiency of supply
8 Lighting of over 2,700 miles of streets, 10 square miles of parks and over 2,500 public buildings
9 Use and transmission of gas, electricity, pneumatic power and steam, and the construction of electric mains, conductors and subways upon or under the streets (except where the public service commission has jurisdiction, as in the case of rapid transit lines)
10 Inspection and testing of gas with reference to its illuminating power
11 Inspection of electric wires, currents and appliances in buildings
12 Licensing of electricians and operators of moving picture apparatus

The department performs its duties through the medium of four bureaus, namely, the bureau of water supply, the bureau of water register, the bureau of gas and electricity and the bureau of administration. The total number of officials and employees is about 2,650.

BUREAU OF WATER SUPPLY

The work of this bureau is performed over an area of more than 600 square miles, and its duties include the care, maintenance and operation of two great watersheds, of nearly 50 reservoirs, lakes and ponds, 150 miles of aqueducts and pipe lines, 40 bridges, 1,000 wells, a number of sewage disposal plants, about 3,000 miles of wate rmains, 67,000 valves and 47,000 fire hydrants.

For years the technical nature of the work of the bureau of water supply discouraged any attempt at outside knowledge of its problems of administration. During the latter half of the first fusion administration, however, a much greater degree of co-operation between the department and the budget-making authorities was established, with the result that substantial economies were effected and a precedent created for the supervision of even its technical work by some independent agency. The present administration insured the continuance and development of this co-operation between the financial authorities and the department and its bureaus.

Defective Administrative Methods and Effort to Correct Them

It was necessary that there should be this co-operation, for several serious defects in organization and practice had heretofore come to light and needed correction. Chief among these was the long-standing practice of charging to corporate stock a large part of the department's engineering payrolls. The engineering cost paid from corporate stock was altogether disproportionate to the amount of new construction work.

Another abuse which had developed in the department's administrative procedure was the practice of charging against corporate stock funds much of the material used in maintenance and repair work. In addition, the department had failed to reduce its technical force as occasion permitted. This was due in considerable measure to the fact that new employees taken on for special work were retained in the service even after the work was completed. It was also due to the absorption of the Aqueduct Commission's force and a part of the special filtration project organization.

Two other major defects at the time of the present administration's assumption of office were the improper housing, inefficient organization and inadequate equipment of the repair companies, and the loose stores and audit systems.

Immediate steps were taken to correct these defects and others that manifested themselves from time to time. Positions formerly paid from corporate stock were dropped completely or transferred to tax levy or water revenue accounts, so that the 1916 budget contains corporate stock schedules of only $61,250 as compared with $458,257.71 in the 1914 budget.

This is partly due to the fact that more construction work was under way in 1914, but the larger portion was due to the old practice of charging overhead expenses to corporate stock. The only corporate stock personal service schedules appearing in the 1916 budget are $47,560 for the construction force and $13,700 for one-half of the designing bureau force, while the 1914 budget provided corporate stock allowances for about one-third of the executive schedule, three-quarters of the designing schedule, all of the construction schedule, one-fourth of the labor force of the water distribution schedule, one-third of the laboratory force, and about one-third of the force engaged in the purchase and storage of supplies. At the same time that this reduction in corporate stock salary appropriations was effected, the total appropriations for personal service from all funds have been decreased by about $444,000, even though much of the former corporate stock payroll cost is now borne by tax levy or water revenue funds. The work of the department is now so organized that the entire cost of the force necessary for its operation and maintenance is met from current funds. The same is true of the purchase of supplies and materials. Prior to 1915 practically all of the pipe, valves, hydrants, etc., used for repair and replacement work were purchased from issues of corporate stock, while the 1916 budget provides tax levy funds for such work.

An index of the curtailment of corporate stock activities is afforded by a comparison of the balances in corporate stock accounts on January 1, 1914, and on January 1, 1916. On the former date there were 72 corporate stock accounts with balances aggregating $3,290,000. On the latter date there were but 22 accounts with balances of only $828,000.

Considerable improvement has been effected in the housing of the department's repair gangs. Two of the companies have been moved from unsatisfactory quarters and consolidated with other companies. Furthermore, good progress has been made in substituting city-owned motor equipment for hired teams, thereby increasing the effectiveness of the repair work and bringing about economies in wages and transportation expense. In addition, steps have been taken to reorganize the stores system. The number of store yards has been greatly decreased and a central control established which minimizes the possibility of supplies being purchased for one borough when an excessive amount of the same article is on hand in another borough. This work was inaugurated prior to 1914 and has been continued by the present administration.

Conservation of Water Supply

In addition to these matters of internal reorganization, the department is concerned with the very important problems of detecting and preventing water waste, and guarding the water supply from pollution. This work was started prior to 1914, but considerable improvement has been made since 1914, particularly in sanitary control. The detection and prevention of water waste is important because under present conditions much of the water is pumped and any saving in consumption means a direct saving in money; also, a reduction in consumption means a postponement of the time when pumping must be resumed or new sources of supply sought. At the time of preparing the 1915 budget, a considerable extension of water waste prevention work, and a material increase in the sanitary inspection force on the Croton Water Shed were recommended. It was also recommended that a systematic study be made of the quantities of water distributed from aqueducts and reservoirs throughout the distribution system, so that a definite knowledge could be obtained of the districts within which waste occurred.

To illustrate the results that may be obtained from careful water waste inspection and correction, the following table, showing average daily consumption per capita and results obtained in Brooklyn, is submitted.

	Average Daily Consumption Per Capita
1910	97 gallons
1911	92 gallons
1912	91 gallons
1913	78 gallons
1914	81 gallons
1915	76 gallons

Waste Channel—Main Dam—Croton Falls Reservoir

With reference to the work of water waste detection, the chief engineer of the department has estimated for the commissioner that the net return to the city for each inspector employed on this work is about $7.75 per day.

The 1916 budget also provides for additional sanitary inspectors on the Croton Water Shed. There is now available an appropriation for thirty-three such inspectors, seven more than were provided for in 1915.

Extensions in Work Program

At the same time that these changes were effected in the administrative organization of the bureau, several important extensions of activity had been started. The distribution system has been extended and the high pressure fire service system has been completed up to 34th Street. In addition, the new Grant City pumping station plant in Richmond has been put into operation. Of course the chief work of extending the water supply system of the city falls to the board of water supply, which is constructing and bringing to rapid completion the new Catskill Aqueduct. When the Catskill water is available for general use and the pressure in the city mains is increased thereby, the department of water supply will have to make numerous adjustments in its distribution system to take care of problems which will then arise. At that time it is probable that some forty pumping stations in the Greater City can be shut down, this being about 80% of the total number. The others will be placed in reserve, with the exception of the 179th Street station, the 98th Street station and the small Clove pumping station in Richmond. It will be wise to maintain a certain stand-by force ready to operate pumping stations in case of any failure in the Catskill supply, but the total allotted to such stand-by service should not exceed $150,000. The 1914 cost of pumping city water in all boroughs was $1,362,495, so that an operating saving of about $1,000,000 should result upon the introduction of the Catskill water system.

The department will, however, have to organize a force for the care and maintenance of the Catskill Aqueduct and the Ashokan reservoir and dam. Funds for this purpose should be provided in the 1917 budget. The greater portion of the Catskill Aqueduct has been completed for two years or more, but the maintenance during that time of buildings and structures, together with the care of the land, has been paid for from corporate stock. The department should soon be able to take over the portions of the Catskill system ready for operation and maintenance, so that the charge of this work against corporate stock may cease.

The above-mentioned saving of about a million dollars in pumping costs will suffer a gradual decrease after 1918 up to 1923, when the Schoharie water will be delivered. While the introduction of the first installment of the Catskill water will result in a considerable reserve in the Croton supply, portions of which can be made available from time to time for Brooklyn, Queens and Richmond, yet as soon as the consumption in these boroughs approaches the full amount delivered from the Esopus Shed it will be necessary again to start the pumps in The Bronx and later in Brooklyn, Queens and Richmond, which will have been shut down because of the new supply. The introduction of Schoharie water in 1923 will make possible the shutting down of all pumping stations in Manhattan and The Bronx. Furthermore, the completion of the Schoharie project will necessitate the employment of only a small patrol force about Gilboa Reservoir and the watershed tributary thereto.

The department of water supply is now concerning itself with definite plans for the distribution of Catskill water and the reorganization of its labor force to meet the new conditions.

A more detailed discussion of the work done in reorganizing the divisions of the bureau of water supply follows:

Executive Division

	1914	1916	Net Decrease
Budget allowance—all funds..........	$121,080.00	$89,920.00	$31,160.00

The principal savings in this division are due to the abolition of the former divisions of values and real estate, resulting in the discontinuance of the services of two division engineers, five assistant engineers and eight draftsmen. In 1914, one third of this schedule was charged to corporate stock, but the 1916 budget provides for charging the entire amount to the tax levy and water revenue accounts on the theory that no extra expense is incurred on account of corporate stock projects and that personal service connected with normal extensions of the system should be a tax levy charge.

Due to the efforts of the present departmental administration and the bureaus of the board of estimate, there is now much closer investigation as to the necessity for new construction work, with the result that the average annual expenditures for corporate stock work have been reduced by more than one-half.

Investigation and Design Division

	1914	1916	Decrease
Budget allowance—all funds..........	$58,540.00	$27,400.00	$31,140.00

The chief positions abolished in this division were one division engineer, three mechanical engineers, two assistant engineers, and seven draftsmen. There is no mechanical engineering work of any considerable magnitude now under way, and the stopping of most of the pumps at the time of the introduction of Catskill water will make the mechanical engineering work of this division of little importance. The purpose of reducing the force has been to keep the cost of the actual designing work within reasonable limits comparable to similar work elsewhere, and to allow a sufficient extra force to do the necessary amount of investigation on projects that may come before the department for determination. The force is considered adequate for all normal requirements, although the commissioner states that he has not sufficient engineers to make satisfactory progress on the valuation of private water companies. A discussion of the department's responsibility in relation to private water companies is included in this report.

Collection and Storage Division

	1914	1916	Decrease
Budget allowance—all funds..........	$345,790.85	$219,293.25	$126,497.60

The water shed work as at present conducted includes repairs to buildings, fences, bridges and structures, the removal of trees and the afforestation of considerable areas adjacent to reservoirs, the mowing of grass and underbrush and the general maintenance of city property. This work is entirely distinct from sanitary patrol. In the past there has either been an insufficient allowance of funds for the proper painting and up-keep of water shed structures or the allowances made for these purposes have been diverted to other uses. Increased provision should be made for the painting and repairing of such structures. A sufficient allowance was made in the 1916 budget to insure the painting of the principal bridges upon the water shed and the repairing of the roofs of certain gate houses, if the money is expended with rigid economy. Several gate houses and bridges and a portion of the fencing in the water shed are in bad condition due to lack of repairs. The maintenance of roads and bridges falls entirely upon the city, and as both require constant repair it is necessary that the money provided in the 1916 budget be expended for these purposes only.

Part of the poor condition of some of this property is due to the fact that money provided in previous budgets for specific repairs was diverted to other purposes. For example, money was provided in several budgets for painting certain of the bridges in the Croton water shed, but was used for such work as repairs to water mains or pumping stations, or some other purpose that the department considered more urgent.

In this connection it should be noted that the present administration has rescinded authorizations of corporate stock made by a former administration for alterations to gate houses and new fences upon the Croton water shed.

From an inspection of all water sheds it would seem that under previous administrations not enough emphasis had been placed upon the sanitary protection of the sources of supply. In view of the fact that the board of estimate has determined not to undertake the filtering of Croton water, it seems particularly desirable that more attention should be given to the sanitary work upon the water shed, so that every source of contamination may be cared for promptly. With this view the present administration of the department is in accord.

The reduction of $126,000 which has been made in the schedules for this division of the department's work is due to the elimination of many foremen, carpenters, painters and laborers engaged upon the water shed, and to the transfer of about $31,000 of the labor force to the distribution schedule. At the same time that these reductions have been made, however, the sanitary inspection force has been increased from 26 to 31, and motor trucks and motor vehicles have been provided in the place of hired teams.

For sanitary patrol the water shed has been divided into districts, each of the patrolmen having definite ground to cover. All nuisances are promptly reported and remedied as soon as possible. In order to increase the influence and effectiveness of the force, the men who were formerly in the labor class, have been put on an annual salary basis and are to be uniformed, the increase in salary being sufficient to enable them to provide the uniforms.

Pumping Division

	1914	1916	Decrease
Budget allowance—all funds..........	$830,442.20	$768,717.40	$61,724.80

The three pumping stations in active operation in Manhattan and The Bronx have pumped an increased quantity of water during the last two years, but the greater portion of such increase has been due to an extension of the areas served by the pumps rather than to increases in population. In Brooklyn the variations in the amounts pumped have been due to monthly or seasonal conditions rather than to a steady increase in demand. The systematic effort made in 1915 to reduce waste in Brooklyn, which resulted in the material savings mentioned elsewhere, has helped to keep down the pumping costs, while in Queens and Richmond there has been an actual increase in demands on the system. The question of pumpage in the various boroughs and provision for the normal increase is complicated by three factors: (1) increased population; (2) waste; and (3) variations in distribution areas. It has been urged that the board of estimate should be asked to approve changes in such areas, for the extension of a pressure area means practically in all cases that the increased pressure must be maintained in the extended area at all times, involving additional expense. **If the water department is permitted to change pressure areas at will without the concurrence of the board of estimate the increasing expenses of the department will be beyond the control of the board.** If, for example, the suggestion is adopted that upon the delivery of Catskill water the pumps in the 98th Street station be utilized to furnish pumped water in the area between 42nd Street and Chambers Street, the increased cost to the city must be borne by the city at large and the economy predicted after the introduction of Catskill water will be considerably reduced.

As part of the program to determine accurately the amount of water supplied to the various street mains, some meters have been installed at the pumping stations to check the pump movements. Repairs to pumps have been made from time to time from current funds, but a considerable portion of the pumping equipment, particularly in the Brooklyn water shed, is not worth extended repair, and with the exception of the reconstruction of the foundation of one Worthington pump at Ridgewood, no extensive repairs have been made.

As stated above, the great economy for the future in this department will lie in the discontinuance of pumping upon the introduction of the Catskill water. The future program of pumping in the borough of Brooklyn involves very serious and careful study, however, because of the increasing population in the borough water shed and the west water shed from which a considerable portion of the Brooklyn supply is now drawn. It seems to be only a question of time when the entire abandonment of the borough water shed will be necessary on account of the increasing contamination due to added population. Furthermore, it may also be necessary to abandon practically all sources of supply west of Milburn as well as all surface supplies east of Milburn for the same reason.

Some years after the introduction of the entire Catskill supply it will undoubtedly be necessary to take up again the question of the water supply from the Brooklyn and Long Island water sheds. But at that time the Brooklyn pumps will have been shut down for a number of years and the supply from the existing wells discontinued, and it is therefore problematical as to whether the repairing of pumps and equipment then existing will be profitable, in view of the fact that the considerable expense involved in remodeling the present stations might better be spent upon a new source of supply free from contamination and equipped with pumps electrically operated from a central station.

Distribution Division

	1914	1916	Increase
Budget allowance—all funds..........	$759,556.00	$773,976.50	$14,420.50

The increase of $14,000 in the 1916 budget as compared with the 1914 budget, shown in the distribution accounts, is due primarily to a transfer of a portion of the aqueduct maintenance force from the collection and storage appropriations to the distribution appropriations. This transfer involved about $31,000. Further transfers were made to this account from the construction schedule previously paid from corporate stock.

Prior to 1914 about one-fourth of the wages account of the repair forces was charged against corporate stock on the theory that during spare time the men were used on water main extension work which was a proper corporate stock charge. The 1915 and 1916 budgets, however, provide for the total wages schedule out of the tax levy on the ground that the force employed was the minimum force necessary for repair work. In general, city work is more expensive than contract work and, except for the spare time of the men required for emergency work, it is not economical for the department force to do construction work.

During the past two years new mains have been laid in all the boroughs of the Greater City. In Manhattan and The Bronx most of this extension has been for improvement purposes and not because of increased demands from consumers.

The board of estimate has recently made available funds for extension of mains in the various boroughs, and it is believed that in view of the early introduction of Catskill water these funds will be sufficient to meet most legitimate demands for increased distribution facilities, although certain cross connections and modifications of the present distribution system may be desirable when the Catskill water is available. It seems almost certain, however, that no very considerable expenditures for extensions of the distribution system will be urgently demanded for the next two or three years.

The department intends to give two important pieces of work special attention. One is the careful mapping of all important valves and connections in the distribution system so that they can be immediately located in case of emergency. The need for such information has been emphasized in the past two years by several serious breaks in sections where the mapping is not up-to-date. The result was a delay in finding the controlling valves and an unnecessary property damage due to the unchecked escape of the water. The other is the organization of a thoroughly equipped force whose entire attention should be given to the location of leaks from large mains in the various boroughs. The determination of the amount of water flowing through the mains in the several sections of the city is essential before any real control can be had through water waste prevention inspection.

An important accomplishment during the past two years with respect to the distribution forces of the department has been a readjustment of the repair gangs and their equipment with motor trucks and motor vehicles so that repairs may be made more promptly and damage through leaks and breaks reduced to a minimum. As previously stated, this work has been prosecuted vigorously and most of the hired teams have been replaced with Ford runabouts having box bodies, and with motor trucks, which has resulted in a saving of $86,000 in 1916 as compared with 1914.

The headquarters of the repair gangs have been improved. Several of the unsatisfactory and unnecessary quarters have been given up and the gangs consolidated. An incidental result has been a saving in rent to the city.

Construction Division

	1914	1916	Decrease
Budget allowance—all funds..........	$211,215.00	$47,550.00	$163,665.00

The large decrease shown in this account is due to a considerable reduction in the mechanical and water main construction forces on account of the lack of extensive construction work authorized by the board of estimate. It is also due to a transfer of some of the engineers previously paid from this corporate stock schedule to the distribution schedules paid from tax levy appropriations. In addition, many positions have been eliminated, such as a consulting engineer, 14 assistant engineers, 2 mechanical engineers, 10 transitmen, 4 draftsman, 3 levellers, 13 rodmen, 2 axemen, 5 inspectors, 5 clerks and 3 stenographers.

All these readjustments were made possible by careful studies conducted by the department of water supply and the bureaus of the board of estimate, resulting in the correction of the long-standing practice of charging against corporate stock the salaries of employees who were not engaged exclusively upon construction work. As pointed out above, the new construction work of the department has been growing less and less each year, but in spite of this decrease the payroll of the department until recently was not reduced correspondingly.

Analyzing and Testing Division

	1914	1916	Decrease
Budget allowance—all funds..........	$34,727.50	$25,415.00	$9,312.50

The decrease of $9,312.50 is made up of $7,500 in salaries and $1,812.50 in wages, due to the elimination of 5 chemists, 1 laboratory assistant and 2 laborers. The bulk of the work done at the Mt. Prospect laboratory has been testing water and coal samples. Samples of the water supply are taken and tested regularly and the treatment of the water with lime, copper sulphate, etc., is regulated by reports on the results of these tests. Prior to 1916 the department also tested in this laboratory all of the water purchased. The 1916 budget, however, provides only for field investigation and laboratory testing of the water supply, all the other work being done at the central testing laboratory. The typhoid death rate, which is generally taken as an index of the quality of the water supply, as well as the general sanitary condition of the community, was, in 1914, 5.9 per 100,000. This rate is much lower than that of other large American cities and compares very favorably with that of European cities.

Private Water Companies

An important function of the department is the regulation of the private water companies, which serve about 400,000 people within the city limits, and an area of about 85 square miles, which is more than one-quarter of the entire area of the city. Under Sec. 472 of the Charter the commissioner "may exercise superintendence, regulation and control in respect of the supply of water by such water companies, including rates, fares and charges to be made thereunder. * * *." These companies are not subject to the jurisdiction of the Public Service Commission or any other state or local body. Prior to this administration the department had never made any systematic attempt to examine into their affairs or apply the law to them.

Soon after taking office the commissioner received formal complaints from citizens of Rockaway Beach against the rates of the Queens County Water Company. As a first step in fixing proper rates it was necessary among other things to value the company's property, examine its accounts, analyze its rates and determine the relative costs of fire and domestic service. After much careful study the commissioner found that the actual cost of fire protection was largely in excess of what the city had been paying, while the company, to recoup itself, had been charging domestic consumers considerably higher rates than the cost of service justified. On June 1, 1915, he issued an order somewhat reducing the company's gross earnings in the Queens area and readjusting its rates as between fire and domestic service upon an equitable basis. This was the first time any commissioner had ever exercised the rate-fixing power conferred upon him by statute.

Similar work has been started as to the Citizens' Water Supply Company, the Jamaica Water Supply Company, the German-American Improvement Company, the Woodhaven Water Supply Company and the Flatbush Water Works Company. Much of this work is rapidly approaching a conclusion. As to the rates charged by several of these companies the commissioner has received complaints upon which he expects before long to take action. All of this work is being done by the regular force of departmental employees. It requires much skill and judgment, and in the case of some of the companies is extremely difficult.

At three successive sessions of the legislature attempts have been made to take the private water companies out of the jurisdiction of the city and place them under a public service commission. This effort to disintegrate and divide the control of the city's water supply has on each occasion been vigorously and thus far successfully resisted by the department. Since the purpose of this work is in part to provide a basis of appraisal of those private water companies that would be of use as parts of the city's water system, it is important that the board of estimate and apportionment determine upon some policy of purchase so as not to render nugatory much of the work of appraisal already done.

Further Steps Necessary Toward Satisfactory Administration of Bureau

The responsible officials of the department fully realize that much remains to be done before the work of the bureau of water supply will be carried on in a manner wholly satisfactory. Some of these steps have already been indicated; others are as follows:

1 The plant, or so much thereof as will remain in use, must be put and thereafter maintained in a proper condition. This includes such matters as replacing defective fencing around reservoirs, repairing gates, gatehouses, bridges, etc.
2 The flowing of all effluent from sewage disposal plants into potable waters should be stopped. This applies to the effluent from the Mount Kisco plant, however well treated.
3 The pressures in lower Manhattan should be increased moderately.
4 The high-pressure fire service system in Manhattan should be extended to 42nd Street and eventually to 59th Street.
5 The many remaining hydrants of obsolete pattern should be eliminated.
6 The work of securing adequate headquarters for maintenance forces and substituting motor transportation in place of horse and wagon transportation must be completed.
7 Land no longer required for water supply purposes should be disposed of or leased for a term of about ten years.
8 The taxation of the department's watershed property lying outside of the city limits should be upon a more equitable basis.
9 Further simplification of the bureau organization. Such organization must necessarily undergo some change upon the taking over of the Catskill supply, at which time a further effort will be made to improve it. In this connection the field of activity of each unit will be made as definite as possible and written rules established for its guidance.
10 There is of course the continuous problem of welding together into a cohesive organization, with one division effectively cooperating with another, the great organization of the department, divided as it is into different bureaus each with separate but interrelated functions to perform. This is a problem of personnel and management as well as spirit and method and is receiving constant attention with increasingly beneficial results.

BUREAU OF GAS AND ELECTRICITY

The work of the bureau of gas and electricity is performed by five divisions as follows:

1 Division of electrical inspection
2 Division of street lighting
3 Division of light and power for public buildings
4 Division of gas examination
5 Division of accounts

Since the present administration took office in 1914, great progress has been made in improving the method of conducting the work of these several divisions, and in reducing the cost to the city of light, power and heat purchased for its streets, buildings and public places from the various public service lighting corporations.

Electrical Inspection

The division of electrical inspection consists of an electrical engineer, in charge, 5 chief inspectors, 60 inspectors, 8 stenographers and typewriters and 22 clerks. **The force is entirely inadequate to perform the duties imposed on it by the charter.**

Under the law inspections are supposed to be made of all electrical construction and appliances in every building not owned or controlled by the city government. The staff of inspectors is too small to do this. At present the division relies upon the inspections made by the Board of Fire Underwriters, checking with its own inspectors only about ten per cent. of this work. As a result, certificates of compliance with the electrical code are issued in most instances upon the underwriters' approval of installations.

The division does, however, make its own inspections of theatres, schools, churches and moving picture shows, where the public gathers in large numbers, and it is about to take over the inspection of hospitals and department stores.

The division also inspects all overhead and underground distribution lines to determine their safety. In doing this the use of overhead lines is limited as much as possible. Wherever practicable the use of underground ducts is required. Such wires as are discovered *to exist* illegally are removed by the department.

Among the other duties of the division are the examination of moving picture operators as to their qualifications, the issuance of permits to those who pass examinations, the application and interpretation of the electrical code, and the examination of all electrical appliances and materials used in buildings. A new activity of the division has been added by the revised electrical code adopted at the initiative of the department, in July, 1915, by the board of aldermen, and providing that "no person shall install, alter or repair electric wiring or appliances for light, heat or power in any building except a person holding a license, special license or special permit." The board which passes upon the fitness of applicants was appointed by the commissioner. From November 1, 1915, to February 15, 1916, this board issued about 1,500 licenses, which brought in a revenue of $15,000. As the code gives the commissioner power to revoke a license at any time, a better grade of work is now ensured.

Street Lighting

The most serious defect, however, which the present administration discovered in the conduct of the bureau of gas and electricity was with respect to the lighting of streets, parks and public places. Street lights had been installed with no proper regard for uniformity of illumination or of

Illumination on Broadway and 7th Avenue, Below 42d Street

equipment. One of the most striking examples of this disregard for any definite program of street lighting is afforded by a large district of the park slope section of Brooklyn bounded by Ninth Avenue, Third Avenue, First Street and 60th Street. The streets in this district are used solely for residential purposes and the blocks are of uniform length, yet the following discrepancies in lighting were found:

5 blocks lighted by 3 Welsbach lights.
106 blocks lighted by 4 Welsbach lights.
85 blocks lighted by 5 Welsbach lights.
25 blocks lighted by 6 Welsbach lights.
6 blocks lighted by 7 Welsbach lights.

Furthermore, the distance from arc lamps at street intersections to the nearest Welsbach side street lamp varied anywhere from 75 to 200 feet. Not only were there these inequalities in street lighting, but on many streets it happened that extra lamps were provided in front of churches and public buildings which were in no way required for the proper illumination of the street. In Queens, 22 out of 194 churches; in Brooklyn, 269 out of 589 churches and in Manhattan and The Bronx 372 out of 711 churches had extra lighting ranging from one to seven lamps. These lights all burned on the regular schedule of 4,000 hours per year, whereas the average number of hours per year that churches are open after dark is but 400.

The elimination of these lamps recommended by the sub-committee on tax budget represented a saving of $22,530 annually. In addition to these examples of carelessness and wastefulness in the arrangement of street lights, the bureau had failed prior to the present administration to take advantage of improvements in the street lighting equipment which were being placed upon the market. Chief among these was a perfection of the nitrogen-filled tungsten lamp, which, because of its high illuminating power, was susceptible of economical substitution for the old-style enclosed arc.

Studies were made during the summer of 1914 by the chamberlain and subsequently by the bureau of contract supervision, as well as the department, to determine the feasibility of substituting these nitrogen lamps for the arc lamps on the streets. The result of these studies indicated conclusively that a tremendous annual saving would result from such substitution, and the budget allowances made by the board of estimate and apportionment to the department of water supply, gas and electricity for street and park lighting were predicated on the prompt substitution of the nitrogen lamp for the arc. At first this plan met with opposition from the former head of the lighting bureau, but as the superiority of the nitrogen lamp was incontrovertible the department, under the commissioner's direction, took up thoroughly the problem of making the changes and has prosecuted the work admirably ever since. For 1916 the city will pay for a nitrogen-filled lamp, giving more light than the arc which it replaces, $75.80 instead of the $90 which the arc lamps cost. At the end of 1916 there will be scarcely a single old-style arc left in service.

The appropriations for street and park lighting for 1916 are approxi-

mately $500,000 less than for 1914 in spite of extensions of service which have been provided in insufficiently lighted sections of the city. This is one of the most striking economies which the administration has effected.

There are still, however, further possibilities for increased economy and efficiency in the lighting of streets and parks. The department has already commenced to substitute on side streets 200-watt nitrogen units, mounted on city-owned posts, for Welsbach mantle lamps. This substitution will result in a saving to the city and will also place the illumination of the streets upon a more uniform basis and thus correct the inequalities previously mentioned. The ratio of substitution is about one 200-watt nitrogen lamp for 2¾ Welsbach lamps. As the annual cost of a Welsbach mantle lamp is about $22.50 as against $45 for the nitrogen lamp the saving is sufficient to pay off in less than two years the cost of the post required. These changes have been practically completed in Manhattan and the work will be extended to the other boroughs in the spring.

It is believed that where such substitutions are made in streets with shade trees, special attention should be given to their presence and, where necessary, mast arms used; otherwise much of the illuminating power of these lamps will be lost in the branches. To be most effective the 200-watt lamps should be elevated at least sixteen feet above the street surface, the height adopted by the department. The Welsbach lamp gives good results when only nine feet above the street, but is less economical than the electric lamp.

Another problem which now confronts the department for solution within the next two years is with respect to the iron posts now owned by electric light companies and at present equipped with nitrogen lamps. Under the terms of the old arc lamp contracts the lighting companies supplied these posts and of course still retain ownership. If the city owned the posts, the fixtures and the wiring from switch to lamp, an allowance of at least $10 would probably be deducted from the present bid prices of the lighting companies. As it is estimated that this equipment could be purchased for about $50.00 per post, and as the life of a post is about twenty years, it would be a very profitable investment for the city to make. The city now owns all posts on the side streets that are being installed in place of gas lamp posts, and should it purchase the former arc lamp posts it would be in a position to ask for a bid for current and a separate bid for lighting, extinguishing, cleaning, glazing and renewing lights. This might well result in very considerable economies inasmuch as the current cost for all sizes of lamps under 500 watts is less than one-half of the present total bid price. At present there is no competition for street lighting work. If the contracts were split as suggested it would be possible to obtain competition on at least half of the work.

Light and Power for Public Buildings

Early in 1910 the board of estimate adopted a resolution requiring all plans and specifications for the installation of gas and electric equipment in public buildings to be approved by the department of water supply before contracts for the execution of the work could be awarded. Until the present administration no attempt was made, however, by the department to adopt standard plans, specifications, materials, fixture designs or uniform methods of procedure, and as a result contractors, architects, engineers and city officials were constantly complaining of the unsatisfactory manner in which the work was being done. In 1914, conditions reached a crisis. About this time the plans and specifications for lighting fixtures in the new Bronx County Courthouse, which had been approved by the department of water supply, were assigned to the bureau of municipal investigations for report. After an examination it was apparent that the plans and specifications contained many errors and that the cost would be excessive. Conferences were held and the entire matter redrawn and the contract amended. This specific case, together with numerous others, led to the creation of the position of electrical engineer under the board of estimate and apportionment when early in 1914 the bureau of contract supervision was established.

The bureau of contract supervision and the department of water supply co-operated in the formulation of the necessary standards, eliminating many of the errors which had previously been of frequent occurrence, and succeeding in reducing the time which formerly elapsed between submission and approval of plans. It is still desirable, however, that the department should adopt printed standard specifications and should promulgate a list of materials suitable and approved for use in public buildings. This would make unnecessary the repeated examination of every type of electrical appliance desired. Only such materials as are not included in the list of approved fittings would have to be submitted and examined and as each passed the test it would be added to the list.

Another defect which was found by the present administration when it took office was the duplication of electrical inspection work. In some cases four sets of inspectors have visited buildings in which electrical construction work was in progress. The installations were checked by one squad to see if they complied with the requirements of the electrical code, by another squad to record compliance with lighting specifications, by a third squad to see if they complied with power requirements, and by a fourth squad to equip the fixtures with lamps. This duplication of work has been eliminated to some extent by requiring those checking the lighting and power specifications to see also that the code requirements were fulfilled, although there are still some instances where two or three groups of inspectors have been assigned to one job. This tends to cause delay and a division of responsibility which could be obviated by making each inspector responsible for a small district under a supervising borough inspector who should be required to be present at or assume full responsibility for the final inspection of any job. If these same district inspectors were required to read gas and electric meters, they ought to be able to detect any unwarranted increases in consumption because of their familiarity with their work, and by stimulating a spirit of rivalry a large degree of saving in gas and electric consumption should be possible.

During the past two years it has been demonstrated that numerous buildings were grossly over-lighted either because of units that were too large or because of too many fixtures. In some cases fixtures are installed not more than eight feet apart. If shifting electric outlets were not so costly, a large number of these excess fixtures could be removed and reinstalled in new buildings. This, however, could be, and is in a degree, being accomplished whenever other alteration work is under way in the particular buildings affected.

The size of lamps in certain buildings has been reduced and through a closer co-operation with other departments and more thorough inspection upon the part of the department inspection force a large amount of wastage of current has been eliminated. This is shown later in a table stating the cost of lighting numerous representative buildings during the past few years. In some cases the cost of lighting has been reduced to one-third of the cost in 1912.

As a result of a report made by the bureau of contract supervision of the board of estimate, in August, 1914, and of the discussion before the subcommittee on tax budget, the department advised the Welsbach Company on March 13, 1915, to discontinue the rental and maintenance service supplied to various public buildings, as the work could be carried on much more economically by the department inspectors, who now replace mantles where necessary on the few remaining lamps of this type much in the same way as the tungsten lamps are renewed. The maintenance cost paid to the Welsbach Company in 1913 amounted to several thousand dollars. The aim of the department is to eliminate as far as possible the use of these lamps and only keep them where they show a saving in operating cost over a tungsten lamp of sufficient size to give the necessary illumination. The tungsten lamp is at least as dependable as and permits of far more flexibility than the Welsbach inverted light.

The 1916 appropriations for public building lighting are about $300,000 less than the corresponding appropriations for 1914, in spite of the erection of many new schools, fire houses and other buildings for which the department has to supply illumination. **In the two fields of street and park lighting and the lighting of public buildings the department has therefore saved about $800,000 a year as compared with the 1914 basis of expenditure.**

The economies which were effected in the lighting of public buildings were due chiefly to a reduction in the size of lamps supplied to many buildings, to changes in fixtures and to more careful inspection to eliminate waste of current. In this latter work the co-operation of the city departments has been invaluable. The following table of comparative costs of lighting typical public buildings gives examples of the financial results obtained by the department's careful, systematic campaign to reduce waste and extravagance in the lighting of public buildings:

Building and Location.	Consumption in Kilowatt Hours			
	1912	1913	1914	1915
Manhattan and Bronx				
Bellevue Hospital Group................	....	1,166,640	1,136,829	904,945
City Prison...........................	....	251,090	189,460	167,650
South Ferry Terminal 39th St. Ferry.....	....	192,833	189,229	133,507
71st Regiment Armory.................	....	145,394	146,720	112,284
Police Department, West 30th St.........	30,216	21,673	20,304	15,379
Street Cleaning Department, 349 Rivington St..............................	24,967	24,673	23,566	11,175
Brooklyn				
13th Regiment Armory.................	85,764	50,890	57,520	56,640
2nd Naval Militia.....................	62,360	51,239	44,200	35,221
Cumberland St. Hospital...............	49,672	29,290	27,860	22,210
Kingston Ave. Hospital.................	49,521	50,183	44,025	29,352
Commercial High School................	54,100	57,404	47,745	32,469
Borough Hall.........................	51,040	50,490	38,744	31,832
Hall of Records.......................	92,860	100,559	80,226	63,498

The department has succeeded in compelling the gas companies to maintain more uniform pressure in their mains and has therefore been able to dispense with the gas regulators formerly used to stabilize pressure. As these regulators were rented and cost about $6,000 a year, the saving effected by this change is considerable.

Another considerable economy has been effected in lighting the East River bridges and the armories. Prior to 1914, the city maintained at its own expense the arc lamps for lighting these four bridges and paid at meter rates for the current consumed by these lamps. The nitrogen filled tungsten mentioned above was of course equally adaptable to bridge lighting. Accordingly, the substitution was made in 1915 and resulted in tremendous savings, as shown by the following table giving the cost of lighting the bridges:

Bridge	1913	1914	1915
Manhattan....................	$15,696.77	$15,212.23	$7,103.87
Brooklyn......................	21,804.03	18,490.38	10,684.67
Williamsburg..................	24,223.65	22,729.07	14,772.53
Queensboro...................	18,410.45	14,128.85	10,958.08

Similar substitutions in the drill sheds of armories have resulted in reducing the cost of lighting about thirty per cent. In most cases the saving in current consumption during the first year more than offsets the cost of changing the equipment. For example, the lighting of the Thirteenth Regiment Armory Drill Shed, by gas, cost during 1914, $4,805. Based upon the same hours of use the lighting by nitrogen lamps should cost only $924, representing a saving of $3,881 per year on an investment of $3,500 necessary to install a modern system.

There are, however, in the judgment of the department, a number of economies yet to be realized. At present there are gas radiators and water heaters used in many city-owned buildings for heating purposes. The water heaters are used in some fire department buildings for heating water in the fire engine boilers. As it costs more to operate such heaters than it costs to heat the entire building, the department is trying to eliminate all gas heaters and substitute coal stoves. Electric heaters used in some offices as radiators are even more expensive and should be dispensed with entirely.

The city at the present time enjoys such rates in the borough of Manhattan that it is somewhat problematical if a saving could be effected by the installation of an isolated plant, except in buildings where the load factor is high, the current consumption about 300,000 kilowatt hours per year, and the building operated for 24 hours a day every day in the year. There are in Manhattan a few such buildings owned by the city, such as Bellevue Hospital, which is ideally situated on the water front, where coal and ash handling would be reduced to a minimum. However, with a little pressure, the rate at Bellevue could probably be lowered to 2 cents per kilowatt hour, which is the Federal rate for buildings of this character.

Other places in Manhattan, where isolated plants might be operated at a saving are:

1 Blackwell's Island and Queensboro Bridge
2 Criminal Courts Building, Tombs and Police Headquarters
3 Municipal Building, Court House, Brooklyn Bridge, Hall of Records, City Hall and Court House

During the past ten years the cost of light has decreased to about one-eighth of its former cost, due in part to the higher efficiency of the lamps, and partly to the lower rates obtained from the lighting companies. While at present rates a plant might show a saving over purchased current in the above groups of buildings, in general, if a plant cannot make a saving sufficient to offset its cost in six years its installation is speculative.

In Brooklyn and Richmond where the rates are higher, it is much easier to show economies provided buildings of the proper size and character can be found. A few cases where plants would probably pay are:

1 Brooklyn Borough Hall, Hall of Records and Court House
2 Kingston Avenue Hospital and Kings County Hospital
3 Richmond Borough Hall, St. George Ferry Terminal, Docks and Ferries, Shops and Viaducts

Gas Examination

Among the duties of the department is that of "inspecting and testing of gas and electricity used for light, heating and power purposes, electric meters, electric wires, and of all lights furnished to said city and of the use and transmission of gas * * *." Section 522 of the charter provides that "The gas manufactured, furnished or sold as aforesaid shall be tested with reference to illuminating power, pressure and purity, in a suitable manner and by proper apparatus, at least once each day."

For the purpose of making the tests required by law, the department maintains 12 photometric stations, located at various points throughout the city. These stations are conducted by 9 inspectors at an annual cost of $11,430. Photometric tests, to determine whether or not the gas is up to the 22-candle-power standard, are made at least once each day at each station. These stations are also equipped with pressure gauges so that the department may properly audit the city's lighting bills as to pressure.

The work of the photometric stations is really a part of the audit of the city's gas bills. Any benefits to the general public accruing therefrom are incidental. The public, as a matter of fact, looks to the public service commission to protect its interests. The public service commission law gives the commission very broad powers with respect to the supervision of gas and electric companies, and the limited powers which the department of water supply, gas and electricity has in relation thereto are also included in the commission's powers. There is, therefore, a distinct duplication of authority. The public service commission has power to fix the standard of the illuminating power and purity of gas, while the department of water supply has authority only to enforce the standard so fixed. The public service commission may, in determining whether the gas sold to the public conforms to the established standard of illuminating power and purity, investigate the methods employed in the manufacturing, delivering and supplying of gas, and it has the right of access to the plants and the books of the manufacturing corporations. There is, therefore, duplication in work between the public service commission and the water department. In the commissioner's judgment, however, the city should continue the gas testing stations if only for its own protection as a large consumer.

In spite of the administrative difficulties in the way, the commissioner has been active since the early part of 1915 in attempting to reach a satisfactory agreement with the gas companies with respect to the quality of gas furnished as evidenced by the department's tests. The photometric stations had been reporting that the tests showed gas inferior to the 22 candle power standard prescribed by law, but as the statute as interpreted in the 80-cent gas case made inadequate provision for the enforcement of penalties, the commissioner found it difficult to determine what damages should be assessed against the companies.

After consultation with the corporation counsel and conference with representatives of the companies the department decided to withhold payment of 20 per cent. of the bills of the companies guilty of serious violations for the period under dispute. This action was taken as the first step towards reaching a definite agreement with the companies as to the amounts to be deducted from the city's bills for varying degrees of inferiority in gas.

Although no schedule of penalties has as yet been agreed upon, the effect of the commissioner's work has been to decrease materially the number of violations of the 22 candle power law and thus to improve the quality of gas supplied not only to the city, but the public.

Division of Accounts

This is not a large division of the bureau of gas and electricity. It is the statistical organization for the bureau and also certifies the bills for lighting submitted for payment. In the past two years much has been done to improve the control over expenditures for street and public building lighting. New records have been installed so that comparative meter readings are available as a check against sudden jumps in consumption. The division thus endeavors to act also as an agency for effective supervision over expenditures.

There does not, however, seem to be any adequate argument against the consolidation of the work of this division with the bureau of audit and accounts in the general administrative offices. Prior to 1914, the work of street lighting and the lighting of public buildings was regarded as the province of a separate organization distinct from the rest of the department. This idea has been outgrown. The commissioner is more and more directing personally the activities of his bureaus. There is greater co-operation and co-ordination, and it seems very proper to raise the question as to whether the time has not come to wipe out the artificial line between auditing water supply bills and auditing lighting bills.

BUREAU OF WATER REGISTER

Reorganization Work Prior to 1910

The reorganization of the bureau of water register dates back to April, 1907, when, in accordance with an offer of co-operation from the then commissioner of the department of water supply, gas and electricity, the Bureau of Municipal Research undertook a study of the activities of the water revenue office in Manhattan. After a period of some eighteen months a report entitled "Collecting Water Revenue," dealing with the methods of the bureau of water register and containing suggestions for complete reorganization, was submitted to the commissioner. This report laid the foundation for consideration and intelligent discussion of the problems involved. Subsequently, the forms necessary to operate the proposed system were prepared and submitted, but little progress was made until April, 1910, when the Bureau of Municipal Research, in co-operation with the department of finance and the commissioner of the water department, undertook to install a complete accounting system. This close co-operation, extending over a period of approximately one year, resulted in drastic changes being made in the offices of the bureau of water register in all boroughs. The results of the work were reflected in the records of the department. In the first ten months during which the reorganization work was prosecuted to the fullest extent, the city raised its water revenue collections over **two million dollars.** Through the efforts of the water department these results were maintained until after January 1, 1914. During the last four years efforts have been concentrated on introducing in the other four boroughs of the city the methods worked out and installed in the water register's office, Manhattan. The system is working now in all five boroughs, but there are some slight variations due to lack of standardization of the forms and procedure.

During the year 1910, a campaign was started to survey every property supplied with city water within the city limits. This work has been prosecuted intermittently. A large percentage of this work was performed prior to January 1, 1914.

During the years 1911-12, a special leak and waste campaign was inaugurated and was the means of conserving the supply at a time when a water famine was threatened. The results were so satisfactory that this work has been continued from time to time with beneficial results.

Several matters, by means of legislation, were placed on an improved basis. Among these may be mentioned the imposition of penalties on unpaid meter accounts which had applied to frontage rates only, and the changing of the water year (May 1st to April 30th) to the calendar and fiscal year of the city.

During the years 1910-1913, considerable work was performed in connection with the testing of water meters which undoubtedly resulted in increased revenues far beyond the cost of the work performed. Most of the meters tested were found to be recording inaccurately. Several were registering only a small percentage of the water passing through them. The meter testing stations were enlarged and properly equipped to handle this important work.

The physical arrangement of the offices of the bureau of water register in the various boroughs was given careful consideration and, in some cases, offices were refurnished. The laying out of the floor space on a scientific plan has resulted in the work of the bureau being conducted under much better conditions and with greater facilities for the handling of public business.

During this period the salaries and grades of employees were considered, with the result that this bureau standardized the salaries and established standard grades of positions even before the bureau of standards commenced its work.

A system of handling complaints was devised and installed and a complaint division was established in the borough of Manhattan. Since its inception this division has done much to avoid the friction formerly apparent between the department and the public; the policy adopted has now permeated all divisions of the bureau. The relationship between the department and the public is a matter on which the department prides itself.

The effect of the reorganization work performed during the years

1910-1911 is clearly indicated on the accompanying chart showing total collections from the sale of water for the years 1905 to 1915 inclusive. The apparent decrease in collections for the year 1912 was due largely to the changing of the fiscal year which necessitated billing for an eight months' period instead of a full year. If a twelve-month rate had been levied the collection would have been approximately as indicated by the dotted lines.

Accomplishments of the Present Administration

Organization and Personnel

During the first two years of the present administration much has been accomplished in eliminating unnecessary positions and in the standardization of salaries of employees.

The organization of the bureau has been studied in more detail than was possible in the earlier days of reorganization work, when there were so many important matters relative to public service which required attention. Instead of five bureaus of registry there is now one directed by the water register who formerly had jurisdiction only over Manhattan. The bureau organization is now practically the same in all boroughs, except that Manhattan has a division which controls the revenue received from water supplied to shipping for all five boroughs, and that some of the smaller boroughs have not yet established complaint divisions as separate units.

There has been a reduction in the number of employees due to the elimination of 135 unnecessary positions, the aggregate salaries of which amounted to $148,500 per annum. A further saving of $8,500 per annum has been made through the reduction of the salaries of 35 employees who were over-paid. On the other hand, 92 increases, aggregating $10,500 per annum, have been made as the result of standardization work. In addition, 33 employees whose salaries amounted to $35,500 per annum, have been transferred to other departments or bureaus. The total payroll for the bureau of water register in 1914 was approximately $680,000 as compared with the appropriation for 1916 of $498,000. This net decrease of $182,000 in the two-year period is equal to a saving of 27%.

Equipment

During the past two years considerable improvement has been made in the equipment of offices. Labor-saving machinery has been purchased with the object of reducing clerical service to a minimum. All equipment purchased has been of the type standardized at the time of reorganization.

Inspection Division

A system of preparing inspectors' reports in the field in duplicate by carbon process has recently been adopted in all boroughs. The saving effected by this change of procedure has amounted to over $15,000 per annum.

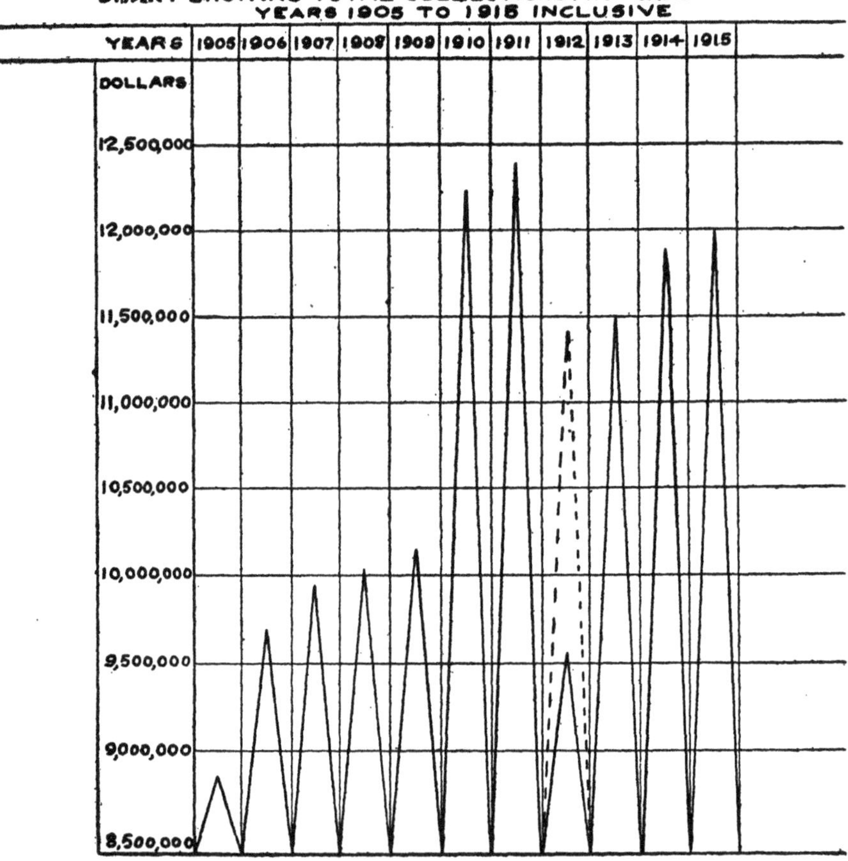
THE CITY OF NEW YORK
DEPARTMENT OF WATER SUPPLY GAS AND ELECTRICITY
BUREAU OF WATER REGISTER
CHART SHOWING TOTAL COLLECTIONS FROM SALE OF WATER
YEARS 1905 TO 1915 INCLUSIVE
YEARS
1905
1906
1907
1908
1909
1910
1911
1912
1913
1914
1915
DOLLARS
12,500,000
12,000,000
11,500,000
11,000,000
10,500,000
10,000,000
9,500,000
9,000,000
8,500,000

The use of the patrol boat " Croton " has been discontinued after several years' service. The operation of this craft has cost the water department approximately $8,000 a year. This expenditure will be eliminated in the future.

The establishment of sub-inspection offices has been the means of adding from one-half hour to one hour per day to the inspectors' time available for inspection work. This addition is equivalent to an increase of approximately 10 per cent. in the amount of work performed by an inspector. A reassignment of area allotted to district supervisors has been made recently.

Over 75,000 premises have been re-surveyed for water revenue purposes and for leak and waste of water in the last two years. This work has resulted in increased revenue, although the actual amount of the increase due to the re-survey cannot be definitely stated owing to the records not being adapted to show this information.

The leak and waste campaign, especially in the borough of Brooklyn, has progressed favorably. The accompanying table shows the amount of work accomplished in this regard.

Borough	No. of Premises Examined for Leaks and Waste	Per Cent. of Premises Examined where Leaks and Waste Were Found	No. of Premises where Leaks and Waste Were Reported	No. of Re-examinations Necessary Before Leaks and Waste Reported Were Stopped	No. of Penalties Imposed	No. of Penalties Subsequently Cancelled
Manhattan	15,220	68	10,330	15,488	507	7
Brooklyn..	131,502	48	63,815	82,960*	5,092	1,918
Bronx.....	9,404	52	4,888	5,843*	143	2
Queens....	9,275	24	2,201	2,850	59	4
Richmond.	14,071	21	2,998	3,604	123	23
Total...	179,472	..	84,232	110,745	5,924	1,954

*Estimated—exact figure unknown

The leak and waste inspection was for a considerable time conducted separately from the re-survey work. Latterly these have been combined, thus reducing duplication of work to a minimum.

Although in connection with the reorganization of the bureau and the need for economic administration several of the inspectors heretofore available have been dropped from the payroll, this division has made commendable advances. The inspectors as a body form an efficient organization and are doing excellent work.

Frontage Rate Division

On December 31, 1915, this division was handling over 250,000 accounts from which revenue was received. In addition, it maintains records relating to properties supplied by meter, exempt properties and vacant lots which are non-revenue accounts so far as this division is concerned.

The most notable advance is the new system of control cards which has been adopted and installed during this administration. These form the permanent record of each service supplied by the city on a flat rate basis. Full particulars of each supply are shown on one of these cards together with data covering all charges and adjustments. From these cards the frontage rate bills and the ledger sheets are prepared in one operation. Thus, a card acts as a continuous record of the charges for a supply, and the necessity of separately writing up new ledgers each year for each piece of property is avoided. This procedure has resulted in an annual saving of approximately $8,000.

Meter Rate Division

The division was handling over 100,000 meter accounts on December 31, 1915. Following out the policy established four years ago the transfer of the data relating to each metered supply to the new loose-leaf ledgers has been continued. Before the end of June 1916, it is hoped that this work will be completed in all five boroughs. This procedure was necessary in order that the meter accounts might be kept strictly in block and lot order, thus facilitating the work both in the office and in the field.

Extension of Policy of Metering Supplies

With the operation of the Catskill supply, the department must face an annual deficit of approximately three million dollars. To overcome these conditions and to conserve the supply, legislation has been secured, in the face of vigorous opposition, authorizing a more general use of meters as a basis of assessing water charges.

It is to the credit of the department that it has taken the initiative in this matter, and the legislation obtained places the responsibility where it properly belongs, in the hands of the board of estimate and the board of aldermen. Upon the action taken by these two bodies will depend the further adjustment of the basis of assessing water charges.

Low Capacity Meter

The department has also prohibited the use of the low capacity meter. It possesses chambers smaller than those of the standard meter, though the inlet and the outlet of the two classes are the same. The effect of the smaller chamber is that the amount of water available on the premises is reduced from thirty to fifty per cent., and the pressure materially lessened. Some of the complaints which the department has received as to insufficient supply of water above the lower floors are due to the existence of these low capacity meters in the buildings in question. Householders rarely knew whether the standard or a low capacity meter had been installed by their plumber and the department believes that the only reason why the objectionable low capacity meter was ever introduced is its smaller cost of manufacture.

The action of the department in abolishing this deceptive type of meter was most important and will do much to obtain better standards of water service.

Plumbers' Work

Plumbers' work ordered through the department is now awarded to some plumber in good standing located near the place where the work is to be done. There are no longer any favored plumbers, and bills to citizens under the new plan are averaging 20 per cent. less than formerly for similar work.

Hose Permits

With the co-operation of the police commissioner the revenue from hose permits has been more than doubled under this administration.

Recommendations for Further Progressive Action

Organization and Personnel

The position of general inspector may be eliminated. Certain inequalities in the salaries of employees should be adjusted at the time the next budget is prepared.

The system of promoting men from the ranks to positions as heads of divisions in the smaller boroughs should be made effective. This procedure should be supplemented by the transfer of men, as vacancies occur, from the head of a division in a smaller borough to a similar position in a larger borough.

The dual administrative control in the revenue collecting function which formerly existed is now supplanted by a single headship of all boroughs. With respect to this the commissioner states:

> "Every employee of the water register's bureau, in whatever borough, reports directly to the water register through official channels, i. e., the water register's chief clerks in the various boroughs. None of these employees report to a deputy commissioner any more than they report to the commissioner. There is no known interference by any deputy commissioner with any of the water register's employees. Written orders that there should be no interference were issued over fifteen months ago."

The abolition of the borough water registerships and the substitution of a single administrative head so long advocated was a commendable step and should lead to continued improvement in the administration of this vital function.

Equipment

The new equipment for filing the new system of frontage rate control cards is now in use. Under the new system the control cards are important documents and should be carefully safeguarded.

The proposed changes in the system of inspection reporting will necessitate slight changes in the internal rearrangement of the files now used for this purpose. An appropriation should be made to cover this expenditure, since the change will save in the first year of operation many times over the original cost of the new equipment.

The new system of prebilling necessitates the purchase of equipment for filing the bills pending their delivery to consumers. Considerable inconvenience and delay has been caused by the lack of proper bill files for the 1916 accounts. The suggestions here contained relative to the reduction of the size of the frontage rate bills should be carried out, the form of bills settled, and an appropriation made for the purchase of suitable files.

The substitution of steel filing cabinets for bulky loose-leaf binders would be a distinct improvement, resulting in economy in cost of filing and in the more efficient handling of the records.

Inspection Division

The most important improvement to be made in this division is the installation of a more detailed system of reporting the work of inspectors so that unit costs of work performance may be obtainable. The system of inspection is not being operated uniformly in all boroughs as it should be. It is also in need of slight revision and standardization. Effectively to administer the large force of inspectors attached to the department, it is necessary that the present system of reporting work performed by each inspector be kept in greater detail, and that comparative statements containing all the necessary data be prepared from information currently reported. In the larger boroughs steps have already been taken looking to the accomplishment of these recommendations, but to effect the same results in some of the smaller boroughs will be more difficult.

Some minor changes should be made in the methods of requesting and reporting examinations and inspection work. This recommendation is made in an attempt to eliminate duplication of work and at the same time to reduce materially the cost of the inspection work. This method is contingent upon the adoption of new inspection forms, and when these forms are provided the cards at present prepared by the clerks can be dispensed with, the information being inscribed direct on the inspectors' report.

In order that the comparative quantity and the cost of work performed by inspectors may be available, it is recommended that the monthly inspection report be revised. As an aid to comparison of work performance a "constant" should be established for each inspection district.

The supervision by inspectors of the tapping of mains should be eliminated. The tappers are employees of the water department and are qualified to perform their work without the supervision of a revenue inspector. This change it is estimated would save approximately $10,000 a year.*

The re-survey of all premises supplied by city water within the city limits can be completed under present conditions in the early part of

*Since this recommendation was made, the plan has been put into effect.

1917. With an efficiently planned organization, this work should be completed by the existing force before December 31, 1916. There are approximately 115,000 premises yet to be inspected by the 44 inspectors available.

The employment of inspectors at meter testing stations is open to criticism. It is considered that better results could be obtained if this work were performed by skilled mechanics. This would permit the inspectors now testing meters to be released for inspection work, and would help to expedite the completion of the re-survey program.

The assignment of inspectors should conform to the adaptability of the employee to the various kinds of work to be performed. Adherence to this rule and other suggestions herein contained, will enable a much greater volume of work to be performed.

Frontage Rate Division

The majority of the water services in the city are supplied at flat rates based on the frontage of the property supplied. These rates were established in 1857 and have not been changed materially since that time. The frontage rate charges are unjust and should be superseded gradually by the more equitable method of charging for water by meter measurement. The department is endeavoring to make this effective by means of the meter law recently enacted. There is lack of standardization in the forms and methods used in the five boroughs. Complete co-ordination of the system of records is desirable.

The rules and regulations relating to the supply of water on a frontage rate basis should be revised completely. This work has now been undertaken.

The form of frontage rate ledger could be improved considerably. The showing of the itemized charges on the ledgers and on the bills is superfluous. This data, unless kept up-to-date on both the ledgers and control cards, is misleading and the duplication of work involves the employment of additional clerks. All necessary information can be obtained from the control cards on which every change is currently recorded. These cards form the logical source of information relative to all supplies on a frontage rate basis.

The elimination of the detail charges on frontage rate bills would reduce the present expense of billing by one-half, would expedite the preparation of bills, would reduce the work involved in checking the bills before issue, and would enable the use of smaller ledgers of a design which would considerably facilitate bookkeeping. The detailed information now shown on the bills only tends to confuse the consumer and to cause unnecessary inquiries. As the charges on the frontage rate bills are the same year after year, except in the case of changes in a service, when the consumers receive a notification giving particulars of the change and the amount of the increase or decrease in the charge, there is no need for itemized bills. The department, however, does not agree with this recommendation.

To obviate the difficulties which arose in the first year of the operation of the new prebilling system, the preparation of the bills should be contracted for on a piecework basis, at a fixed price per complete and corrected bill. It is stated that this procedure will be adopted with regard to the 1917 billing. A large percentage of the saving which could be effected was lost last year because the work took so long that the appropriation therefor was exhausted before the billing was completed.

The various boroughs have been provided with files for the frontage rate control cards. It is very essential, however, that these cards be kept under lock and key, as they are original records. The main advantage to be gained from the installation of the new control cards has been negatived to a great extent by establishing these card files in the frontage rate division. They should be transferred to the control division where they could be used as a medium of accounting control. This matter is under consideration.

The assessment of water revenues depends largely upon the accuracy and completeness of tax maps. It is essential, therefore, that these be available in all boroughs and that they be kept up-to-date. Certain of the outlying boroughs are not at present provided with such maps. These should be provided and maintained by the city surveyor.

In order to build up a complete history of the apportionment of lots and blocks, especially in Richmond, the use of a card index file is recommended.

A change in procedure has been made eliminating the penalty memoranda which were formerly sent out to water consumers whose accounts were in arrears. The reason stated for this elimination was that penalties were imposed on meter rates by means of legislation recently obtained. The object of these cards is not only to prevent the consumers from being called upon to pay a penalty. The principal reason for their use is to keep a check on the cashier in regard to water rates receivable. They are the means adopted commercially to insure the integrity of collectors. As recently as 1910-1911 cashiers in two of the boroughs misappropriated funds of the city. It is not considered good policy, therefore, to eliminate this method of protecting the city's interests.

Under present procedure, over 100,000 of the accounts carried on the frontage rate ledgers relate to metered property for which there is no charge at all on a frontage rate basis. There is no good reason why these accounts should be shown year after year in the frontage rate ledgers. The accounts for metered supplies can be found in the meter rate ledgers where they are kept in the same order—by section, block and lot—as in the frontage rate ledgers. The control cards also are filed by section, block and lot, and show both frontage and meter accounts, so that there are two other places where these records are maintained. The new meter law passed in April of this year will enable the department to eliminate the metered accounts from frontage ledgers. This will take effect in December of this year when the books for 1917 are prepared.

Meter Rate Division

The procedure now effective in this division in the five boroughs varies slightly owing to incomplete co-operation between the various boroughs. Apparently a change in procedure was permitted in one borough and no proper notification of the change given to the others. This matter is receiving the water register's attention.

Several desirable changes could be made in the meter rate bill. It should be reduced in size and rearranged. Another form of bill is needed where more than one charge on the same meter is to be billed at one time and a special form of meter bill in billing "averaged" accounts should be provided.

The present form of meter-reading sheet should be discontinued and the form of independent and individual reading sheets substituted therefor. The latter system is being very generally used in commercial circles for the reason that no previous readings are shown. One of the greatest disadvantages of the present system is that the meter-reading sheets show all readings for the last three or four years. The proposed system would insure better meter reading than can be expected under the present methods of meter reading. The department is in accord and is preparing to make this change.

Owing to the constant additions to the number of meter supplies, some of the new ledgers are growing cumbersome. It is suggested that a reapportionment of the accounts be undertaken so that as far as possible work may be equally divided between the clerks whose duty it is to keep these ledgers. This is now being done.

The criticism made with regard to the transmission of notices relative to unpaid frontage rate accounts applies equally well to unpaid meter accounts. The valuable check which this procedure furnishes should be reinstated.

Permit Division

This division, owing to many minor changes, is now operating under a procedure which is neither standard nor effective in all boroughs. The forms and procedure should be standardized and established forthwith. Several of the borough offices have installed forms without reference to the general system. There is apparently little co-ordination in this work in the different borough offices. The re-establishment of the conferences of heads of divisions at stated intervals would enable the water register to make further headway in straightening out most of the present difficulties.

Wherever possible, charges should be pre-billed. This would eliminate the charge slips now used for meter setting, meter repairs, etc.

The installation of a card system with respect to properties on which leak or waste of water is discovered is suggested as a substitute for the present register of reports of leak or waste and unnecessary use of water.

The method of assessing charges for building purposes supplies leaves much to be desired. Several years ago an attempt was made to appoint official estimators of quantities, but without success. Efforts are being made by the department at the present time to adjust definitely the question of estimators as employees of the bureau.

The charges for water supplied for building purposes are unsatisfactory both from the point of view of the contractor and of the city. At the present time water for building purposes is not supplied on a metered basis. If it is possible to install a meter and the revenue can be fully protected thereunder, the supply should be furnished on a meter basis. When it is impossible to install a meter and water is supplied on the basis of estimated consumption at flat rates, the charge should be fixed sufficiently high to cover waste.

Collection Division

The collection forms and procedure are being revised as recommended, segregating the accounts to show: (a) income from the sale of water; (b) non-revenue items, and (c) other miscellaneous receipts. A few of the forms now in use could be eliminated, notably the present system of charge slips.

It has been the custom to refuse payment from persons (other than plumbers) after 2 p. m. daily, except Saturdays. This practice has now been stopped and the time extended to 4 p. m.

The transfer of the collection function to a central collecting agency for all departments of the city would result in a saving to the city through a decrease in the number of employees in this division. It is desirable that this be done for the reason that in some of the borough offices the accommodations are extremely limited. The additional space available, if the collection function were transferred, would facilitate the work of the bureau and at the same time be a convenience to the public because both tax and water bills would be payable in the same office. The department does not agree with this recommendation.

Control Division

There is duplication of work relating to the control of water revenues. In the office of the auditor of receipts of the department of finance, records almost identical with those kept in the water department are maintained. There is no necessity for this duplication, and action should be taken to centralize accounting control over water revenues in one office. As this is primarily an auditing function, it is recommended that control be vested in the department of finance, which is the official auditing department. The water department does not agree with this recommendation.

Charter changes and other matters beyond the jurisdiction of the department have affected the control division records installed in 1910. It is suggested that the present records be studied carefully with a view to complete revision. The allocation of revenues by classes and kinds of supply (commercial, residential, etc.) would be a distinct improvement.

The method of handling papers in the general file room can be greatly improved. Outgoing material should be registered to prevent loss of important papers. A new location for the filing room is badly needed in the borough of Manhattan, where the file clerk works in an inside room without windows or proper ventilation. Action is being taken to remedy these conditions.

Complaint Division

Some slight revisions should be made in the forms and procedure in the complaint division. This criticism applies more particularly to the form of monthly report, which needs reclassification and rearrangement. At the present time it does not show all the significant data which should be available to the administrative head of the bureau.

Conclusion

The comparative statement below shows, for the past five years, the earnings of the department from the sale of water and revenues from miscellaneous sources. It forms a valuable index to the department's operations.

Department of Water Supply, Gas and Electricity.

Statement of Revenues from January 1, 1911, to December 31, 1915.

	1915	1914	1913	1912	1911
Sale of Water:					
Frontage rates*	$6,327,702.50	$6,142,618.88	$6,005,010.43	$5,861,174.46	$4,150,569.13
Frontage penalties	184,832.69	158,072.32	140,509.89	87,996.96	131,457.24
Total—Frontage	$6,512,535.19	$6,300,691.20	$6,145,520.32	$5,949,171.42	$4,282,026.37
Meter rates**	6,308,104.62	6,354,037.60	6,301,171.98	6,212,971.99	6,019,111.10
Meter penalties	93,219.54	92,909.32	93,532.33	10,925.30	....
Total—Meter	$6,401,324.16	$6,446,946.92	$6,394,704.31	$6,223,897.29	$6,019,111.10
Miscellaneous:					
Building purposes	167,838.74	180,818.32	181,779.10	245,064.48	217,592.01
Shipping	46,087.06	46,220.66	43,982.66	44,842.78	38,496.82
Street sprinkling	4,795.10	4,867.31	5,372.32	3,844.94	....
Hose permits	20,335.00	19,232.62	9,835.00	6,545.00	....
Total—Miscellaneous	$239,055.90	$251,231.91	$240,969.08	$300,297.20	$256,088.83
Total—Sale of Water	$13,152,915.25	$12,998,870.03	$12,781,193.71	$12,473,365.91	$10,557,226.30
Other than Sale of Water:					
Miscellaneous Operating Revenues—					
Meter setting and repair charges	$6,481.33	$11,319.32	$15,004.56	$18,945.95	$21,267.70
Meter glasses	909.00	1,164.00	1,060.00	691.00	....
Pipe fittings	19.93	31.71	71.22	23.72	....
Labor and material	46,050.74	14,726.01	16,065.76	15,638.25	17,738.31
Taps and plugs	43,980.35	39,595.05	35,385.75	41,914.25	38,712.30
Locating taps	501.00	336.00	87.00	....	....
Meter testing	59.29	49.61	21.75	....	....
Sale of ashes	2,668.19	1,624.00	892.75	1,213.00	972.55
Sale of old material	15,483.92	16,137.56	8,454.62	2,620.30	422.51
Total—Operating	$116,153.75	$84,983.26	$77,043.41	$81,046.47	$79,113.35
Miscellaneous non-operating revenue	17,493.72	3,688.56	2,907.52	401.29	416.25
Total Other than Sale of Water	$133,647.47	$88,671.82	$79,950.93	$81,447.76	$79,529.62
Total Revenue, All Sources	$13,286,562.72	$13,087,541.85	$12,861,144.64	$12,554,813.67	$10,636,755.92

* Frontage accounts adjusted, for all years, to December 31, 1915.

** Meter accounts adjusted, for all years, to December 31, 1915, with exception of 1915, in which year there is included an estimate of the

PARKS AND RECREATION

Introduction

The problem that confronted the park departments when the present administration took office in 1914 was two-fold in character. In the first place, the need for economy in the conduct of the city's business made it imperative that every possible reorganization be effected which would decrease the cost of running the park systems without in any way impairing their public service. In the second place, the rapidly growing population of the city, together with the increase in demands upon the public park facilities, made it equally imperative that park properties be developed to their highest usefulness.

It was obvious that if the city were to have a comprehensive plan of park development some steps must be taken to work out a program for each borough in its relation with the other boroughs as well as with regard to local borough needs.

There were, moreover, other matters of administration to be considered if the park departments were to be freed from operating details in no way connected with the proper problems of park management and development.

The park departments should be recreational departments. Their efforts should be centred on matters of public recreation rather than on matters of engineering routine. Furthermore, they should be responsible for all of the recreational work of the city save, possibly, that under the control of the board of education.

As an example of what could be done to relieve the park departments from duties not germane to their principal function, it is suggested that an arrangement be effected whereby repairs to asphalt pavements in the parks be made by the borough presidents' forces. It is wasteful to maintain two plants to carry on the same sort of work in the same locality. It is no less wasteful to divide jurisdiction over comfort stations, bath houses, playground lots and the like, as is now done. It is desirable to centralize control over these activities under the park departments.

The only machinery that exists for co-ordinating the park and recreational work of the five boroughs is the Park Board. A discussion of its organization, of its defects, and of the work of the individual departments whose commissioners constitute the board follows.

THE PARK BOARD

The park board is composed of four commissioners, each of whom has jurisdiction over one borough, except the Manhattan commissioner, who also has jurisdiction in Richmond. Its duties are confined to making ordinances, awarding contracts and generally acting on the requests of the individual members of the board. These functions are carried forward in a routine manner. The board now requires, however, that each commissioner present the details and defend the need of each contract before it is acted upon, whereas formerly contracts were approved on the log-rolling principle.

The staff of the board consists of a secretary, a landscape architect, an assistant landscape architect and a photographer. The budget figures for the last three years are as follows:

1914	$30,349 00
1915	30,300 00
1916	31,475 00

The expense figures are practically the same as the budget figures, all but about $200 being expended in salaries, the office being administrative, not operative. The increase in 1916 is due to the transfer of the photographer, formerly on the payroll of the Manhattan and Richmond division, to the park board.

Administration

Theoretically the secretary of the park board is the executive officer of the board, but actually his duties are confined to the Manhattan and Richmond division. He is assigned to the supervision of concessions and music for that division, and this important work has occupied the major portion of his time. In addition, he has completed the recodification of the park board ordinances, bringing them up-to-date, and has secured the change of certain ordinances in order that uniform rules and regulations might apply to the parks in all boroughs. He has been assigned to keep in touch with park work in other cities and collate this information for the benefit of the commissioners. He occasionally represents the board at meetings and conferences.

The secretary should be assigned by the park board to study the methods and practices of the four divisions, for the purpose of recommending action by the board to secure uniformity of procedure and methods wherever practicable and to eliminate duplication of services. He might also conduct a publicity campaign for the four divisions to bring to the attention of the public generally the numerous attractions in the parks in order to stimulate interest in and use of the parks provided by the various boroughs.

Landscape Designing

The charter requires that the approval of the landscape architect " shall be requisite to all plans and works or changes thereto respecting the conformation, development or ornamentation of any of the parks, squares or public places of the city, etc." This has not been secured in all the boroughs. For example, only a few visits have been made to the Queens division during this administration, although in the meantime extensive development work of a more or less permanent nature has gone forward without the landscape architect's approval. Similar conditions in this regard have existed in The Bronx division. His advice and approval should always be secured when any permanent development work is undertaken. Most of the time of the landscape architect has been spent on work for the commissioners of Manhattan and Richmond, and Brooklyn, and his advice has been of great value.

In explanation of this apparent inequitable use of the landscape architect's services, the commissioner for the borough of Manhattan states:

" The Manhattan division has been under particular stress because of the great activity and large number of different points where operations for subway construction, or construction and restoration by the board of water supply, affect park areas.

" To make clear the park department's point of view, and limit the area of destruction, to secure proper restoration, and modification of the plans regarding gratings, subway entrances, etc., within the park limits, require a great deal of detail work and study, besides vigorous opposition at times.

" Furthermore, the same situation in regard to Manhattan exists with regard to monuments and their settings and proposed new park lay-outs made necessary by gifts to the city.

" These questions arise in a very large majority of cases in Manhattan borough alone, and the landscape architect's time is greatly taken up in meeting committees to secure a modification of their views and protect the city.

" It should also be remembered that the commissioner of Manhattan has felt obliged to call on the landscape architect for immediate attention in connection with matters of restoration in many Manhattan park areas which had been allowed to run down, before these areas became desolate and unserviceable.

" Despite these conditions, the landscape architect's time has been divided, by agreement with the park board members, so that under ordinary conditions the commissioner of Manhattan has first call on him for two days in the week, Brooklyn two days, and The Bronx and Queens the remaining two.

" The landscape architect is also subject to the call of all of the commissioners at all times whenever necessity requires. The only way in which conditions (under existing laws) could be bettered, would be by giving the assistant landscape architect sufficient salary and allowing him to do a large portion of the detailed work of landscape features in the field until the extraordinary conditions now existing in Manhattan shall have subsided, meanwhile providing a draftsman of experience to do the office work.

" It need only be pointed out that such questions as were raised by the proposed arrangement between the New York Central Railroad Company and the City of New York, made necessary many hours of work and study on the part of the landscape architect, but resulted in the new gifts to Isham Park and the new Dyckman House and Park."

Reorganization

This subject has been discussed from many angles. The time available for this survey has not permitted of any definite comparison of present costs with possible savings under a consolidated or a further decentralized plan, but several suggestions for reorganization occur:

1 Retention of the present park board and the consolidation under it of the accounting, engineering, forestry and recreation bureaus.
2 Abolition of the park board and the substitution of a single commissioner. Under him there would be a superintendent or an engineer of operation and maintenance in each borough in charge of the details of the work.
3 Actual decentralization with a separate departmental organization for each of the present divisions.

Under the first plan central control would be obtained. No great saving in money would be possible, however, and this plan seems to be impracticable. It is a half way measure and would increase rather than decrease any lack of harmony or co-operation now existing.

Under the second plan absolute central control would result. A considerable saving would be effected, notably the salaries of three commissioners and their secretaries and the maintenance cost of separate offices. It has been estimated that a total saving of $150,000 per year could be effected.

The third proposal would eliminate any central control. This scheme would preclude the possibility of studying and developing the parks of the different boroughs with relation to the park problem of the Greater City unless it could be done through an appropriate committee of the board of estimate or by a special planning board.

DEPARTMENT OF PARKS—MANHATTAN AND RICHMOND

Cost

As the following table shows, very considerable economies have been effected in the administration of this department:

Comparative Budget Appropriations

	1914	1915	1916
Personal service	$908,593.56	$914,758.50	$693,406.08
Supplies	81,926.78	68,849.25	67,030.50
Equipment	19,778.05	18,040.00	16,875.00
Materials	41,225.25	34,575.00	21,608.50
Contract or open order service	80,572.15	48,660.00	65,274.00
Contingencies	406.00	369.00	344.00
Departmental Total	$1,132,501.79	$1,085,251.75	$864,538.08

The reduction shown represents a saving of 19% of the total budget. This result has been brought about chiefly by the following means:

1 Consolidation of bureaus and offices and reorganization of the department's administrative work, saving $70,000.
2 Economies in floral display, saving $30,000.
3 Extension of motorization, saving $30,000.
4 Use of contract instead of departmental labor on large repair jobs, saving $20,000.
5 Drastic economies in the purchase and use of supplies and materials, saving $80,000.

Internal Reorganization

As an incident to these economies the work of the department has been rearranged on a much more practical basis. The stables in Central Park which were found to be badly located and in unsanitary condition have been removed to a more desirable place and supplied with modern equipment, and as indicated above the number of horses has been reduced by partial motorization. The shop work of the department had been carried on at several widely separated points and storage places were filled with junk and useless material while valuable equipment was left exposed to the weather. The shops have now been combined and placed at one point in the 86th Street transverse road, and a new system has been installed so that their administration and operation can now be carried on more economically. Modern machinery has been placed in service so that the work done by the shops has been increased at the same time that the labor force has been decreased. The store yards have now been concentrated at the location of the new stables and a better control is afforded. The preparation of fertilizing material is now handled exclusively at the 97th street stables, saving hauling costs, while the old stable built at 86th street has been

Track Meet—Chelsea Park

remodeled and now provides an adequate storehouse for stores formerly scattered throughout the parks. The 79th street storage yard has been turned over entirely to concrete and masonry work.

In addition, considerable construction and repair work has been undertaken. Riverside Drive has been repaved with asphaltic concrete as far north as Manhattanville Viaduct, and the department is desirous of repaving the upper drive and the east drive of Central Park with a similar surface. Both of these roads now require heavy maintenance expenses. Requests have also been made for funds to repave the 65th, 79th and 97th street transverse roads through Central Park, but action is now pending whereby jurisdiction for paving and maintaining all four transverse roads will be transferred to the borough president, all other matters remaining in the jurisdiction of the park department.

The department has also erected new comfort stations at Cooper Square and John Jay Park, and the authorization of another comfort station at Madison Square Park has been approved. Work has been started on a comfort station in Isham Mansion. The dairy building in Central Park is being renovated and the Gracie Mansion, mineral springs house and other buildings are being painted and newly roofed. Many useless, ugly and tumble-down structures have been removed and the areas restored to park use.

Care of Park Areas and Street Trees

One of the greatest park problems is the care of trees, particularly those on city streets. When the present administration took office it found that the condition of the trees was most unsatisfactory. The number of street trees in the residential sections of Manhattan was being reduced each year by several thousands. Furthermore, the department had made no attempt to advise citizens who wanted to plant trees. As a result, in many cases the kind of tree selected was not adapted to local conditions and shortly died. The fact that streets and sidewalks in Manhattan are everywhere paved adds to the difficulty of the problem. In the outlying boroughs the large stretches of unpaved soil along the sidewalks makes planting much simpler and cheaper.

Although the service with respect to trees had been inefficiently carried on in the past, there was the foundation of an organization for proper work. The commissioner is attempting to centralize responsibility and devise a thorough program for both remedial and constructive measures. Through the co-operation of the New York State College of Forestry a forester was assigned to the department and a census of street trees taken. A study was also made to determine the kind of tree suited to particular localities. As a result of this study a definite plan for street tree planting will be submitted in connection with the 1917 budget.

The park plant has been brought up to normal by the restoration of lawns, shrubs, trees and rearrangement of layout wherever this could be accomplished within the limited appropriations and labor schedule. A survey of the parks of Manhattan and Richmond, shortly after this administration took office, revealed the fact that in many places the park areas had been reduced to a desolate condition. Such areas no longer served the useful purposes for which the city had made large original expenditures. It was a serious problem, without special funds, to know where to attempt to redeem these areas, especially since any restoration must be done during the few weeks of the planting season. However, careful planning has resulted in transforming a number of parks to their proper condition and usefulness.

The physical problem of Central Park has been largely solved, except the northerly portion, by restoring it to its condition of ten or twelve years ago. In the northerly section special funds will be needed for restoration, since destruction in that region has been so serious as to require practically reconstruction. The same is true as to areas in Carl Schurz, Mt. Morris, Colonial, Morningside and Corlears Hook Parks.

Subway work has rendered impossible the present improvement of a number of park areas where construction work is in progress.

A number of small triangle park areas, such as on Canal Street, Beach Street, Grand Street, etc., have been entirely restored to usefulness, and this is true of the larger type of park, such as Seward, Tompkins Square, Stuyvesant, Madison, Hudson, Chelsea, Bryant, etc.

Numerous lawns have been restored, new trees, shrubs, and sod provided and this work has been accomplished by a reduced departmental labor force and no increase in appropriation. In many cases, conditions have been improved by changing the layout after consulting the landscape architect so that actual needs were better served. After a number of experiments, a method was found for restoring deep gulleys and washouts in Riverside Park so the restoration would remain permanent. The employment of deep rooted ground covering plants has proved most successful in this respect.

Park Concessions

In line with the extension of park facilities to the public is the need for proper control over the concessions furnishing public service in the parks. When the present administration took office the letting of park concessions in Manhattan was in such a confused condition that there was need for the immediate establishment of a consistent policy which would protect the city's interests and furnish the best service to the public. The studies which were carried on by the department in co-operation with the Bureau of Municipal Research resulted in the establishment of a definite policy of concession granting which provided for proper control by the city and incidentally increased park revenues by about $50,000 a year.

Concerts

For many years the department was accustomed to appoint band leaders and give them engagements for two or three concerts apiece. The

Basket Ball Game—Tompkins Square Park Playground

technical qualifications of the bands and their leaders were not passed upon and the system resulted in wasteful expenditure and favoritism.

In 1914 an expert citizen music committee was appointed to pass on the names of all applicants for positions as leaders of park music, and to advise the department as to the general composition of the programs and the personnel of the musicians forming the respective orchestras and bands. Standard instrumentation was prescribed for bands employed. A band of less than standard instrumentation was not assigned to any concert.

The boroughs of Manhattan and Richmond were divided into four districts, and a band of twenty-one men and a leader was assigned for the music season to each district. These men were employed by the week, the members of the band receiving $28.00 per week, and leaders $56.00 per week. A schedule was made up for each district so that the band played in a different park in the district on each night of the week during the season. This method of employment resulted in two distinct advantages:

1 Leader and musicians became accustomed to each other with the result that a much higher quality of music was secured.
2 A saving of 20% was made in the appropriation so that the department was enabled to give forty more concerts than if the leaders and different members of the band were employed for each concert or group of concerts.

Future Development of Park System

The past two years have thus been given over to a reorganization of the department within the limits of its 1914 appropriations. As a result of this reorganization economies of over $250,000 have been effected. The commissioner now feels that the attention of the department should be given to a greater degree to a program such as the following for the future development of the park system:

1 *Paving*	
Relaying the walks in Central Park and other city parks	$250,000 00
Repaving upper Riverside Drive, 135th to 158th Streets	150,000 00
Repaving east drive of Central Park	350,000 00
2 *Park Restoration*	
Morningside Park	$40,000 00
Central Park	15,000 00
Mount Morris Park	75,000 00
3 *Resurfacing Playgrounds*	16,000 00
4 *Construction and Development*	
10 comfort stations	275,000 00
Playgrounds at Cherry and Market Sts., Jasper Oval, 67th and 68th Streets and First Avenue, and Highbridge Park	150,000 00
Completion of Harlem River Bulkhead	310,000 00

It also includes plans for the wide development and extension of the city's park areas, as follows:

1 Preserve what can be saved to the city of the banks of the Harlem River, and develop them in connection with the existing parcels of park land which adjoin the present Speedway. This latter with restrictions removed could then be developed as one park together with Highbridge, Washington Bridge and Fort George Parks.
2 Connect by a parkway Washington Bridge and Fort Washington Parks.
3 Prolong by a parkway or boulevard street the existing Speedway from its termination northwesterly, so as to join the present northerly terminus of Lafayette Boulevard at Broadway and make a connecting link with the new park to be created at Inwood Hill, continuing along the line of the Harlem Canal to Isham Park, by connections with Van Cortlandt Park.
4 Acquire additional park lands between Lafayette Boulevard and the Hudson River front. This is now private property, which may at any day be built upon to the permanent detriment of the city. New York could ill afford to acquire some years from now at an almost prohibitive cost, this property which can now be saved to the city at a reasonable figure.
5 Furnish Central Park with more adequate connections with Riverside Drive, thus making it possible to use more intensively the existing park and recreation facilities. A study is being made for such a connection just north of 77th Street. Morningside, St. Nicholas and Colonial Parks should be connected with boulevards or additional park space, so as to join Central Park with the Speedway at 155th Street.
6 Make a real parkway connection from the northerly terminus of the straight strip of viaduct at 155th Street and Riverside Drive so as to prolong it over the railroad tracks, and provide a physical connection with moderate curves and grades joining Lafayette Boulevard at a point in the southerly portion of Fort Washington Park.
7 Transfer the present activities of Blackwell's Island (which is not suitable to modern needs for charities and correction) and turn it into what would be a most beautiful island park—such as the Belle Isle Park of Detroit.

Other recommendations which the commissioner makes are as follows:

1 Make an extensive study of the park problems of the borough of Richmond.
2 Create a special park squad for police work in the parks.
3 Permit the park department to be represented on the committee on city plan, the committee on port and terminal facilities and the borough presidents' committees on street changes.
4 Reconstruct old bulkheads along the river front at Thomas Jefferson Park, Corlears Hook Park, Carl Schurz Park and at 77th Street and the Hudson River. The construction of a concrete bulkhead to replace the old wooden bulkhead along the river side of the Harlem River Speedway should be completed.
5 Complete the irrigation and watering systems in the parks.

Anemic Children—Thomas Jefferson Park

6 Make a city-wide recreation survey for the following purposes:
   a To disclose actual work accomplished and deficiencies in service.
   b To determine specifically how far present recreation agencies (private, public or commercial) meet the needs of the city at large and also each community.
   c To show what sections lack certain recreation facilities, and why and when these should be provided.
   d To compare conditions in New York with conditions in other cities and with generally accepted standards.
   e To show wherein the recreation needs of children, young people and adults are supplied and not supplied.
   f To illustrate in as many different ways as possible, by map, chart, table or picture, each of the conclusions reached.
   g From the sum total of this information to base extension work under the supervision of the department of parks.

7 Plan for the consolidation and centralization of certain existing separate park and recreation administrative units. This would include consolidation and centralization of the city's present scattered zoological and menagerie plants and botanical exhibition plants; the centralization of the administrative, engineering, recreation and other park functions; the centralization of comfort station administration; also further concentration of recreational facilities already partially completed and co-ordination of city and voluntary recreational activities.

8 Transfer to the park department areas now controlled by other departments within and outside existing park areas which are no longer needed for the operation of these departments, and which can be carried on as a part of the department's recreation plant.

9 Complete the reorganization and systematization of the department. This will include motorization, cost and expenditure accounting systems, new standards and qualifications of playground force, recreation program, better distribution and control of non-directed recreational activities, more intensive use of existing playgrounds, development of community centers in park playgrounds.

10 Develop a definite policy regarding the city's attitude toward the works of art in or to be placed in parks, and regarding the museums, or other institutions already located therein. A definite policy should be established which can be made applicable to all such institutions coming within certain well-defined classifications. The present method is haphazard and unsatisfactory, both as to the share the city will bear in annual maintenance, construction of buildings, etc., and the consequent authority of the city's representatives in the affairs of the institution. A plan is now being prepared along these lines which will be submitted to the mayor for consideration.

11 Carry on a public educational campaign to secure better care and protection of park property by citizens, and to bring home to the people how this will provide for better and more intensive use of the parks.

   This includes the holding of a city-wide park campaign—" Know the parks " and taking other measures to secure dissemination among the citizens of information as to how to reach the parks and what facilities are provided.

These suggestions are submitted without comment at this time. There is no reason why most of them should not be put under way at once.

DEPARTMENT OF PARKS—BROOKLYN

Cost

In 1914 when the present administration took office the budget for the Brooklyn park department was $868,843.60. The new commissioner realized the imperative need for economy and immediately undertook the reorganization of his department with a view to widening, if possible, its usefulness without increasing expenditures.

The following tables of budget appropriations and expenditures show that the department has made a practical demonstration of its appreciation of the need for economy and of its ability to effect such economy through the introduction of business methods:

COMPARATIVE BUDGET APPROPRIATIONS

	1914	1915	1916
Personal service	$626,441.00	$586,351.15	$556,874.25
Supplies	50,740.54	46,559.96	43,746.81
Purchase of equipment	6,655.53	9,906.26	8,897.55
Materials	37,196.68	26,490.12	30,194.08
Contract or open order service	147,559.85	103,997.78	121,220.52
Contingencies	250.00	240.00	240.00
Total Budget	$868,843.60	$773,545.27	$761,173.21
Revenue bonds	....	17,475.00	....
Corporate stock (engineering)	15,281.05	13,547.00	....
Grand Total	$884,124.65	$804,567.27	$761,173.21

COMPARATIVE EXPENSE FIGURES, 1914, 1915

	1914	1915
Personal service	$591,038.08	$556,294.99
Supplies	57,709.79	46,166.36
Purchase of equipment	16,981.61	21,186.49
Materials	45,648.05	47,725.68
Contract or open order service	137,925.21	100,514.93
Contingencies	1,608.70	133.92
Total	$850,911.44	$772,032.37

The decrease of over $100,000 made in the 1916 tax budget appropriations to the department as compared with the 1914 appropriations has been effected in spite of largely increased activities. This saving has been brought about by careful attention to administrative detail and by a painstaking reorganization of the department's methods of operation.

Tennis Field—Prospect Park

Principal Administrative Defects

The chief defects which the commissioner found to exist at the beginning of his administration were:

1 Inefficient business methods
2 Inadequate recreational facilities
3 Lack of program with respect to and inadequate use of existing recreation facilities
4 Inadequate comfort station facilities coupled with excessive cost of operation for those in use
5 Lack of definite program of park work
6 Neglect of street trees which were disappearing at the rate of 2,500 per year, with no effort to replace them
7 Unbalanced labor force
8 No systematic and equable employment of per diem workers
9 Excessive cost of supervision of labor
10 Disproportionate expenditures for team hire
11 Lack of a central planning organization to correlate all park work in the several boroughs
12 Lack of cordial relationship with the public

Substantial improvements have been made in the past two years in respect of all of the above items. Not only have those conditions been remedied which were known to be defective when the administration came into office but other defects discovered in the course of the reorganization work have been corrected as they appeared.

Results Accomplished

The following examples indicate the methods through which administrative defects have been corrected and economies obtained:

1 *Supervision*

The supervision of all maintenance and operation work in the department is now handled directly by the superintendent. Under him, the handling of the force in the parks is taken care of by one general foreman who is in direct touch with 19 section foremen in charge of sections or groups of parks. In addition to this force there is under the superintendent directly a foreman of greenhouses, a foreman mechanic, a foreman of stables and three arboriculturits, in charge of the care of trees. This scheme of operation has enabled the department to make a saving of $15,000 annually in the cost of supervision.

2 *Comfort stations*

A saving of $12,000 per year has been made in the operation of these stations, in spite of the fact that six new stations have been opened and that the hours of operation of a number of the stations have been lengthened. This saving resulted through making the care of these stations incidental to other duties in a number of cases, instead of keeping a laborer stationed in the building all the time, and through providing one attendant to care for several adjacent women's stations in Prospect Park instead of an attendant for each station.

3 *Policing and watching*

By new arrangements for storing equipment, and by changing conditions generally, the cost of conducting this work has been reduced by $15,000 a year. This has been partly accomplished by educating park employees and the public to protect park property. The use of signs and the aid of the schools have been of material assistance in educating the public.

4 *Care of buildings*

The majority of departmental buildings were badly in need of repair on January 1, 1914. These buildings are gradually being put in condition and considerable savings have been effected through the adoption of an improved system of making repairs. Whereas formerly there was no definite system of inspection, and repairs were made spasmodically as they became imperative without proper regard for their cost or quality, the department now makes repairs wherever possible as soon as needed. Estimates are made of the probable cost and actual costs checked up as the repairs are going on, so that records may be kept for use in estimating on future work. The result of this systematic method has been an increased amount and better quality of work done, and a considerable decrease in the size and cost of the departmental mechanical force.

5 *General cleaning*

This work is now carried on continuously throughout the day whereas it was formerly done only once a day. This has resulted in great improvement in the appearance of the parks, especially in the afternoon. In spite of this continuous operation a saving of about $15,000 per year has been effected.

6 *Stores*

The stores system was found in good shape on January 1, 1914. The commissioner was able, however, to effect a saving of $1,000 per year in the cost of operation. By more careful buying and the installation of work programs, it has also been possible to reduce the amount of stock carried on hand by $25,000.

7 *Stables and garage*

By motorizing the department a branch stable was abolished at a saving of $1,500 per year. The cost of operating the remaining stable has been reduced, up to date, by about $2,500 per year. This does not include the amount saved on drivers and hired teams through motorization, but is due to a smaller number of stable employees. Economies would be greater were it not for the greatly increased cost of forage during the past two years.

A well-equipped garage was established but when the central motor service was installed the department turned over all of its motor equipment, with the exception of one 3½ ton motor truck, to it.

8 *Repair gang*

This gang covers all road patrolling and repairing. $1,200 per year has been saved by dropping one foreman and providing the foreman in general charge with a Ford car. Efficiency has been greatly increased by concentrating responsibility for all of the work under this foreman. Although no reduction in the size of the gang has been possible, the force has at certain seasons been put to other and unrelated work which has resulted indirectly in an appreciable saving of departmental funds.

9 *Mechanics*

By changing the method of supervising repair work, and having mechanics work from a detailed plan and estimate of cost for each job, the payroll for mechanics has been reduced by $12,000 per year, despite a considerable increase in quantity and improvement in quality of work done.

10 *Equipment*

A high power tree sprayer has been purchased. This has resulted in doubling the number of trees sprayed with no increase in the spraying force. 30,000 trees were sprayed in 1914 and 63,000 in 1915. A paint sprayer has been purchased which has reduced the cost of painting park benches 40 per cent., and enabled the department to paint all of its benches each year, which was formerly impossible. Portable bandstands have been constructed by departmental labor, which resulted in lowering the cost of concerts. All playground equipment is now constructed by departmental labor for less than it could be purchased in the open market, and of greater durability. Shops have been equipped with modern machinery mostly by transfer from other departments where it was no longer needed. Increased efficiency was secured with a greater range in the possibilities of the use of the shops.

11 *Team Hire*

The 1914 appropriation of $105,000 for hired vehicles has been reduced to about $66,000 for 1916 by the exercise of strict economy.

12 *Care of Lawns*

The cutting of grass more frequently than formerly resulted in a saving due to elimination of the former expense of raking and carting away grass, now unnecessary. The department now grows and cuts its own sod instead of purchasing it and has also inaugurated a compost pit from which several thousand cubic yards per year are spread on the lawns for their betterment.

13 *Labor Force*

Relations with the working forces in the department have been greatly improved. A readjustment of pay schedules has resulted in increases for more than seventy-five of the outdoor men, while the cost of clerical work and engineering services has been reduced. The department has done away with the old practice of hiring from one hundred to two hundred raw men in the spring for temporary work and laying off a large number in the summer and fall.

The temporary men so employed were of comparatively little value and all the men in the department were made uncertain of their positions when lay-off time approached and naturally concerned themselves with efforts to influence their own tenure.

The present method is to have a continuous force working on full time during the summer and on shortened time during the winter. The undesirable men have been weeded out. Those who remain feel that they have a steady job and give gratifying support. In 1915 the heavy spring work, including greatly enlarged activities was done with one hundred fewer men than the previous year. Furthermore, the men have come to realize that they are dealt with on their merits without regard to outside influences. The increased rate of pay for men previously underpaid has made it possible to do away with Sunday time except where the need for it is genuine. The working time of the playground attendants has been readjusted so as to make the hours more reasonable. Those who formerly worked 365 days at $2.50 per day now work 300 days per year at $3.00 per day. This enables the department to give each playground worker an occasional day off without pay and to concentrate and expand its work in the summer and reduce it to a minimum in the winter time.

These definite achievements have been made possible by the fact that the commissioner has familiarized himself with the details of each park activity and has assigned his private secretary as secretary to the department with entire charge of filing, civil service matters and concerts. The clerical work of the administrative office is now closely supervised by the commissioner and, as a result of transferring a portion of the work to the finance department and improving office equipment, a saving of $5,460 has been made.

As stated above, all these changes have been coupled, not with decreased service to the public, but with widely extended activities both with regard to the upkeep of the parks and their wider use by the public, and the permanent upbuilding of the department's equipment. The recreational facilities, which will be discussed in greater detail elsewhere, have been doubled since 1914. Additional playgrounds, tennis courts, baseball diamonds and farm gardens have been provided. Dreamland Beach has been cleaned and opened for public use. A new carousel has been provided in Prospect Park, together with an additional boat house. A new Zoo building and additional animals have been provided by public subscriptions. The services of the department have been offered to the public in planting street trees. About 2000 orders at a cost to the property owner of $8 per tree have been taken, and about 1000 trees have already been set. New skating ponds and new coasting slides have been constructed.

Improvements to park equipment have been no less noteworthy. In addition to the boathouse, carousel and zoo building mentioned above, a children's farm garden building has been erected at McCarren Park, an open pavilion, refreshment pavilion and comfort station at Dreamland Beach, and new potting sheds at the greenhouses.

School Farm—McCarren Park

Wading Pool—Bushwick Playground

New roads, walks and lawns have also been constructed as follows:

About one mile of walks in Sunset, Tompkins and Prospect Parks
3,000 feet of new boardwalk at Dreamland Beach
New granite steps and walk at Highland Park
Seven acres of new lawn at Highland Park
One acre of new lawn at Sunset Park
Three acres of lawn restored in Saratoga Park
One and one-half acres of lawn restored in Irving Park
Three acres of lawn restored in Prospect Park
New service road at the store house

Other structural improvements in the parks include new wading pools at City Park and Bushwick playground, open pavilions in Prospect and Bensonhurst Parks, and refreshment stands in Sunset and Highland Parks. Improvements have been made at the greenhouses resulting in savings of $5,000 a year in operating costs and $10,000 a year in botanical supplies, plants, shrubs and the like.

The following table shows a considerable increase in the amount of revenue received by the department in 1915, as compared with 1913. It does not, however, give as accurate an impression as it should, for, in addition to the cash receipts, the city obtained in 1915 as part payment for a carousel concession the new building erected by the operators of that privilege at a cost of $10,000. Two buildings erected by the operators of the boating privilege at a cost of about $2,500 were also turned over to the city in the same year.

REVENUE RECEIPTS FROM PARK PROPERTY

	1913	1914	1915
Concessions advertised	$19,275.00	....	....
Concessions not advertised	....	$18,487.00	$14,084.92
Permits	6,058.67	5,398.62	4,538.15
Lockers	....	408.50	347.75
Sale of materials	756.45	717.42	693.37
Bathing facilities	....	....	65.41
Miscellaneous	4.01	761.49	780.87
Planting trees—City streets	....	1,880.00	13,224.00
Total	$26,094.13	$27,653.03	$33,734.47

Program for Next Two Years

The progressive work of the past two years is to be continued during the remainder of this administration. Already certain definite phases of the problem of proper park management have been considered for 1916 and 1917. Among the improvements which the department plans to make are the following:

1 Improvement of Dyker Beach Park, to make it available as an athletic field and playground.
2 Development of the strip along New York Bay between the present Shore Road and the sea wall as a park and playground.

3 Opening up for recreational activities the plaza of Fort Greene Park.
4 Extending the movement of tree planting by property owners by offering the services of the department to the owner at a nominal fee on request, for the furnishing, planting and caring for, of street trees.
5 Extending the animal collection and improving the menagerie facilities.
6 Construction of new bridle paths and walks in Prospect Park and opening an automobile road to the menagerie.
7 Motorization of the department's vehicle equipment.
8 Construction of shed to enable the department to keep its entire plant under cover.
9 Establishment of a series of small yards for the storage of material, thus reducing the transportation charges for material.
10 Laying more permanent pavements on park roads and drives, thus reducing maintenance charges to a minimum.
11 Moving certain shrubs now poorly located to better locations, thus improving the appearance of the parks.
12 Construction of additional fences around parks and plots.
13 In addition to the above the department has requested $1,000,000 in corporate stock for various permanent public improvements which are subject to the policy of the city government in appropriating funds.

DEPARTMENT OF PARKS—THE BRONX

Administrative Defects Found and Efforts to Correct Them

When the present administration took office in January, 1914, the incoming commissioner of parks found the following defects in his department:

1 Insufficient recreational facilities.
2 Inadequate maintenance of roads and parkways.
3 Lack of exact information regarding street trees and their care.
4 No attempt at checking the ravages of insects and fungus in the park trees.
5 Insufficient fencing.
6 No definite plan for park development.
7 Too great an extent of available park area undeveloped so as to be unavailable for public use.
8 Insufficient revenue from privileges and concessions.
9 Insufficient bathing facilities to meet the public demand at Pelham Bay Park.
10 A departmental organization without centralized responsibility.

The past two years have been devoted to making progress in correcting these defects and others. Although the budget appropriations to the department have been decreased since 1914, and although the department's expenditures for 1914 and 1915 have remained almost stationary, as shown by the following tables, very considerable progress has been made in improving the departmental service.

COMPARATIVE BUDGET FIGURES, 1914, 1915 AND 1916

	1914	1915	1916
Personal service	$358,971.50	$337,745.50	$319,607.50
Supplies	14,451.22	14,795.11	12,906.69
Purchase of equipment	4,867.80	11,350.23	5,619.02
Materials	25,970.51	17,363.57	36,363.04
Contract or open order service	49,387.76	52,185.25	53,848.30
Contingencies	50.00	....	....
Departmental Total	$453,698.79	$433,439.66	$428,344.55

COMPARATIVE EXPENSE FIGURES

	1913	1914	1915
Personal service	$345,498.64	$352,764.75	$336,561.71
Supplies	13,915.53	16,313.00	13,314.52
Purchase of equipment	7,622.78	5,630.99	11,299.39
Materials	24,274.87	44,370.55	49,447.36
Contract or open order service	57,605.04	55,477.20	59,865.74
Contingencies	....	....	....
Total	$448,916.86	$474,556.49	$470,488.72

For example:

1 *Recreation*

Six new playgrounds have been opened and sixty-one new tennis courts have been constructed. The new Mosholu Golf Links have been opened and a new golf house has been provided in Pelham Bay Park.

2 *Roadways*

A patrol and repair gang operating continuously throughout the year has been established and a definite program laid down for all necessary road reconstruction and preservation based on careful inspection and the preparation of estimates of probable cost.

3 *Care of Street Trees*

A census has been taken of all street trees and a system established dividing the borough into fourteen sections for trimming and spraying purposes. As a result twice as many trees are being cared for with the same force.

4 *Park Trees*

Park trees are now sprayed against insects and a large number of trees affected by fungus have been removed. Furthermore, considerable underbrush has been cleared away in the wooded sections of the parks.

5 *Fences*

Four miles of fence have been constructed by departmental labor and plans have been made to erect several thousand feet of fence in 1916.

6 *Park Development*

Twenty-five acres of Crotona Park have been developed and made available as a ball field, playground, etc. The athletic field at Macombs Dam Park has been put in usable condition, and general improvements have been made at Fulton, Echo and Pelham Bay Parks.

7 *Revenues*

Revenues received from privileges, concessions, permits, locker fees, etc., have been increased from $18,000 in 1913 to $35,000 in 1915. This was done by calling for competitive bids for privileges and concessions and by establishing new privileges at a few points; also by making a charge of one dollar for annual golf permits and 50c. per day for daily golf permits.

8 *Bathing Facilities*

The capacity of bath houses in Pelham Bay Park has been increased by about thirty per cent., and the beach has been cleaned up so that the available area for bathing has been largely increased.

9 *Departmental Organization*

A definite scheme of organization has been worked out providing for the adequate supervision of every activity and centralizing responsibility in the commissioner for all the details of park administration. The commissioner now is in direct touch with park work and his private secretary handles all permits and receives

Pelham Bay Park—Orchard Beach

St. Mary's Park Playground

all revenue. In this way more effective administration has been obtained. In the course of reorganization the positions of chief clerk and chief engineer were dropped and their duties distributed among the remaining employees. The overhead cost of administration has thus been reduced without any sacrifice of efficiency.

At the same time that these steps have been taken the general work of the department has been improved. Four times as many plants and twice as many flowers have been put out as ever before. Five acres of new lawn have been opened to the public, nineteen new drinking fountains have been constructed, and the boating and skating facilities have been extended.

Operating economies have been effected in the care of park comfort stations, in the policing of park property, and in the care of buildings. The shop system has been improved by the installation of several thousand dollars' worth of machinery transferred to the department by the sinking fund commission, and a repair gang of five men and a foreman has been organized to make day-by-day repairs on roads.

One of the two stables formerly maintained has been abolished and converted into a garage. A partial motorization of the department has resulted in a considerable saving in the cost of hostlers, stablemen and drivers, while the number of horses has been reduced about one-half. Other improvements are the purchase of five new snow plows, which have reduced the cost of snow removal about one-half; a new motor lawn mower, which replaces three horses; the stone-loading machine, and the conversion of old automobiles into motor trucks.

The department has constructed two new storage sheds, four bath houses, three additional greenhouse buildings and ten new tool houses. In addition, sixteen miles of road have been reconstructed and resurfaced by departmental labor, and twelve miles of macadam road never before treated have been given tar treatment each year. One mile of new bridle path has been constructed and eight miles of new walk have been opened in Crotona, Van Cortlandt, Pelham Bay and Bronx Parks.

An appropriation has been granted for filling in swamp lands in the southwesterly portion of Van Cortlandt Park to make available a site for a playground and to eliminate the mosquito nuisance. This work will be carried out with all possible expedition.

These accomplishments are all the more significant in view of the magnitude of the park problem in The Bronx. There are 3,555 acres of park property under the control of the department, of which 1,436 are improved. There are 45 miles of paved roadways, 22 miles of walks and 12 miles of bridle paths. In the near future the improved areas will have to be enlarged to accommodate not only the increased population of The Bronx, but also to take care of the growing number of persons from other boroughs who use The Bronx parks. Central Park has long since become inadequate for the residents of Manhattan, and to a greater and greater extent the overflow is being absorbed by the system in The Bronx.

Work Remaining to be Done

If the parks of The Bronx are to be developed to their full usefulness the commissioner feels that a very comprehensive program must be initiated. This program includes the following items:

1 Laying 15,450 square yards of asphalt pavement on Bronx and Pelham Parkway from Southern Boulevard to Butler Street. The estimated cost is $36,500. No roadway in The Bronx is used more than this, and none has cost more for repairs during the past ten years. As a matter of economy this expensive repairing should be ended and a substantial wearing surface substituted.

2 Construction of roadway from new subway station at Jerome and Bainbridge Avenues to Grand Avenue. The estimated cost is $17,000. There is at present no park entrance to this place.

3 Improvement of Clay Avenue side of Claremont Park at an estimated cost of $10,000. Half of the work has already been done.

4 Improvement of shore front and bathing beaches at Pelham Bay Park. There has been a tremendous increase in the number of people using the pier, and an improvement of the shore is necessary. Some work along this line has already been completed, but an additional appropriation of $5,000 is required.

5 Construction of golf house at new golf links in Van Cortlandt Park. At present there is no shelter of any kind on the new links. The estimated cost is $20,000.

6 Construction of a road on the northerly boundary line of the Bronx and Pelham Parkway at an estimated cost of $50,000.

In 1909, the grading and paving of a roadway along the southerly boundary of the Bronx and Pelham Parkway from the White Plains Road to the crossing of the Parkway over the tracks of the New York, New Haven & Hartford Railway, was completed, at a cost of $100,000, and thrown open to automobile traffic, leaving the main roadway for the use of all manner of horse vehicles and automobile trucks. This road has become immensely popular with the owners of pleasure automobiles, and has at the same time become exceedingly dangerous, owing to the congested condition of traffic at certain hours of the day, especially between the hours of 5 and 8 in the evening. The whole cost of constructing this road, which will have a length of 10,375 feet is $106,000, which will include 34,580 square yards of asphalt block pavement, at a cost of $2.50 per square yard. $50,000 could properly be expended on it this year, $30,000 in 1917, and the balance, $26,000, in 1918.

The estimated cost of grading is fixed at $20,000, which it is proposed to expend in the first six months of the year, and the balance used in paving the roadway from Bronx Park East to the Williamsbridge Road. A portion of this proposed roadway, that from the easterly boundary of Bronx Park to the Bear Swamp Road, is already graded.

7 Completion of Crotona Parkway, including entrance to Crotona Park, and exclusive of additional lands which will cost approximately $38,000.

8 Improvement of Easterly and Westerly sides of Crotona Park which would cost approximately $20,000.

9 Re-paving with permanent pavement, the roadway of Bronx and Pelham Parkway, from N. Y., N. H. & H. R. R. bridge to Eastern Boulevard, and the Eastern Boulevard from Bronx and Pelham Parkway to Prospect Hill Road at a cost of approximately $72,000.

10 Improvement of Southerly, Westerly and Northerly portions of Claremont Park at an estimated cost of $5,000.

Caring for Old Elm Trees in Flushing

DEPARTMENT OF PARKS—QUEENS

Cost and Scope of Activity

Prior to 1912 the parks in the borough of Queens were administered in conjunction with the Brooklyn parks. My judgment is that the separation of the two boroughs for park management was never justified. The budget for that year for the first time provided a separate allowance of approximately $165,000 for Queens parks, and a fourth commissioner was added to the park board. The problem of the new department was then, as it still is, chiefly a matter of forestry and general development. Only a few of the city's park holdings in Queens have reached a finished state, so that there is a great deal of development work to be done. The large wooded acreage in Forest Park and the 300,000 trees which the park department must care for in the public streets make the forestry problem particularly important. Attention has therefore been justifiably centered on these two matters.

When the present administration took office in 1914 comparatively little had been done toward the solution of these two pressing questions. The need for economy in administering the city's business had led the board of estimate to keep the appropriations to this newly formed park department down to the lowest possible point as shown by the following table:

Year	Appropriations and Expenditures			
	Budget Appropriation	Revenue Bonds	Total Appropriations	Expenditures
1913	$186,972.84	....	$186,972.84	$181,081.40
1914	180,130.29	$10,000.00	190,130.29	182,141.60
1915	171,283.89	10,975.00	182,258.89	186,071.23
1916	171,595.72	None to Mar. 1	171,595.72	....

Annual appropriations of less than $200,000 do not permit intensive development of park property when applied to the care of 1,213.66 acres of parks and 300,000 street trees. Nevertheless effort has been made to utilize this comparatively small sum so as to get the best results. The quality of labor employed has been improved due to a more careful selection of laborers and the raising of labor standards by the municipal civil service commission. Care has been taken to prevent the transfer from other departments of men physically incapable of doing the best work. In addition, the overhead cost of administration has been reduced. The following summary shows the percentage of budget appropriations for overhead service, productive service and the purchase of supplies and materials:

Character of Service	Budget Allowances					
	1913	Per centage of Total	1914	Per centage of Total	1915	Per centage of Total
Overhead and non-productive.....	$44,600.00	22.1	$30,200.00	16.8	$27,100.00	15.5
Productive.......	90,737.50	45.1	93,393.50	51.8	113,803.12	65.2
Supplies and materials...........	66,035.34	32.8	56,536.79	31.4	33,692.60	19.3

In analyzing the budget appropriations in this manner the item of overhead has been made to include all expenditures, not directly productive, for personal service above the grade of foreman, so that the foresters and arboriculturists, clerks, etc., have been grouped in the overhead or non-productive service.

The productive service which shows an increase of 13.4 per cent. for 1915 as compared with 1914 consists of the active working force. The principal increases have been for laborers and for climbers and pruners. In March, 1915, there were 37 laborers and 70 climbers and pruners as against 20 laborers and 39 climbers and pruners in January, 1914. The care of trees is the largest and most important function which the Queens department has to perform. The additional labor has also been used to a considerable extent in producing lumber and fire wood, so that the expenditure for lumber has been reduced and the departmental revenues have been increased by the sale of fire wood to the board of education.

The mechanical equipment of the department consists chiefly of carpentry and blacksmith shops, a shop for repairing tools and two portable saw mills. The most important work done by the mechanical force since 1914 has been the construction of a garage and of an addition to the storehouse, the rebuilding of the greenhouses and the building of a portion of the new house, the installation of a heating plant and toilets at the greenhouses, the construction of about two hundred benches, a small amount of playground apparatus and back stops for baseball diamonds, the erection of a coal trestle and the construction of a concrete well pit, a pagoda and steps and a rustic shelter at Kissena Park, the extension of the boardwalk at Rockaway Park and the construction of a bandstand at Kings Park. The two saw mills have produced a large amount of lumber and fire wood. The trees felled on the new links of the golf course furnished raw material for most of the lumber used in constructing the coal trestle and coal pockets mentioned above, and 179½ cords of firewood were cut and supplied to the public schools.

A reduction in the number of horses owned by the department and in the amount of money paid for hired teams has been made possible by the introduction of motor trucks. There is opportunity, however, for further

Wood-yard in Forest Park

motorization of equipment. A pick-up truck, similar to the one used in Manhattan, would probably reduce materially the number of hired and owned teams. Motorization is particularly desirable in Queens parks because the department is without a central service plant. While the solution of the forestry problem is more urgent than the erection of a central service plant at this time the need for centralizing the department's working forces should not be lost sight of.

Substantial decreases in expenditures for supplies, materials, etc., have been made in the past two years. With the exception of equipment for the proper care of trees the department is fairly well supplied with apparatus, so that this reduction does not represent an injurious curtailment. The reduction in the amount expended for highway materials is due to the fact that the roads apparently will not require as much maintenance in 1916 as in 1914. The general work of park maintenance requiring the greatest amount of labor does not entail a great expenditure of material, because the cost of supplies for the care of trees and lawns is small compared with the labor cost. This reduction in appropriation, therefore, does not indicate necessarily an excessive proportion of labor expense.

This readjustment of the budget for Queens parks has unquestionably resulted in a better balanced program of work.

Steps Necessary for Fuller Utilization of Parks

As pointed out above, however, the attention of the commissioner is necessarily centered upon a better utilization of existing facilities and the most effective expenditure of the small annual appropriations which he receives than upon any program of constructive work. Furthermore, the financial condition of the city since 1914 has made the board of estimate reluctant to authorize the issue of corporate stock for permanent improvements in the parks. In 1914 there were but two comfort stations in the Queens parks and although there is great need for the construction of additional stations at Kissena, Flushing, Rainey and Astoria Parks, which are entirely without facilities, only one additional station has been built.

The proper cleaning of parks, particularly Rockaway Beach, is a problem of the department. Five men, with an extra man on Sundays, are required to keep the 17.87 acres of Rockaway Beach clean during the bathing season. Flushing Park also is used so intensively by the public that it is difficult to maintain a cleanly appearance.

A central service plant with facilities for handling the large quantities of road oil required annually in taking care of the department's roads would facilitate the maintenance work on the Forest and Kissena Park roadways. On the former a very heavy automobile traffic is carried and a considerable expenditure must therefore be made each year to keep the surface in proper condition. In addition to the maintenance work needed on park roadways, the department must soon obtain funds for completing the construction of roads in Forest Park. There are still 30,000 feet of thirty-foot roads to be surfaced. In view of the very rapid deterioration of the present surface roads and the constantly increasing automobile traffic, a very careful study of traffic conditions and needs should be made before any additional temporary pavement is laid. This study should primarily determine whether it would not be more advisable to lay permanent pavements of asphalt, or other lasting material than to continue the laying of macadam.

Closely connected with the need of improving the roadways in the parks is the need for walk construction in Forest Park. At the present time there are many trails through the woods and it is important that the lines of the paths to be substituted for these trails be carefully studied from the standpoint of landscape design in order that the exceptional natural beauty of the forest may not suffer.

An improvement of the landscape work in the parks means, of course, that additional attention must be devoted to the planting of trees and shrubs. To this end better working methods have been introduced in the greenhouse in the past two years. The area available for propagation has been practically doubled. A large number of vines and perennials are being grown for use on the steep slopes in Forest Park. The tree nursery, which was in deplorable condition, has been thinned out as much as funds would permit. Some new stock has been purchased and planted in the parks and a large number of pines, sycamores and oaks have been transplanted. As a result the nursery has increased in value and excellent stock has been obtained. As now operated it more than pays for itself. One of the most profitable things which the city could undertake would be to continue the nursery work which has been started and to provide sufficient funds for the proper development of scientific forestry in Forest Park.

The Queens parks are not as yet productive of any substantial amount of revenue. A very great increase has been made, however, since 1913 in the amount of revenue received. In that year the department's income amounted to but $70.23. In 1915 it had grown to about $9,000, due primarily to the revenue received from golf permits and from the sales of firewood and trees. Revenues could be further increased by raising the charge for annual golf permits from $1 to $5. This would be justified because of the high maintenance cost of golf links as compared with the rest of the park areas.

A summary of the steps which must yet be taken to provide for the proper utilization of the natural facilities of the Queens parks and for their constructive development in the future follows:

1 Serious and systematic consideration should be given to the forestry problem with reference not only to the Forest Park forest but to the maintenance of the 300,000 street trees.

2 A program of structural improvements should be formulated.

3 Definite plans should be formulated and a program adopted for the development of all park properties.

4 The tree nursery should be regarded as an asset of the city's parks. Its proper development would make possible the utilization of trees grown therein by the parks of the other boroughs.

5 A prompt determination should be made of the proper pavement to be laid on Forest Park roadways.

6 If possible, the city should by some means obtain more complete control over Rockaway Beach. At the present time, under the terms of the deed, the city can do nothing to add to the convenience of the public. Anything in the nature of a concession is reserved to the former owners.

Especially important is the consideration of central management of the Queens and Brooklyn park systems.

RECREATION

Increased Facilities

The provision of adequate recreation facilities for the citizens of New York is one of the most important duties of the park departments.

During the past two years the city has greatly extended the recreational work of the park departments. The general supervision of playgrounds has improved, especially in Brooklyn, where for the first time a general supervisor has been employed who has arranged schedules and trained workers so that more effective work has been done. In addition, the following extensions of service in all boroughs have been made:

1 The number of playgrounds has been doubled since 1913.
2 The number of ice skating places, by use of artificially flooded areas, has been doubled.
3 The number of athletic fields has increased 20%.
4 The number of school farm plots in use has increased 50%.
5 The number of tennis courts has increased 50%.
6 The number of permits issued for golf, tennis, baseball and the like has increased from 23,823 to 64,603.
7 The number of special celebrations has increased from 90 to 233.

The following table shows in detail, by boroughs, the increases in recreational facilities since 1913.

Cost

At the same time that these extensions in activity have been made, the recreational work in general has been reorganized in the interests of centralized control. Recreation piers have been transferred from the jurisdiction of the dock department to the park departments, and the four gymnasiums formerly under the public recreation commission have also been transferred to the park departments. The public recreation commission has been abolished and a Committee on Recreation of the board of estimate and apportionment substituted therefor. This committee can do what has never before been done in New York, namely, prevent duplication of recreational activities by the park departments and the board of education, and work out a plan whereby all facilities may be used to the limit of their capacity.

The receipts from golf permits and the like in The Bronx and Queens have been increased from $5,795.75 to $17,028.55. Not only has the revenue been thus increased but distinct economies have been effected, the cost of band concerts in Manhattan having been reduced 36%, and a saving of from $20,000 to $30,000 effected in Brooklyn by the rearrangement of the care-taking service in the small parks.

Table 1—Active Recreation in Parks

Summary of Facilities and Activities by Years

	Manhattan & Richmond			The Bronx			Brooklyn			Queens			Total All Boroughs		
	1913	1914	1915	1913	1914	1915	1913	1914	1915	1913	1914	1915	1913	1914	1915
Playgrounds	41	62	76	....	7	7	7	16	21	....	2	4	48	87	108
Athletics and ball fields	15	15	17	9	9	10	3	4	5	1	1	2	28	29	34
School farms	3	5	5	....	3	3	....	1	2	....	....	....	3	9	10
Golf links	....	....	....	2	2	3	....	....	....	1	1	1	3	3	4
Ice skating	5	5	5	3	5	5	1	10	14	6	6	6	15	26	30
Tennis courts	100	100	100	37	50	94	229	343	364	2	2	8	368	495	566
Baths—Shower	8	10	15	1	1	1	1	2	3	1	1	1	11	14	20
Baths—Beaches	....	....	....	2	2	2	....	1	1	2	2	2	4	5	5
Concerts	287	308	246	62	59	71	93	91	97	26	26	30	468	484	444
Special celebrations	70	85	150	3	4	3	17	24	80		No record		90	113	233
Recreation piers	....	8*	8	....	....	....	....	....	1*	....	....	....	....	8	9
Indoor recreation centers	2	2	7	....	....	....	....	....	1	....	....	....	2	2	8
Permits	8,750	19,458	29,207	7,362	19,723	22,756	5,847	10,448	10,256	1,864	2,271	2,384	23,823	51,900	64,603

* Transferred from Dock Department.

The following table shows the comparative expenditures, by boroughs, from 1913 to 1915, for active recreation, band concerts and general park purposes:

TABLE 2—ACTIVE RECREATION IN PARKS

Summary of Maintenance Expenditures of All Boroughs for Active Recreation and Budget Allowances for All Park Purposes

Expenditures—Active Recreation

	Manhattan and Richmond	The Bronx	Brooklyn	Queens	Total
1913	$124,475.21*	$36,043.25	$17,910.95	$6,420.92	$184,850.33
1914	125,913.71	54,850.92	41,979.77	7,968.17	230,712.57
1915	149,160.69	74,877.72	57,128.25	8,500.00*	289,666.66

*Estimated.

Expenditures—Band Concerts

	Manhattan and Richmond	The Bronx	Brooklyn	Queens	Total
1913	$49,493.00	$5,935.07	$14,586.20	$3,399.61	$73,413.88
1914	56,654.40	5,825.11	20,205.73	4,221.26	88,906.50
1915	26,188.19	6,237.82	15,339.30	4,396.50*	52,161.81

*Estimated.

Total Expenditures for Active Recreation and Concerts

	Manhattan and Richmond	The Bronx	Brooklyn	Queens	Total
1913	$173,968.21	$41,978.32	$32,497.15	$ 9,820.53	$258,264.21
1914	182,568.11	60,675.92	62,185.50	12,189.43	317,618.96
1915	175,348.88	81,115.54	72,467.55	12,896.50*	341,828.47

* Estimated.

Budget Allowances for All Park Purposes

1913	$2,698,290.53
1914	2,630,565.97
1915	2,461,550.57

1915 expenditures for active recreation and concerts per capita of population of each borough, based on 1915 state census:

Manhattan and Richmond	.079
Bronx	.132
Brooklyn	.040
Queens	.032
Entire City	.283

Percentages of total budget allowances for all park purposes were as follows for active recreation and concerts:

1913	9.5%
1914	12.0%
1915	13.8%

Expenditures for active recreation in 1915 were 56.7% more than the expenditures for active recreation in 1913, and expenditures for active recreation and concerts in 1915 were 32.3% more than expenditures for the same two purposes in 1913; while budget allowances for all park purposes in 1915 were 8.7% less than budget allowances for all park purposes in 1913.

Improvements Necessary

The following recommendations for the further extension and development of the recreational facilities of the city are made:

1 The principle of charging for certain activities should be extended, and the revenues so received used partly in improving the service and partly in reducing the cost of allied recreational activities.

2 Evening recreation in small neighborhood parks should be extended by the introduction of sufficient lighting equipment for out-door play and by the provision of trained workers in recreation to supervise.

3 Dyker Beach Park should be developed, making possible a large number of additional athletic fields.

4 The Plaza at Fort Greene Park, which has been graded without expense to the department, should be used for playground purposes.

5 Athletic facilities for South Brooklyn in the area between the recently completed sea wall and the shore road should be developed.

6 If the Gary plan is further extended in schools near parks, the recreational work of the park department should be so arranged as to coincide with the plans of the board of education.

In addition to the foregoing specific items there are other improvements which should be made. Chief among them is the complete centralization of recreational facilities under one authority. The abolition of the public recreation commission was a step in this direction, and the transfer of the recreation piers from the dock department to the park department a further step. Furthermore, the playgrounds formerly administered by the bridge department, water department and other departments are now under the park department's direction. There still remain, however, public bath houses containing swimming pools which are under the jurisdiction of the borough presidents. As the gymnasiums in these same buildings are administered by the bureau of recreation of the park department, and as in almost every case the swimming pool is situated in the immediate vicinity of a park playground, it is obvious that much better results could be obtained under a single management. The public baths situated along the water front should also be turned over to the park department as a part of the recreation plant of the system.

It is equally important that there should be better co-operation and co-ordination between private and city agencies working on the recreation problem. For example, co-operation with the steamship companies and the Interstate Park Commission would make it possible for cheaper rates to be secured for the transportation of children and young people to Bear Mountain. Already the New Jersey authorities are willing to co-operate in regard to the Essex Reservation. If the public is advised of the facilities existing, not only outside the city limits and within a reasonable distance, but also in the outlying districts of the Greater City, much relief from congestion now existing in the parks and playgrounds in the heart of the city can be obtained.

DEPARTMENT OF BRIDGES

Scope of Activity

In response to a suggestion made by the chamberlain, the mayor recommended to the legislature and there was established by act of the legislature in 1916 a Department of Plant and Structures to supersede the department of bridges, taking over the existing functions of that department and assuming important new ones in addition. These functions are to consist of the construction and maintenance of the physical plant, including buildings and appurtenances thereto of all departments of the city other than dock facilities and the buildings of the department of education. The transfer of the building function is to be made from time to time by the Board of Estimate and Apportionment. Thus the city has undertaken a businesslike program of central control of its physical plant. The existing organization of the bridge department is a splendid opportunity for effective constructive service.

The department of bridges, as constituted prior to July 1, 1916, had jurisdiction over the construction, repair, maintenance and management of all bridges that now exist, may be constructed or acquired by the city, which extend across the waters of a navigable stream or have a terminus in two or more boroughs. The department is also permitted by the charter to construct, repair, maintain and manage all tunnels that may be constructed in whole or in part at the expense of the city or that may be acquired by the city which extend under the waters of a navigable stream or have a terminus in two or more boroughs. None of these powers, however, limit or affect those possessed by the public service commission. By special acts of the legislature this department was permitted to construct the Municipal Building and the subway connection under this building to the Brooklyn Bridge.

There are forty-two bridges under the control of this department. These bridges represent an investment of about $120,738,354.59, of which $78,864,379.24 is represented by the structures alone and $41,873,975.35 by the land. For years the expenditures of the department had been predicated upon the capital invested in bridge properties rather than upon the proper operating requirements. For example, when the present administration took office it found that a part of the engineering force which had been engaged on the construction of the Williamsburg, Queensboro and Manhattan bridges, and also on some smaller bridges that were constructed over the Harlem River, Pelham Bay and Newtown Creek, was still on the rolls of the department. It was also found that the maintenance and operating forces engaged on the bridges and in the various shops were excessive and that the revenues over which the commissioner had control were small in comparison with the possibilities.

In addition to these difficulties resulting from long-standing disregard of economy in administration, the commissioner was confronted with many important technical problems, such as the need for better bridge pavements, the need for more efficient methods of making repairs, the reorganization of painting methods, the possibilities of economy in coal consumption and the ever-present requirement that the safety of the bridges be insured for the traveling public.

Internal Reorganization

Steps were taken almost immediately to bring about a more efficient organization of the administrative force. The commissioner abolished two divisions, " division of East River bridges " and the " division of shops and stores." With the abolition of the positions of engineer in charge of the East River bridges, deputy chief engineer and engineer in charge of shops and stores, the line of responsibility for the operation and maintenance of these bridges and the construction and design of new bridges ran directly from the commissioner to his chief engineer and thence to the engineer in charge of the different divisions. There is now no overlapping of responsibility. The large shops and stores at Brooklyn Bridge were placed under the control of the engineer in charge of that bridge, and the small shops and stores were likewise placed under the control of engineers in charge of the other divisions.

The design and construction forces of the department were placed under the direct supervision of the chief engineer. The principal construction jobs in 1913 were the Municipal Building and the Manhattan bridge, both constructed under contract. The former, with the exception of the tower, was rapidly nearing completion and the latter was in its final stage of construction. At that time the corporate stock allowance, as set up in the budget, amounted to $375,439.50. The budget for 1916 shows the corporate stock allowance as $37,905, a reduction of $337,444.50 under 1913 and $211,811.50 under 1915.

In January, 1914, there appeared on the construction rolls, in addition to the ordinary operation and maintenance forces of the department, a chief engineer at $10,000, three consulting engineers at $7,500 per annum, an assistant engineer in charge of design at $6,000, and four assistant engineers at $4,000 per annum. All of these positions and many others have since been dispensed with. To-day the construction force of the department is based on actual current requirements.

In addition to effecting these changes in the engineering force the commissioner directed his attention to a reorganization of the entire personal service of the department. This reorganization work has been carried on during the whole of the past two years. At the beginning of the administration a large portion of the operation and maintenance forces was composed of men well advanced in years. By a gradual reorganization and the elimination of vacant positions, caused by death, resignation, dismissal and retirement, the department has been able to reduce this force considerably. Notwithstanding the reduction in force, it is believed that the service of the department is far more efficient than in 1914. The reductions made are shown by the following table:

Division	January 1, 1914					January 1, 1916				
	Supervision	Operation	Maintenance	Construction Design	**Total**	Supervision	Operation	Maintenance	Construction Design	**Total**
Executive	4	..	..	..	**4**	3	..	..	..	**3**
Clerical	1	..	34	..	**35**	1	..	23	..	**24**
Engineering	1	..	7	..	**8**	1	..	6	..	**7**
Design	1	..	..	24	**25**	1	..	..	7	**8**
Construction	7	..	..	84	**91**	3	..	..	25	**28**
Brooklyn Bridge	14	7	209	..	**230**	8	4	190	..	**202**
Manhattan Bridge	4	..	56	..	**60**	2	2	43	..	**47**
Williamsburg Bridge	15	..	155	..	**170**	6	2	112	..	**120**
Queensboro Bridge	6	4	87	..	**97**	4	7	44	..	**55**
Harlem River	9	134	88	..	**231**	5	110	79	..	**194**
Manhattan and Bronx, Brooklyn, Queens and Richmond	5	118	27	..	**150**	4	110	26	..	**140**
Shops and stores	4	..	32	..	**36**	..	..	..	..	..
Painting	..	..	..	..	..	7	..	107	..	**114**
Total	71	263	695	108	**1,137**	45	235	630	32	**942**
Municipal garage	..	4	11	..	**15**	..	32	12	..	**44**
Grand total	71	267	706	108	**1,152**	45	267	642	32	**986**

With this decreased force the department undertook many improvements with departmental labor in place of contract labor, such as changing the lighting system on the various bridges, in co-operation with the department of water supply, gas and electricity, which resulted in a considerable money saving and more effective service.

The following tables show the economies in appropriations to the department and expenditures by the department represented in part by reductions in force mentioned above and in part by other changes to be described later.

Appropriations

	1913	1914	1915	1916
Tax levy	$922,255.25	$871,699.85	$802,205.09	$609,269.45
Bridge revenue	440,253.94	438,433.95†	403,082.33††	432,946.98
Corporate stock	375,349.50	249,716.50	75,000.00	37,905.00
Special account*	11,507.50	11,465.50	12,877.00	....
Tax levy (municipal garage)**	....	....	13.00	137,500.50
Total	$1,749,366.19	$1,571,315.80	$1,293,177.42	$1,217,621.93

*Old municipal garage.
**New municipal garage.
†Actual appropriation by board of estimate was $410,025.97.
††Actual appropriation by board of estimate was $365,215.66.

EXPENDITURES

	1913	1914	1915
Tax budget	$878,449.64	$844,883.30	$797,597.78[1]
Bridge revenue	419,785.49	404,772.68	361,043.30[2]
Corporate stock	336,960.03	241,266.66[3]	85,926.09[4]
Special account	10,752.86	10,217.10	12,057.57
Totals	$1,645,948.02	$1,501,139.74	$1,256,624.74

[1]Includes outstanding encumbrances.

[2]Special revenue bonds to amount of $27,563.65 were provided and are not included in this amount to meet a deficiency in the appropriation of Williamsburg Bridge revenues.

[3]About $8,500 was not set up in the budget and is for wages of a force engaged on structural changes to Williamsburg Bridge to permit of the operation of the new 10-foot-wide subway cars across that bridge.

[4]This figure includes the sum of $10,426.09 added for salaries, temporary employees, engaged in construction, over the amount provided in the budget; and also does not include the sum of $36,983.86 for the wages of a force engaged on the structural changes to Williamsburg Bridge as stated above.

These tables show that the 1916 budget carries tax levy appropriations less by $312,985.80 than the 1913 budget and that the total budget schedules (including corporate stock, bridge revenue and municipal garage appropriations) are $531,744.26 less for 1916 than they were for 1913. These reductions have been made in spite of the addition of over $125,000 to the 1916 municipal garage account because of its extended activities, and in spite of the fact that the Manhattan Bridge did not go into practically complete maintenance until 1915. This bridge was opened to vehicular traffic in 1909 when yet uncompleted.

Specific Economies Effected

Some of the specific improvements in organization and economies in operation are described below:

1 By a redistribution of the work in the executive office, the position of secretary to the department at $4,000 per annum, was dispensed with.

2 A gradual reorganization of the division of audit and accounts, has resulted in a saving of about $13,050. The payrolls which were formerly made up in this office from the time sheets submitted by the engineers in charge of the various divisions are now submitted by the central payroll bureau to this department, to be in turn transmitted to the foreman in charge of the various gangs or to the person who has immediate supervision over a force, for the purpose of inserting on the roll the amounts due to the various persons working under them. Part of the force engaged in making up these rolls has been transferred to the department of finance. The payrolls were prepared in duplicate by hand; now they are prepared by machine.

3 Supplies on open market orders are now purchased by one instead of by two employees, as formerly. This consolidation effected a saving of $3,000 a year. All the supplies for the department and for the municipal garage are bought in one office. Certain articles such as coal, gasoline, lumber, etc., are bought under a general contract for the various departments under the mayor, through the central purchase committee.

4 The office of the chief engineer of the department has been reorganized, at a saving of $9,220. The commissioner now places the responsibility of all engineering matters on a single individual, who is required to supervise all corporate stock work both as to design and construction, and to see that the operation and maintenance of the various bridges are carried on in an efficient manner.

5 A reorganization of the painting force has resulted in a large saving. The 1914 appropriations for salaries and wages for this force were $161,400, in 1915 they were $107,740, and in 1916 they are $92,040, a reduction of $69,360 in two years. Prior to 1914 the painting forces were divided into five separate units—one in each of the five departmental divisions. The separate units made for wasteful and ineffective work, so much so that some structures were more frequently painted than necessary and others did not receive the attention they required due to the unequal distribution of the forces. This new division is under the immediate supervision of an assistant engineer who reports directly to the acting chief engineer.

6 At the beginning of the present administration there were full operating crews both day and night on nearly all the smaller bridges over the Harlem River and Bronx, and on some of the bridges over Gowanus Canal and Newtown Creek. At night the traffic over these bridges and on these waters is considerably reduced. With due regard to public safety, the night crews were reduced to a minimum, effecting a saving with other changes of about $20,000.

7 During the past two years various changes were made in the lighting system of these bridges, in the method of both illumination and wiring, which improved the lighting of the bridges and resulted in a considerable saving. This saving on the four East River bridges already amounts to $22,000 and will probably be further increased.

Revenues

At the same time that these efforts towards greater economy were being prosecuted, the department devoted much time to the problem of increasing its revenues. The following summary of revenue receipts indicates a gratifying increase in the annual income obtained for the general fund:

	1913	1914	1915
Railroad tolls, etc.	$361,390.80	$334,077.15	$336,043.49
Rents and privileges	102,495.05	113,000.19	126,859.43
Market stand fees and rents	10,276.00	9,777.00	33,763.76
	$474,161.85	$456,854.34	$496,664.68
Railroad tolls due and uncollected	19,776.90	53,643.40	56,889.00
Total	$493,938.75	$510,497.74	$553,553.68

From the Brooklyn Bridge, revenues from railroad tolls and privileges have increased from $77,680 in 1913 to $100,501 in 1915. The revenue from the Manhattan Bridge amounted to $5 in 1914. In 1915 this was increased to $1,015. The commissioner, under authorization of the sinking fund commission, has been able to sell at public auction a lease of premises under the Manhattan approach of the Manhattan Bridge for $16,000 per annum, for the first ten years, and $17,600 per annum for the next ten years. The maximum price fixed by real estate experts as to the leasing value of these premises was $9,000 per annum. There are certain recapture clauses which will safeguard the city's interest in this property.

For the Queensboro Bridge, excluding the railroad tolls, the revenue from rents and privileges increased from $1,000 in 1913 to $3,729.18 in 1915. During the early part of 1915 a public market was established by the borough president with the co-operation of the bridge commissioner under the Manhattan approach of this bridge. Lately it has been enlarged. The revenue from this source amounted to $15,364.76.

During the past two years considerable thought and attention has been given by the commissioner of bridges to the subject of rebating tolls paid by the railroad companies for the use of the Brooklyn and Williamsburg Bridges, with a view to not allowing credits which some of them had received through an interpretation of Section 48 of the tax law.

The contention of the commissioner that these tolls should not be credited against special franchise taxes was confirmed by a decision of Supreme Court Justice Whitaker, which was afterward affirmed unanimously by the Appellate Division, Justice McLaughlin writing the opinion. This decision in favor of the city was given in the case of the New York Railways Company against the city for tolls paid on account of surface cars using the Williamsburg Bridge, and the facts brought out in this instance could be equally applied to all the companies of the Brooklyn Rapid Transit system which are now receiving such credits.

The companies using the Brooklyn and Williamsburg Bridges are operating under agreements entered into in 1897 and 1904, respectively. The tolls collected, namely, five cents per round trip for surface cars, and ten cents per round trip for elevated cars, are paid by the railroad companies for the privilege of operating on tracks that have been installed and paid for by the city. The amount of these tolls is afterwards deducted from the amount of the franchise tax against the companies, as required under the interpretation of Section 48 of the franchise tax law, the city suffering a loss on the entire transaction, as it has to assume the expense of employing clerks, etc., in the collection of these tolls.

The importance of this matter to the taxpayers is evident from the fact that during the period from 1904 to 1914 the sum of $2,786,300 was paid to the city by these railroad companies and later deducted as credits from their special franchise tax. When the new law takes effect,* the city will be

* Bill passed by the Legislature at the last session.

able to retain its revenue of $240,000 to $300,000 annually, collected in tolls from the railroad companies as rental for the use of the Brooklyn and Williamsburg Bridges as well as the full proceeds of the special franchise tax.

Although these credits have for many years been granted to the railroad companies, the present commissioner was the first to take this matter up with a view to having the city retain moneys justly earned and due it.

In order further to preserve the city's rights the bridge commissioner early in 1915 protested to the state tax board against the inclusion as a part of the value of the special franchise, of the privilege of the railroads to cross these bridges. The contention of the commissioner has been sustained by the state tax board, and in the 1916 assessment this privilege has been specifically excluded from the value of the franchise.

Bridge Pavement

Another very important problem which confronted the incoming administration was that of bridge paving. The department has now adopted the policy of using on all bridges either granite block or wood block pavement. All other kinds have been found to be unsatisfactory. In accordance with this policy nine of the smaller bridges or parts thereof have had the wood plank, sheet asphalt or asphalt block removed and wood block substituted. All these bridges have been maintained at a slight cost as to repairs insofar as the wearing surfaces are concerned. Two of the bridges are of the rolling lift type and the wood block pavement has given entire satisfaction. There has been no heaving or bulging of the blocks on either of these bridges.

The pavements of the large East River bridges, particularly the Queensboro, Brooklyn and the Williamsburg bridges, have caused considerable criticism.

The Queensboro Bridge is paved with wood block for its entire length of 7,449 feet, all of which, with the exception of 1,486 feet which is the length of two of the approaches to the bridge, has almost completely failed. This failure is due to the foundation of the pavement and is in no way concerned with the wood block itself. The department would have reconstructed this pavement long before this time had the board of estimate and apportionment rendered a decision as to the crossing of this bridge by rapid transit trains as provided in the dual contract.

The department in its design for the repaving of the roadway contemplated the removal of the surface car tracks within the roadway limits and the operation of all the trolley lines, three in number, on the outside brackets. This decision was arrived at after long and mature investigation. The mayor designated a committee of engineers from other departments of the city to report on the bridge department's design of reconstruction which included the removal of these tracks. The report as made fully approves the bridge department's design.

The original pavement of this bridge cost $3.50 per square yard. The pavement which the department proposes, of which over 2,000 square yards have been laid, costs $3 a yard. It is proposed to reinforce the buckle plate floor of the roadway. This will mean an additional expenditure amounting to approximately a dollar a yard of roadway surface. The department had to deal with a condition which is nowhere to be found in any of the large bridges of the country; and in the design a foundation was necessary that would not diminish the carrying capacity of the structure. The design is a rather unique one—never having been attempted on any bridge to the knowledge of the engineers of the department.

The Brooklyn Bridge presents a peculiar condition. This bridge has two roadways each 16 feet 9 inches in width. Within the limits of each there is a surface car track leaving about 10 feet for accommodation of vehicles. The bridge was opened to traffic in 1883 and from that time until 1914 no attempt had been made to reduce the very heavy annual cost of maintaining the spruce plank which provides the wearing surface of the roadway on the main span. The renewal of the spruce plank has cost about $25,000 a year, as it is necessary to replace the planks about twice a year. The department has requested the sum of $70,000 for the reconstruction of its part of the roadway. The present spruce plank wearing surface is set on a creosoted yellow pine timber underdeck about four inches in thickness. The department's design provides for a creosoted wood block pavement with an underdeck of untreated yellow pine timber varying in depth from four to five inches.

In the reconstruction of the roadway floor it is contemplated that the present "T" rail is to be removed and a grooved girder rail installed. The department expects the railroad company to do this part of the work.

The Williamsburg Bridge roadway also requires considerable attention. The design of the roadway between the anchorages consists of wood block pavement laid on a steel channel floor. These channels are 12 inches wide with webs laid longitudinally, the supports being taken care of by the flanges. These webs owing to the continually increasing heavy vehicular traffic have deflected for almost the entire length of the bridge and in many cases these deflections have produced ruptures. The department has removed during the past two years twenty-five of these channels annually. Many plans were thought of with the view of reconstructing this pavement, and one that offered the least interference to traffic as well as the most economical provided for the laying of wood block 2¼ inches in depth cut from 2 x 6 plank on 2½ x 12 yellow pine timber laid transversely to the center line of the bridge and securely bolted to the roadway channels which are laid longitudinally. The department has put in over a thousand yards of this pavement and up-to-date the result has been satisfactory.

Brooklyn Bridge Subway Connection

The subway connection at the Manhattan terminal of the Brooklyn Bridge was completed in 1914. The construction work cost $588,330.41 and land and easements cost $152,967.49, a total of $741,297.90. Early in 1915 a representative of the Brooklyn Rapid Transit Railroad interviewed the commissioner about the operation of this connection, but as the law provides that the commissioner *must charge* an annual rental equal to the interest on the bonds required for the cost of construction plus 1% for amortization, and as the railroad company is unwilling to pay such a charge, no progress has been made towards operation. Operation would permit a connection of elevated trains on Fulton street, west of Manhattan crossing, with the Broadway-Seventh Avenue-59th Street subway. Further, this connection would make possible the running of trains or cars of the present weight to the Municipal Building, relieving the New York station of some of the congestion during rush hours by operating empty trains through the subway connection from New York to Brooklyn, where these trains may have come in over the Williamsburg Bridge. In case of congestion in the station at the New York end of the Brooklyn Bridge the subway connection would make possible the operation of trains into the underground station in the Municipal Building and the delivery of passengers there.

This would afford a *partial* loop service with the Manhattan and Williamsburg bridges. It is not believed feasible to operate a full train of the new steel cars across Brooklyn Bridge on account of the requirements for the structure's safety.

Proposed Work for Next Two Years

Brooklyn Bridge

1 Further changes in the lighting system to reduce the cost of current.
2 Repavement of roadway with a pavement of a more durable character.
3 Reconstruction of the Brooklyn approach of Brooklyn Bridge. It is proposed to remove the present terminal and train platform, to make changes affecting the elevated and surface lines now using the bridge and to construct a new station building.
4 Reconstruction of Manhattan terminal of Brooklyn Bridge. It is proposed to remove the present train shed extension across Park Row. The plan devised is to construct a building of an ornamental passenger promenade crossing over Park Row to City Hall.

A new design of support has been perfected for the short suspension rods at the center of the river span.

Manhattan Bridge

An effort should be made to induce the Brooklyn Rapid Transit Railroad to operate some of their surface lines intersecting Flatbush Avenue extension, over the Manhattan Bridge. This would be an excellent service to the public and would make the new civic center more accessible to Brooklyn. A terminal is now being constructed on the Manhattan Bridge at Bayard street which could accommodate added lines.

Williamsburg Bridge

Wrapping main cables to stop rusting.

Substituting some permanent fireproof construction on footwalks. Designs have been made.

Continuing repaving of roadways, main and end spans.

Repaving at least one half of roadway pavement on approaches; approximately 50% complete at the present time.

Widening the south outside platform at Bedford Avenue station and extending the present roadway over the south clearance to permit of this change. The necessity for this improvement depends on the development of this neighborhood as a factory center, and on the increased use of the present platform. The platform is small and the traffic at night considerable.

Improving the south clearance property from Bedford Avenue to New Street.

Designing and constructing the traveling scaffold under bridge floor.

Designing and constructing cross walks between footwalks, main span.

Designing and installing an electrically-operated two-leaf runaway gate at north roadway Manhattan end.

Constructing bulkheads at river on Brooklyn side.

Waterproofing roof of Bedford Avenue stairs; also footwalk walls between Bedford and Driggs Avenues.

It has been suggested that a comfort station be established on the New York side of this bridge in the vicinity of Clinton and Delancy Streets.

It is suggested that a new station on the Brooklyn Plaza of this bridge between Roebling and Havemeyer Streets be installed, which would accommodate the express as well as the local elevated service, if satisfactory arrangements can be made with the company for the payment by them of a rental.

It is also suggested that the north foot walk of the bridge be repaired and converted into a recreation centre.

Queensboro Bridge

The present paving is to be replaced by a new kind specially designed by the department. The wood block now in use on this bridge extends from Second Avenue, Manhattan, to Crescent Street, Queens. From the Manhattan anchor pier to Ely Avenue, in Queens, the pavement rests upon a concrete foundation of varying thickness which in turn is supported by buckle plates riveted to the floor beams and stringers. This section has presented the greatest difficulty in the matter of proper repair, practically all of the expenditures for upkeep having been confined to this portion.

Since the proposed repaving requires the reconstruction of the floor system, the existing tracks between the trusses must be removed during such operation. In order to obviate the expense of relaying new rails, it is proposed to transfer the street railway service now operating over these tracks to the tracks supported on the outer brackets of the bridge over which two other companies now operate. The greatest density of travel so far reached on the Queensboro Bridge is 180 cars per hour in one direction over two tracks. At the peak of the rush hour on the Brooklyn Bridge, 360 cars per hour per single track were operated in one direction. Further, the operation of the Second Avenue elevated trains over the Queensboro Bridge, the newly constructed elevated lines to Queens, and the proposed tunnel connection between Manhattan and Queens will all tend to relieve any future possibility of surface car congestion. In addition to these facts, the rapidly increasing amount of vehicular traffic on the bridge demands as wide a roadway as can be provided.

Harlem River, Manhattan and Bronx Division

Apart from the necessary changes and repairs in the operation and maintenance of the fifteen bridges, the department proposes to change the lighting system on the Willis Avenue Bridge, 135th Street Bridge and City Island Bridge and to install new navigation lights on the Third Avenue, Madison Avenue, 145th Street, Washington, University Heights, Ship Canal, Westchester Avenue and Eastchester Bridges.

PROPOSED NEW BRIDGES

Morris Heights Bridge over the Harlem River

This bridge is to cross the Harlem River from West 177th Street in the borough of The Bronx to the Harlem River Speedway in the borough of Manhattan. It will provide a direct connection between The Bronx and the Dyckman Street section and the upper end of Riverside Drive on the west. Surveys and soundings have been made for this bridge.

174th Street Bridge over the Bronx River

This bridge will be located on the extension of one of the main cross streets in this district. It will open up connections with a large section lying east of the Bronx River which at present is very inaccessible. The existing bridges at Westchester and Tremont Avenues are nearly one mile apart. The proposed bridge will be about half way between the two. Surveys and soundings have been made for this crossing.

Unionport Bridge (Bascule)

This is now under construction. Funds have been provided. This structure is to cross Westchester Creek at East 177th Street ($195,511 contract bid). Ludlow and Tremont Avenues converge near this crossing and both are important highways in The Bronx. The new bridge is to replace the old one which was antiquated and inadequate for present traffic. Tremont and Ludlow Avenues are graded on both sides of the creek and the New York City Interborough Railroad Co. has the franchise for extending this line across the creek to Long Island Sound. The new bridge will be able to accommodate this traffic and assist in the development of the large district lying easterly. This, for some time, will be the only crossing over the navigable portion (about 3 miles) of Westchester Creek.

A contract has been entered into for the construction of this bridge.

Eastchester Bridge

The designing of this structure is about to commence, $180,000 of corporate stock having been authorized for this work.

The proposed new bridge will be on the line of Boston Post Road, one of the main arteries of travel to towns lying eastward on Long Island Sound. It will relieve the present heavy traffic over Pelham Bridge, by affording a shorter route to remote points. At present a temporary bridge is located here which will be removed upon the completion of the new one, for which plans are now in preparation.

Municipal Building

At the beginning of 1914 the Municipal Building had been advanced to 86.1 per cent of its present state of completion; $10,175,466.33 had been certified for completed work. At the close of 1915, a total of $11,818,305.29 had been certified for completed work and there remained an outstanding obligation amounting to $177,313.29. There is an unencumbered authorization of $404,696.41. It is estimated that this balance will be sufficient for all construction necessary for the full completion of the building as contemplated in the original plans.

The rentable area of the building is 633,319 square feet, of which about 22,722 square feet is unfinished and unoccupied. At the beginning of 1914, 45 departments were assigned to the building—to about 28.2 per cent of space available. Changes in assignments were made with a view to effecting the greatest possible utilization of the building. At the close of 1915, 59 departments were housed and all of the main part of the building, 96.4 per cent, was occupied.

The cost of the building to date, as represented by all obligations liquidated or outstanding is $11,995,618.56, exclusive of site, or at the rate of 61 cents per cubic foot.

The completion of a passageway connecting the Brooklyn Bridge station of the Interborough Rapid Transit subway with the Municipal Building station of the New York Municipal Railway Corporation adds greatly to the convenience of about 25,000 persons daily.

Proposed work on building

Safety devices for elevators (in progress)
Studies of space assignment
Construction and equipment of women's lunch room
Construction of storage room in basement
Placing of weather strips on east and west windows
Storm doors for west vestibules
Fire prevention appliances
Changes in lighting fixtures

Municipal Garage

This garage is part of the Brooklyn Bridge division.

The old organization was under the control of the engineer in charge of the Brooklyn Bridge, and was operated originally as a small garage for the benefit of bridge department cars. Its efficiency caused other departments to take advantage of it until it developed into a garage storing and supplying 28 cars and making repairs and furnishing supplies to an average of 22 more which were stored outside. It had a repair force of machinists, cleaners and washers performing the work of the average public garage. Economies were effected in repairs to cars, purchase of supplies, handling of work, and centralization of purchasing with accompanying reduced prices.

At the request of the mayor, the chamberlain caused records to be kept in the various departments for a period of four months to show the exact use and operating cost of each car. A report was made to the mayor showing a disproportionate use of cars for the transportation of officials to and from their homes, a disproportionate amount of idle time for cars exclusively assigned to a particular official or department; and that economies to the amount of $76,866 would be effected if the service were centralized and placed under the control of a single department, and cars assigned to officials as required, on a livery basis. Upon recommendation to the board of estimate and apportionment funds were provided in the 1916 budget for the establishment of this garage, which effected a saving in appropriation for this purpose in the various departments under the mayor of $94,000. However, certain cars were not included in this service, those for fire chiefs, police patrol wagons, ambulances, motor trucks, etc. The cars brought under the municipal garage are passenger cars used by administrative officials for occasional trips of inspection and for transportation about the city.

The new organization of the municipal garage is operated under the supervision of the engineer in charge of the Brooklyn Bridge and consists of a garage foreman, a clerk, a dispatcher and a repair and cleaning force.

It has taken over about 90 cars from 18 different departments under the mayor's jurisdiction, and is designed to supply service to all departments requiring motor car service on call, keeping a record of the cost of maintenance of cars and the number of hours of service provided to each of the different departments served by it. The appropriation for 1916 provides a schedule of the hours of service to which each department will be entitled.

DEPARTMENT OF STREET CLEANING

Introduction

The department of street cleaning of the city of New York is the largest single municipal sanitation department in the world. It serves a population of over 5,000,000 individuals living in a territory of 140 square miles with an average density of 58 people per acre.

Its functions as defined in the charter comprise the cleaning of streets, removal of snow, collection and disposal of ashes, garbage, street sweepings, rubbish and roadway incumbrances. The department exercises these functions in three boroughs of the Greater City, namely, Manhattan, Brooklyn and The Bronx. In the other two boroughs, Richmond and Queens, these functions are under the jurisdiction of the borough presidents.

The present commissioner has realized from the first that if the business of the department is efficiently managed the municipality will reap benefits in the shape of improved public health, comfort, convenience, and greater civic reputation. He has felt that to achieve these results the department must be organized and operated along the lines of a successful commercial enterprise rather than as a political institution.

The magnitude of its work can be realized from the fact that in 1915 it involved the collection and disposal of 8,704,316 cubic yards of waste (an average of 1,200 pounds per capita), the removal of 4,972,307 cubic yards of snow and the daily cleaning of more than 1,500 miles of paved streets used by upwards of 100,000 horses. Incidentally it is interesting to note that in the last ten years despite the enormous increase in the use of motor vehicles the number of horses in use in this city has not decreased.

Aside from the work involved in the direct exercise of its charter functions, but constituting a very important feature of the actual conduct of that work, the department provides its own auxiliary service, which includes among other things the care of some 2,500 horses, the maintenance and repair of practically all the departmental structures and equipment, and the purchase, storage and distribution of all its equipment and supplies.

The appropriations made for this department, which for the last six years have averaged $7,500,000 per annum, serve to indicate the volume of work in a general way, although they do not adequately reflect either the quality or quantity of work done in that period.

For the three years prior to the present administration these appropriations were:

1911	$7,233,000
1912	7,422,000
1913	7,710,000

Each succeeding increase represents in a measure the increment made necessary by the growth in population, and the rise in cost of commodities. During this period, however, it may fairly be said that no scientific attempts were made to reduce the unit cost of any feature of the work either by securing an increased output from the laboring force or by the adoption of more economical methods; nor were any improvements made in the quality of the work to meet the widespread demand for higher civic standards resulting from a growing realization of the close relationship of cleanliness to health.

In contrast with the above, the departmental appropriations for the first three years of the present administration were as follows:

1914	$7,682,000
1915	7,646,000
1916	7,571,000

These reductions have been made possible despite the normal increase in population and in the cost of commodities. Moreover, it is believed that the quality of work has been greatly improved and undoubtedly the quantity increased.

The efforts of the commissioner to bring the department up to an acceptable standard of efficiency have been seriously embarrassed by the fact that, while the department of street cleaning is mainly responsible for street sanitation in the broadest sense of the word, the charter grants to other city departments control over many of the conditions which directly affect its work.

Responsibility for Sanitation Decentralized

At the present time, for instance, the cleaning of sidewalks is not a part of the work this department, or, for that matter, of any department, although control of other sidewalk conditions is under the jurisdiction of the several borough presidents. Yet it is obvious that roadways cannot be thoroughly clean if the sidewalks are neglected. It might be expected that the city ordinances would place responsibility for the cleanliness of sidewalks definitely upon the shoulders of the property owner, but this is not the case, and attempts to remedy the matter by the adoption of suitable ordinances by the board of aldermen have failed on two occasions during the present administration. Even with an appropriate ordinance, the difficulty of enforcement by the police is apparent, and while the co-operation of the police department in enforcing minor ordinances relating to street sanitation has noticeably improved in recent years, it is clear that much better results would be secured by including the cleaning of sidewalks among the functions of this department.

No less requisite to the proper performance of its work is the cooperation of other departments whose functions are intimately related to the work of street cleaning. Among those functions, jurisdiction over which is vested in the borough presidents, may be mentioned the construction and repair of pavements, supervision over the use of streets for storage of building material—in itself a source of much street dust—as well as the construction, maintenance and cleaning of sewers and catch-basins, the latter process being only another means by which the street dirt is removed to the street cleaning dumps. The department of health is charged with the removal of dead animals from the streets and the licensing of private refuse collectors. The cleaning of some streets, as well as the entire sanitation of parks and parkways, is controlled by the departments of parks. The department of water supply has control over the use of water for street flushing and for augmenting sewer flow during periods of snow removal, increased utilization of which processes have, under the present administration, resulted in great economy as well as in improved conditions of cleanliness.

Quit easide from the departmental co-operation above mentioned, the work of street cleaning is further dependent upon the co-operation of every individual citizen, and if this city is to be the model in street sanitation that is desired it is essential that the public come to a full realization of its share in the responsibility for maintaining a high standard of street cleanliness. The department of street cleaning may be said to have a contract with the people of the city under which it performs certain work for which the residents pay. It is to their interest that this work be reduced as much as possible in order that the cost to them may be correspondingly lessened. They should therefore understand and live up to the laws and ordinances which have been devised to control the inclination of the individual in the general interest of the community.

The fact that this relation of the individual to the city in matters of street sanitation has not in the past been properly understood or fully realized has led the present commissioner to inaugurate an active public educational campaign. The activities of a division of the department previously established for this purpose but operating in a restricted field have been greatly extended and the entire time of one man is now employed in organizing juvenile leagues in the schools of the city and instructing them in matters of street sanitation. There are now over three hundred of these juvenile leagues pledged to aid in keeping the streets of the city clean. Attempts have also been made to educate the public in these matters by the use of signs placed on collection carts or painted on refuse cans. A popular phraseology is used, such as, " Help keep the street clean—use this can," " This is your city, make it the cleanest in the world."

Auxiliary Service Inadequate

Although the population has been growing rapidly and demands for more and better service have been made on the department, the physical means for accomplishing its work, namely, its plant and equipment, as well as the methods employed in its performance, had been improved but little in the seventeen years prior to January 1, 1914. Up to the beginning of this administration practically no change had been made in the type of equipment installed by Commissioner Waring in 1897.

The only mechanical equipment for combating the dust evil consisted of four flushing machines and a few squeegee machines, all horse drawn.

Only two motor-drawn vehicles were in service despite the demonstration of their profitable use in large private enterprises. At five of the twenty-six stables owned or leased by the department individual shops were located for the repair of equipment, and each stable also maintained its own separate shops for horse shoeing and harness repairs. Furthermore, the repair procedure then employed made repairs to equipment expensive and uneconomical.

The stores service, likewise, was carried on in an extremely unsystematic way, partly through lack of suitable facilities and organization and partly through the failure to establish a definite, logical system of stores control.

The results accomplished during the past two years in remedying these defects in plant, equipment and stores service are shown in the following report.

General Organization

During the past two years much has been done to improve the organization of the department. This organization which has always been of a military character, with executive control vested in a commissioner appointed by the mayor, consists of a uniformed force performing the functional work, and a non-uniformed force performing the clerical and other auxiliary service.

Prior to 1914 the commissioner's authority was exercised through three deputy commissioners appointed by him, one for each borough. The form of organization for work control then in existence may be described as partly geographical and partly functional in character. The boroughs were, as at present, divided into districts, each in charge of a district superintendent. The organization for each of the three boroughs differed slightly. Under the deputy commissioner was the general superintendent, to whom the district superintendents and the stable foremen were directly responsible. In Manhattan the general superintendent also reported directly to the commissioner on many matters and exercised a nominal control over district superintendents and stable foremen in the other boroughs. The district superintendent controlled the operations of street cleaning, refuse collection and carting, but had practically no authority over the stable in his district, or over the drivers when they were in the stable, and his control over refuse disposal terminated upon the arrival of the carts at the dumps. Here the superintendent of final disposition, responsible to the commissioner only, was in control, both of the unloading of the carts and of the loading of the scows and final disposition of all refuse by the contractors.

It will readily be perceived that this form of organization afforded countless opportunities for conflicts of authority, with the result that not only was there great difficulty in fixing responsibility for unsatisfactory work, but also in giving credit where due. Another disadvantage was that owing to the short term of office of the deputy commissioners a large part of their time was occupied in becoming thoroughly familiar with the routine work. Hence it was found necessary with each change of administration to assign an experienced officer, usually a district superintendent, to each borough office to act as virtual head of the borough organization and to instruct the deputy commissioner in the details of his work.

To remedy these defects in organization, the present commissioner held a series of conferences with the officers of the department, at which the defects were analyzed and a new plan outlined. It was decided that the functional type of organization, on account of the wide distribution of the work, and the greater expense entailed, would not be so well adapted to the work of the department as the geographical type. The commissioner enlisted the help of the Bureau of Municipal Research and the efficiency staff of the commissioner of accounts for the development of reorganization plans, which during the past two years have been gradually perfected and put into operation.

To relieve the commissioner of administrative details in order that more of his time might be devoted to matters of policy, a fourth deputy commissioner was appointed, who has been placed in charge of the central office functions.

This deputy commissioner was given direct supervision over all of those auxiliary services noted in the first part of this report, with the exception of the care of horses, which was made a district function. Veterinary care of horses, however, and the maintenance and repair of equipment which were formerly borough functions, have been put by the present administration under the control of the central office in order to secure greater uniformity of method and, in the case of equipment and repairs, a more economical operation and an organization more readily adjustable to varying conditions.

The jurisdiction of the general superintendent of Manhattan was restricted and clearly defined.

In the boroughs of Brooklyn and The Bronx two positions of borough superintendent with the civil service title of "district superintendent" were established, thus insuring greater continuity to the executive work of these boroughs and enabling the borough deputy commissioner to keep in closer touch with all activities of the department within his borough. The functions of the superintendent of a district were extended to include control over all departmental activities within the district. At the present time, therefore, the district superintendent is in charge not only of the foremen of sections, but of the stable foremen and all the forces employed at the dumps for unloading the carts, etc. Final disposal is made by contract as formerly, and the superintendent of final disposition is responsible for the enforcement of contract provisions, and the physical condition of the dumps.

These changes in organization have resulted in a stronger and more definitized control and have freed the higher officials from unnecessary petty detail, permitting them to devote more of their time to general improvements.

A planning and engineering division has been established, consisting of an examining engineer and seven technically trained subordinates. This division has proved of great assistance to the department in designing new equipment, working out improved methods of procedure, conducting tests, and furnishing exact data for comparative cost analyses. The wisdom of establishing the planning division has been demonstrated by the great saving of both time and money effected by the new methods of snow removal which it worked out and by the success of the so-called model district.

Model District Organized

For the purpose of demonstrating the greater economy and better results obtainable by the employment of scientific methods and modern equipment, the sixth district, bounded roughly by the East River, 12th Street, 5th Avenue and 40th Street, was selected for the experiment because it was believed that the varied character of its structures and general conditions were typical of those in the entire city.

To the people in the model district the most noticeable change so far has probably been the disappearance of the objectionable open ash and garbage carts, and the use in their place of large trucks or trailers (drawn by motor tractors) which collect ashes, garbage and litter simultaneously from each house, the ashes and garbage being carried in closed receptacles. The tractors can be equipped with snow plows instead of trailers and used for snow removal, but for the daily work of the department they are fitted with three or more different types of trailers, one for refuse collection, one for street flushing or sweeping and one for sweeping and hauling snow. A gradual reorganization of the collection service has been progressing for the last seven months and complete elimination of horse drawn collection vehicles in this district was effected last May. On the basis of results thus far accomplished, an annual saving of some $34,000 is indicated for the collection service alone, after allowing the usual depreciation charges on new equipment purchased. In addition, it has been found possible to return to the department from this district for use in other districts or for sale, equipment of the old type valued at approximately $600,000.

Standard Procedure

At the beginning of the present administration there existed in the department practically no code of standard procedure, nor was any systematic method employed in instructing new men in their duties. To devise means for remedying these defects, twenty-one committees, composed of officers of the department, were formed early in 1914. These committees have been engaged during the past two years in summarizing, analyzing and criticizing present methods of sweeping, refuse collection, the care of horses, stables, equipment, etc., in recommending improvements, and finally

Collecting all Three Classes of Household Waste Simultaneously by Tractor-trailer

Tractor of the Model District Used as Snow Plow, Trailer Having Been Detached

in submitting written reports which contain conclusions as to the best methods of performing stated classes of work. No such undertaking had ever before been attempted in the department, and no uniformity existed in methods of hand sweeping, flushing, etc., in different districts of the city, so that district superintendents were not agreed at first as to the one best way of performing the usual set tasks. As a result of the committees' work, however, and the general discussions that followed, explicit instructions for standard practices are now available in the form of printed handbooks.

Up to the present time there have been issued for the instruction of the departmental forces about a dozen of these handbooks of standard procedure, which cover the majority of routine operations performed by departmental forces, including the new methods of snow removal. In addition, there have been issued handbooks containing other information and regulations of importance to all employees, among which may be mentioned "Summary of Laws and Ordinances Relative to Cleaning of Streets and Sidewalks," "Definition of Terms for Departmental Employees" and "Code of Discipline." It is the intention of the present administration to have this series continued so as to include all operations performed by the department. When published together as one book on "Street Cleaning, Standard Methods and Procedure," the volume will have a unique value as representing the recorded experience of men who are devoting their life to street sanitation problems.

To combine the function of instruction in standard procedure with that of an independent inspectional service, a superintendent of instruction and inspection has been provided, and a school of instruction established where both old and new employees may be thoroughly drilled in the work to be performed and the best methods to be followed. This school has daily sessions in a room with appropriate equipment in the headquarters building of the model district, and has resulted in a more intelligent interest in the work, and its consequent performance with greater efficiency by the members of the force.

Personnel

During the last seventeen years the administrative control of the department has changed, on an average, once every two years. In the four-year term of one mayor five different commissioners were appointed. This, together with the fact that with possibly one exception none of the commissioners had had any previous experience in work of this character, prevented the development of any definite policies or standards of work. The time of the higher administrative officials was principally taken up with straightening out the tangles in current work due to lack of proper organization and rules of procedure.

At the beginning of the present administration, the majority of the officers and men in the department were found to be conscientious, hard working, and willing to give their best efforts in the interest of the service, and in general, the personnel of the working force of 7,000 men was satisfactory. But because of confused methods of control, frequent overlapping of authority and general lack of system, it was impossible for them in many cases to use their abilities to the best advantage.

Realizing this, the new administration conducted a series of officers' conferences at which each man was urged to make whatever suggestions he might have for the improvement of the service. Many of these suggestions were immediately adopted. In this way the service was much improved, and at the same time the men were directly interested in seeing that those changes for which they felt responsible, were effectively carried out.

To regulate, control and secure the best results from the force by obtaining their confidence through "square deal" methods was one of the first objects of the present administration. The success of this effort is now apparent. The next step was to set up a tangible, practical ideal of service to the community. In these directions much was accomplished by the officers' conferences.

With the help of the bureau of standards, standard grades of salary were established for the labor services, rates being based on length of service, records of conduct and quality of work; and a somewhat similar method of salary regulation for the supervisory force has been put into effect this year. It is expected that this will be formally adopted by the board of estimate and apportionment in the near future for most of the positions in the service. According to these new salary schedules, while men on entering the service will receive less than formerly in most positions, they may after satisfactory service receive considerably more than was possible under the old flat rate system, but no reduction in the pay of the existing labor forces will be made. An incentive in this way has been provided to employees to better their positions and increase their salaries by establishing good records for length of service, conduct and work.

Welfare Work Among Employees

It has not been found possible in the department of street cleaning to organize a welfare bureau similar to those found profitable in private corporations, or to appoint any one person to conduct work of this kind, but in several specific matters the interests of the men have been well served and much thought is still being given to this important phase of administration. Such welfare work as had been done in the past was carried on by various separate units of the department. It has now been placed among the duties of the so-called personnel division under the supervision of the deputy commissioner at the central office. The duties of this division include administration of the pension fund, medical care of the men, keeping service and disciplinary records and other work of a similar character.

Up to the present year, the medical care of the men, if such it may be called, consisted solely of examinations of applicants for positions in the department or for admission to the pension roll, and of employees reported as incapacitated for work. For this purpose four physicians were employed on part time at a nominal compensation. In the past two years over 16,000 such examinations were made of the regular force of approximately 7,000 men. It was therefore almost impossible to care for the large number of the men who became ill or were injured through exposure or dangers incident to their work, and no attempt was made to do this. In this two year period, 2,040 employees were injured and 11 killed in performance of duties, a relatively greater proportion of casualties than in the police department.

As a result of these disclosures the medical staff was increased at the beginning of 1916 to one full time physician and four medical examiners, and it is expected that this force will more than pay for itself in decreasing the service loss to the city due to incapacitation of the labor forces, and in preventing illness by educating the men to take more intelligent care of themselves.

Discipline of Force

In the matter of disciplinary measures, a system has just been put into operation which it is believed will be advantageous to deserving men as well as the department as a whole. Until the present time officers brought charges of misconduct before the commissioner. A great deal of time was wasted by the trial of such charges and probably many men were needlessly tried for petty offenses partly owing to their unpopularity with the foremen.

According to the new regulations, it will not be within the authority of any officers other than the commissioner or his deputies to make a charge against an offender necessitating a trial, and such charges will be occasioned only by major offenses. A schedule of demerits for various offenses has been established and penalties for minor delinquencies will be imposed in this form by the borough commissioner. Conduct ratings based on these demerits will be employed in determining salary increases. If during the year the demerits imposed on any individual reach a certain maximum, a trial will be ordered and the usual penalties inflicted, varying from suspension to dismissal. In cases of exceptionally deserving conduct, merit marks will be added to the conduct record of the men.

Other benefits obtained for the men have been changing the pay period from a semi-monthly to a weekly basis, securing better terms for the men in the purchase of their uniforms, and granting audiences once a week to employees who may wish a confidential hearing on any matter relating to the service. The welfare work inaugurated for the employees has resulted in a better *esprit de corps* and consequent better quality of work and more faithful service.

Departmental Budget

As in all other departments, the segregated form of budget has been in force in the department of street cleaning for a number of years. Although a great improvement over the previous condition of uncontrolled expenditure which was subject to serious abuse, it has, nevertheless, placed many restrictions upon the ability of the commissioner to meet successfully the working conditions encountered.

Probably no other department is affected by varying conditions due to seasonal and weather changes, etc., to the same extent. The department must deal continually with constantly changing conditions which seldom occur in any expected sequence. The segregated budget has been found to lack that elasticity which would permit a prompt adaptation of funds to such wide and frequent variations. In consequence, the board of estimate and apportionment has recently considered certain radical changes in the form of this department's budget which, if adopted, will not only provide such elasticity, but at the same time form the basis for a much better administrative control of the department's operations.

The present form of departmental estimate, which has heretofore been considered an essential prerequisite to the proper preparation of the segregated budget, may fairly be said to have been equally responsible in embarrassing departmental operations because it does not demand that the relation between the amount of work to be done and the quantity of articles or services to be purchased be clearly shown.

The present commissioner has attempted to supply this deficiency by securing permission to change the form of estimate, not only with a view to clarifying it, but more particularly to satisfy himself that the items therein contained are requested in proper proportion, and to secure for the future administration of his budget that degree of control which is obviously necessary.

Functional Work

More significant to citizens than betterments in central organization and auxiliary service are the following improvements in the functional work of the department, resulting from the present administration's successful study of the problems involved.

Cleaning Streets

Street cleaning, which consists in removing from the roadways of the streets the daily accumulation of refuse, and in the winter includes also the removal of snow and ice, represents usually about 50% of the department's total expenditures. This branch of service has probably been most open to criticism in the past, and still presents the greatest difficulties, because of the numerous conditions militating against its proper performance, over which the department has no control. It is particularly unfortunate that responsibility for such activities as repairing streets and sidewalks, cleaning sewers and catch basins and tearing up the pavement by gas, electric light and telephone companies, etc., which are prolific sources of street dust, is not properly correlated with responsibility for street cleaning.

If, for instance, the roadway is poorly constructed, or poorly laid out so that its drainage is insufficient, the difficulty of cleaning it may be increased many times. Disintegration of pavement due to its bad state of repair is a common source of street dust and mud, as are also openings made in pavement to give access to sub-surface structures or building construction. Where, as is often the case in building operations, large quantities of building material are allowed to be dumped on the roadway, much of this becomes scattered over the road for long distances at a time. By far the worst conditions with which this department has to contend are those caused by subway construction. Other sources of street dust and dirt are sand, cement, sawdust, etc., dropped from overloaded trucks; excelsior and straw scattered when carts are loaded and unloaded in the wholesale and factory districts, cinders from smokestacks, dirt of all kinds swept by the householder from the sidewalk into the gutter or thrown from the houses directly into the street, and litter, especially fruit skins and paper, dropped by pedestrians. Many of the causes for these conditions are fully covered by ordinances and have been under the present administration considerably ameliorated owing to more active police enforcement. Also, as has already been stated, the public educational work conducted by the department has borne fruit. There is still, however, much room for improvement.

The organization of the street cleaning branch of the department has been little changed during the past two years except for the increased responsibility placed upon the section foreman by reducing the number of assistant foremen. The districts are divided for street cleaning purposes into several sections, each in charge of a foreman, with headquarters in a so-called section house which is used as office, locker room for the sweepers and storehouse for equipment. Each sweeper with the exception of those working in gangs is given a route consisting of one or more blocks of roadway to clean and keep clean.

Standardizing Sweepers' Routes

The method of assigning and carrying on the work has, however, been materially changed. Formerly the determination of the length of each sweeper's route as well as the degree of cleanliness to be attained was left to the discretion of the section foreman, with the result that some sweepers were given considerably more surface to clean than others, and some sections of little importance and low traffic density received relatively more care than others where traffic was more dense or the character of the abutting property such as would warrant more frequent cleaning.

With the idea of standardizing the amount of work involved, and the amount of cleaning which roadways of like character and traffic should receive, an inspection was made at the direction of the present commissioner of every block of roadway in Manhattan, covering the kind of pavement, character of abutting property, amount and character of traffic, and various other factors affecting the rate of accumulation of street refuse. Blocks were then classified according to these characteristics into approximately 300 classes, and an inspection of one or more blocks typical of each of these classes was made to determine the amount of refuse removed per day per 1,000 square yards and the amount of time spent in cleaning. When the observations thus obtained have been completed in the three boroughs it is intended to standardize the day's work for a sweeper, and to lay out the sweeper's routes on this basis on street maps on which roadway areas are marked.

By this means all blocks falling within each particular class will receive a standard amount of cleaning, that is, will be cleaned the number of times per day which it has been determined is advisable for that class of street. Thus inconsistencies of the former cleaning schedules will be eliminated.

Flushing Streets

The work of the sweeper, supplemented by that of the so-called litter squads, will take care of the large particles of refuse in the street. But no matter how efficiently performed, it cannot do away with most of the fine dust which accumulates in large quantities during the day time and blows or drifts about, rendering the streets unsightly and spreading disease germs. Unless most of this dust is removed each day, the streets can hardly be said to have been thoroughly cleaned.

Because of the many difficulties the attempts of past administrations to lessen the dust evil have met with little success. Attempts to design a machine which would remove this street dust in the same way that a vacuum cleaner removes the household dust have so far failed. The best means at present available for removing the dust from the roadway is by a thorough flushing supplemented, in the case of smooth pavement, by scrubbing machines fitted with rubber-shod revolving brushes called squeegees. This means had been employed, prior to 1914, to a limited extent and without the most suitable flushing equipment. The efforts of the present commissioner were directed to improving the methods employed in washing and scrubbing pavements, and toward making it possible to extend this service to all paved streets under the jurisdiction of the department. With the co-operation of the Bureau of Municipal Research and the department of water supply, experiments were made to determine the methods and equipment not only most effective in cleaning the pavement, but also most economical in the use of water.

As a result of these experiments and of further study by department officers it was found possible greatly to improve the flushing process. New forms of hose reel, hydrant equipment, and shut-off nozzles were employed, new methods of procedure established for handling the hose, and the work was so routed as to save retracing steps.

While prior to the adoption of these new methods it was seldom found possible to flush more than 25,000 square yards of pavement effectively per day, it is now possible for a two-man gang to cover from 30,000 to 45,000 square yards in an eight-hour day. Another advantage is that owing to the new designs of reel and the use of more suitable size of hose as well as to improvements in procedure, the wear and tear on the hose, which is the most expensive part of the equipment, is considerably lessened, and in addition 50% less water is required to produce a desired degree of cleanliness. This means a saving of nearly 3,000,000 gallons of water a day.

In May, 1916, and for the first time in the history of the department the practice was inaugurated of giving all paved streets in Manhattan and many in Brooklyn and The Bronx a thorough cleansing by this flushing process every night. Flushing at night is not only more economical in the use of water but is also done more rapidly owing to lower traffic density.

The force employed for flushing and for the preliminary pick-up work is about one-third of the total force formerly employed in the day sweeping, and it has been found that the thorough cleansing which the streets receive each night so improves their early morning condition that the remaining two-thirds of the force can handle the day sweeping without difficulty, keeping the streets even cleaner than before flushing was established since refuse may be picked up before it becomes widely scattered.

The method of flushing now applied to the streets, known as hand-flushing, is the only possible method of flushing all streets, within the limits of the present appropriation. It is believed, however, that it will in the end be more economical to use machine flushing. This would involve an original expenditure considerably greater than that needed for hand flushing, but should result eventually in as great economy as has already resulted from the use of motor vehicles in the model district. For this district, money has recently been appropriated for four combined flushing and sweeping machines for use with the standard tractors already employed for refuse removal. The latter when used with flushing machines will furnish power for operating the pump and revolving brooms. If they prove efficient it is hoped that appropriations may be secured to extend their use to all districts.

Snow Removal

The removal of snow from the streets has constituted a more difficult problem than the daily cleaning, chiefly because snow-filled streets create an emergency condition which cannot be anticipated much in advance of a storm yet which must be met promptly to prevent monetary loss to the citizens through interrupted traffic and consequent injury to all business. The direct cost of snow removal for the five years from 1910 to 1914 was over $6,200,000, and it is estimated that the indirect loss due to interruption of business was several times this amount.

Efforts by past commissioners to improve snow removal methods were sporadic and productive of little good, and it was not possible for the permanent officers in the department experienced in snow work to divert time from routine work to develop new methods or inaugurate advantageous changes in policy. In past years, with the exception of snow removed from gutters and cross walks by the department's regular force of sweepers, assisted by about the same number of laborers hired in such emergencies, practically all of the snow was removed under contract. Such men and teams as could be spared from the department's collection service were also employed in carting away snow from those streets not cleared by the contractor, but only a very small proportion of the work could be thus handled. The city, therefore, depended chiefly upon the contractors to haul snow from the streets to waterfront dumps, the work not starting as a rule until the storm was over and traffic already retarded or in some cases even completely blocked. No other method was considered feasible, and the time elapsing before streets were again in good condition after a storm depended largely upon the supply of trucks which the contractors could secure.

Such was the state of affairs early in February, 1914, when, just after the present administration took office, there began one of the longest and most difficult storm periods ever experienced by the city. For five weeks the department was engaged in a struggle to open the streets for traffic and to remove the accumulation of snow resulting from eight different storms, with a total snow fall of 38 inches. For all but three days of this period the mean temperature remained below freezing, so that little relief was afforded by the melting of snow.

The new officers thus had full opportunity to test the procedure and organization which had been handed down to them, and before the snow was half gone, a beginning was made in devising and testing cheaper and more rapid methods of doing the work. These were subsequently worked out by the planning division assisted by members of the Bureau of Municipal Research, and applied to snow removal the following winter (1914-1915). During this winter and that of 1915-1916 when these methods were still further perfected, the new procedure proved superior to former methods in every way.

New Method of Snow Fighting

One of the two principal features of the new plan originated by the present commissioner is the organization of a " snow fighting force " composed of regular officers and sweepers of the department and a large number of emergency laborers, working in squads under the direction of sweepers. The members of this force do not wait until the storm is over, but, if indications point to a real storm, start work as soon as snow begins falling, and work in continuous shifts of nine hours each, day and night, until the streets are cleared for traffic.

The second of the two principal features is the greatly increased use of sewers for carrying away the snow. Formerly only a few of the large trunk sewers had been so used, and the several sewer bureaus at first refused to allow the more general use of sewers advocated in 1914. The commissioner, however, succeeded later in obtaining permission to use all sewers adaptable for this purpose. An investigation was then made of the average

Use of Sewers for Snow Removal by the "Snow Fighting Force"

velocity and depth of flow of 1,098 miles of sewers in the three boroughs. The results showed that it would be practicable to place snow in sewers on at least 37% of the total street area scheduled for snow fighting. As a matter of fact, it was found possible by augmenting the flow with water from hydrants, to sewer snow from about 60% of the total area cleared.

It was not found practicable to have all of the operations of snow removal conducted by the "snow fighting force" on account of the necessity of obtaining trucks for use on some of the principal streets where snow cannot be sewered directly, but it was arranged last winter to have almost all snow on such streets piled by city forces, contractors being employed only in removing snow to sewer manholes or waterfront dumps. In opening up lines of traffic expeditiously the work was greatly facilitated by the employment of some 70 private motor trucks fitted with departmental snow plows.

Economy Resulting From New Methods of Snow Removal

The results of the plans originated and put into effect during the past two winters by the present administration are strikingly shown in the last column of the following table:

Season	Snowfall in Inches	Cubic Yards Removed (to nearest 10,000)	Total Cost	**COST PER CUBIC YARD**
1909–10	30	1,870,000	$1,405,873	$0.75
1910–11	25	2,630,000	1,475,985	0.56
1911-12	23	1,640,000	893,233	0.55
1912–13	12	500,000	249,307	0.50
1913–14*	38	5,180,000	2,473,334	0.47
1914–15	22	4,320,000	523,892	0.121
1915–16	48	11,910,000	2,521,299	0.212

*All snow removed fell in 1914.

It will be observed that the cost last winter was 21 cents a yard against 12 cents in the winter before. This is explained partly by the scarcity of labor, which necessitated a greater proportion of the work being done by contract than in the previous winter, but mostly by the nature of last winter's storms. Several of these storms began with rain, followed by dense, ice snow which, owing to a sudden fall in temperature, froze to the pavement before the work of snow removal had much more than started. The result was a condition extraordinarily unfavorable for rapid snow removal. Yet on the basis of the cheapest contract work during the four years prior to 1914, that of 1912-13, it would have cost the city $5,955,000 to remove last winter's snow fall. There is indicated, therefore, a clear saving of $3,-433,000 by the present methods for last winter alone.

The rapidity with which the streets were cleaned is shown by the fact that the average amount of snow removed per day was 269,905 cubic yards in 1914-15 and over 198,000 cubic yards in 1915-1916. Prior to 1914 the best record since the adoption of the present method of estimating quantities by truck loads was 62,006 cubic yards, made in 1912-13. This indicates that this "snow fighting" method besides costing only one-quarter as much, is from three to four times as rapid as the former method of snow removal. As a result of the economy effected through the new method the cost per cubic yard of snow removal was reduced more than 50% below prior years.

The problem of the department for the future lies in determining when, where and how to remove snow from the hundreds of miles of paved streets and the adjacent areas of paved sidewalks. These decisions must be made regardless of individual demands. There is great question now as to whether the city is not doing more cleaning than is absolutely necessary, and complaints as to unsatisfactory conditions are fully as often due to selfish and unreasonable demands as to actual inefficiency in the work. Many of the details of snow work must be improved upon and it is expected that with the accumulation of experience and careful planning by qualified men even greater strides may be made in the future in improving conditions.

A continuance of the present method of piling snow so as to leave crossings clear immediately after the storm commences, upon those streets where it cannot be immediately placed in the sewers, and to prevent the formation of compacted snow and ice upon the pavement, especially if this work is so far as possible done by mechanical means, should produce economies and result in greater satisfaction on the part of the public.

A more extensive development of organized co-operative effort not only between the various city departments, but between the public service corporations, especially the street railway companies, and the department of street cleaning, should help to reduce the number of men employed on purely inspectional service to a minimum, such as those from the water department and the sewer bureaus.

The street railway snow removal forces still work almost entirely independently from the other forces on snow and without much effective co-operation. During the winter of 1915-1916, perhaps partially on account of legal proceedings which had been brought against them during the previous season, the work done by street railway employees was improved over that previously done, but there still remains much opportunity for improvement through more cooperation with the street cleaning force.

Collection of Household Wastes

Since January 1, 1914, several improvements have been made in the service of collecting ashes, garbage and other household wastes. An improved form of cart cover has been introduced which permits keeping the ash and garbage vehicles covered while the drivers make their rounds, and enough of these covers have been purchased to equip all of the 2,200 carts now in service. The open ash and garbage cart, so long an eyesore to the critical public, will soon be a thing of the past.

Ash and Garbage Carts Fitted with New Covers

The improved form of tractor trailer used in the model district has already been mentioned. This type of apparatus has been in successful operation now for seven months. In all other districts of the city the collection service is performed in the same manner as formerly by two sets of carts; the steel dump cart of about 1½ cubic yards capacity collects from each building ashes on one trip and garbage on another, and the paper cart makes still another visit to each building for paper and other light and bulky refuse. The new trailer especially designed for collection service makes but one visit to each building, and collects at one time ashes, garbage and other refuse. The trailer is fitted with eight separate detachable pockets, each of 1 1/3 cubic yards capacity, in which either ashes or garbage may be put, and two detachable rubbish containers, resting on top of the above mentioned pockets and serving as covers for them. The ash and garbage pockets which are fitted with vertical doors, closing by gravity, form dust and water tight receptacles. It is intended to have these trucks make collection visits on a regular time schedule. In this way householders may know the exact time to place their refuse on the sidewalk, thus shortening the length of time that the sidewalks of the city must daily be disfigured by the ugly ash and garbage cans and the uglier bundles of refuse.

Transferring the contents of the collection trailers to the contractors' scows for final disposition is accomplished by means of electrically operated locomotive cranes, which lift the compartments from the trailer and dump their contents directly into the scows. From 25 to 45 minutes is required to unload the ordinary horse-drawn rubbish cart of 7½ cubic yards capacity. The time taken to transfer the contents of the compartments of the trailer, consisting of 15 cubic yards of refuse and upwards of 10½ cubic yards of ashes and garbage to the scows averages now about 15 minutes.

Another very considerable advantage in the use of motor equipment is the fact that it can be operated continuously, thus securing a much higher percentage of productivity per day of 24 hours than can be obtained from horses, and resulting in a corresponding saving in original investment.

Collection and Disposal of Trade Wastes

The collection and disposal of trade waste were for a long time the subject of controversy between the department of street cleaning and business concerns, and between the department and contractors for refuse disposal. In 1915, the Supreme Court decided that the department was not obliged to remove such waste. But until recently the term "trade waste" was never clearly defined, and the charter in defining the duties of the department makes no mention of such waste. The department has for many years collected and disposed of trade waste without charge from small business houses, and has also disposed of waste collected from large corporations by private carts and delivered at its dumps under permits issued by the department. The number of business houses served by the department's carts has depended on the amount of appropriation available. This system has resulted in unavoidable yet seemingly unfair discrimination, and in endless complaint from the larger business houses, stores and hotels.

The present commissioner came to the conclusion that because the city had fallen into the error of disposing of trade waste free of charge there was no reason why it should continue to do so. In 1915, the passage of a bill was secured which granted to the department (1) the right (already exercised without express legal sanction for many years) of disposing of trade waste at its dumps; (2) the right to charge for this service; (3) the right to collect trade waste and to charge for its collection at rates fixed by the board of estimate and apportionment. Recommendations on this subject made by the present commissioner are now awaiting action by that board.

An extensive investigation of the amount of trade waste involved and its present cost to the city is now in progress. A canvass of the larger business houses already completed shows that the department disposes of 846,198 cartloads of trade waste annually, of which 683,434 loads are delivered at the dumps by private cartmen. If the latter were charged the amount which this service costs there would be an annual saving to the city of approximately $200,000.

Final Disposition

As far as this department is concerned, the city's refuse is finally disposed of when delivered to contractors at some seventy points within the city limits. These points are mostly land or waterfront dumps, but in some cases dumping stations maintained by the street railway companies are used. The contractors in turn dispose of the garbage at reduction plants, and the other refuse at various places where filling material can be used to advantage. For this service the contractors are paid at fixed rates established in their contracts.

At the beginning of the present administration all of the waterfront dumps were unsightly and unsanitary, consisting of open platforms from which the carts dumped their contents into scows, spreading dust and dirt far and near. They were lighted by lanterns or even torches, and as no adequate fire protection was provided frequent fires occurred and the city suffered considerable loss in this way. During the past two years electric lights have been installed at most of the dumps and contracts for a complete fire sprinkler system are pending. Two covered dumps have been built of fireproof construction and of practical, yet pleasing, architectural design, and two others of similar design are soon to be constructed. Dumping at land fills in Manhattan has been entirely discontinued.

Contracts for the disposal of refuse other than garbage which are in force until next January, were entered into on the date of the appointment of the present commissioner. The contracts provide as formerly for the payment by the city of a definite rate per truck load delivered at the dumps. The total cost of final disposal is in excess of $1,000,000 a year. The commissioner, together with the superintendent of final disposition,

Covered Fireproof Dump for Unloading Refuse Recently Built at 72d Street and East River

is making a careful study of these contracts so that future specifications may be more complete and more definite, and so avoid the lawsuits and frequent disputes concerning contract provisions which have occurred in the past.

Until three years ago the city also paid for garbage disposal. Twelve years ago the cost was $280,000 a year. Under the last administration a contract was entered into which provides that during 1916 the city shall receive $112,500 from the contractor for the privilege of garbage disposal.* The present contractors have been disposing of garbage at their reduction plants at Barren Island. This has long been obnoxious to adjoining sections of the city on account of the method employed, which permitted the escape of fumes incident to the reduction process. Under the new contract for garbage disposal which has recently been awarded, the objectionable plant at Barren Island will be discontinued and an improved process employed at a plant in an isolated part of Staten Island. The new process of garbage reduction will be carried on mainly in air-tight containers and so conducted that, according to investigations carried on in New Bedford, where the same process is in use, no objectionable fumes will escape. For the privilege of garbage disposal under this contract the contractors have agreed to pay the city an average of $180,000 a year, or a total of $900,000 during the five years' life of the contract.

Removal of Incumbrances

A service performed by the department, perhaps little appreciated, but of considerable value to the city, is the removal of unlawful street incumbrances.

Those incumbrances which come within the jurisdiction of the department comprise vehicles of every description, and all push carts, bags and bales of merchandise and similar articles found upon any public roadway which interfere with the work of cleaning the streets—not including, of course, vehicles attended by their users, or articles for which permission to occupy the street has been granted. This work is under the control of the district superintendents. The department employs in each of the more thickly populated districts of the city a regular squad for the purpose of seizing these incumbrances and transferring them to the nearest of the four yards which the department maintains expressly for the storage and redemption of such articles. The equipment of the incumbrance squad consists mainly of a wide double truck, ropes, chains and an assortment of tools for handling and transporting articles seized. Incumbrances are tagged and numbered and may be redeemed by the owner on payment of a fine in accordance with the fixed scale, the amounts ranging from 15 cents for milk cans to $10 for automobiles and double trucks. Articles unredeemed after sixty days may be sold at public auction or, if of no monetary value, be disposed of at the department's dumps.

* Payment of this is at present the subject of litigation.

Auxiliary Work

Accounting and Statistical Service

Prior to 1914 the accounting work performed in the department included only the regular procedure for keeping track of expenditures chargeable to appropriation accounts and the maintenance of a set of expense records prescribed by the finance department. The statistical work comprised the collection and compilation of a large amount of data relating to the physical work performance.

Except that these records made it possible for the department to avoid an improper exhaustion of its budget appropriations, they provided practically no other means for the exercise of administrative control. Despite the fact that both expense and work data were collected, in neither case was the information properly arranged or logically compiled; and the financial data were absolutely unrelated to the work data. In other words, unit costs, the only means of testing the comparative efficiency of various methods of work, or the efficiency of different bodies of men, were not compiled for administrative use.

Inasmuch as the prime function of this service was thus emasculated, the efforts of the present administration have been directed towards the introduction of remedial measures. Accordingly, a system of cost and expense records was designed to combine the physical and financial statistics in such form that they could be made to show *currently* as well as at periodic intervals the degree of efficiency with which the operations of the department were conducted. This involved the definition of the various kinds of work which the department is called upon to perform, and the determination of suitable units which could be used in measuring the volume of each. It also involved a very careful determination of the logical order in which the expense actually incident to the work should be recorded and thereafter compiled to show for each unit of the functional organization, as well as for each auxiliary service, a comparison of the results actually accomplished. Furthermore, this system of expense records has been designed in such a way as to simplify the preparation of departmental estimates and make possible a complete analysis of these estimates in the most minute detail.

The stores and equipment records, elsewhere described, which provide for physical control of departmental property and furnish all pertinent information with respect to the cost of plant and equipment service, are subsidiary to and properly articulated with the new system of expense accounts above mentioned.

The whole system, which was put into operation on January 1, 1916, is designed to permit the use of punch card records, and the necessary apparatus for mechanically sorting and tabulating the data contained on these cards has been installed. Without these mechanical aids it would be infeasible to secure the statistical detail needed for complete administrative control.

Plant, Equipment and Stores Service

To provide the facilities necessary for the conduct of its functional work, the department, as already stated, maintains its own plant, equipment and stores service. Except for the erection of new buildings and other large structures nearly all of this service is performed by departmental forces. This work includes the purchase, custody, distribution and care of stores and equipment, the repair of practically all its equipment and plant structures, and the manufacture of certain supplies and minor equipment used.

Without attempting to describe in detail the chaotic status of this whole service at the beginning of the present administration, it may be said that the defects were so serious as to demand a complete reorganization, not only because the service was improperly equipped, poorly organized and very badly managed, but also because, until these conditions could be corrected, it was impossible to secure a degree of control over the conduct of the functional work which would insure its efficient performance.

Arrangements were accordingly made to centralize the control of this service, then partly a borough and partly a central office function, in the main office and place it under the general jurisdiction of the deputy commissioner in charge of administrative matters.

The work thus centralized was divided into three parts:

1 Purchase of supplies and equipment
2 Stores service
3 Plant and equipment service

Purchase of Supplies and Equipment

The purchase of supplies and equipment has been delegated to a purchasing agent who co-operates with the central purchase committee. The stores service has been placed in charge of a general storekeeper, with headquarters at the main office, who is responsible for the receipt, custody, issuance and distribution of all articles carried in stores, returned thereto or condemned. The plant and equipment service, with the exception of that involving care and control of live stock, has been placed in the hands of a mechanical engineer whose responsibilities include, (a) custody and care of plant structures and equipment not in stores; (b) inspection of the current condition of equipment in use, together with the technical instruction of departmental employees with regard to the operation and care of such equipment; (c) repair and maintenance of plant and equipment, and the conduct of all other work done at repair shops, including the manufacture of new articles. In this way, instead of the former condition of independent jurisdiction and divided authority over similar activities, which resulted in inadequate performance and general irresponsibility, there has been substituted the necessary machinery for properly co-ordinating these activities and definitizing responsibility therefor.

Aside from the matter of general organization, it was apparent that successful control over the auxiliary service above outlined could not be obtained without a reliable inventory of all departmental property and complete facilities for its accurate identification. The first step taken in this direction was the establishment of a complete and logical classification of all material, supplies and equipment owned, or likely to be acquired, by the department. The application of a system of numerical codes to this classification provides the means for its practical use as a medium of identification.

A printed code book alphabetically arranged, and a card catalogue arranged in accordance with a basis of classification which groups the various articles according to their distinctive characteristics in such a way as to make possible the logical codification of any subsequent additions, have been devised. The codification in both forms was placed in service January 1, 1916.

With the facilities thus provided a complete inventory of departmental property was taken on January 1, 1916, and for the first time in its history the department can show by its records what property it actually possesses, where that property is located and its actual value.

Stores Service

The next step was to devise improved methods for the administrative control of this auxiliary service. In the early part of 1916 a complete system of stores procedure, together with the necessary forms, was installed. This system articulates properly with the other records of the expense accounting system, gathers all information which can possibly be desired for any purpose, and is susceptible of easy analysis at budget-making or other periods. At the same time, complete physical control over material can be currently exercised by the officials in charge.

Standard quotas of stock for each section, stable and repair shop have been established and will be maintained by replenishment at uniform intervals.

Contemporaneous with the establishment of centralized control over stores, steps were taken to improve the facilities for storage and handling of reserve stock. To that end, an abandoned school building on West 20th Street, Manhattan, has been remodeled and equipped as a central storehouse to replace the storerooms formerly located at separate stables in the three boroughs. The storehouse at Stable "A," Manhattan, will be used as a sub-storage point, carrying only those articles whose bulk prohibits their being kept at the main storehouse. At both of these points a certain amount of space has been definitely assigned for the receipt of articles prior to their arrangement in bins and for the assembly of outgoing shipments.

Equipment has been provided to reduce labor in handling stores, and electric motor trucks have been purchased for the purpose of distributing stores and collecting articles to be returned, this service being under the control of the general storekeeper.

While great improvement has already been made in providing better plant and equipment facilities for the stores service there is still opportunity for further improvement, since the present facilities were designed to serve only as a temporary expedient pending the completion of an elaborate plan under which the departmental stores points would become part of a central stores service for all departments of the city. Before this plan can be made effective, however, it will be necessary to perfect many of the facilities now in use.

Plant and Equipment Service

At the same time that the new stores system was put into effect, an allied procedure for controlling the plant and equipment service was also installed. This procedure, together with the necessary forms of record was designed (a) to present a complete history of the equipment assets of the department, and (b) to furnish detailed information regarding the investment value, depreciation, maintenance expense, and service output of all the major pieces of plant and equipment in the department. It is related directly to the new system of cost and expense accounting and conforms to advanced theories of budget-making.

The new procedure enables the administrative officials to exercise a very close control over the current operations of this part of the auxiliary service, assists them in securing the best disposition of available equipment as well as economy in its maintenance and use, provides a basis for determining the relative cost of different methods used in the performance of the functional work and is indispensable in arriving at proper budget allowances. The value of these records will increase with use since they are built up on a comparative basis.

One of the most important features of the plant and equipment service is the repair work. Plans for the control of this work contemplate a predetermination of the character, volume and relative importance of the repairs to be made. Furthermore, by inspecting equipment while still in usable condition, provision is made for anticipating a serious break-down. This planning of work in advance is no small undertaking on account of the enormous quantity of departmental equipment. The procedure for this work requires that requests for repairs shall be followed by careful inspection of the defective conditions and an estimate of the cost of rehabilitation submitted to the proper authority, who, in case the repairs are not excessive, will authorize the issuance of definite written work orders specifying the exact work to be done, the materials to be used, and the assignment of mechanics to be made. No mechanic is allowed to perform work not specifically covered by a work order. The procedure further requires an accurate report of the time of employees, material consumed and equipment used on each repair job, which information is submitted to the main office for the compilation of expense statistics.

Many improvements have been made in shop methods, especially in the matter of systematizing the progress of work through the shops and assembling in advance the material and tools required in work performance.

The shop methods, however, are still far from perfect, owing to inadequate shop facilities. With regard to these shop facilities, much has been done in the last two years to improve the very unsatisfactory conditions which previously obtained in the repair shops, but these improvements were undertaken only as a temporary expedient pending a radical revision of the entire repair plant of the department.

As soon as arrangements can be made to finance a new investment in repair plant, and plans can be prepared, it is proposed to establish a central repair shop in the borough of Manhattan with a complete equipment of new machinery systematically arranged for the convenient and expeditious handling of repair work. At this point it is proposed to handle all heavy overhauling jobs, all jobs requiring special machinery, all repairs which involve work on large quantities of the same kind of minor equipment, and all manufacture of new articles. Supplementing this main shop, three other shops are to be established; one in Brooklyn, one in The Bronx, and the third in the upper part of Manhattan. These subsidiary shops will be located in stables or adjoining structures, and, although a certain amount of machinery will be installed in each, they will be designed to handle work on a much smaller scale than the main repair shop. The primary purpose of establishing these smaller shops is to avoid heavy transportation charges and loss of time when large pieces of departmental equipment are in need of minor repairs which require shop facilities.

In addition to the above facilities it is planned to supply each of the stables of the department with an outfit of small tools and spare parts sufficient to enable the district forces to attend promptly to any simple and minor defect in structures and equipment which can readily be handled by the unskilled labor located at those points. It is further planned to provide portable repair facilities, including such power equipment and hand tools as are needed to meet the demand for emergency repair service which frequently arises in the department.

Much yet remains to be done to bring the shop methods and procedure up to an acceptable standard. The most important part of this task is planning the work in a way to secure the most expeditious and economical performance, bearing in mind the most seasonal demands of the functional work. It must be clearly understood that efforts so far in this field have been directed only at the cruder defects evidenced by existing conditions and that further development towards what may be termed really scientific methods of management in shops will be a relatively slow process.

When the repair shop work has reached a point where the attention of the mananging officials is not entirely confined to the immediate work in hand, it is proposed that such officials shall undertake a study of the various types of departmental equipment with a view to ascertaining whether or not the present types are satisfactorily adapted to the work in hand and what improvements in design will produce more satisfactory results in the functional work.

Care of Horses

The live stock equipment of the department, comprising over 2,500 horses, is one of its most important physical assets. While the routine care of these animals is still entrusted to stable foremen under the direction of district superintendents, control over the acquisition, current condition, upkeep and disposal of the horses is now vested in the central organization, and a staff of veterinarians under the jurisdiction of a chief veterinarian is maintained to facilitate this control.

With regard to the live stock service it may be stated that formerly little or no control over the condition or care of horses was exercised, no careful inquiry was made to determine the reason for the death or disablement of a horse, and many of the drivers were totally ignorant of the simplest precautions governing the care and treatment of a horse when at work. Moreover, drivers and stable employees were not held responsible for their delinquencies in these respects. The selection and condemnation of horses was also a matter that was very carelessly handled, and the shoeing was especially unsatisfactory on account of vague specifications and lack of proper control over the horseshoeing contract.

A marked improvement in all these conditions has been brought about since January 1, 1914, by the administrative heads of the central office aided by the department's veterinaries. The cost for draft horses was reduced from $340 per head in 1913 to $285 per head in 1914. At the same time, a better grade of animals was secured by the appointment of three stable foremen to act as judges in the premliminary choice of animals most suited to the work of the department. Animals accepted by the judges were in turn subjected to a rigid examination as to soundness and fitness by the department's chief veterinarian and, finally, the horses were given a ten days' trial before being purchased by the department. In 1914, in order to obtain 373 horses, it was necessary for 1,058 horses to be thus examined.

In the care of horses, many steps have been taken to increase the years of service obtainable from them, and to decrease losses due to sickness and accident. A handbook written in clear and simple style, has been issued for the special use of drivers and stablemen, called "Sick Horses—How to Prevent, How to Tell and What to Do." Shoeing, which is still done by contract, has been more carefully provided for by wording specifications with greater care and completeness. Experiments in the value of different foods for horses have been started, but these are not yet far enough advanced to be utilized. Complete records are kept of all horses as to sickness, length of time worked, etc., and these are used as a basis for condemning horses as unfit. Still further improvements in the selection and care of horses are believed possible for the coming year as a result of the careful attention bestowed upon the subject in the past two years.

Summary of Accomplishments

The principal improvements made in the department of street cleaning during the two and a half years that the present administration has been in office may be summarized as follows:

1 The department has been put on a more thorough business basis by the establishment of a strongly centralized organization which has made possible increased administrative efficiency. A definite program covering every branch of the service and designed to increase the departmental output of work, improve its quality and reduce its cost, has been developed and inaugurated.

2 Particular attention has been given to the personnel of the department. The *esprit de corps* has been improved by "square deal" methods, and through the incentive to do good work provided by a new standard of wages based on individual performance.

3 Greater public co-operation with the department has been secured through an educational campaign, which has resulted in the more faithful observance of ordinances in regard to keeping the streets clean.

4 A means of trying out new procedure and new equipment has been furnished by the establishment of the model district, and a force for working out scientific methods and designing improved appliances has been provided by the organization of a planning division. A departmental school has been started where recruits are thoroughly taught the essentials of their work and where regular members of the force are instructed in new and improved methods.

5 Definite steps have been taken to modernize the departmental equipment by motorization of the collection service, which has been already effected with successful results in the model district. Improved covers have been provided for all garbage and ash carts.

6 All paved streets in Manhattan and in parts of Brooklyn and The Bronx receive a nightly "washing" as well as a daily sweeping. Improved methods of hand flushing have been adopted and the quality of work improved.

7 A probable average annual saving of from one to two million dollars has been assured by the introduction of new methods of snow removal, which enable the clearing of streets in one-third of the former time.

8 A new contract for garbage disposal by methods of practically odorless reduction has been awarded on terms which will bring in an increased revenue to the city, and which will do away with the present nuisance-creating reduction plant on Barren Island.

9 A central repair shop and a central storehouse have been established, and repair and stores procedure have been systematized and put upon a more efficient basis.

10 The accounting and statistical methods have been reorganized so that compilations now furnish a means of current work control and at the same time a rational basis for future budget-making.

11 The annual departmental report has been improved. Information furnished in the last two annual reports of the department has been so compiled and so presented as to furnish not only a record of expenditures and quantity of work performed, but information which can be used by the citizen as an index of the efficiency of the department.

Program for Future Work

Plans of the present administration contemplate the fulfillment of the program already laid down for the improvement in personnel, methods and equipment of the department. In addition thereto the program for future work will include:

1 The training of officers and present employees, as well as new recruits, at the school of instruction, for the purpose of developing a more highly trained force.

2 An extension of the present system of paying men in accordance with their period of employment, conduct record and work record, so that satisfactory service will entail a more prompt reward in the way of a direct salary payment.

3 Improved facilities for the personal comfort of employees at the various section stations, stables, dumps, etc., through the installation of proper washing and bathing apparatus.

4 The creation of a co-operative purchasing division, organized and maintained by employees of the department, for securing uniforms, shoes, rubber boots, rubber coats, and other equipment in large quantities, and at the lowest possible cost to the employee.

5 Intensive study of work methods through the engineering staff, for the purpose of reducing the labor, and at the same time producing a better quality as well as quantity of work.

6 The revision of ordinances for decreasing litter on the streets, and for controlling the unlawful practice of street littering, either through citizens' co-operation or police power.

7 Modification of present charter provisions permitting the department to conduct all work in connection with the final disposition of refuse as a business proposition, involving the production and utilization of by-products which are necessarily a direct result of the treatment of the wastes, and the sale of all products under the most advantageous market conditions.

8 The gradual elimination of assorted and ill-adapted cans for holding refuse and the adoption of a standard type receptacle with cover attached to prevent odors and dust from escaping while refuse is being handled.

9 The gradual elimination of horse-drawn vehicles for collecting refuse, cleaning streets and removing snow, and the adoption of power-driven auxiliaries for this work following the plan of the model district. This substitution will require a number of years and the total investment will aggregate $6,000,000, but the saving in annual operating expense will more than justify the change.

10 The gradual elimination of all contract work for the final disposition of refuse and the performance of this service by city forces. Recent experience with the contract for garbage and the history of refuse disposal by contract, point to the necessity for municipal ownership and operation of this sanitary utility, not only on the grounds of health, comfort and convenience, but for commercial reasons.

An investment of $9,000,000 for a complete utilization works to treat all classes of refuse should net an annual profit of $1,000,000, and in addition save the present cost of disposal amounting to $1,500,000. An annual saving of $2,500,000 on a $9,000,000 investment is possible with efficient management, a consistent policy, and the development of processes over a series of years. This plan was reported to and approved by the board of estimate and apportionment in 1912, but failure to secure legislation prevented the adoption of the program on a contract basis. The only alternative (and a proper one) is municipal development, ownership and operation of the utilization works.

Excluding the cost of snow removal, appropriations for street cleaning, refuse collection and disposal aggregate $7,500,000, in round figures. It is estimated that $15,000,000 will be required in the near future to motorize the apparatus and provide a sanitary and profit-making disposal system. Such an expenditure should reduce the net cost of operating the department to $5,000,000 per annum. At 10% for interest and sinking fund the reduction of $2,500,000 in annual expense would justify an investment of $25,000,000 or $10,000,000 more than is necessary to produce the desired results.

11 Coincident with the motorization of the department apparatus and plans for the utilization of refuse, the present waterfront dumps should be removed from the North River to the East River, borough of Manhattan. In Brooklyn and The Bronx inland stations for the reception of refuse should be constructed by the city and operated by the municipality. This phase of department betterment will depend upon the success of the utilization

work for the disposal of refuse, and the net revenues from the treatment of refuse should be appropriated for improvements in the handling of wastes.

12 Eventually, the city should assume the duty of cleaning sidewalks, as nobody now is obligated to do this work and a consistent standard of street cleanliness cannot be secured without complete responsibility for the whole street surface. This additional work will cost approximately $600,000 per annum.

13 The continuance of intensive studies by a competent technical staff will reveal further economies or improvements in standards with present expenditures.

14 The development of mechanical devices for snow removal and the construction of new sewers, specially adapted to snow disposal, will save the city millions of dollars directly, and the commercial interests much more by rapid and economical clearing of roadways during and after a snowfall. An appropriation of $100,000 for water connections to sewers and $25,000 for the design and tests of mechanical loading and hauling apparatus has been requested, and if the funds are provided, the results of this expenditure should become available next winter.

15 Time, a consistent policy, effective management, technical ability, hard work and an investment of about $15,000,000 will place the department of street cleaning on the highest plane of public service where it belongs as the general city housekeeping division, whose work affects most directly and intimately the convenience, comfort and health of all residents of the municipality.

INDEX

www.ingramcontent.com/pod-product-compliance
Lightning Source LLC
LaVergne TN
LVHW020558110826
845149LV00002B/295

* 9 7 8 1 4 1 8 1 8 8 3 6 8 *